Praise for *Speaking Torah: Spiritual Teachings from around the Maggid's Table*

"Insightful ... puts in dialogue the thought of the most original and formative group of Hasidic masters, demonstrating the nature of their spiritual aspirations and the dynamics of the laboratory that produced the leadership of Hasidism as a movement. A fresh and inspired project that brings to life the spirituality of an unprecedented constellation of religious geniuses."

—**Moshe Idel**, Max Cooper Professor of Jewish Thought, Hebrew University, Jerusalem

"Sparkling translations, judicious selections, wise-framing comments, comprehensive scope, with an authoritative historical introduction that masterfully summarizes a lifetime of scholarship: Rabbi Arthur Green and his students have produced the most insightful, valuable and accessible presentation of early Hasidism available in the English language, an indispensable resource for study and devotional work."

—**Nehemia Polen**, professor of Jewish thought, Hebrew College

"As heaven and earth met in creation, so too does scholarship and true passion of the love of the Hasidic masters meet in this monumental work of devotion and wisdom. If you were to commit to learning one book, this should be it!"

—**Reb Mimi Feigelson**, Mashpia Ruchanit

"In a world which too often feels fractured and dark, these precious teachings come along to lend clarity, light and hope. This extraordinary work stirs the mind, uplifts the spirit and makes age-old wisdom accessible in a way which liberates us from our most narrow places."

—**Matthew D. Gewirtz**, senior rabbi, Congregation B'nai Jeshurun, Short Hills, New Jersey

"Magnificent ... a treasure for all who seek to understand the rich variety of spiritual worldviews and religious experiences of the people who created the Hasidic movement. The world of those sitting around their master's table comes alive in this book. The multiple levels of interpretations offered in their teachings allow us to encounter these incredible personalities in their own world and to then explore the vitality of their teaching for our contemporary Jewish life."

—**Melila Hellner-Eshed**, research fellow, Shalom Hartman Institute

ALSO BY ARTHUR GREEN

Ehyeh
A Kabbalah for Tomorrow

Seek My Face
A Jewish Mystical Theology

These Are the Words
A Vocabulary of Jewish Spiritual Life

Tormented Master
The Life and Spiritual Quest of Rabbi Nahman of Bratslav

Your Word Is Fire
The Hasidic Masters on Contemplative Prayer

Speaking Torah

Spiritual Teachings from around the Maggid's Table

Volume 2

Numbers • Deuteronomy • the Holiday Cycle

Arthur Green

with Ebn Leader, Ariel Evan Mayse and Or N. Rose

For People of All Faiths, All Backgrounds

JEWISH LIGHTS Publishing

Woodstock, Vermont

Speaking Torah:
Spiritual Teachings from around the Maggid's Table—Volume 2

2013 Hardcover Edition, First Printing

Library of Congress Cataloging-in-Publication Data
Green, Arthur, 1941–
[Commentaries. Selections]
Speaking Torah : spiritual teachings from around the Maggid's table / Arthur Green with Ebn Leader, Ariel Evan Mayse, and Or Rose.
volumes cm
Includes bibliographical references and index.
ISBN 978-1-58023-694-2 (alk. paper)
1. Bible. Pentateuch—Criticism, interpretation, etc. 2. Hasidism. 3. Hasidim—Biography. I. Leader, Ebn D., 1969– II. Mayse, Ariel Evan. III. Rose, Or N. IV. Title.
BS1225.52.G732 2013
222'.106—dc23
2013017622

10 9 8 7 6 5 4 3 2 1

Manufactured in the United States of America
Jacket Design: Tim Holtz
Jacket Art: "Jerusalem Sunset" © 1998 was painted by Michael Bogdanow. His art, much of which is inspired by Judaic texts and spiritual themes, can be seen at www.MichaelBogdanow.com.

For People of All Faiths, All Backgrounds
Published by Jewish Lights Publishing
A Division of LongHill Partners, Inc.
Sunset Farm Offices, Route 4, P.O. Box 237
Woodstock, VT 05091
Tel: (802) 457-4000 Fax: (802) 457-4004
www.jewishlights.com

Contents

Volume 2

Volume 1

במדבר

Sefer Be-Midbar

The Book of Numbers

Be-Midbar

No'am Elimelekh

> Y-H-W-H spoke to Moses in the desert of Sinai, in the Tent of Meeting, on the first day of the second month [*hodesh*] of the second year since they had left Egypt.
> (Num. 1:1)

With this sentence the Torah is teaching correct conduct. The words **the desert of Sinai** are a reminder that the Torah was given on Mount Sinai in order to teach you to be extremely humble and self-effacing. Remember that God rejected all the high mountains and chose Mount Sinai, which was the lowest of them all.

But take care that this submissiveness not lead you into depression, for that is a great obstacle to God's service. The Torah teaches that you should always be joyful. The *shekhinah* is not present amid sadness. The words **in the Tent of Meeting** (*be-ohel mo'ed*) imply that you should enter the tent of joy, for the word for meeting (*mo'ed*) is also the word for festival.

On the first day of the second month [hodesh] ("renewal"). But should you say, how can I rejoice when I have sinned so extensively? The Torah teaches that you should nevertheless engage in repentance with joy. Encourage yourself by saying, "I am reborn this very day and I will never return to my foolishness." Renewal (*hiddush*) is about becoming a new person, and this is alluded to in the words **the first day of the second month [*hodesh*]**. Indeed this is the second new start—the first was when you were born, and the second is when you repent and are forgiven.

The second year since they had left Egypt refers to the same thing. For the blessed Holy One took us out of Egypt, meaning the terrible shells, the forty-nine gates of impurity. The Exodus from Egypt happens again whenever a person breaks the shells on the way toward holiness. Our reality is referred to as "year" (*Sefer Yetsirah* 6:1), so **the second year** comes to teach that there is a second Exodus from Egypt that happens in our own times, whenever a person repents.

This is a powerful example of the upbeat message that the Hasidic masters sought in even what seem to be the most bland and ordinary words of Torah. They see nothing in Torah as "ordinary," of course. Think how this verse might be "translated" in accord with R. Elimelekh's reading. It would go something like: "Y-H-W-H tells us that even while we are to be lowly and humble, we should fill ourselves with joy. There is always a chance to begin again and change, since we are ever being liberated anew from whatever enslaves us." Wow, what a message!

Rav Yeevi

> Y-H-W-H spoke to Moses in the desert of Sinai, in the Tent of Meeting, on the first day of the second month of the second year since they had left Egypt.
> (Num. 1:1)

We have not found reference anywhere else in the Torah to a "desert of Sinai," only to the mountain. But we have to interpret the word *Sinai*, as did the *Zohar*, by noting that its numerical value is 130, identical to that of *sulam*, or "ladder" (*Zohar* 1:149a). The mountain was given that name when God descended upon it to give Torah to Israel. Y-H-W-H, who is supremely transcendent and elevated, spread down to earth, metaphorically speaking, like a person descending from heaven to earth would come down on "a ladder stuck into the ground whose head reached heaven" (Gen. 28:12). It is called Sinai because it is a ladder-mountain, its head reaching into heaven. Thus "God came down ... upon Mount Sinai" (Ex. 19:11).

But sometimes it is called the desert (*midbar*) of Sinai, for a person can cleave to God and attain the holy spirit by means of speech (*midbar/dibbur*). Every letter of the alphabet is attached to God above. When you speak here below employing those letters, their source rises upward; your speech itself becomes "a ladder ... whose head reaches heaven." Your words ascend and come before God. This is called the *midbar* or speech-act of Sinai.

The play of *midbar* and *dibbur* is irresistible and is widely found in Hasidic teaching. The sacred power of speech is extended already by the Ba'al Shem Tov from the holy words of Torah and prayer to include all of human speech, including the vernacular. *Leshon ha-kodesh*, the holy tongue, no longer means only Hebrew as distinct from other languages, but pure human speech in any language, kept free from sin.

Ginzey Yosef

> Y-H-W-H spoke to Moses in the wilderness of Sinai ... saying: "Lift up the head [i.e., count] of the community of the Children of Israel according to their families, their fathers' households, counting [*be-mispar*] the names of all the men, counting their heads."
>
> (Num. 1:1–2)

RaSHI says that because He loves them, He repeatedly counts them.

But the real counting of Israel points upward, toward their Root above. The six hundred thousand Israelite souls have their source in the six *sefirot* [from *hesed* to *yesod*], the "six directions." That is why the text says **Lift up the head** and not simply "count." This act of Moses's counting awakened the light of that Source, shining down brightly upon Israel. It raised them up to the highest rungs of awe and love, directing their hearts to the ever-present God. **Lift** (*se'u*) is to be taken as in "Israel lifted up their eyes" (Ex. 14:10).

This is **Lift up the head**: Raise Israel to its highest Root. **According to ... their Father's household**, the Source of their souls. [***Be-mispar***] means "shining." **The names**, for a person's name represents the life-force within. Thus the light of their upper Source comes to shine within them, each according to their name or essential flow of life.

Each of us has a unique light, shining in upon us from the Source of all life. Moses—or the inner sage—is called upon to lift us upward toward that Source. Here the act of counting, sometimes superstitiously suspect as bringing curse, is itself raised up to the highest blessing.

Kedushat Levi

> As Y-H-W-H commanded Moses, he counted them in the wilderness of Sinai.
> (Num. 1:19)

The verse would have made more sense in reverse order: Moses counted them, as God had commanded him. But this appears to be the meaning: God gave the Torah to Israel, and the souls of Israel form the body of the Torah. There are six hundred thousand Jewish souls, parallel to the number of letters in the Torah. Israel, in other words, *are* the Torah. Each one of us constitutes one of Torah's letters.

By counting Israel, therefore, Moses was learning the Torah. This is the meaning of the verse's order. **As Y-H-W-H commanded Moses** means that the Torah's commandment to Moses was the very act of counting Israel. That is also why it says "but do not count the tribe of Levi or lift up their heads among the Children of Israel" (Num. 1:49). Israel represents the Written Torah, while the Levites stand for the Oral Torah. Therefore, of the Levites it says: "He counted them *by the mouth of God*, as he was commanded" (Num. 4:49).

Counting Jews is a way of learning Torah! The translation of this teaching is offered as a gift to our Jewish demographers and social scientists. But they have to remember, of course, that such learning is a *mitsvah*, a sacred act, to be undertaken only for the sake of heaven.

Be-Midbar
Round Two

AG: You might take these comments as a Hasidic object lesson in how to make Torah interesting. *Parashat Be-Midbar* is a preacher's nightmare, almost entirely taken up with census figures. And here it is enlivened with lessons about humility, penitence, rebirth, the ascent to God, and lots more.

EL: The second and third texts are both about ascent and uplifting, Sinai as a ladder and *mispar* ["number"] as the shining light. But the homilies are themselves upliftings of this prosaic text. Here the method and the message seem to reflect one another!

AG: Is the *Kedushat Levi* also an "uplifting" text? The Children of Israel are being raised up to the level of Torah.

OR: The Hasidic master, as always, is telling us to look beneath the surface and to raise everything up. The exegetical project and communal project are in that sense the same. Raise both text and people to a higher level!

EL: Yes, you are to love the people and reach out to them. But the purpose is not just accepting them as they are. You are always there to raise them higher. The *tsaddik* sets a high bar as the standard for himself, then draws others upward. But that role sets him apart in a certain way; he stands midway between the people and the heights toward which he is raising them.

OR: But I think Levi Yitshak is different here. He's not telling you to raise them up. They already *are* Torah. To engage with Jews—even just counting them—is to be engaged with Torah. If you can't see this, you have to raise *yourself* up, transform your vision, so that you can see this truth.

AG: Yes, that's the *Kedushat Levi*; it fits with lots of the stories about him. But other members of the group were not so sure. Does the *tsaddik* then give up any role as reprover? How far would you go with this? Discovering holiness in ordinary people is wonderful. But is *anything* they do to be seen as holy?

Naso

Or ha-Me'ir

> "As these curse-bearing waters come into your loins ..." the woman shall say: "Amen, Amen."
> (Num. 5:22)

RaSHI says that she is thereby placing herself under oath, saying "Amen" if I am pregnant by this man [her husband], and "Amen" if I am pregnant by another.

This verse reminds us of a teaching by our sages: "Rabbi Yose ben Yehudah says that two angels accompany a person on the way home from synagogue on the Sabbath eve. One is for good and one is for ill. If they arrive and find the candles lit, the table set, and the bed prepared, the good angel says, "May it be God's will that you have another Sabbath like this one," and the bad angel is forced to say, "Amen." But if not, the situation is reversed, and the good angel is forced to say, "Amen" (b. Shabbat 119b). All the *mitsvot* of the Torah have angels appointed over them, as is known, one from the right and one from the left. When a person fulfills a *mitsvah* in love and awe, the left is incorporated into the right and joins with it....

Now it is known that the reciting of "Amen" effects the union of the two names Y-H-W-H and Adonay, standing for love and judgment (*Tikkuney Zohar* t. 10, 25b).... Even though the sages said that whoever responds "Amen!" with all his strength has his ill-fated decrees torn up (b. Shabbat 119b), this is not a matter of simply crying out in a loud voice. The mouth has to follow one's innermost thoughts. We have to remain aware of God's oneness and unity even when engaged in the worldly deeds that we need to sustain ourselves. There too we should be seeking out God's oneness, our thoughts not being separated from the One even for a moment. Wherever we go, whatever we see, we should perceive it as a garbing of divinity, a limb of the *shekhinah*, who is called Adonay. From there we should raise that up to the name Y-H-W-H. This is the way an enlightened person says "Amen," uniting the two holy names.

You should do so even when engaged in those twenty-eight varied "times" [described in Ecclesiastes 3 as "a time for ... "], fourteen for the good and fourteen for ill. You serve God through all of them, raising up *shekhinah*'s limbs. A person like this, when coming to pray, is truly able to say "Amen" with "all his strength" (*koah* = 28), bringing along all those twenty-eight times that seem so opposite to one another. Even from there [the harder times], one calls out "Amen," joining judgment to compassion, linking the two names. That is the main thing we pray for, as in "May the Master of heaven aid you in all times, and let us say, 'Amen.'" May God give us the strength of heart to be able to say "Amen" in all those twenty-eight times....

The final lesson is this. Your human task is not fulfilled unless you serve your Creator with such effort that you force the bad angel to say "Amen." Now you can see how deeply the sages were thinking when they said that the woman's saying "**Amen, Amen**" was placing herself under oath. This is the full acceptance of God's kingdom, the uniting of those two names Y-H-W-H and Adonay. This is possible only if we work so hard at it that the bad angel is forced to go along. That is the meaning of "**Amen**" if by this man, referring to Y-H-W-H, who is called "Man," or "**Amen**" if by the other man, the "other side," for he too will be forced to say "Amen."

We include this text to show how even a very harsh and problematic biblical passage like the ordeal of the suspected wife may be transformed in the Hasidic reading into a paradigm for God's service. All of us, as understood here, are the suspected wife, standing between the pulls of good and evil. The two "angels" are our own good and evil urges. But our ultimate embrace of the good needs to be so strong that we join it as whole selves, our inner "evil angel" forced to come along.

Orah le-Hayyim

> Y-H-W-H spoke to Moses, saying: "Speak to Aaron and his sons, saying: 'Thus shall you bless the Children of Israel. Say to them....'"
> (Num. 6:22–23)

Why is the word **saying** repeated? And since the words **Thus shall you bless** [referring to Aaron and his sons] are in the plural, why does the text then switch to the singular form in **Say to them**? RaSHI notes that the verb **say** is in a grammatical form called the "source" (infinitive absolute), vocalized with a *kamats* and a *holam*, as in such words as *zakhor* and *shamor.*

Holy books teach us that God created the world so that His kingdom [would] be revealed over Israel. For their sake were all the worlds created and linked to one another, reaching down to this world where God's kingship would be revealed through them. The last link in this chain is the aspect of *malkhut* ("kingship"). All the upper worlds and their lights are manifest in it, and all beings above and below are included within it. *Malkhut* is the image or mirror in which all are reflected, as the *Zohar* teaches (*Tikkuney Zohar* t. 18, 31b).

Y-H-W-H gave blessing to Abraham our Father, who passed it on to Isaac, and he to Jacob, and then his sons. But God then gave the act of blessing to the *kohanim* ("priests"), since they represent divine compassion (*hesed*) and love. When the *kohanim* arouse themselves in love to bless Israel, they awaken love far, far above in the uppermost Source, showering goodness and blessing upon Israel. That is why the form of their blessing is uniquely coined as "who has commanded us to bless His people Israel with love." In arousing their own quality of love to pour blessings upon Israel, they cause love and blessing to flow from that highest Source into *malkhut. Malkhut* is indeed called *kenesset yisra'el*, "the assembly of Israel." Thus all Israel, but also all the worlds and all creatures that are rooted in *malkhut,* receive that blessing [of love] from the uppermost Source....

But how were the *kohanim* able to attain a state of such pure love? Surely they had to repent completely, seeing themselves in an absolutely humble way. This was like Sinai, when all of Israel stood at the level of total love and unity, because they had returned to Y-H-W-H.

Speak to Aaron and his sons, saying. This act of "saying" takes place within the heart, as in: "Should you say in your heart" (Deut. 7:17). The heart is the seat of *binah*, the place to which we turn in repentance. They should repent in order to come to love all Israel....

Say to them, in the realm of thought. This form, vocalized with a *kamats* and *holam*, is indeed a "source." By reaching there they were able to draw blessing upon Israel and upon *malkhut*, from the highest Source. All worlds and all creatures partook of that blessing.

Note the repeated insistence that blessing was to flow both to Israel and to all creatures, since *malkhut* contains all the worlds and all creatures within it. This dual sense of Israel-centered piety and a desire to bring about universal blessing is typical of the best of Hasidic teachings.

Divrey Emet

> Speak to Aaron and his sons, saying: "Thus shall you bless the Children of Israel. Say to them...."
> (Num. 6:23)

In the following Torah portion, Moses is first told, "Take the Levites ... to purify them" (Num. 8:6–7), and only afterwards, "Thus shall you do to them." But here Moses says, "Thus shall you bless," without previously having commanded Aaron to bless them.

We know that Aaron's actions brought him to his rung. Because he loved peace and was always trying to make peace between people, he merited to bring about peace between Israel and their Father in heaven, as the *Zohar* teaches (3:88a). All this came about because he loved God and therefore loved His creatures. He always wanted them to be at peace and to love one another. This all derived from the root of love.

That was how he came to bless Israel, because of his great love. This is **to Aaron and his sons, saying: "Thus...."** Aaron and his children, meaning his followers, have it in their very nature to bless. [They do not have to be commanded to do so.] To them it is fitting just to say: **"Thus shall you bless...."**

We have all met such people in our lives, those whose very nature brings them to bless others. All they need to be taught is how to do it in such a way that the blessings will be heard and uplift those who receive them. This in itself is no small trick.

HAYYIM VA-HESED

> May Y-H-W-H lift His face to you.
> (NUM. 6:26)

This is difficult. Does the blessed Holy One, God forbid, have any likeness or **face**? The **face** here comes from the side of the receivers [of God's blessing]. They picture the divine light in accord with their own degree of clarity. The verse means "May Y-H-W-H lift up your perception of His face."

This is the meaning of "At the Sea He appeared to them as a youth, but as they stood before Sinai, He appeared as a compassionate white-haired elder" (*Pesikta Rabbati* 21). When they came out of Egypt, [the people] Israel were in a childlike state of mind, like a "youth." That was the level on which they could access God's light. But by the time of Sinai, their minds were expanded; they could see the whiteness and clarity of the light. *They* were in the category of "white-haired elder." That is how it can say that there God's face appeared to them as that of a compassionate old man.

This explanation of a well-known midrash answers explicitly a question the midrash itself leaves open. Was it God who changed appearances, or was it the mind-set of Israel that received the divine presence through different projected images of its own? Here it is clear that the "face of God" is none other than our own. Maimonides would be proud of this Hasidic follower!

NO'AM ELIMELEKH

> To the children of Kehat he did not give (wagons); theirs is a holy burden, they carry it on their shoulders.
> (NUM. 7:9)

Regarding Saul it says: "From his shoulders up, he was taller than any of the people" (1 Sam. 9:2).... The Talmud teaches: "Why did Saul's kingdom not continue? Because there was no blemish in him" (b. Yoma 22b). This is very strange. If there was no blemish in him, his kingdom should have continued forever! This can be understood based on the Talmudic teaching

"A sin done for [God's] sake is greater than a commandment fulfilled for ulterior motives" (b. Nazir 23b). This too is difficult to understand. How could "God's sake" apply to a sin? Who ever commanded one to sin so that it could be called "for God's sake"?

The truth seems to be as follows: Everything that the Holy Blessed One created in the world was created to benefit the creatures by way of a flow of blessing coming from above. This flow must be awakened from below; [this awakening] is known as "female waters...."

The *tsaddik* facilitates the flow of blessing. A *tsaddik* who wants to benefit people must cleave to them in order to bring about the good that they need. Any person who wants to benefit another cannot do so fully unless they are connected in total unity. A *tsaddik* must therefore connect to all the people of Israel in order to benefit them. Yet how can the *tsaddik* do this with a sinner (heaven forbid)? Even a sinner needs the divine flow and vitality, but how can the *tsaddik* connect completely to the sinner?

This is why the Talmud speaks in praise of "a sin for (God's) sake." For the *tsaddik* also sins, albeit in God's service, and through this creates the possibility of a connection with the sinner and can help him as well.

This matter of sinning for God's sake can be demonstrated in Saul's case as follows.... It seemed to Saul that killing the livestock of the Amalekites [as Samuel had commanded him to do; 1 Sam. 15] would be a great sin. If he had been capable of sinning for God's sake, he would have killed the animals. He would have reasoned that even if it seems like a sin, if God commanded it, let it be a sin for God's sake. But he was so righteous and without blemish that he was incapable of sinning even for God's sake. And since he could not sin for God's sake, he would not be able connect to sinners to bring the divine flow to them, as they had no point of connection.

Yet a king has to benefit all of Israel equally, including the sinners. And this is why his kingdom did not continue: because there was no blemish in him. He did not have the capacity to benefit everyone.

That is why Saul is referred to as "from his shoulders up—higher than all the people." The "shoulders" refer [in Lurianic Kabbalah] to extending one's arms in giving ... but what Saul had to give was higher than all the people. There was no blemish in him, and he could not unite with the people because he was above them. The only way they could receive from him was by becoming righteous people and connecting with him at his level. But he could not come down to them....

This is the meaning of the verse **To the children of Kehat he did not give (wagons); theirs is a holy burden, they carry it on their shoulders.**

The children of Kehat are the *tsaddikim*, and they must do their holy work. They must bring down the flow of blessing, bearing it on their shoulders.

Saul held his "shoulders" too high; broad shoulders are intended for bearing the people's sin and thus connecting with them. The *No'am Elimelekh*'s choice of example to demonstrate sinning for God's sake may be somewhat disappointing (the seemingly senseless slaughter of all those animals), but the message of this teaching is still clear: a person who holds by absolute principles cannot be a leader, no matter how just and right those principles may be. One wonders toward whom, across the Maggid's table, these words might have been directed.

Naso
Round Two

AG: The final piece is a great warning to the would-be leader not to stand too far above the people. But at the same time, we do want leaders who stand firmly for something. Too much willingness to come down to the "lowest common denominator" level is also wrong.

OR: I wonder if this comment really is addressed "across the table" to someone or to a "someone" within his own self. Might it be a call for course correction after some particular event, now lost to us? The would-be *tsaddik* who holds himself too high might indeed lose followers, who choose to pursue a less demanding path.

EL: We also have to look at the priestly side of the *tsaddik* in these texts, especially those on the priestly blessing. To be a *tsaddik* is to help open the channels of blessing for people, to help them feel God's presence in their lives, materially as well as spiritually. This requires a great deal of love.

AG: The *Divrey Emet* (by the Hozeh [Seer] of Lublin) seems to depict a perfectly compassionate priest; you need to be quite perfect in order to be a source of blessing.

EL: His own master R. Elimelekh never would have said that.

AM: That's why the whole Polish school rebelled against the Hozeh. He both posited and demanded so much perfection that it came to seem unreal.

AM: The "face" you need in order to receive blessing means that the process is a two-way street.

OR: Receiving is an active part of the process, not mere passivity. The one who receives the blessing does so in an act of giving, putting forth a "face" or a vessel in which to receive the light.

AG: So both are needed. Just as the *tsaddik* cannot be too high to reach people with blessing, the recipient can't be so low in his own sight so as not to offer such a vessel. Without it there can be no blessing.

Be-Ha'alotekha

Or Torah I

> When you raise up the lamps, all seven lights shall be facing the *menorah*.
> (Num. 8:2)

Read this in accord with the verse "The commandment is a lamp; Torah is light" (Prov. 6:23). The commandment is like a lamp, inside which there dwells a light. That inwardness is composed of love and awe.

When you raise yourself up by means of **the lamps**, the commandments, **all seven lights shall be facing the *menorah*.** These refer to the seven qualities, beginning with love and awe. This is parallel to our reading of "God spoke all these words [i.e., all of the commandments] in order to say: 'I am Y-H-W-H your God who brought you forth from the land of Egypt'" (Ex. 20:1–2). When you perform *any* of the commandments, you should be thinking "I am Y-H-W-H your God," representing love, and "You shall have no other gods facing Me," meaning awe. "Who brought you out of the land of Egypt": I have redeemed you from all your woes. "Do not have any other gods facing me," do not follow your desires, which constitute "another god." "Facing me" really refers to your inwardness (*panay/ penimiyyut*), which is God's holy Self. **Facing** [*peney*] **the *menorah***: this also refers to inwardness. [All the qualities need to be directed toward God, who is the *menorah* within, the Source of light.]

This teaching was preserved in fragmentary form and the translation represents an edited surmise as to the original. It seems to be saying that all the commandments are to be performed for the sake of arousing that inner light that is God's presence. The way to do this is ever to be in quest of love and awe, the combined key emotions of the religious life. These lead to *penimiyyut*, the inwardness where God is found. Have no other god but this One.

No'am Elimelekh

> God spoke to Moses ... "Tell the Children of Israel to offer the *pesah* at its time. On the fourteenth day of this month in the evening...." Moses told the people of Israel to offer the *pesah*. And they offered the *pesah* on the first month ... in the evening ... and the Children of Israel did everything that God had commanded Moses.
>
> (Num. 9:1–5)

Why does the description of God's commandment include specific details regarding the time of *Pesah* while Moses's instructions to the people are described without details? Following that, the time of the actual offering is again described in detail. If there is no need for detail in describing Moses's instructions because we assume he followed God's word precisely, wouldn't we also assume that Israel followed the instructions they received? Also, why do we need **the Children of Israel did ...** at the end of the sentence if it already says **and they offered the *pesah*** at the beginning of the sentence?

This is something essential to all time-defined *mitsvot* such as *pesah, sukkah, shofar,* or *lulav*. You must fulfill these *mitsvot* at a very high spiritual level, with joy and cleaving to the Divine. In doing this you can create an ongoing connection to the Holy, not limited by time. The word *mo'ed* is used in the verse (**at its time**, *be-mo'ado*) because it has two meanings. It means time, but it also means "festival," thus alluding to joy and divine connection. All time-defined *mitsvot* are enacted in their specific times but create potential for the future, referring to the holiness you have stimulated that stays with you.

This is why Moses told them to offer the *pesah* without giving the details of time. He meant that they should constantly be doing the *pesah*, created by action on its specific date, and sustained afterwards by means of the holiness they aroused, continuously awakening them to God's service. That is why in the description of Israel's celebration it says that they did it *be-mo'ado* ["in its time," not in our verse] with great joy and divine connection.

That is also why it says both that **they offered** and they **did**. It teaches that their doing had a double [effect]; one for the time they did it and another for the potential that they created for the future.

As this teaching reminds us, the success of our year-cycle celebrations is not measured only by our experience of the holidays. It is also measured by the impact these celebrations have on our daily lives.

Or Torah II

> Make for yourself two trumpets of silver.
> (Num. 10:2)

The phrase *shtey hatsotserot*, **two trumpets**, is to be read as linked with "On the image of the throne was an image with the appearance of a man, from above" (Ezek. 1:26).

A person is really only made up of *dalet* and *mem*, two letters that may be taken to stand for *dibbur*, speech, and *malkhut*, God's kingship that dwells within it [but together also composing *dam*, or "blood"]. But when you attach yourself to the blessed Holy One who is the cosmic *aleph* [representing the oneness of all being], you become *adam*, a full human being [i.e., the divine presence turns "flesh and blood" into humanity].

The blessed Holy One entered into multiple contractions of His own self, coming through various worlds, in order to become one with humans, who could not have withstood God's original brightness. Now the person has to leave behind all corporeality, also traveling across many worlds, in order to become One with God. Then our own existence is itself negated. Such a person is truly called *adam*, the one on the image of the throne, or *kisse*. That word can also refer to "hiding," for God Himself is hidden (*kissui*) there. This follows the prophet's description of "cloud and crackling fire." At first the person is in a "cloudy" state, filled with darkness, unable to pray with enthusiasm. But then along comes the "crackling fire," when we attain ecstasy. This is the "image of the throne," where our blessed God is hidden. We discover it in a *mar'eh* ("appearance"), a word that can also mean "mirror." Whatever is awakened in us is awakened also within God. If love is aroused in the *tsaddik*, so too is it aroused above. The same can be true of any quality. This is true of those who are very pure, rising across all those worlds to become one with God....

These are the two *hatsotserot* (**trumpets**) of *kessef* (**silver**). A person is only a *hatsi tsurah*, a half of the whole form—*dam*, or blood. But the *aleph* by itself, as it were, is also an incomplete form. But only when attached to one another are they made whole. *Kessef* can mean "longing." When you long for the blessed Holy One, God loves you as well....

The theological statement here is quite a bold one: both God and the human are "*hatsi tsures*," as it was pronounced; they are both "half forms," each needing the other in order to be complete. We humans may be mere flesh and blood, needing God's presence to be whole. But God without us is "merely" an *aleph*, not yet a whole word, unable to be manifest in speech or to bring about God's earthly kingdom. We thus need to long for one another, in order to make for wholeness both "above" and "below."

Torey Zahav

> If you come to war in your land against the enemy who confronts you, blow the horn. You will be recalled by Y-H-W-H your God and saved from your enemies.
>
> (Num. 10:9)

... "Draw redemption near to my soul; for the sake of my enemies, redeem me" (Ps. 69:19). Exile really belongs to each individual, based on [our struggle with] personal qualities and evil desires. In order to call out for collective redemption, a person first has to be personally redeemed, free from all of these. Then all the accusing forces vanish; enemies turn into friends. "Once God accepts a person's ways, even one's enemies follow suit" (Prov. 16:7). Then, once redeemed from all judgment, you may cry out for the redemption of all Israel. But not so if you yourself are still in exile, hemmed in by the "shells" of moral inadequacy and desire. This is the meaning of "Draw redemption near to my soul." Help me to break their hold, so that I may be delivered from all my enemies.

This is **If you come**; if you desire to come before Me, see that first you have **war in your land.** Do battle with the earthly forces, your evil and ugly desires, your corporeal self, the evil urge **who confronts you**. That one comes to destroy you, to deprive you of both worlds, [this and the next]. That one is the homegrown enemy, residing within the self.

Blow the horn. I heard in the name of our master Dov Baer that the word "trumpet" (*hatsotserot*) can be read as referring to "two half forms" (*hatsi tsurot*). I think this can be taken as referring to the verse "For a hand is upon the throne of God [*kes YaH*]; that Y-H-W-H does battle with Amalek in each generation" (Ex. 17:16). [The word "throne" is missing its final *aleph*.] "My name is not whole, and My throne is not whole" [say the sages on this verse, as long as Amalek persists (cf. RaSHI)]. They are both half forms. **Blow the horn** in order to break through yourselves, not to prevent some ill from coming upon you, but for the sake of God's great name, so that it and God's throne might become whole. Blow on these two half forms, to make them whole and complete....

Your own inner battle is only preparation for the real task, which is the struggle to bring about divine wholeness, but you cannot engage in that unless you are properly purified.

Dibrat Shelomoh (from *Ki Tavo*)

> The manna's ... appearance was that of bedellium.
> (Num. 11:7)

All the worlds were created with letters and speech-acts, as it says: "With the word of Y-H-W-H heaven and earth were created" (Ps. 33:6). This utterance is the animating force that gives everything life, and God's word is the appearance, taste, smell, and the pleasure within it. The brilliance of this force is referred to as the "eye" (*'ayin*) of each thing, as in the verse "**its appearance** [*'eyno*] **was that of bedellium**" (Num. 11:7). The divine life-force sparkles and glimmers through it, just as the vitality of your intellect twinkles through your eyes. This is why it says of all creations, "God saw that it was good" (i.e., the divine appearance within it is good)....

Yet these "eyes" can also tempt you into being seduced by physical cravings, as it says "his master's wife cast her eyes upon Joseph" (Gen. 39:7). The sages taught, "[You should not stare at inappropriate things,] even if you were as full of eyes as the Angel of Death" (b. Avodah Zarah 20a/b). That is, if you see every pleasure on its own [superficially separate from all others], it is as if you are full of eyes, seeing things as would the Angel of Death.

This is the meaning of Rav Hisda's statement in the Talmud, "Had I been married at the age of twelve, I would have said to the Accuser, 'an arrow in your eye!'" (b. Kiddushin 29b–30a). That is, I would have paid no mind to the physical pleasures of this world, realizing full well that they are all expressions of God's light—all have a single Parent.

On the verse "[Tamar] sat down at the crossroads" (*petah 'eynayim*, lit. "open eyes," to seduce her father-in-law Judah; Gen. 38:14), the sages remind us that all eyes are trained upon the blessed One [i.e., that one can see God, the "eye," within each thing (*Bereshit Rabbah* 85:7)]. This is the meaning "those who fear God are looking toward the divine eyes" (Ps. 33:18)—all of which are embraced in His Oneness....

The manna shows us that the physical world indeed twinkles with divine brilliance, hinting at an all-inclusive illumination just beneath the surface. Don't see the world as full of endless temptations, be they spiritual or carnal, each of which can pull you from the path at any instant. That's the superficial paradigm of the proverbial Angel of Death! The deeper truth is that the sights, sounds, and tastes of this world are a colorful representation of divine light refracted through the prism of the physical realm. The radical example of Tamar serves as a reminder that the "eyes" of God are indeed everywhere, meaning that one can seek out the divine presence even in the most unlikely places. The "eyes" that lead you astray are the same eyes that allow you a vision of the divine presence amid this world. Be careful, but don't be afraid!

Be-Ha'alotekha
Round Two

EL: The call to turn inward is heard very loudly here, the inner self as the meeting-place between God and the person.

AM: But the work is to purify yourself before going any farther, either toward union with God or toward working to uplift others.

EL: The *Torey Zahav* text insists on that. You have to "do war in your land," struggle with your own earthly self, before you can "blow the horn" and see that God and man are two halves of the same cosmic self.

OR: But does it always work that way? Aren't some people purified and uplifted within themselves through turning outward? Isn't there a back-and-forth between personal and collective redemption?

EL: These are two modes of worship. For some, or in some situations, the self is transformed from without, sometimes by the influence of others and sometimes by joining in a collective task.

AG: Hasidic wisdom makes room for both of those. The *tsaddik* can indeed uplift you, if you allow that to happen. But often the wise *tsaddik* tells you that you have to do the inner work on your own.

EL: But we're losing focus on the really earth-shattering words of the Maggid here. God and the person are both incomplete without one another. We are mere *dam*, flesh and blood, without the divine *aleph*. But God too is "half a form" without us. What does that say to this whole conversation about how to become pure?

AG: It raises up the importance of the task. If you make yourself into a proper vessel, you really can be joined to the One, fulfilling God's longing as well as your own. Then together you can really do the work of outward transformation.

AM: If you purify and open your heart, God becomes accessible to you. This is the gift of *tsimtsum*, the cosmic Source of our lives acting like a loving parent who simplifies his mind so that the child can understand. Our Creator wants us ordinary flesh-and-blood humans to succeed in doing God's work.

Shelah Lekha

Or ha-Me'ir

> They spoke to him, saying: "We came into the land where you sent us. It indeed flows with milk and honey, and this is its fruit. But the people dwelling there is strong...." But Caleb silenced the people for Moses, saying: "We will indeed go up and inherit it, for we are able."
>
> (Num. 13:27–28, 30)

The meaning in our terms of Moses's wanting them to scout out the land of Canaan was to teach Israel to scout out all the letters that are dressed in "land" or earthly things. To this they replied: Yes, **we came into the *land* where you sent us.** We indeed do want to see our King, to grasp divinity even as found within earthly matters and human pleasures. We do not want to cheat at the service of God, doing things that alienate us from Him. But we find it difficult. Not every mind is capable of this acting in the lower world while pointing toward the upper. It is all too likely that we will fall, remaining almost completely sunk in corporeality. Not only will we fail to lift anything up, but we will bring down those sublime letters of Torah, just making things worse. "Only few can rise high" (b. Sukkah 45b), having that power to uplift the letters of Torah.

This was "the ill report of the land that the Children of Israel scouted, saying: 'The land you sent us to scout is one that consumes its inhabitants'" (Num. 13:32). I heard the Maggid explain that the distinct character of earthliness is that it destroys those who become too much at home in it, filling themselves with earthly pleasures. The word *yoshveha* ("its dwellers") implies delay ... destroying a person in both this world and the next. This happens to those who allow themselves to tarry, getting stuck in the physical world....

But Caleb silenced the people for Moses, saying: "We will indeed go up and inherit it, for we are able." RaSHI says that he silenced them all, since "Caleb had a different spirit within him" (Num. 14:24). His heart was truly whole with God. His soul deeply knew that the blessed Holy One does not seek confrontation with people, but gives each one of us the sort of burden we are able to bear. Each is given a heavier or lighter burden of service in accord with our degree of awareness and understanding. If only we turn our hearts toward heaven, we too can bring about ascent, lifting the limbs of the *shekhinah* to Her elevated home. This is the meaning of **We will indeed go up**. It is not as you said: **The people dwelling there is strong**, and therefore whoever does not have great awareness is as useless as a dry twig, unable to raise up the lower rungs. **We will indeed go up**, said Caleb, counting himself among them. Each of us on our own level can raise up the *shekhinah*. **We will indeed go up and inherit** Her (*otah*). We will all act as one person, together inheriting *otah*, the letter *heh*, *shekhinah*.

There is not one among Israel who does not have a place to hold on [to] the embodiment of *shekhinah*; each of us can do the work of cosmic repair corresponding to that particular hold. That proper work is easy to do, because we were not created in this world with a task harder than we can accomplish.... This "silenced them all," because the blessed Holy One does not impose service on people that is too hard for them to do.

Yes, there is a "right" place for each of us—all of us humans, not just Jews—to hold fast to the *shekhinah*. Once we find it, we will learn how each of us has to serve and what our task is in this world. But finding that place can be a lifetime's labor! The *Or ha-Me'ir* struggled mightily with issues raised as Hasidism grew into a widespread popular movement. This text is his answer to his own inner doubts about whether the community to whom he was preaching was up to the task.

Or Torah (from *Massa'ey*)

> A land [*erets*] that consumes those who dwell in it [*yoshveha*].
>
> (Num. 13:32)

Every thing contains the ten [moral, human, and divine] qualities. That is what we mean when we say that the entire Torah is God's delight. Even its narratives speak of some quality like love or fear. The blessed Holy One is cloaked in each of them. You just have to take care to raise up every thought. If thoughts of love come to you, lift them up. The same with fear [and all the rest]. Don't just **dwell** or sit there with them! That would be really foolish.

A man travels to a city to do some business. [Instead of engaging in business,] he just "sits" there, having left his family behind. Can you imagine any greater folly? In the same way, the blessed Holy One sends you to a certain thought, in order that you raise it up. It would be really foolish of you to just **dwell** there with it and not restore it to God.

That is ***erets***, the corporeal realm, that consumes those who just **dwell in it** forever.

Like Moses's spies, we too are sent into the land, the world of our physical selves and worldly thoughts, in order to do the "business" of uplifting and transformation. How easy it is, like the ten spies, to become intimidated. Or even worse—to just forget what we were sent here to do.

Tsemah ha-Shem li-Tsevi I

> Moreover [*ve-ulam*], as I live, the glory of Y-H-W-H fills all the earth.
>
> (Num. 14:21)

The sages taught (b. Hullin 89a): What should a person do in order to live? Make oneself as though mute (*ilem*). But might this apply to Torah as well? Thus Scripture says: "Of justice, you shall speak" (Ps. 58:2).

... The life-energy for this one who chooses silence also derives from words of Torah. They represent the letter *vav* of God's name, the Tree of Life. On this the *Zohar* (3:2a) quotes the verse "Give me a sign [or, "letter"] of truth and you will be kept alive" (Josh. 2:12–3). This refers to the letter *vav* [*tif'eret*, truth], upon which life depends. That is the *vav* that differentiates *ulam* ("moreover") from *ilem* ("mute" [distinguishing speech from silence]); life is drawn forth through this *vav*.

The glory of Y-H-W-H fills all the earth. Our sages read "Who is like You among the mighty" (Ex. 15:11) as "Who is like You among the mute" (*elim/ilmim*; b. Gittin 56b). He hears Himself cursed and is silent! In this way the glory of Y-H-W-H fills all the earth: even in the place of curses and disrespect, the glory of God hears and is silent. This is the source for the "mute" person's ability to remain silent and not feel those curses, to maintain balance whether praised or denounced. This is one of the most praiseworthy and exalted human states.

This is the meaning of "Open your mouth wide and I will fill it" (Ps. 81:11). The three letters of *ilem* ("mute") will be turned around to form *male'* ("full"). "Full is the blessing of Y-H-W-H" (Deut. 33:23). In this way, **the glory of Y-H-W-H fills all the earth**.

Hasidim were (and are) often mocked by both Jews and gentiles for their extreme displays of piety. The ability to maintain silent balance in the face of attacks, an ancient teaching of Jewish and other moralists, came to be highly praised. The cultivation of inner stillness, to nourish that balance, requires great skill. Here the silent one is seen as deriving that strength from Torah, the Tree of Life. The verse is being read to say, "In the silent one, I Y-H-W-H am alive; through such people, My glory fills the earth." How might this lesson apply to us today?

No'am Elimelekh

> But my servant Caleb, because he was imbued with a different spirit and remained loyal to Me....
> (Num. 14:24)

There are two kinds of *tsaddikim*. There are some for whom it is necessary to be separated and apart from people. When they are among people they may fall from their appropriate spiritual level. Then there are those who do not fall from their spiritual level even when involved in the community and talking to people. Actually, they have a positive impact on others.

This is similar to something I heard from my master and teacher, the great and holy R. Dov Baer of Rovno, whose soul rests in heaven. Regarding the statement "the holy flesh [of the sacrifices] never [*me-'olam*] spoiled" (m. Avot 5:5), he explained that a person who is "holy flesh," meaning a totally righteous person, never spoils, even when involved with the public (*'olam*) and conversing with them.

This is the meaning of the phrase **but my servant Caleb, because he was imbued with a different spirit**. He did not fall from his spiritual level even though he spoke with them (the other spies). On the contrary, he **remained loyal to Me**.

The Maggid is certainly attempting to encourage his disciples to take on leadership roles, and not to fear engagement with the broad community. However, one must imagine that even among Hasidic *rebbes* there are very few "totally righteous" people, so the challenges of communal service and the dangers of corruption must have felt very real.

Tsemah ha-Shem li-Tsevi II

> Speak to the Children of Israel, telling them that they shall make themselves fringes on the corners of their garments throughout their generations ... they shall be fringes for you, and you shall see it [or "Him"].
> (Num. 15:38–39)

Why is the word **themselves** needed in this verse? "They shall makes fringes" would have sufficed. This hints that they should make *themselves* into a way to see God. Thus RaSHI interpreted the word *tsitsit* ("fringes") as related to "gazing," as in "Behold He stands behind our wall, gazing [*metsits*] through the latticework" (Song 2:9). This brings about the fear of God, since "fear" (*yir'ah*) and "seeing" (*re'iyah*) are made up of the same letters. Therefore if you lay a garment down in a box, it does not require fringes (b. Menahot 41a), for the essence of the *mitsvah* lies in **themselves**....

At first, speaking of fear alone, the passage speaks in the third ("hidden") person, for out of fear a person hides from the King. But when you love, you join yourself to the King. This is **and you shall see it**, referring to Y-H-W-H....

First it says: **they shall make themselves fringes** (= "gazers"), meaning that they shall seek ways of seeing for themselves. But then it turns into **they shall *be* fringes** ("gazings") **for you**; this can be read to mean that you yourselves shall *become* ways of seeing.

This can be understood through the comment of *Midrash Shemuel* [Rabbi Shmu'el Uceda, sixteenth century] on "a seeing eye," [as a quality that a person should choose—m. Avot 2:1]. In the physical realm, the eye does not really see. Light shines into the eye, and one sees by means of that light. That is why, scientists tell us, we do not see the air, since it is everywhere and lies directly upon the eye.... The *shekhinah* too fills all the earth, and that is why we are unable to see it. The physical person has no light in the eye but sees by virtue of this external [lit. "hidden"] light. But if we had essential light, from within the eye, we would see the air as well....

Thus Scripture says: "They will see eye to eye as Y-H-W-H returns to Zion" (Is. 52:8). Even though the eyes of God are everywhere, lying directly upon the human eye, we will be able to see them because we will have light in our eyes' own essence. This is seeing "eye to eye."

First fear alone: They shall make themselves gazing—drawing forth light so that they may look upon God. This can only be from a distance, as in "From afar Y-H-W-H appears to me" (Jer. 31:2). They could not see closer up, having no essential light within their eyes. But then, when they come to ... the level of love, it says, **They shall *be*** [gazings, tsitsit] **for you**, meaning that you make yourselves into seeing, the light coming from within you, so that you may see close up.

The *mitsvah* of *tsitsit* is here transformed—as all the *mitsvot* are supposed to be—into a path toward mystical insight, a transformation of the person (or community) as a vehicle of insight itself.

Tsemah ha-Shem li-Tsevi III

> They will be fringes for you, and you will see it and remember all the commandments of Y-H-W-H, and do them. You will not turn to follow your heart or your eyes, after which you go whoring.
> (Num. 15:39–40)

This means that you will attain the qualities of humility and lowliness, one before the other. **They will be fringes**, meaning that they will make themselves into such [lowly beings] as are dragged along on the edges of the garment.... Such humility will surely lead them to fulfill "Love your neighbor as yourself" (Lev. 19:18), which contains the entire Torah (b. Shabbat 31a). Thus **you will ... remember all the commandments of Y-H-W-H**, which lie within this general rule....

When a person fulfills this commandment to "love your neighbor as yourself," it means that you love the other as though he or she were you. When you give alms to that person, it is as though you were giving to yourself. You can't stand seeing that person being disgraced any more than you could stand such disgrace to yourself. In this way you will come to see the face of the *shekhinah* without being ashamed. This is the word *tsitsit*, derived from "gazing [*metsits*] through the latticework" (Song 2:9), a way of looking....

You will see it and remember all the commandments. The sages taught (b. Berakhot 63a): "Upon what short phrase do all the great bodies of teaching depend? 'Know Him in all your ways' (Prov. 3:6)." Indeed the entire Torah depends on this. They also spoke of that would-be proselyte who said: "Teach me the entire Torah while I stand on one foot." [Hillel's answer was] to fulfill "Love your neighbor as yourself" by means of not doing to others what is hateful to you (b. Shabbat 31a)....

This is the impact of **Remember all the commandments of Y-H-W-H**, embodied in loving your neighbor as yourself. **After which you go whoring** represents the opposite of love. By following this path you will reach the high state of "Know Him in all your ways," which is the entirety of Torah....

Really "Know Him in all your ways" is directly hinted at and included in "Love your neighbor as yourself," since RaSHI interprets "neighbor" to refer to the blessed Holy One....

These readings of *Parashat Tsitsit* (the teaching on the fringes) represent a remarkable drawing together of the mystical and the ethical realms, a union that itself may be the most important task of religion.

Shelah Lekha
Round Two

AG: The first and last teachings in this group tie together in a very powerful way. The real world of *artsiyyut*, daily living, is not a "land that consumes" us, because we're promised that no person is given a task that is too hard to bear. We just have to stretch to carry the burden and make it a way of service. Then the last text reminds us that it's all about loving our neighbor (and our Neighbor!); that alone will lead us to "know Him in all your ways."

AM: The same is true in the little *Or Torah* passage. All of life is a series of occasions to uplift and serve. Don't miss the opportunity! Everything depends on us and how we do our "business." Yes, if you just sit there with *artsiyyut*, it will indeed consume you. So get to work!

AG: The positioning of this discussion in *Shelah Lekha* is especially powerful. Yes, it's about you and your struggles with corporeality. But here is the people of Israel about to enter the Land. "Don't let it drag you down!" is the message they are to hear. Being in the Land will mean lots of daily responsibility on the physical plane. See it all as an opportunity for service.

OR: Hear this as a religious Zionist—whether Rav Kook or Martin Buber—would. How will our coming into the Land become an opportunity for uplifting? And how will we avoid the pitfalls of being consumed by it?

AM: That sounds lofty. But what do you do when your *artsiyyut* comes in the form of a tank or a gun? That kind of "worldliness" is not so easy to uplift.

OR: The ten spies are usually depicted as wicked or ill-willed. But here they're not. "It's just too hard for us!" is all they're saying. They're giving up.

AG: That's why they need Caleb to say to them: "You *can't* give up!" His message is one of reassurance; the enemy he's fighting is not wickedness, but despair.

OR: How do you know how to counsel people? When should they admit that the burden they've been given really is beyond them? And when is reassurance the right thing to offer?

AG: Yes, but remember the beautiful teaching about *tsitsit*: you can find God there, anywhere. Especially within yourself, using yourself as a way to "gaze" and find God.

OR: The simplicity and intimacy of *tsitsit* make this all the more powerful.

AM: And the love. Through your *tsitsit*, you gaze back at the Lover, who is peering at you through the latticework of the Song of Songs.

Korah

Hesed le-Avraham ha-Malakh

> And in his anger Moses said to God, "Do not heed their offering; I have not taken a single donkey from them, and I did not wrong any one of them."
> (Num. 16:15)

The Talmud interprets Moses's statement as "I have not taken a single object of desire [*hemed*]" (b. Megillah 9b). This can be understood through reference to the statement by the woman of Shunam [Tsarafat]—"You have come to me, to recall my sin" (1 Kings 17:18). You should always rouse your good side, because when you don't, your bad side awakens. However, when you are at a low spiritual level and in the presence of an elevated *tsaddik*, you may not be able to arouse your good side. The greatness of the *tsaddik* may overwhelm you. Then, heaven forbid, your evil side could awaken. This is the meaning of the Shunamite woman's complaint—"You have come to me to recall my sin." [Your coming to me has awakened my sinful side.]

But if the *tsaddik* is humble this will not happen. Moses was the most humble of all people, and the meaning of **I have not taken a single donkey** [*hamor*] is to say that I have not caused any person to raise their corporeal (*homer*) side. And according to the Talmud it is to say, "I have not provoked the desires [*hemdah*] of any person." **And I did not wrong any one** [*ehad*] **of them** means I did not damage the One (*ahdut*), the life-force within them.

An important reminder for people in positions of leadership. Take care that your strengths support and encourage other people to be the best that they can, rather than overwhelming them.

Yosher Divrey Emet (#30)

> Why do you uplift yourselves over the congregation of Y-H-W-H?
> (Num. 16:3)

Korah's conflict with Moses took place despite the fact of Moses's great humility, as the Torah declares ["Moses was more humble than any person on the face of the earth"] (Num. 12:3). Nevertheless, some grandiosity remained in certain things he did. He was ruler over Israel, and he conducted himself like a king over his people. Yet he did all this for God's sake, to guide people in God's service. This would not have been possible without someone to take the lead. Still, at first he did not want it. He refused, saying to God, "Send whom You will" (Ex. 4:13), until God forced him to accept the office.

Even though Korah possessed both intelligence and the holy spirit, a spark of envy remained within him. He had not purified his heart of it in a total way. Envy derives from that sense of grandness; he could not believe that Moses did everything by the word of God and that he was in truth so humble and lowly. He thought that Moses was using his exalted role in a way that opposed truth, that he had strayed from truth and erred in aggrandizing himself. It was Moses's sense of his own greatness, Korah thought, that caused him to exalt himself over God's community, as he said: **Why do you uplift yourselves over the congregation of Y-H-W-H?**

Regarding himself, Korah never imagined that he might bear a sense of grandiosity. He thought that his desire to rule derived entirely from the side of truth. On the verse "His heart rose high in the ways of God" (2 Chron. 17:6), I have taught that such a sense of greatness is permitted. Korah did not want to attribute any lack to his own sense of greatness, when really the proper greatness belonged to Moses. Korah thought just the opposite, as the evil of envy caused his heart to see bad as good and good as bad....

The struggle between them was over deep matters. It requires great faith to always assign the lack to yourself, ever seeking submission and humility, even when it comes to doing good. Take care: it might be sinful self-exaltation that makes you want to do a *mitsvah* that is not required of you and that might be performed by somebody else. Do not think that you are more the right person to do it than your fellow, for that is grandiosity....

[Learn from Moses's own reluctance to lead] not to compete for any *mitsvah* that has an aspect of authority about it. Flee from such a thing. If it is right for you, God will force the whole world to make that opportunity for leadership come your way. But weigh this matter with deep thought and a sense of pure justice, asking God's help that no evil urge lead you to oppose His will....

Ah, if only this advice were heeded by today's generation of leaders—both within the Hasidic community and far beyond! The evaluation of Korah offered here is unusually generous among those found in traditional sources. He was not a person of wicked intent, but simply one who did not turn his sharp eye of critical judgment inward on himself. Do you known this person? Are you, in part, such a person?

Tsemah ha-Shem li-Tsevi

> ... A service of giving I shall make your priesthood; the stranger who approaches shall die.
> (Num. 18:7)

This may be understood through a parable: A king gives his noble servants gifts of cities and towns. But the one who is most beloved to him is given none of these. The king tells him instead to come close, to serve and wait on him. He is to set the king's table and light the king's lamp, fulfilling all of his personal needs. Finally this servant says to the king: Why have you given gifts and property to all the other nobles, but not to me? He answered: They serve me through my government, paying fees and taxes. But you serve me in my own body. Is there any reward greater than that of being so close to the king himself? You need no other payment; all those nobles who see your honor will bow before you. They will provide you with anything you want. The service you offer is itself your reward.

This is "You shall not inherit within their land; you shall have no portion among them. I am your lot and portion amid the Children of Israel" (Num. 18:20). **A service of giving I shall make your priesthood**; the giving itself is the service. Why? Because such is your priesthood, your reward. **The**

stranger who approaches shall die. But you have been drawn near. There is no greater honor.

This description of the Levites within the community of Israel came to be a paradigm for the way the Jewish people ideally understood its own role of priesthood among the nations, including the reality of temporary but long-extended landlessness. For such a priesthood to function, however, the laity has to buy into the model. This was never quite the case with the Jewish diaspora, certainly not once Jews came to live as minorities in two supercessionist religious civilizations, each of which in turn sought to inherit this same model, seeing themselves as missionary priests to the rest of humanity.

Ma'amarey Admor ha-Zaken

> The service of the Levites is thus....
> (Num. 18:23)

The service of the Levites is in song, to arouse such [emotional] qualities as love, awe, and joy. Their arousal below brings about their arousal above. This is also the quality of *binah*, or contemplation (*hitbodedut*), since the emotions arise from the contemplative self.

But *kohen* ("priest") refers to the aspect of mind (*hokhmah*) that lies beyond all these qualities, since they do not exist on the rung of "there is nothing else [but God]" (Deut. 4:35). When you see that there is nothing but God, and all existence is truly negated, then there is no one to love, no one before whom to stand in awe, nor any other emotion. This is "priest of the heart's desire," beyond all such qualities (*Zohar* 3:39a). This is the meaning of "Silence is a guard for mind" (m. Avot 3:13). Silence reaches higher than sound, which is the Levites' song. Here you cannot raise your voice, since your existence itself has been negated....

Both of these rungs of service, those of priest and Levite, exist in the mystic devotee's life as Hasidism understands it. Song and silence exist in a fructifying dialectic with one another, each aspect giving birth and renewed energy to the other.

Korah
Round Two

EL: Quite naturally, the subject on their minds is leadership and humility. Korah brings that up for them, but it is never far from their concerns.

AG: Let's ask a broader question. What does Hasidism—both text and history—have to teach us about leadership? The movement was born, after all, amid a great critique of failed leadership. The writings of the *Toledot* are filled with biting comments about inadequate leaders. Both Jewish society and the Polish state in which they lived were suffering from this crisis.

EL: The most important key to real leadership is reluctance to take it on. Watching today's candidates for political office, in Israel as well as in America, you can't help but see how eager they are for the office. Is it really then "public service"? Hasidism teaches that a real leader is there to serve both God and the community. But this is not a high office you are to strive for; it is one to which you are called, sometimes kicking and screaming.

OR: Wait a minute! That's a very idealized view of Hasidism. Look at the outrageous claims—miracles, spiritual perfection, and all the rest—that are being made for the Hasidic *tsaddik*. How much room for humility and reluctance do they really leave? On the other hand, we can say that if you have the talent to lead, you should feel obligated to use it, to offer it.

EL: But how do you deal with the problem of ego and ego needs in putting forth a claim to lead? Should you look for balance, for a golden mien? Or should you follow someone like R. Elimelekh, who goes to extremes to deflate your ego—knowing that the other side is also going to assert itself to an extreme degree?

AM: It's worth recalling that these men are disciples of the Maggid, who seems to have offered a somewhat reluctant model of leadership.

AG: He was quiet enough in his charisma to allow room for the big personalities among his disciples to emerge in all their variety. In the image of Moses they also see a reluctant and humble leader.

OR: Yes, but Moses is really a more complicated figure. They pick up on that side of him because they are struggling with the pedestal on which their disciples have placed them. But a potential leader needs to accept and "own" some sense of potential, a willingness to step forward. Without that you remain isolated, just a "*tsaddik* for yourself," but not for others. Leadership does require boldness and self-assertion, alongside humility.

EL: That's why the rabbis taught that a sage should be allowed a small bit—"an eighth of an eighth" of pride.

Hukkat

Me'or 'Eynayim

> Y-H-W-H spoke to Moses and Aaron, saying: "This is the statute of the Torah.... Speak to the Children of Israel and let them take unto you a perfect red cow, having no blemish and never yet yoked."
> (Num. 19:1–2)

The Torah is composed of letters, vowel points, musical notations (*te'amim*), and crownlets. But this is only the revealed Torah; all of it can be accessed by the human mind, each according to one's own level. But the light within Torah, that of which the sages said, "The light within it will bring them back to goodness" (*Eikhah Rabbah* Petihta 2), is the quality of Nothing, that which cannot be grasped. It is beyond any reason (*ta'am*); it is the source from which Torah flows, the Creator. In this way Y-H-W-H and Torah are one.

Everyone who engages with Torah has to vitally engage with its inner light, the Nothing beyond all reason. This is why the musical notations of Torah are called *te'amim*: even though they are a subtle matter, it is still possible to find meanings in them. But that inwardness called Nothing is beyond any such access. The learner has to cleave to the light that flows forth from it; this will surely restore you to goodness. When your inner self cleaves to Torah's inner light, you become a throne for God's presence as it flows through Torah. Yes, it is true that when learning you need to exercise discernment and to seek out reasons. But in order to attain wholeness, you need to do this too, for this is the "light hidden for the righteous" (b. Hagigah 12a) [within the Torah]....

So if you want Torah to be effective in making you good, seek out the flowing light within it, that from which Torah itself is formed (*nigzerah*). This is referred to as a "cow," as in the sages' teaching that "more than the calf wants to suckle, the cow wants to nurse" (said of students and teachers; b. Pesahim 112a). The source of flow is called "cow," and in this case so too is the hidden light flowing forth from Torah, [the "milk" of wisdom].

Now Torah itself is called by Moses's name, as in "Remember the Torah of My servant Moses" (Mal. 3:22). When we engage in Torah, we need to take the Nothing discussed here and attach it to the revealed Torah, the Torah of Moses. Thus will Torah itself become whole, as God intended it, a pure and brilliant light shining through the letters called "Torah of Moses."

This is **Speak to the Children of Israel and let them take unto you**. To that Torah called by your name, the revealed Torah of Moses, they have to **take ... a perfect red cow**, the flowing source that shines within Torah, called **red** because of its brilliant color and inconceivably pure light. Then it will be **perfect**, with the wholeness God intended. It may also be called **perfect** in the sense explained by the Ba'al Shem Tov, who said that the hidden light remains perfect in innocence, since only very few people have ever reached it. "The Torah of Y-H-W-H is perfect" (Ps. 19:8) means that the quality of Torah that is called "Torah of Y-H-W-H" and not "Torah of Moses" remains pure because so few have trod the path to it or reached its rung.

But in these generations, every whole person has to make the effort to get there. This is **having no blemish**: "blemish" is a lack, and the Torah of Moses will be lacking until the whole person becomes aroused to be attached to this quality of Nothing. Why is that? Because she is **never yet yoked**: such a person has not yet taken on the yoke of heaven's kingdom and thus become whole. But that is indeed the only way to wholeness. Onkelos translated **statute of the Torah** as "the cut decree [*gezerah*] of Torah as God commands it," meaning that you have to reach toward that source from which Torah was cut or hewn. Then you may be called a complete servant of Y-H-W-H.

This passage that is seen as locus classicus for the mysterious nature of Torah is a good occasion for the *Me'or 'Eynayim* to return to one of his favorite themes, the insistence that true Torah study is a contemplative exercise and that without this it has little meaning. Like some others in the early Hasidic world, he must have been fighting a significant battle with Torah scholars who he felt just missed the entire point. The final paragraph opens with a clear invitation to end the esoteric quality of the Jewish spiritual quest and to demand that it be accessible to everyone. This was the true revolution of Hasidism.

It is also noteworthy that here the typical gender roles (male = active, giver of blessing; female = passive receiver) are shifted. The cow, source of milk (nourishment, blessing), is the giver. God as Mother (*binah*, *shekhinah*) could also be depicted in this way.

Torey Zahav

> This is the statute of the Torah: If a person dies in a tent, anyone who enters the tent, along with anything in it, shall be defiled for seven days.
> (Num. 19:14)

Our sages [defining "tent" as "the tent of Torah"] read this to mean that "Torah is fulfilled only in those who [metaphorically, referring to intense learning] kill themselves for it" (b. Berakhot 63a). Following this interpretation, however, we still need to understand the latter part of the verse: **anyone who enters the tent ... shall be defiled for seven days**.

We are taught that a person should study Torah even if that study is not for its own sake, because such study will lead to "for its own sake" learning (b. Sotah 22b).

God has structured the cosmos in parallel form. Just as there are seven *sefirot* of holiness, so are there seven of defiling shells. The shell surrounds the fruit, as is known.... You have to pass through those shells and break them in order to get to the inner tent. That tent is holy *malkhut*, the Oral Torah, the fear of God. From there you can proceed to *tif'eret*, the Written Torah, the quality of love.

To do this, you need the devotion to "kill yourself," that is kill off all the "shells" and evil parts of your own bodily self. You need to break through the lusts, the false motives, and all the other nonsense you have about you until you can reach that inner life-flow of soul, a part of transcendence that is within you. As you do this, you do the same reaching upward, breaking through the shells until you reach that inner tent of true undeterred awe and love, wholly directed toward Y-H-W-H.

Until you break those shells, your learning and worship are not "for their own sake"; you are still within the husks of selfhood.... Only when you are willing to surrender your life for each act ... do you really attain that rung. That being the case, it is unreasonable to say to yourself that since you are still in a corporeal state and unable to break through, "Why should I study at all?" You can't start out in the highest state, but need to work your way through the shells. Only after some time will you be able to rise above the confusion they cause and reach the "for its own sake" stage. But if you don't set out to study at all, you will never pave the path for that journey. You therefore *must* begin at the "not for its own sake" level.

In this way I have also interpreted the verse "Speak of them when sitting in your house and when walking by the way; when you lie down and when you rise up" (Deut. 6:7). You need to speak of them "when you lie down." When you are in a lesser state of mind you need to serve God in fear, love, and joy, so that you will "rise up," having those same qualities on a higher rung. You may not say that since I am now "lying down," in a low place, I will not study. It is only from lying down that one comes to rise up. Keep learning, even when your mind seems small....

Though not fully spelled out, the preacher seems to be saying that in order to enter the inner tent of *malkhut*, or soul, you need to begin from a place of defilement, traversing the seven "days" of the shells until you can break through to find the light. The path has to be one of inner struggle. Do not expect to start on too high a rung.

Both this and the previous teaching are reading the opening words of the *parashah* to mean "this is the way of Torah." From this obscure passage about ritual defilement, we are to learn profound lessons about the process of Torah study itself.

MEVASSER TSEDEK

> Y-H-W-H spoke to Moses, saying: "Take the staff and assemble the community, you and your brother Aaron. Speak to the rock before their eyes, that it give water...." Moses and Aaron assembled the congregation facing the rock. He said to them: "Listen, you rebels! Shall we bring you water out of this rock?" Moses raised his hand and struck the rock twice with his staff. Water came forth and the

> community drank, they and their cattle. Y-H-W-H said to Moses and Aaron: "Because you did not have the faith in Me to sanctify Me before the eyes of the Children of Israel, you will not bring the congregation into the land I have given them."
>
> (NUM. 20:7–12)

A *tsaddik* who wants to bring about some change in the order of creation needs to go to the root of the thing that is to be changed. Suppose someone made a vessel out of clay. If you wanted to change its function, you would go back to its maker and ask him to change it to suit your purpose.

When Moses wanted to get water for the people to flow miraculously from that rock, he had to raise the people up to the rock's own Source. Everything can be transformed at its root. This is what the blessed Holy One intended, that Moses uplift the people; then speaking would have been sufficient. Moses did so. But the ordinary folk also needed water, and he was unable to raise them up to that high level, the Source above. Thus he did not succeed and was forced to strike the rock, representing a lower level [of religious action], as is detailed in the *Selected Teachings* of Rabbi Isaac Luria.

The *tsaddik* was punished for this. Even though it was impossible to raise up the masses, he should have elevated the *tsaddikim*, who are called "the eyes of the community" (*Shir ha-Shirim Rabbah* 1:15), so that Y-H-W-H would be sanctified in their sight. Thus the verse says: **Moses and Aaron assembled the congregation**, including the ordinary masses. **Facing the rock**: having them look into the rock, toward its Source. In this lay their failure; the ordinary folk were just not able to rise up that high. Once Moses saw that they were unable to concentrate on the Source, but only on the rock below, he said to them: **Listen you rebels! Shall we bring you water out of *this* rock?**, meaning the rock that you see. This is indeed impossible. And since you are incapable of rising to the Root, it will not bring water forth for you. Therefore he **struck the rock**, acting at a lower level. Then **the community drank**, including the masses.

Y-H-W-H said to Moses and Aaron: "Because you did not have the faith in Me to sanctify Me before the eyes of the Children of Israel." These are the community's "eyes," the *tsaddikim*. Even though you couldn't succeed with the ordinary people, you needed to **sanctify Me before the eyes**, the proper leaders. Because of this, **you will not bring....**

But Moses's intent was really for the good of Israel, for those ordinary people.

There is certainly an inner Hasidic "address" behind this homily. The *tsaddik* becomes frustrated when he tries to offer the sort of mystical teachings that will raise people up to the great Source of life. He sees that they are not with him, that he cannot succeed in bringing them to that level. Instead, he gives them what they want: visible miracles, "striking the rock." Such a *tsaddik*, the author tells us, is not fit to lead, to bring the people into the Land. Find those with whom you can communicate on a deep level; raise them up to the highest places. Perhaps they will be the ones capable of taking the next step and bringing "water" to the masses through their holy words, not needing to lower themselves by resorting to the outward sign, the "cheap trick" that lies within the holy man's powers.

To whom, "around the Maggid's table," were such comments being addressed? Who is this well-meaning would-be miracle worker who is pitching his message too low?

Tsemah ha-Shem li-Tsevi

Speak to the rock before their eyes....
(Num. 20:8)

Before their eyes should be understood as in "All flesh together shall see that the mouth of Y-H-W-H has spoken" (Is. 40:5). This is also like: "All the people saw the voices" (Ex. 20:15); the voice was so holy that they could experience it with the sense of sight. So too "David blessed Y-H-W-H before the eyes of all Israel" (1 Chron. 29:10). Here too **before their eyes** means that [the people] Israel were to see the act of speech. That is why both Moses and Aaron are commanded; **speak** is in the plural form. The sages refer to this in teaching that "whenever two are engaged together in Torah, the *shekhinah* is present between them" (m. Avot 3:2). Here the whole intent was to invoke the *shekhinah*'s presence.

In this spirit the *Zohar* teaches that "had Moses spoken to the rock, there would have been no forgetting [i.e., Torah would never be forgotten]" (*Tikkuney Zohar* t. 21, 44a). Forgetfulness is a fall from awareness, as is written in the copies [manuscripts of the Maggid's teachings].... The reason is that all the miracles Moses performed were accomplished by speech alone; he did not belong to the realm of action. He was told to lift up his staff (Ex. 14:16), but the Sea was subdued by the word alone, [with no need to strike it]. This was not the case with Joshua. Moses represents the category of mind or awareness; as such, he was drawn toward speech. His generation was also called "the generation of awareness." For this reason they are referred to as *dor ha-midbar*, which can mean "the generation of speech" (b. Sanhedrin 108a). Speech is drawn forth from the mind. Hence they received the Torah in speech....

When this first generation was dying out and another coming along, Moses thought that they were people more related to action. They were going to inherit the Land [i.e., earthiness]. That was why he struck the rock. But the blessed Holy One said just the opposite: his task was to uplift that second generation, to raise them higher. They were to inherit it [by following] in the way of their fathers (Gen. 48:6). Speech alone would have brought water out of that rock, as for the generation of the *midbar*. In this way they too would have become a generation of awareness. By hitting the rock he brought about forgetfulness, a fall from speech to action, as the *Zohar* teaches. Thus far have I seen in the copies.

Had all Israel seen this act of speech, there would have been no fall, since speech flows forth from mind. But because they saw no speech, but only the striking, they fell from mind to action....

The whole point, however, was to draw forth divine light from the upper Mind to the exquisite Dwelling, the *shekhinah*, the World of Speech. But Moses became angry, and "whoever is angry, the *shekhinah* disappears from him" (b. Nedarim 22b).

The notion that Moses wrongly changed his behavior in an attempt to suit a younger generation is a fascinating one. The teaching quoted here from manuscript is also found in the Maggid's own published writings. Might it have to do with their own times, a sense that the popularizers of Hasidism were already changing or watering down the message in an attempt to reach a younger and more worldly generation than that of the Maggid, when really they should be making an effort to raise them up? Does this conflict somehow apply to our own generation as well?

KEDUSHAT LEVI

> Speak to the rock before their eyes ... because you did not have faith in Me, to sanctify Me in the eyes of the Children of Israel.
>
> (NUM. 20:8, 12)

RaSHI and RaMBaN are divided as to the sin of Moses. One says it is that of saying, "Listen, O you rebels!" (Num. 20:10), and the other defines it as striking the rock. But they really are the same, for one led to the other.

There are two sorts of preachers who address Israel to get them to do the Creator's will. One speaks to them in a positive tone, telling each one of Israel what a high rung is his, how the souls of Israel are truly hewn from beneath the Throne of Glory. [He reminds them] of the Creator's great pleasure in a *mitsvah* performed by any Jew, how all the worlds are joyous at seeing God's command fulfilled. This kind of preaching bends the heart of Jews to do God's bidding and to accept the yoke of God's kingdom. But other preachers reprove Israel with tough language, shaming them until they are forced to do God's will.

The difference is that the one who approaches them with goodness, uplifting their souls to such great heights ... is a fitting leader for Israel. Not so the one who speaks harshly. The preacher who speaks so well of Israel ... all the world's creatures [on hearing this] necessarily turn of their own accord to doing Israel's will, since it was for Israel's sake that they were created. But if one doesn't speak well and lift up Israel's righteousness, each creature will have to be forced to do their bidding, that for which they were created.

When Moses said, "Listen, O you rebels!" he was reproving Israel with harsh words. That was why he had to strike the rock in order to fulfill its created purpose. Had he uplifted Israel as the blessed Holy One intended by saying **Speak to the rock**, he would have been saying this: "You, O rock, who were created for the sake of Israel! They are on such a high rung that you have to do that for which you were created, to bring forth water for Israel!" But now that he had reproved Israel harshly, he needed to strike the rock....

Because you did not have faith in Me, to sanctify Me in the eyes of the Children of Israel. The one who approaches Israel through goodness can pass this understanding on to them, **sanctify[ing] Me in the eyes....**

Our sages say that "eyes" refers to the wise within the community (*Shir ha-Shirim Rabbah* 1:15). They too would be able to attain this understanding.

This is a predictable Levi Yitshak response to the Torah's classical discussion of Moses's failure in leadership. It was Moses's lack of patience with the people that led him to sell them short, rather than uplifting their holiness for all the world, including the forces of nature, to see. He is insisting that ordinary people can and indeed must be raised to the highest rung.

No'am Elimelekh (from *Balak*)

> Moses raised his hand and struck the rock with his staff twice; abundant water came forth, and the community and their animals drank.
> (Num. 20:11)

Why was Moses punished for striking the rock at "the Waters of Conflict"? Doesn't the fact that abundant water came forth prove that the blessed Holy One agreed with his actions? Surely God would not bring about a miracle to support a falsehood (b. Berakhot 58a)!

Heaven forbid that the "Man of God" (Deut. 33:1) would go against the will of the Creator.

Rather, a *tsaddik* always seeks out good for the people of Israel. Even if this requires doing something that might be a minor sin, if it is for the benefit of Israel—do it. Accept that you may be punished in hell for their sake because all you desire is their good.

The truth is that a *tsaddik* can bring blessing to the world just by means of holy speech without recourse to any physical action. There are times, however, when you must engage in physical action. This is because your words will work only for people who believe that a *tsaddik* can act through speech. In order to help people who do not believe this, you must act in accord with their nature and engage in physical deeds. This is like a sick person who cannot take a medicine that would cure the illness because it is too strong. You have to find a lighter medicine that the patient can take even though the strong medicine would have been a better cure. What can you do?... the comparison is clear.

Moses thought—it is true that by speaking to the rock I will be fulfilling God's will. But that would only work for the righteous people. It is better that I do something physical that everyone can relate to, and all will benefit. That is what the blessed holy One supported, for that intention was very good. That is why it says **abundant** [*rabim*] **water came forth**; it was for the community (*rabim*), for everyone.

In this teaching Moses is being presented as a model of a sort of "civil disobedience." Do what is best for the people and accept the consequences. What makes this interesting is that the disobedience is directed toward God. In effect the *No'am Elimelekh* is teaching that as a leader your first commitment is to the welfare of the people and only secondarily to follow God's instructions.

Hukkat
Round Two

AG: The challenge raised here is around the question of popularization. We, like the Maggid's disciples, want to reach a broad audience, hopefully to affect their spiritual lives. But the tools we have for doing this are highly intellectual, requiring deep knowledge of sources and commitment to deciphering them. How far are we permitted to go in bridging this gap?

EL: The Maggid's students went very far, some even claiming the ability to perform miracles.

AG: That reminds me of some of the popular "Kabbalah" outfits that we see today, offering all kinds of lavish claims to be able to solve all one's personal problems.

EL: But let's not let ourselves off the hook that easily. We go out to congregations and "perform," using our own charisma, lots of personal charm, and all our most appealing teachings to the first-time hearer. They get very "turned on" and enthusiastic. Isn't that our form of "miracle working"? Aren't we selling short the path that has been our own, one of hard work and struggle with learning the sources over so many years?

AG: Levi Yitshak would say that we've got to do it. He believes that you really can raise people up to a higher plane, if only you approach them with love and support, bringing out the best that is already there within them. If you can do that for people, you *must.* If it does not succeed, the failing is ours, not theirs.

OR: As we go forth in these situations, my question is whether there is a constant core that stays with us. Are we being true to ourselves, to our own sources of nurturance and paths of growth? It's my attachment to the inner light within Torah that the *Me'or 'Eynayim* describes that allows me to keep going. If I stray from that, I'm in trouble.

EL: In spending so much of our lives training future rabbis, we seem to be following the advice of the *Mevasser Tsedek* here. "Don't stretch farther than is natural for you," he seems to be saying. You train the "eyes of the community," the future leaders. Let *them* go the next step of reaching out to ordinary people.

AG: But we have to see our own ability to teach, including the "charisma" we bear, as a gift of God. If it is, we are given it for a reason. The question is how to use it well, which means responsibly. The same is true of popularizing these teachings. How do we do it responsibly?

EL: Remember the *Tsemah* here, who quotes the Maggid as saying that Moses is punished for the sin of being too willing to go down to the people's level.

AG: He's arguing with Levi Yitshak, saying: "Remember that your job is to raise them up, not to go down to where they are." It's too easy and comfortable to just fit in with the group that you're there to teach.

EL: But R. Elimelekh has the last word. Yes, reaching too far out to people may be a sin. Maybe I'll be punished for it. But I've got to do it anyway!

Balak

Ginzey Yosef

> Balak son of Tsippor saw all that Israel had done to the Amorites.
> (Num. 22:2)

The *Zohar* (3:199b) notes that the name Balak can be derived from *ba lak*, short for *ba lakuta*, "defeat comes." In this way he hoped to defeat Israel. Balaam is from *bal 'am*, "no people," seeking to destroy the people of Israel.

"Balak" refers to the evil urge, lying in wait and laying a trap at each person's feet. "Like birds [*tsipporim*] caught in a trap, so do they hunt humans" (Eccles. 9:12). The evil urge begins its attack by entering the mind, since it is easiest to get a person to begin having [questioning] thoughts. Our sages in fact said that there is no person who can escape these, even for a day (b. Bava Batra 164b). From thoughts we move on to words, beginning with a light dusting of evil speech, another thing that engages us every day. From speech we turn, God forbid, to deeds. "Do not let your mouth cause your flesh to sin" (Eccles. 5:5).

Balak ... saw. The evil urge sees how to make people stumble. **Son of Tsippor** ("bird"): we are "like birds caught in a trap...."

Once evil thoughts turn into speech, deeds will surely follow. This is **all that Israel had done to the Amorites**. The deeds one does come from "Amorites," derived from *amar*, "speaking," words that come forth from the heart, [beginning in thought]. "He [Esau] said in his heart" (Gen. 27:41).

That is why we are taught, "O my son, give me your heart" (Prov. 23:26), since everything depends upon the heart.

Hasidism seeks to construct a Judaism that is all about the heart. Although *halakhah* insists that we judge people primarily by their deeds, the Hasidic ethos wants to show that human wickedness takes root first within the heart, and it is the heart that has to be given to God. Purity of speech is the first real test of the heart's intentions. The rest will follow.

Kedushat Levi

> Moab feared [*va-yagar*] the people greatly, for they were many; Moab abhorred [*va-yakats*] the Children of Israel.
>
> (Num. 22:3)

Why does Scripture first refer to "the people" and afterward to "the Children of Israel"? The Midrash (*Shemot Rabbah* 42:6) and the *Zohar* (2:45b) say that "the people" refers to the "mixed multitude" [that had come out of Egypt with Israel]. This is *va-yagar*: Moab feared Israel because they saw that wherever Israel dwelt they received proselytes (*gerim*) who joined them, like the mixed multitude. That's why Moab was afraid to have Israel enter its borders; they feared that some of their own people would become converts.

But should you ask, "What difference would that make to them? [Why should they object?]," the answer is clear: **Moab abhorred [*va-yakats*] the Children of Israel**. They hated Jews greatly....

A person who is returning to God, namely [in this case] the proselyte, has an easier time uplifting fallen sparks than does one who is righteous from birth. That wicked man Balak feared Israel [coming into his realm] since wherever they walked, they would raise up sparks. This wicked one despised such holiness; becoming a Jew, he thought, was the end (*kets*) of a person.

This is why **Moab feared the people greatly**, meaning the mixed multitude, the proselytes who were joined to Israel. **For they were many**, and they were especially talented at raising up sparks....

There is a veiled but obvious historic reference here. The Russian empire absorbed a huge Jewish population following the partition of Poland after 1772. The Berdichev district was annexed in 1793. Previously Russia had been closed to Jews, precisely because of an old fear of "Judaizing," a tendency within some circles in Russian Orthodoxy that reputedly had flirted with conversion to Judaism. Balak, in late eighteenth-century eyes, must have seemed very like Russia, both fearing and hating these Jews who were now "passing through" its territory.

At the same time, this teaching also shares what has become an open secret in our own time: converts to Judaism often have an easier time with the devotional work of uplifting sparks than do born Jews, for whom the *mitsvot* are too easily seen as "mere" tradition.

Teshu'ot Hen (from *Balak/Massa'ey*)

> Balaam said to the servants of Balak: "Even were Balak to give me his houseful of silver and gold, I cannot transgress the mouth of Y-H-W-H my God.... Who can count the dust of Jacob and the fourfold number of Israel?..."
>
> (Num. 22:18, 23:10)

There are four elements in the world: earth (*'afar*, dust), air, fire, and water. Parallel to these are the four sorts of persons we have within Israel: the pious, the righteous, the ordinary, and the wicked....

The blessed Holy One smells the [sweet] aroma that arises even from those who betray Him [a play on Gen. 27:27, reading *begadav* ("his clothing") as *bogdav* ("his betrayal"); cf. b. Sanhedrin 37a]. Even from the sins of Israel very great things emerge, as the Midrash tells us. The selling of Joseph led to the sustaining of a great many people [during the famine]. The sin of the Golden Calf brought about the shekels given to build the Tabernacle. There are other cases like this as well (Gen. 50:20; *Tanhuma Yashan* 8; *Tanhuma Ki Tissa* 10). Thus we pray: "Before You may our judgments come," for the blessed Holy One looks at what "comes forth" from the transgressions....

The entire purpose of humanity is to join the lower world to that which is above, to turn transgression into merit, matter into spirit. This is called joining Y-H-W-H and Adonay [the transcendent and indwelling aspects of

God]. This is the meaning of **I cannot transgress the mouth of Y-H-W-H my God**. The *shekhinah* is called "mouth [the source of divine speech]." She is the lowest of the seven "days" of the *sefirot*, also called Adonay. Of this the sages said: "My name is not spoken as it is written. I am written Y-H-W-H, but pronounced by the mouth 'as Adonay'" (b. Pesahim 50a).

Now Balaam wanted to curse Israel by means of those who are on the fourth and lowest rung, [the wicked who are called "earth"]. He was not able to do so, however, because the blessed Holy One "smells the sweet aroma" that will arise from their sins. Thus he said: **I cannot transgress the mouth of Y-H-W-H my God**, meaning that I cannot separate Adonay from Y-H-W-H, because they uplift even the lowest of rungs....

The *rebbe*'s task is to find merit, or at least the potential for goodness, even in the greatest of sins. Balaam, seeking to curse, looks toward the weakest link, the "earth" among Israel. But the whole thrust of Hasidism is to show how even that "earth," the lowliest, is capable of being uplifted.

Dibrat Shelomoh

> How can I curse [*ekov*] whom God has not cursed, how can I doom [*ez'om*] when Y-H-W-H has not doomed? As I see them from the rocky summits, gaze on them from the hills, they are a people that dwells apart, not reckoned among the nations.
> (Num. 23:8–9)

We know that ***ekov*** refers to cursing, since it derives from a word meaning "lessening" and "limitation." A *kav* is a tiny vessel with a limited capacity. ***Ez'om*** also refers to cursing and limitation, as we see in the sages' teaching "How long does His anger [*za'amo*] last? For a single moment" (b. Berakhot 7a)—for an extremely short and restricted time.

The opposite of this limitation is nullifying oneself by connecting to the Source of all kindness and compassion, which is never-ending and infinitely expansive. This is how we should understand **How can I curse** [or, "limit"] **whom God** [*El*] **has not cursed?** The divine name *El* alludes to the source of kindness, as in the verse "the kindness of God [*El*] endures forever" (Ps.

52:3). This same teaching is also found in the book *Likkutey Amarim* [by the Maggid] on the verse "God [*El*] who took them out of Egypt" (Num. 23:22).

How can I doom [*ez'om*] when Y-H-W-H has not doomed means that when you cleave to the blessed One, all stern judgments and limitations are nullified. Yet the very existence of judgments and limitations [is difficult to understand]: if everything comes from God, whence do these judgments originally derive? The Creator constricted the brilliance of His infinite light, as it were, and used the twenty-two letters of the Torah to fashion [the world] "in order He might be known to it," as it is taught in the *Zohar*. And yet "in them You are concealed from human beings" (*Tikkuney Zohar* 17a).

I heard this idea from my teacher the Maggid as well, regarding the sages' explanation of how the first light was created (*Bereshit Rabbah* 3:4): The blessed Holy One adorned Himself in light and created illumination, as the verse says "wrapped in a robe of light" (Ps. 104:2). This process of self-limitation continued from level to level until reaching the lowest of the low, where *Gehinom* and the stern judgments were created. This is the world of fragmentation, from which emerge the Other Side and the wicked, who follow the base desires of their hearts. But such is not the case for Israel, who received the holy Torah and divine commandments with which they bind themselves to the Creator, standing in great awe of God. In this way Israel cleave to the very Source from which the original limitation derived, attaching themselves to the One from whom all limitation and judgment come. Their great awe before the Creator nullifies all judgments and limitations, which are called the "slag of gold." Thus did Rabbi Isaac Luria teach us that judgments must be sweetened at their root.

But there is more. Through awe you will necessarily come to love and cleave to the Creator. My teacher the Maggid taught us as follows (cf. b. Kiddushin 2b): It is the way of the world for a man, symbolizing love, to court a woman, who represents awe, as in the verse, "a woman in awe of Y-H-W-H is to be praised" (Prov. 31:30).

Through this type of love and attachment to God, kindness and mercy are drawn into all of the worlds from the infinite Source of all benevolence, thus sweetening the judgments.

This is the meaning of **As I see them from the rocky summits** ["**see them**" may also be translated as "see Him"]. Rock represents strength and limitation, and the **rocky summits** [*rosh tsurim*] means the first (*rishon*) moment of limitation. **From the hills** refer to the matriarchs (*Be-Midbar Rabbah* 9:13), who represent the female aspect of holy awe. Israel cleave to the Source of unity and oneness [that precedes] the first limitation and are therefore not a part of this world of fragmentation and multiplicity. This is the how to understand **they are a people that dwells apart**—Israel exist[s] in the world of true unity. **Not reckoned among the nations** refers to multiplicity [i.e., they don't engage in typically divisive human behaviors].

Balaam's words remind us that God created the world by restricting His undifferentiated divine brilliance. This act of self-contraction into finite vessels (the *sefirot* and the letters) allows us to know the One, for without them the light would be unbearably strong. Yet the diminished divine presence in our reality also allows for negative forces and stern judgments, the improper machinations we humans sometimes pursue as a result of free choice. Therefore, we are called to ascend to a higher (or deeper) consciousness, transcending God's initial self-limitation and connecting ourselves directly to the unlimited Source. Only thus can we sweeten the "stern judgments."

How is this to be accomplished? Torah and the *mitsvot* are a bridge between our temporal reality and the divine Infinity that infuses it. When performed with awe, here employed with both meanings of "fear" and "wonder," these sacred actions bring us to an intense love of God. This love enables us to draw divine mercy and compassion into the world.

Ah, if only we had an Israel—indeed a Jewish people—like the one he describes as "not reckoned among the nations." Have you met a community that doesn't "engage in typically divisive human behaviors"? Teachings like this remind us just how far we have to go.

Or Torah

> Balaam raised his eyes and saw Israel encamped by tribes, and the spirit of God came upon him.
> (Num. 24:2)

Our rabbis taught that Balaam saw that the openings of Israel's tents were directed away from each other [a sign of modesty] and said, "These people are worthy of having *shekhinah* rest upon them" (b. Bava Batra 60a).

This may be applied to a group of scholars who sit around one table. They all offer teachings about a particular verse or rabbinic statement, one explains the verse one way and another explains it differently. If, heaven forbid, they are in competition with each other, each claiming, "My explanation is better than the others"—woe to them, it is better they had never been born. But if their sole intention is to develop and enhance Torah, they are very fortunate.

The "openings" Balaam saw were their mouths, as in the verse "guard the openings of your mouth" (Micah 7:5). He saw that their "openings" were not directed toward each other, that they had no intention to oppose each other. Rather each person offered a teaching and explanation only for the sake of heaven. Such people, he said, are worthy of having *shekhinah* rest upon them.

One cannot but wonder what was going on "around the Maggid's table" on the day he offered this teaching. He too must have "raised his eyes" and have seen something that did not please him. Even in so loving a group as the Maggid's circle, it is not surprising to learn that competition sometimes broke out. But as leader of the little circle of scholars editing this volume, smaller by every measure than the group we study, I can testify that it has not happened here.

Balak
Round Two

AG: The *Torah Or* passage is especially impressive. I hear the Maggid talking to his disciples, telling them that they need one another's support and that competition between them will undermine that.

EL: We see the same thing in the *No'am Elimelekh*. He is a master of disciples who is trying to create a community of *tsaddikim*.

AM: In other contexts too, the Maggid seems to decry controversy or competition. That may be why he tried to avoid conflict with the anti-Hasidic forces.

AG: Look how different he is from the *Toledot*, the Ba'al Shem Tov's other main disciple. The *Toledot* is always fulminating against false leaders, communal corruption, and lots more. The Maggid never does that. He preaches *for*, not against.

EL: Yes, here he is setting a warning in positive terms. But the negative consequences are also very clear.

AG: The typology of "two types of *tsaddik*" that we see so frequently, especially in Levi Yitshak, comes to mind here. One type reproves Israel with harsh words, the other only with goodness. This may have come right out of the experience of the Maggid's personality and his abhorrence of conflict.

AM: So what can we learn from all this history? How do you build a religious movement or community? Not by attacking others, but by being a living exemplar of the values you want to put forth. People will notice and will be attracted.

EL: You need both. Sometimes it's very important to stand up and say what's wrong. Doing it all with love and patience can be an excuse for not having the backbone to oppose evil. Even Levi Yitshak says that you need *yir'ah*, awe before God, as well as *ahavah*, service through love.

AM: Throughout the teachings, those always need to be kept in balance.

AG: But *yir'ah* is not the same as harsh rebuke. It's about our fearing God, not making others fear us!

Pinhas

Tsemah ha-Shem li-Tsevi

> Pinhas the son of Eleazar, son of Aaron, withheld My wrath from upon the Children of Israel by his zeal for My zealotry in their midst, and I did not destroy the Children of Israel in My zeal. Therefore say: "Behold I give him My covenant of peace."
> (Num. 25:11–12)

Our sages (b. Sanhedrin 44a) teach that he came and threw them [Zimri and Kozbi] down on the ground, saying: "Lord of the world! Shall twenty-four thousand of Israel die because of these?" This is the meaning of "Pinhas got up and prayed [*ve-yefalel*], stopping the plague" (Ps. 106:30). We need to understand the nature of this prayer.

We are taught (*Tanna de-Vey Eliyahu Zuta* 8) that when Elijah said, "I am indeed zealous!" (1 Kings 19:10), God raised him up to heaven, saying, "You and they cannot dwell in the same world, since you are being an accuser of My children." The same applied to Hosea and Isaiah (b. Pesahim 87b). Y-H-W-H seeks to love His children, as in "the prayer of the upright is His desire" (Prov. 15:8), meaning that God desires us to pray *for* Israel.

That is why Moses was willing to offer his own life for them; that is what Y-H-W-H desires. Moses said: "Why, O Y-H-W-H, should Your fiery anger burn against them?" (Ex. 32:11). The Midrash (*Shemot Rabbah* 43:6) on this gives the following account:

When Israel performed that deed [making the Golden Calf], Moses stood up to appease God. [He said: "Master of the world, they sought to help You and You are angry with them? This calf they made will be a help to You. You will make the sun shine, and he the moon. You will attend to the stars, and he to the constellations. You will make the dew fall, and he will blow the winds; You will make the rain fall, and he will grow the plants." The blessed Holy One replied: "Moses! Have you fallen into the same error as they! There is nothing to him!" Moses replied: "In that case, why are You so angry at Your children? 'Why, O Y-H-W-H, should Your fiery anger burn against them?'"]

Shouldn't a sage be jealous only of another sage?

Moses, in other words, made naught of God's anger, for the sake of loving Israel....

But in this case [of Pinhas] anger had already done its deed; divine wrath had already been aroused. Twenty-four thousand of Israel had died. Moses's means were exhausted, and "the people were in tears" (Num. 25:6). Then Pinhas, seeing that divine anger had already begun to take its toll and could not be stopped, came up with this idea. Even were he to take up God's zeal, it would have no effect, for that is not God's desire, as we have said. So he started out to be zealous, killing Zimri [and Kozbi], throwing them to the ground, and calling out, "Should twenty-four thousand die because of these?" This means that he was also being zealous for Israel, who shouldn't have to die for these sinners. Thus he joined together zealotry for God and for Israel.

This is "Pinhas got up and prayed." The form *va-yefalel* [a form nowhere else used for "pray"] refers to joining, as RaSHI reads the word *niftalti* (Gen. 30:8). Pinhas didn't just pray to God, but set up a legal case (*pelilim*) before his Master, linking zeal for Israel to zeal for Y-H-W-H, making love for them equal to love for God. This is like the link that pious writers make between love for one's neighbor and love of God. This was the legal case Pinhas brought before God. This follows "there is friendship toward heaven" (cf. b. Berakhot 34a, which says the opposite!).

This is **by his zeal for My zealotry in their midst**. My zeal was placed amid [the context of] zeal for Israel. Thus: He **withheld My wrath.... Therefore say: "Behold I give him My covenant of peace."** He linked and made peace between these two zealotries, bringing about peace between Israel and their Father in heaven. For this **I give him My covenant of peace....**

We see the Hasidic author struggling mightily, as we do, with this difficult text. Hasidism makes it clear repeatedly that love and defense of Israel is the leader's task, an understanding that stretches back to Moses on Sinai. The reshaping of Pinhas the zealot into a Hasidic *rebbe* who stands up for Israel is no small task.

ME'OR 'EYNAYIM

> Therefore say that I grant him My covenant of peace.
> (NUM. 25:12)

Midrash Tanhuma: Great is peace, for the prayer service [*'amidah*] concludes with peace. Torah is also called "peace," as in "All her paths are peace" (Prov. 3:17). A person returning from the way is greeted with "peace."

To understand this, we begin with the verse "Behold I send you My prophet Elijah before the coming of God's great and awesome day" (Mal. 3:23). "Send [*sholeah*]" is in the present tense, meaning that even now God is sending Elijah. It does not say, "I *will* send."

All the desire of God's servants Israel for their Father in heaven comes about through the quality of Elijah, the herald of all that is whole, including Torah and prayer, in which thought and speech are fully united. But before reaching this, you need great passion and longing. It is this Elijah quality that first arouses such passion, leading to the quality of messiah.

Surely in every proper prayer, one that unifies thought and speech, some restorative step toward messiah is taken. When our righteous redeemer comes (speedily, in our day!), this unity will be both whole and constant. All the thoughts and letters that together constitute speech will be uplifted. But the same thing happens in every person's prayer and study. This aspect of the inner upbuilding of messiah's form is present. Thus taught the BeSHT: Every one of Israel needs to restore that part of the messiah's form that belongs to that person's soul. The word Adam ("person") consists of the letters *aleph, dalet, mem*, standing for Adam, David, and messiah. The form of Adam, we are told, extended from one end of earth to the other; all the souls of Israel were included within Adam. Only after he had sinned was his form diminished. So too messiah will be of such a full structure, containing all the six hundred thousand souls of Israel, just like Adam before the sin.

Thus every one of Israel has to prepare the part of messiah belonging to his particular soul.... This cannot take place absent the passion aroused by Elijah the herald. This is called "messiah" (*mashiah*), related to the word *mesiah*, meaning speech.... Thus whenever thought and speech are united, messiah is restored. But this is not yet constant, as it will be when messiah actually comes. Before the arrival of such wholeness, there will need to be a heralding by Elijah, to arouse the passion of Israel.

The reason why Elijah arouses all this passion is that Pinhas is Elijah. He inherited [i.e., absorbed] the souls of [his uncles] Nadav and Avihu, the sons of Aaron. The reason they died was the great fiery intensity of their worship of our blessed Creator. They so cleaved to the pure, shining light, because their passion was so strong, that their souls departed from their bodies. This is the meaning of "A fire came forth from before Y-H-W-H as they drew near to Y-H-W-H and consumed them" (Lev. 10:2). They drew so very near, with such intensity, that "a fire came forth" from their being so very directly "before Y-H-W-H." It was their drawing so near in fiery passion that consumed them. Their souls just cleaved to the pure light. Afterwards Pinhas, who is Elijah, inherited those souls. That's why he embodies a state of unity and passion; the great unification will take place through him....

Wherever there is such unity, there is peace, because of the wholeness (*shalom/shlemut*). Torah and prayer are both peace; that is why the *tefillah* concludes with a blessing of peace, since it unifies thought and speech....

This is "behold I send you"—always, in the present—"Elijah the prophet"....

Every moment of true prayer and Torah study bears the presence of Elijah and messiah, along with the passion of Aaron's sons, all in anticipation of the great unity that is to come.

Dibrat Shelomoh

> And Y-H-W-H said to Moses, "The plea of Zelophehad's daughters is just: you should give them a hereditary holding among their father's kinsmen; transfer their father's share to them."
>
> (Num. 27:6–7)

... It is written earlier that "Moses brought their case before Y-H-W-H" (Num. 27:5). But why didn't Moses say, "Stand by, and let me hear [what instructions Y-H-W-H gives about you]" (Num. 9:8), as he did [when asking God about *Pesah Sheni* in] *Parashat Be-Ha'alotekha*?

The truth of the matter is that the daughters of Zelophehad loved the Land of Israel, as our sages have taught (RaSHI on Num. 26:64; *Tanhuma Pinhas* 7). Their longing inspired the entire Jewish people to feel the same way. This is the meaning of "Moses brought their case before Y-H-W-H"—their "case" of intense love brought all the others before Y-H-W-H, since due to their great love and desire, God hastened to give them the Land of Israel.

We know everything relies upon our love and desire for the word of God, acting as the "female waters." Therefore God says: **you should give them** (*naton titen la-hem*), which grammarians call the *makor* verb form (infinitive absolute). Since they had already opened up the source (*makor*) of giving the Land of Israel, therefore, [God told Moses] to **give them** [i.e., the people] the Land.

Perhaps we can say that our teacher Moses's longing for the Land was not sufficient to his great righteousness. Had he fully desired to enter the Land, surely it would not have been withheld from someone of his stature and God would have brought him in. Even though it was ordained [that he couldn't], "you shall decree and it will be fulfilled" (Job 22:28)—the *tsaddik* decrees [and the blessed Holy One fulfills!] (b. Ta'anit 23a). But God was the source of Moses's insufficient desire. When the blessed Holy One wants a *tsaddik* to act, He instills the will and longing within him, as it says, "He makes the will of those who fear Him," so that "He may hear their cry [and save them]" (Ps. 145:19). This is how the sages interpret the verse "prepare your hearts, incline Your ear" (Ps. 10:17)—[God both prepares your heart for prayer, and will surely listen] (b. Berakhot 31a; *Va-Yikra Rabbah* 16:9).

This was not the case with the daughters of Zelophehad. On their own they longed greatly [for the Land] through receiving their inheritance, and they paid attention to every detail concerning it. Thus the sages taught: [God said to Moses, "The daughters of Zelophehad have spoken well and demand the right thing,] for so it is written [in My Torah in heaven]" (*Sifrei* 134). This is why RaSHI says that their eyes saw that which Moses did not....

What an interesting interpretation of why Moses could not enter the Land! Here the reason is not the "sin" involved in drawing water from the rock, but rather that Moses's own desire was insufficient. Had he truly wished to be let in, the divine decree would surely have to be overturned.

The daughters of Zelophehad, on the other hand, loved the Land of Israel so completely that their portion in it was assured. Their longing both inspired the Jewish people and aroused the divine source of giving.

There is an interesting, if difficult, theological claim being made here as well. Since human desires are instilled by God, Moses's lack of longing actually had a divine origin. If so, to what extent was he culpable for this shortcoming? Are the daughters of Zelophehad, whose request God agreed to fulfill, a model of spiritual agency, or is their claim only valid because "it is written in My Torah in heaven"? The teaching leaves this interesting tension unresolved.

Or Peney Mosheh

> Moses spoke to Y-H-W-H, saying: "May Y-H-W-H God of the spirits of all flesh appoint a man over the community, one who will go forth before them and come back before them, bring them out and bring them in, so that the community of Y-H-W-H not be like a flock that has no shepherd."
>
> (Num. 27:16–17)

Commenting on the verse "Who is it who ascended and came down?" the Midrash answers: "This is Moses" (*Yalkut Mishley* 30:4). Rabbi Moshe Alshekh noted (*Shemot* 9) that both Enoch and Elijah also ascended to heaven, but they did not come down. Instead, their bodies were turned into flaming torches. Perhaps this is what Moses meant when he said: **one who will go forth before them and come back before them,** meaning one who could rise to heaven and return. In his heart he knew that he was the only human who could do this. He hoped that God might restore things to the way they had been and cancel His decree [of Moses's dying before they entered the Land].... **One who will ... bring them out** also refers to himself; the one who had already done that, bringing them forth from Egypt, should be the one who brings them into the Land of Israel....

Now we understand why the angels did not object when Enoch rose into the heavens. Once turned into a torch, he was not going to go back down! But they saw Moses standing in heaven with his body unchanged, ready to go down again. This is why they asked, "What is one born of woman doing among us?" (b. Shabbat 88b–89a). He stands in our midst while still in his human body, not having been turned to flame. God answered that "he has come to receive the Torah." He has to bring that strong assurance to Israel, and he must do so together with his body. In that case, said the angels, since mortals can ascend to heaven and go back down, as we see Moses has done, then why should you give the Torah to earth? "Give Your glory to heaven" (Ps. 8:2), meaning that Torah should stay in heaven and whoever wants to fulfill it could rise up to heaven and study it there, then go down and teach it to others, and they to yet others.

God said to Moses: "Give them an answer!" Moses replied: "Did you ever go down to Egypt? Is there any evil urge within you?" Torah does not belong up here, but down below....

Perhaps Scripture is here referring to Moses's modesty, for it says that he was "most humble." Therefore he brought an answer that applied to "any person on the face of the earth" (Num. 12:3). He told them that people are unlike angels. He did not give the other answer that could have countered the angels' claim, namely that he was the only human who could rise to heaven and return. He did not raise that to his lips, for it would have shown his superiority to all other humans. This shows that he was indeed "most humble."

This teaching reflects one pole in the Hasidic dialectic between seeing the *tsaddik* as nearly divine and creating a teaching accessible to ordinary humans. No, the Torah is not meant only for those who can rise to "heaven" and reach it there. It is intended precisely for flesh-and-blood non-angelic human beings.

Kedushat Levi I

> Moses said, "Let Y-H-W-H, the God of the spirits of all flesh, appoint a man over the congregation."
> (Num. 27:16)

The verse instructs us to judge the people of Israel favorably, even if they are unable to do the will of the Creator at all times, as angels do. This is so only because they are preoccupied with making a living.

This is why Abraham our Father, a man of mercy who judged people favorably, gave food to the angels who came to visit him (based on Genesis

18:5–8) [though he knew that angels do not eat]. He did so in order to teach the angels about human needs, in order that they not judge Israel harshly.

This is why Moses said, **God of the spirits of all flesh** (Num. 16:22): because a person is flesh and blood, he must labor for his livelihood and therefore does not serve God consistently.

And this is why Moses said, **Let Y-H-W-H, the God of the spirits of all flesh, appoint**—that is, appoint a judge and leader who will deal with Israel favorably, just as You do with a person who does not serve You consistently.... Just as You are the God of the spirits of all flesh and You judge Israel favorably, so shall You **appoint a man over the congregation,** a leader, who will also speak favorably of them.

This text represents a central theme in the Berdichever's teachings: to be a spiritual leader means that one must be a compassionate guide, who understands the challenges people face as embodied spiritual seekers. Here Moses, nearing the end of his tenure as the leader of Israel (and having struggled at various points with the misbehavior of his people), pleads with God to appoint a successor who will deal favorably with the community. In so doing, Moses points out that the ultimate model for this leadership style is none other than the Divine.

Judaism has always insisted on being a religion for householders who bear the responsibility of supporting themselves and their families. The *Kedushat Levi*, living in the Ukraine, saw a surrounding civilization that had strong a monastic culture. As it happens, the Russian Church especially venerated the story of Abraham and the angels as prefiguring the Visitation; it is often depicted in icons. Could it be that there is a polemical touch to Levi Yitshak's insistence that Abraham is teaching the angels about real humans and their needs?

Kedushat Levi II

The God of the spirits of all flesh....
(Num. 16:22)

The essential longing of the human soul is for the service of God. It is only the body that longs for physical pleasures. In truth, both body and the soul are God's works, and just as God endowed the soul with the power for divine service, God could have endowed the body with the very same desire.

On this basis, we have a claim against the blessed Holy One to forgive us for our misdeeds, for He could have given the body the power to submit to God.

Now the soul, which longs to serve God, is called "spirit," as in the expression "The spirit of Y-H-W-H has spoken through me" (2 Sam. 23:2), and the body is called "flesh." And this is the meaning [of Moses's plea]: just as you are **the God of the spirits**, of those who long to serve you, also be [the God **of all flesh**, that is, the body].

Tales of R. Levi Yitshak's defense of the people of Israel against human and celestial foes abound in the Hasidic tradition. Like Abraham, the Psalmist, and Job, the Berdichever is described in these stories as being so bold as to challenge and chastise God when the *rebbe* felt that heaven was not treating the people of Israel fairly. Interestingly, this text is one of the very few places in R. Levi Yitshak's own writings where he speaks of having a "claim" against God. As in the previous text, the Berdichever uses this rhetorical device to elicit God's mercy. After all, if God wanted us to be "purer" or more spiritual beings, the blessed Holy One could have made us so!

Torey Zahav

> Command the Children of Israel, saying to them: Take care to offer My sacrifice, the food of My fire-offering with its sweet savor, at its appointed time. Tell them that this is the fire-offering you should sacrifice to Y-H-W-H: Perfect year-old lambs [*kevasim*], two each day, constantly. One is to be offered each morning, the other at dusk.
>
> (Num. 28:2–4)

I heard this explained morally by the faithful old *hasid* R. Yitshak, called Itzik Drobyczer, of blessed memory. People generally hold in the anger they feel toward others until the eve of Yom Kippur. Then they appease one another. This is not the way light shines. Rather you should forgive your fellow person each night before you go to sleep for any ill done to you that day. You should say: "May God forgive anyone who has harmed me." If a person transgressed against you during the night, forgive before the sun rises, as the *Zohar* teaches (1:201b). You should not bury (*kavash*) your anger against your fellow for an entire year.

This is **My fire-offering with its sweet savor** (*reah nihoah*), bringing pleasure (*nahat ruah*) to God. **Year-old *kevasim*** ("lambs") means that things kept buried (*kevushim*) all year, until Yom Kippur eve, should instead be offered up twice each day. That which is buried within you at night should be offered in the morning; prepare the second offering each day before sunset.

I would explain it in a different way. Most ordinary people make no effort to pray intensely all year. Only on the Days of Awe do they suddenly make a great effort and put all their strength into their prayers.

I heard that holy man R. Dov Baer of Mezritch, of blessed memory, say the following about the teaching: "Israel sustain their Father in heaven" (*Zohar* 3:7b). A person who is truly to be called "Israel," namely the righteous, serves God with love and fear, a heart aflame with passion. This is considered "sustenance" for God, as it were, in the form of the pleasure and delight God receives from such worship, as in, "They gazed upon God and they ate and drank" (Ex. 24:11). The Targum renders it: "They rejoiced in their souls as though they had eaten and drunk." Another verse says: "Y-H-W-H your God is a consuming fire" (Deut. 4:24), meaning that the fiery offering of a person's worship is considered by God as food [reading the verse to say: "Y-H-W-H your God is a Consumer of fire"]. I heard all this from that holy man himself.

This is why Scripture says **My sacrifice** (*korbani*), referring to your drawing near (*hitkarvut*), which is **the food of My fire-offering**; My sustenance in your passionate devotion. **Take care to offer** it ... **at its appointed time.... This is the fire-offering**, this is the fiery passion **you should sacrifice**. Don't offer **year-old lambs**, intense devotion buried within you all year, waiting for the Days of Awe. Rather offer it **two each day, constantly**. Offer one of those "lambs" **each morning** in your dawn prayers, **the other at dusk**, in your afternoon and evening prayers.

We think of "three-day-a-year" Jews as a recent phenomenon. But when it comes to real worship of the heart, our preacher tells us, this has been going on for a long time. Regarding both aspects of the sacred season—forgiving others and praying with real devotion—we are being told here that the true fires of religious life need to be tended every day.

Pinhas
Round Two

AG: The theme of leadership stands out in these texts. What kind of leader is the *tsaddik* to be?

AM: It's most explicit in the *Kedushat Levi*. The leader needs to be a real flesh-and-blood human being, sharing in the earthly concerns of the disciples.

EL: I love the description of Elijah as carrying a spark of Nadav and Avihu in him. It's that passion that makes him the herald of redemption, always in the process of bringing it about. But the leader has to be a Moses, not turning into flame but coming back to earth.

AG: In these early masters, the *tsaddik* shares in his followers' earthiness sometimes by falling, by sharing in their failures. Later it changes: the issue becomes whether the *tsaddik* is willing to pray for earthly things, whether he will come down from his high rung to concern himself with real people and their needs.

EL: The *No'am Elimelekh* still talks about "sin for its own sake," the *tsaddik* deciding to transgress some small sin in order to be one with his people.

AM: It's very hard. The leader needs to be a step ahead of the people in spiritual development, but also needs to be connected to them, not creating a gap between them.

EL: But how can these models work in our day? We are not simply democratic about this. Not anyone can be a *rebbe*. Yes, I can say that you are my *rebbe* in such-and-such a quality, that I learn a particular value from you, and you may learn another from me. But that is not really being a *rebbe*. On the other hand, we are not ready to put a single person on too high a pedestal. We have seen too many disappointments come from that.

AG: But modeling leadership is terribly important, and people like us generally miss the boat by holding back too much, by being too afraid that our clay feet will show. Sometimes we need to be pushed into letting ourselves be *rebbe*, even if we are far from being *tsaddikim*.

AM: As the youngest participant in these conversations, I give lots of thought to what sort of leader I want to become in the world of Jewish spiritual teaching. The image of a *rebbe* with clay feet is one I find encouraging. It gives me the hope and strength to think that I might aspire to such a role as well. If it required perfection, I wouldn't even be able to try.

Mattot

No'am Elimelekh

> And Moses spoke to the heads of the tribes of the people of Israel.
> (Num. 30:2)

A *tsaddik* who wants to benefit the people of Israel must join together with other *tsaddikim*. Through the conversations you have with other *tsaddikim* you can bring good to all of Israel. They support your efforts toward that good end, and your collective merit silences the adversary.

However, when working alone, you need great power and a strong hand to keep the adversary from overcoming you.

This is why our master Moses said: "How can I alone carry your burden?" (Deut. 1:12). He meant—when I am alone, without connection to other *tsaddikim*, taking care of all your needs becomes a burden to me.

This is also the meaning of the verse **And Moses spoke to the heads of the tribes**, implying that he joined with other *tsaddikim*.

Of the people [*li-vney*] **of Israel**, meaning for the sake of Israel, in order to benefit them.

Like others in the Maggid's circle, the *No'am Elimelekh* saw himself as part of a group of *tsaddikim* trying to transform the spiritual life of the Jewish people. The notion that any individual might proclaim himself *tsaddik ha-dor*, the single figure who stood in the role of Moses (or inherited the mantle of the Ba'al Shem Tov), did not please him. It is also clear that he, like the Maggid before him, referred to his own disciples as *tsaddikim.*

Me'or 'Eynayim

> And Moses spoke to the heads of the tribes ... saying: "... If a person utters a vow ... forbidding a certain matter to himself, his word may not be profaned; he shall do all that he has said."
>
> (Num. 30:2–3)

We must first consider our sages' teaching regarding the Nazirite. On the verse "The priest will offer him atonement for his sin" (Num. 6:11), they asked: "What sin has he committed?" They replied: "That of causing himself pain by abstaining from wine" (b. Ta'anit 11a).

To understand this matter:

The world and everything within it, both great and small, was created by the word of God. "By the word of God were the heavens made, and all their hosts by the breath of His mouth" (Ps. 33:6). That word also sustains them and gives them life. "You enliven them all" (Neh. 9:6). Were it not for the life-force within each thing, it would vanish from existence. But [we see things that are] in a broken state in this lowly world, having come about through the sin of Adam and the generations that followed. Sparks of fallen souls became encased in things of this world, including food and drink. There is nothing in this world that does not have a holy spark within it, proceeding from the word of the blessed Holy One, making it alive.

That divine spark is the taste within the thing, that which makes it sweet to the palate. "Taste and see that Y-H-W-H is good!" (Ps. 34:9). This means that when you taste or see something good, it is Y-H-W-H, the holy spark garbed within that thing, appearing before the eye.

After a person partakes of food, the sustenance remains within, while the waste, that which does not give life, is expelled. That is something worthless and negative, since the main purpose of food is that the person be sustained and given strength. That derives from the holy spark, the good taste one enjoys in that food or drink. Therefore when you eat something, the spark within it is joined to your own life-energy, and you become nourished by it.

When you have complete faith that this spiritual sustenance is indeed God's presence hidden within that thing, you will turn your mind and heart entirely inward. Linking both those aspects of yourself to the sustenance coming from that spark, you will join them all to the Root of all, that One from whom all life flows. Then you bring that broken, exiled spark before God, causing great delight. The whole purpose of our religious life is to bring those holy sparks out from under the "shells," those broken places, into the realm of the holy. Thus is holiness raised from its broken state.

This is especially true because so much of our worship and study consists of speech. The strength and sustenance that we derive from the taste of food, which is the holy spark within it, unites with our speech as we speak holy words, raising up that spark that is also the word of God, since all is derived from fallen letters [of divine speech].

Therefore everyone who serves God needs to look toward the inner nature of things. Then all our deeds, including eating and drinking, are being done for the sake of heaven. Holy sparks are thus redeemed from their broken state, brought forth from exile or captivity, led into sublime holiness. This takes place in the blessings we recite, proclaiming God's sovereignty over that item. Later too, when we serve God with that energy, speaking further words ... we continue to raise up those fallen letters or sparks....

Now this is **If a person utters a vow ... forbidding a certain matter to himself**. In doing so, he is forbidding his soul to approach that holiness, the soul encased in that object that might belong to the root of his own soul. His has the ability to draw it near and raise it up. But now he is forbidding himself and refusing to approach it! Therefore Torah said that ***His* word may not be profaned**, referring to the spark that came forth from the mouth of Y-H-W-H. Do not leave it to be profaned! Treat it like **all that He has said**, everything that comes forth from God's mouth, as something exalted. Find the Creator's intent in having clothed a spark in that food or drink. Act so as to raise it up....

One could hardly imagine a more complete reversal of the apparent meaning of Scripture. Instead of encouraging one to keep his vow in refraining from worldly pleasures, the author suggests that such a vow denies God's intent in creation, keeping one from discovering the holiness to be found throughout the world, to be tasted in everything the Torah permits.

Ginzey Yosef

> If a woman makes a vow, forbidding something to herself while she is yet in her father's house, in her youth, and her father hears ... and her father was silent to her, then all her vows and that which she has forbidden to herself shall stand.
> (Num. 30:4–5)

This refers to the soul, who is called "the daughter of Abraham our Father." Before she comes forth into the air of this world, she is taught the entire Torah. Before coming forth she is given an oath (b. Niddah 30b): "Be righteous, not wicked!" "Even if the whole world considers you a righteous *tsaddik*, be like someone wicked in your own sight."

This is **If a woman makes a vow, forbidding something to herself while she is yet in her father's house**. Before coming into this world, the soul is shown rows of *tsaddikim* in the Garden of Eden and their glory. She accepts upon herself the good qualities of those righteous ones **while she is yet in her father's house**. The blessed Holy One comes into that Garden each midnight to take delight in the souls of the righteous. **In her youth**: these are the youthful (or "waking") days of the soul, when she dwells in goodness more than at any other time.

And her father hears. The *Zohar* tells us that the soul has a Father and Mother, just like the body (2:12a). But the evil urge is "crouching at the entrance" (Gen. 4:7), present as soon as you are born. The good urge comes along only [with maturity], when you are thirteen years old. For those thirteen years, the parent has the responsibility to stand in for the good urge, getting the child used to doing good and guarding the child's mouth, and especially not leading by the hand to do evil....

You especially have to teach a child silence, resisting evil talk, talebearing, and vulgar speech. This is the meaning of **and her father hears**, referring to the [earthly] father. The father needs to hear the soul's vow and take it to heart. She is already under oath, having forbidden something to herself while she was yet soul without body, in the Garden of Eden. **And her father was silent to her**: Cause your child to have silence, the fence that guards wisdom. **Then all her vows ... shall stand.** That soul will stand up with goodness.

Wise counsel about parenting is widespread in the Hasidic sources, which sought to bring profound insights into the lives of ordinary people. A good parent takes to heart the pure soul of a child, helping that soul follow its own truth and protecting it from the many brutalizing influences found in daily life. How important this message is in our age, when unimaginable violence and destruction are available to children with the flick of a switch!

The fact that the soul is here described as "she," while in other sources the body is "female" while the soul is "male," shows us how flexible these gender categories are in religious literature.

Mattot
Round Two

OR: I am moved to hear R. Elimelekh telling his disciples that they need one another. The Hasidic path is an internal one, but it is not meant to be a lone one.

AG: That's part of the worldliness of Hasidism. Yes, you need human companions. But you also need the corporeal world, the place where you have to go in order to find God. The *Me'or 'Eynayim* is really attacking the Nazirite, who must be a stand-in here for the old type of ascetic mystic. To abhor the world, he says, is to profane the creative word of God.

AM: How does that work in real life? Do we really know how to eat and drink for the sake of heaven?

AG: You raise a huge question here. We have these sources, but do we really follow them? What would it be like to eat—and live—that way? These texts cry out to be turned into spiritual exercises.

AM: There were some—I think of the Piasecner Rebbe in pre-war Poland—who seemed serious about doing that. We need a setting where we can re-create such practices.

OR: It's hard because of the hectic pace at which we live. But of course that's all the more reason to do it.

AM: In taking something like this on, we too need the support of other "*tsaddikim*," a community of fellow seekers.

AG: This is a dream of religious community that I've pursued throughout my life, but only lived out in rare moments. Perhaps you will make it become more real.

OR: There is a link in current thinking between this pursuit of inwardness and the growing spiritual awareness of the environment. Both seek out a life of greater simplicity and harmony. Perhaps the growing urgency of the environmental crisis will create an opening for this sort of "slow down and live" spiritual awareness as well.

Massa'ey

Or ha-Ganuz la-Tsaddikim

> These are the journeys of the Children of Israel who came forth from the land of Egypt in their hosts, by the hand of Moses and Aaron. Moses wrote their comings forth and their journeys by the word of God. And these are their journeys and comings forth.
> (Num. 33:1–2)

... What value is there in having these stories in the Torah, which is to serve all generations as a guide to God's service? That is what the word "Torah" means. What happened happened, after all.

In the name of the Ba'al Shem Tov: When you are traveling and therefore cannot pray and study in your usual way, you must serve Y-H-W-H in other ways. Do not be distressed by this, for God needs to be served in all ways, sometimes one and sometimes another. That is why it came about that you needed to travel, in order to serve God in this way.

These are the journeys of the Children of Israel. Their journeys too were for the sake of serving Y-H-W-H; that is why they were written in the Torah. **Who came forth from the land of Egypt**, because there they were not located directly below the Upper Land of Israel [*shekhinah*, hovering above the earthly Jerusalem], where the roots of souls, **their hosts**, are to be found. They **came forth** *to* **their hosts** (*le-tsiv'otam*). **By the hand of Moses and Aaron**, who embraced within them all the souls of Israel.

All their journeys represent sublime rungs and aspects through which they merited to come into the Land of Israel. Had they not sinned by the

Golden Calf and the spies, they would not have needed so many journeys and rungs; just a few steps would have brought them to the Land. Because of sin, however, they had to go rung by rung in order to reach that goal.

The same is true of every person. All our journeys are for the sake of heaven. In accord with good deeds done, some people need only a few such journeys to reach a place of constant rest, both in this world and the one that is to come. "The burdens of livelihood and worldly matters are lifted from him" (m. Avot 3:5) in order to attain that place.

And these are their journeys and comings forth. [The **and** shows that] the journeys of the ancestors are a sign for their children. **These are** a person's **journeys**, even in later times. They are **journeys and comings forth**: we journey as things come forth, including adventures and woes. "The reward matches the pain" (m. Avot 5:22). According to the pain we take on to attain perfect service, so do we journey toward attachment to Y-H-W-H and constant rest.

There is a simple faith-centering here that lies close to the heart of Hasidic teaching. Everything that happens to us, including life's burdens and woes, comes about in order to give us an opportunity to seek and to serve God in unique and diverse ways. Embrace your own life's journey and make it your path to God.

Divrey Emet

> Moses wrote their comings forth and their journeys by the word of God. And these are their journeys and comings forth.
> (Num. 33:2)

Duties of the Hearts [by Rabbi Bahya ibn Paqquda, eleventh century] teaches that there are two worthy rungs. Some people are aroused by Torah or teachings to become deeply attached to Y-H-W-H. Among these are the prophets. This attachment is the [ultimate] "duty of the heart." But there is a higher order, that of those who out of their attachment to God come to attain Torah. This is the rung of Abraham our Father, who attained the entire Torah before it was given. But in the exile of Egypt our ancestors became coarsened. We needed to receive the Torah first, in order to become attached to God.

This is **Moses wrote their comings forth** [*motsa'eyhem*] **and their journeys**. The written form of Torah was a source (*motsa*) of attachment for them, as they went in their wanderings from strength to greater strength. **By the word of God** refers to Oral Torah, the process of interpreting the written Word. Our sages said the same on the verse "By the mouth of these words do I make a covenant with you" (Ex. 34:27), referring to the Oral Torah (b. Gittin 60b). But ***and*** **these** adds something to this. The order **their journeys and comings forth** refers to those who find attachment to God from within themselves and through that come to Torah.

This is a very revealing statement about the value system of a Hasidic master. Unlike the early rabbis, he places Abraham on a higher rung than [Moses and] the prophets. His devotion to God was spontaneous, coming from within himself, and that led him to discover all of Torah. It was only the coarsening effect of slavery that caused Israel to need laws and teachings as a pathway to discover God. It is no surprise that the Hozeh of Lublin attributes this teaching to a *hasid* of a much earlier era, Rabbi Bahya, author of *Duties of the Hearts.*

Kedushat Levi

> Moses wrote their comings forth and their journeys by the word of God. These are their journeys and comings forth.
>
> (Num. 33:2)

Why does the order change? First the verse refers to **their comings forth and their journeys**, then to **their journeys and comings forth**.

It is known that all the Children of Israel's journeys in that great and awesome wilderness were designated by Y-H-W-H; they were for the purpose of bringing forth holy sparks that had fallen into the "shells" there, to take what [the evil one] had swallowed from his mouth.

This is why Israel camped at some places for a long time, while other stops were brief. All was in accord with the redeeming of sparks that needed to happen there....

Of the forty-two wanderings of Israel, Scripture says, among others: "They camped at Haradah" (lit. "trembling"); "they camped at Mitkah" (associated with "sweetness"); "they camped at Har Shafer" ("Mount Beauty") (Num. 33:23–24, 28). This means that when Israel camped at a place where there was a bad sort of fear, they would worship Y-H-W-H with an exalted fear, filled with awe before God's overwhelming majesty. This was their encampment at Haradah, representing the quality of fear, the place where they had to serve God in fear. When they camped in a place where there were bad sorts of love, fallen there in the "breaking," as is well known, they needed to serve God in true love. This was their camping in Mitkah, the quality of love. So too at Har Shafer, referring to the quality of beauty, or *tif'eret*.

In this way they raised up all the sparks that had fallen there, restoring them to their Root, the place of the Holy. This was the purpose of their wanderings in the wilderness. Moses wrote of **their comings forth**, meaning their bringing forth and uplifting the sparks from their shells along **their journeys**. This was all **by the word of God**, in the course of their journeys. Then it details: **These are their journeys**, saying that the purpose of those journeys was the **comings forth**, bringing forth those sparks and raising them to the Source of holiness.

In this description of Israel's ancient wanderings, Levi Yitshak offers a rather clear description of an essential trope in the Hasidic devotional method, one we have seen frequently. Follow the list of essential divine/human qualities. Wherever you find them in a fallen state, raise them up through your own turn toward them in their highest form. As a paradigm, the "places" where Israel camped, whether for days or for years, may refer to your own inner "places," including the ones where you have to do your greatest battles.

Tsemah ha-Shem li-Tsevi

> Moses wrote their comings forth and their journeys by the word of God. These are their journeys and comings forth.
>
> (Num. 33:2)

Objections are raised as to why the order is reversed in these two verses.

In my homily on the Passover Haggadah, I wrote that there is an upper Exodus from Egypt [as well as a lower, earthly one]. Originally all things, even those that are opposite to one another, were jumbled together. As they emerged, each one went and was settled in its own place.

Moses wrote their comings forth, the emergence of individual souls from that upper "Egypt." **And their journeys** refers to their descent through the various realms. Each one was then established in its own place.

But [then the reversal begins]. In the same [ordered] way, each of us has to raise up our soul to the place from which it was drawn. This is the "returning light." That is why the order [of the words] is reversed. We need to journey toward that place from which our soul came forth.

Speech is spread out through every worldly matter. But we uplift it through the twenty-two letters. These then are absorbed into the five verbal categories or parts of speech. That "five" is represented by the letter *heh*, the final letter of Y-H-W-H. It has to be united with its Source, which is Y-H-W. Thus the order of **journeys** toward their **comings forth**, [progressively toward the Source]. The same is true of all uplifted—eating, drinking, and all the rest—these too are called **journeys** back to the place whence they all came forth.

The verses are depicted as a good summary of this key Hasidic teaching. The journey is a circular one. We are given life, energy, breath, speech, and Torah, and our job is to reshape them as they flow through our thoughts, words, and deeds, offering them back up to God their Source.

Or Torah

> They journeyed from Marah and came to Elim [*elimah*].
>
> (Num. 33:9)

This recalls the verse "They came to Marah, but were not able to drink the waters, because they were bitter" (Ex. 15:23). "Bitter waters" may refer to mind that has come into the lower realms [i.e., "distracting" or evil thoughts]. We are told that [after God in Creation divided the "upper" from the "lower" waters] the lower waters cried, saying, "We too want to be close to our Master!" (*Tikkuney Zohar* t. 5, 19b). This reminds us too of the waters in the *sotah* trial, where they were to take dust from the floor of the *mishkan*, the Tabernacle [here your inner *mishkan*], that had been taken on pledge (*nitmashken*) or "broken" (*Tanhuma Pekudey* 2). If the thought you had was found "not guilty," it could be transformed from a mere distraction into a source of creativity (*zarah/zera'*). It could become a way to strengthen your religious life. All evil things contain something good within them, as is known. [The only question is whether] you are "impure" in your approach to them. If so, you are in trouble!

This is "They came to Marah"; they fell into something evil. They "were not able to drink the waters," to find the love within that harsh place. "Because they were bitter" refers to *them*, the people. They were just not good. Otherwise they would have been able to find great goodness, for every negative force contains love within it. Had they broken the negativity open, they would have found the good within.

So **They journeyed from Marah and came to Elim**. The word *elimah* contains the letters of *elohim*, God, in garbled order. *Eli mah*, "My God is in 'What?'" The "What?" is that which we can't grasp, like the love within that place of negativity....

That's the job: to take the "What?" that we can't understand—including pain, emptiness, a sense of God's absence, and all the rest—and uplift it, seeking out the hidden love within that husk. If we ourselves are bitter, we are not able to draw the nourishing waters of *hesed* out of those bitter places.

Massa'ey Round Two

AG: The journey is from our Source in God out into the world, but then back to God as well.

OR: The journey is a very real one, embracing all of our lives. The point is that it is filled with constant opportunities to find and serve God in endlessly varied ways.

AM: I'm struck by the *Or ha-Ganuz*'s phrase "journeying toward attachment." *Devekut* is where we are going. Some of us need a longer path to get there; others need less of a journey. It depends how far and how frequently we wander off our paths.

AG: But the length and difficulty of the journey may pay off in the long run, opening us more deeply to *devekut.*

AM: Yes, but look also at the *Kedushat Levi.* How easily we turn bitter along the way! How do we make our way back from that bitterness, which we know does us no good?

OR: We can accept the value placed on suffering, so long as it is descriptive or after-the-fact, not prescriptive.

AG: That's entirely in the spirit of the Ba'al Shem Tov, who did not want his disciples to seek out suffering.

OR: The figure of Abraham that the Hozeh (*Divrey Emet*) describes, the one who wandered and sought first, then found Torah within himself, reminds me of so many seekers in our own day.

AM: And remember that it was only our enslavement in Egypt that made us need to go in the other direction, to receive Torah first. The moral breakdown caused by enslavement and personal degradation meant that we needed the gift of law.

AG: Yes, I think the Hozeh indeed foretold two ways to see our contemporary spiritual situation. You may say that we are so enslaved to the chaos and materialism of secular life that we need to be given the immediate gift of Torah, law and discipline. Only then can we truly embark on a path of spiritual growth. Or you may say that many in our day are privileged to be in the camp of Abraham our Father, seekers on the path before they have a Rule, but knowing they will need to find one.

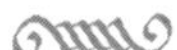

דברים

Sefer Devarim

The Book of Deuteronomy

דברים

Devarim

Me'or 'Eynayim

> In the land of Moab Moses set forth to explain this Torah, saying.
> (Deut. 1:5)

The Midrash (*Rabbenu Bahya al ha-Torah*) says that Torah was given in such a way that it may be seen to have 49 "faces" toward the pure and 49 toward the impure [i.e., that each law or passage may be interpreted in multiple ways]. The word "Moab" has the numerical value of 49. Scripture also refers to this in the verse "If you seek wisdom like silver and search for it like hidden treasure" (Prov. 2:4). The word "treasure" is *MaTmonim*, and M-T is 49 [thus reading *matmonim* to mean "counting 49"].

Now why should the land of Moab be related to the forty-nine ways in which Torah is interpreted, making the numerical association? To understand this, we need recall that the Torah was given to Israel only after seven weeks of wandering through the Sea of Reeds and various other places listed in the Torah. They walked through various deserts until they came to Mount Sinai. All this was in order to cut off the outer shells, the superficialities that formed a curtain dividing them from the Written Torah. Israel were sunk deep in defilement and "shells," as is well known. By traveling through those deserts before coming to Sinai, as well as by witnessing the miracles and wonders at the Sea and afterwards, faith in the blessed One became rooted in their hearts. It was through these journeys across desolate wilderness, the very dwelling-place of those "shells," that they gained the power to defeat them and lay them aside, so that there [would] be no curtain dividing Israel from the Written Torah.

Now Torah was given to Moses at Sinai both in its general principles and its detailed rulings, both written and oral, including "everything a faithful student was ever to innovate" (*Va-Yikra Rabbah* 22:1). But this Oral Torah, the explanation of the Written, was not yet revealed to all of Israel. They would not be able to penetrate its secrets until they removed the additional veil of shells that separated them from Oral Torah....

They were unable to explain or reveal the [Oral] Torah until they had traveled through all those deserts, the dwelling of their own shells. By means of these wanderings and the act of serving God in their course, they were able to defeat the shells, breaking through the veils that separated Torah's multiple faces from those who study her. That is why we refer to the forty-nine faces, pure and impure. It is by means of interpretation that the hidden faces of Torah are revealed. The Creator's incomprehensible wisdom saw that it would be impossible to get beyond those divisions except by travels through the wilderness at that very time when Torah had begun to be revealed.

This is the case today as well. The challenges we have regarding Torah are there because of our "shells." A certain place remains hidden from us, causing an objection in our minds. But when we raise ourselves up to the place of *binah* [the fiftieth gate, beyond the forty-nine] and there confront the pain of that objection, we come to see it from the viewpoint of *binah* [from a deeper perspective] and thus defeat the shells. Then the truth is revealed; it was our own inner harshness that had set the curtain in place, dividing us from truth. When we set about contemplating and hold fast to *binah*, we take that harshness along with us and come to sweeten it in its deeper root.

Now that the collective shells have been defeated and set aside, it is up to every person who studies Torah to defeat his/her own inner harsh places, so that we [will] not be separated from the faces of Torah....

Now Moab was the last stop on Israel's journey, after crossing all the deserts. "They camped in the plains of Moab, across the Jordan" (Num. 22:1). This is the border of the Land of Israel....

Until now Torah had truly been revealed only to Moses, because of his high rung. But this day all Israel are able to attain it, since the dividing veil has now been cast aside.

The personalizing of Israel's wanderings is very strong here. We, like our ancestors, have a wilderness we need to cross before we can fully receive Torah. The stopping places along our journey consist of questions, objections, confusion, doubt, temptation, and the like. Only when we get through these will we be able to live fully in the land of Torah. We each also have a Moab, a seven-times-sevenfold final stretch to cross before we break through and complete our journey.

This radical interiorization of the process should not be dislodged as we confront biblical criticism. That is yet another outer "shell" that has to be broken through as we seek the inner light of Torah. But the path suggested here is one that deals with struggles on a much deeper and more personal plane.

No'am Elimelekh

> You all approached me and said, we will send people out before us, to explore the land for us.... And I said to you: do not fear.... Y-H-W-H, your God who goes before you, will fight your battles, as you saw God do in Egypt ... and regarding this matter, you do not trust Y-H-W-H your God, who goes before you along the way seeking rest for you....
>
> (Deut. 1:22, 29–30, 32–33)

Why did the Israelites send the spies, and why did Moses agree to this plan? Their intention was good; they wanted to clear the [spiritual] way into the Land, to destroy the demonic forces [lit. "shells"] that were in Canaan. That being done, they would easily overcome and kill their enemies. Without the power and vitality that derive from these shells, they would be like dead bodies.

That is why the Israelites chose the best and most important people among them, *tsaddikim* who through their great holiness had the power to destroy the shells. They sent one from each tribe—the best of them. RaSHI says that at the time they were sent they were all still righteous. But when the spies failed, Moses rebuked the people. He said to them: Your intention was good, but you should have trusted Y-H-W-H your God, who performed so many miracles for you and took you through the desert full of snakes and scorpions. These allude to the shells [of that place]. God went before you there and destroyed them and will do the same for all kingdoms you have to go through. **Seeking rest for you** (Num. 10:33, but similar to Deut. 1:33), making it easier for you to overcome your enemies by uprooting their vitality.

Thus **You all approached me and said, we will send people out before us** describes the intention that these people would clear all the obstacles on the road, the shells that still encamp there. **And I said to you: do not fear ... regarding this matter, you do not trust Y-H-W-H your God.** It would have been better for you to trust the blessed Holy One to go before you to clear the way and bring you to the Land.

This teaching is another example of the Hasidic tendency to spiritualize biblical stories. The real battlefield is the spiritual one, and worldly conquest is but a reflection of inner victories. But perhaps even more interesting is the implied critique against *hasidim* who count on the *tsaddik* to go in advance of them and do the spiritual "heavy lifting" for them. It is much better to rely on your own relationship with God.

Torey Zahav

> You have had enough of going around this mountain. Turn yourselves to the north.
> (Deut. 2:3)

We are taught that to the righteous the evil urge appears like a mountain (b. Sukkah 52a).

I heard in the name of that wondrous *hasid* R. Nahman Kossover a reading of "The holiest offerings are slaughtered to the north [of the altar]" (m. Zevahim 5:1). The evil urge entices people to commit serious transgressions. But in the case of a *tsaddik*, who has already overcome him several times, the evil one begins by convincing him to do a *mitsvah* that really turns out to be a great sin. It might involve informing on a person or publicly shaming someone. Sometimes just a bit of improper motivation is brought in, something you don't realize unless you look into it with great care. Only then do you feel it. Because of this, the *tsaddik* has to be vigilant always, not letting go of this self-awareness even for a minute. Of this a *hasid* once said: "You may be asleep, but he [the evil one] is awake;

you may be distracted, but he is always attentive, seeking to expel you from both this world and the next" (*Hovot ha-Levavot*, Sha'ar Yihud ha-Ma'aseh 5).

This is the meaning of "entirely holy offerings"—those are the *tsaddikim*—"are slaughtered to the north [*tsafon*]." The evil urge "slaughters" them in matters that are hidden (*tsafun*). He knows the *tsaddik* won't follow him into obvious sin. The same is not true, however, of ordinary people. Therefore "offerings of lesser holiness are slaughtered anywhere" (ibid. 5:7). People of little awareness can get caught up in obvious transgressions, so they can be "slaughtered" anywhere [by the evil urge]. This much I heard.

In this way we can read our verse: **You have had enough of going around this mountain**. You do constant battle, trying to distance yourself [from evil]. You go "round and round" that mountain, not going near to any major sin. But now, **Turn yourselves to the north** [i.e., the hidden]. Pay attention to those subtle sins and wrong ways of turning, those things you don't notice in the course of turning around and keeping far from major transgressions.... Come to serve God in truth and wholeness, even when it comes to those hidden things.

The path of the *tsaddik* has to be one of constant self-examination and questioning of motives. How to do this without undercutting the wholeness and simplicity needed to serve God in joy is itself a secret, one of the great balancing acts of the religious life.

Mevasser Tsedek (from *Va-Yikra*)

Purchase food for silver, that you may eat.
(Deut. 2:6)

I heard in the name of the Maggid Dov Baer, of blessed memory, that this verse should be read in accord with the teaching of the *Shulhan 'Arukh* (*Orah Hayyim* 571, *Magen Avraham*) that when you see desire overpowering you while eating, you should stop, breaking that desire. The words **food for silver** (*kesef*) can also mean "desire for food" and the word used for **purchase** (*tishberu*) can be derived from *shavar* or "break." When you see yourself eating with too much desire, break down that lust. Thus far the Maggid.

But to me it appears that the verse can be read another way. The word *okhel* ("food") is numerically equal to two divine names, Y-H-W-H and El [fifty-seven]. When you are eating and turn your attention to the holiness contained within your food, so great that it bears two holy names, the food itself will break down your desire. Then you will be able to eat in a state of piety and great shame [before God's presence], in true holiness. Your intent will be to raise up those holy sparks that are found within the food.

This is what it means to offer a sacrifice. In this situation you are *commanded* to eat, just as you are commanded to study, for eating too has become a form of God's service. When you call to mind the great holiness that lies within your food, the lust for eating ceases. You are offering a sacrifice, of which you must eat.

This is the meaning of **Purchase** ["break"] **food for silver** ["desire"]. The food itself breaks the desire!... **That you may eat**: then you are commanded to eat. In your eating, you are like one offering a sacrifice to God, raising up those sparks of holiness that lie within.

Here we see the live conversation going on between master and disciple, even after the master's death. Although the Maggid came to the Ba'al Shem Tov to be cured of an illness brought on by excessive fasting, he never completely absorbed his teacher's dismissal of ascetic practices. Despite the Hasidic emphasis on service in joy, we see in the Maggid and certain of the disciples an ongoing attraction to ascetic teachings. R. Yissakhar Dov of Zloczow dares to take on the master and offer an opposing teaching, one of which the BeSHT would probably have been proud.

Devarim Round Two

OR: These teachings all seem linked in urging us to turn inward and to pay attention to what we find. We need to break through our blockages to find the inner Torah, to pay attention to our hidden temptations, to seek God within the simple human act of eating.

AG: Yes, but they are also all about working on yourself, struggling against ourselves to make the breakthrough.

EL: You wonder whether you are reading Hasidism or *mussar*, tough-minded moral preaching. The *Torey Zahav* text is the strictest here, warning us about those hidden sins that are always there, even when we think we're doing good. Doesn't that sound more like Novarodek, the great *mussar* center, than it does like the Ba'al Shem Tov?

AG: But there is a strong element of *mussar* within Hasidism, the demand that we elevate our moral qualities. The difference is that the Hasidic masters talk about this mostly in a positive way, telling us of the potential we have for greatness, rather than putting us down.

OR: We need to find the holiness within ourselves; that search itself is uplifting. But vigilance is a part of it. They saw self-satisfaction as a great danger. When you think you're doing well, you stop moving and growing.

AG: As soon as you stand still on a single rung, you begin to fall. Human beings, they tell us, have to keep walking; that is *halakhah*. Only angels are called "standing"; they stay always on the same rung.

OR: This is a real challenge to our neo-Hasidic approach to Judaism. We seem to avoid this side of Hasidism, that which makes tough demands of us.

EL: Absolutely. Here we are challenged to take ourselves seriously as religious people, and that means constantly working on ourselves.

AM: Yes, but remember the Ba'al Shem Tov's rejection of ascetic practices. We need to draw a line between honest self-questioning and self-punishment. If we do, I think we can incorporate these teachings. But how would they change us? Would they make any visible difference in the way we behave?

EL: It doesn't have to be visible to others. We ourselves are the challengers here! We know whether we are demanding growth of ourselves.

OR: The question is self-indulgence. We are sometimes accused of trying too hard to create a "happy face" Judaism. It's all fun, it's all about celebration. Is there any real depth to the unchallenged religious life? We need to be reminded of the hidden "shells" and dark places within ourselves.

AG: Wait a minute. Hasidism saved Judaism for me because of the Ba'al Shem Tov's radical sense of self-acceptance. All love, he taught, derives from the love of God, even if we encounter it in a fallen state. Every desire you have is ultimately rooted in holiness; all you need to do is uplift it. This is breathtaking and liberating if taken seriously. But now we're being warned, "But watch out for that evil urge! Be ever on your guard!" Doesn't that undercut the BeSHT completely?

AM: I too was attracted to Hasidism by this vision. But we need to find the balance between self-acceptance and the call to work on ourselves. (To use Heschel's language, all of Hasidism contains both Miedzybozh and Kotsk.) The wholeness of growth lies in that balance.

EL: Levi Yitshak, somewhere else in this volume, talks about two kinds of preachers, *mokhihim*. One approaches people harshly and puts them down, while the other does his work by seeking to build them up. But they are both called *mokhihim*, "reprovers." They are both calling on you to become a better person.

Va-Ethanan

Kedushat Levi

> See, I have taught you goodly statutes and judgments, as Y-H-W-H my God has commanded me, to perform in the land you are coming to inherit.
> (Deut. 4:5)

This may be interpreted in the way we have also understood "The Children of Israel did as Y-H-W-H had commanded Moses" (Ex. 12:28). The principle is that God spoke the commandments to Moses to be said to Israel. But in truth, "hearing from the Master is not the same as hearing from the disciple" (b. Ketubot 111a). They did not attain the expansion of mind that came with God's speaking to Moses until they actually acted out the commandment. Only then did they reach that state.... This is the meaning of "Israel *did* as Y-H-W-H had commanded Moses." They did it with the same expanded mind that Moses had when God commanded him....

Now Moses spoke each commandment to Israel with the same mental state in which he had received it from the mouth of God. This is the meaning of our verse: **I have taught you goodly statutes and judgments, as Y-H-W-H my God has commanded me**, that is, I speak the commandment to you with that same mind. And if you should say that Moses himself only attained that state of mind because he had [already] fulfilled the commandments, the verse goes on to say: **to perform in the land you are coming to inherit.** Moses never came into the Land and thus never fulfilled

[all] the commandments. This clearly indicates that he attained the mental state implicit in the commandments on his own, without acting on them.

Faith that the *mitsvot* are filled with secret meaning is part of Hasidism's legacy from the traditions of Kabbalah. But can these meanings be attained without actually doing the commandments? Are the contemplative contents separable from the deeds themselves? This issue is debated in the Maggid's circle. Here Levi Yitshak answers in the affirmative—but only for Moses. Or does he mean to include the *tsaddik* who is like Moses?

Torat ha-Maggid (from a Manuscript of R. Hayyim Hayka of Amdur)

What great nation has deities as close to it as Y-H-W-H our God is to us, whenever we call upon Him? (Deut. 4:7)

... Note that the verse changes its language. First it uses *elohim* ("deities") in the plural form, but then goes on to use it as "God" in the singular. The fact is that this word *elohim* is a general term. Even a judge is referred to as *elohim*. So too are all the heavenly "princes" [or angels].

Now by logic it would seem that we could be closer to these princes than to Y-H-W-H, asking our petitions of them, since God is so very elevated. Scripture says: "There are guardians higher and higher" (Eccles. 5:7) [seemingly indicating a hierarchy above]. This was in fact the error of the generation of Babel.

The truth is not that way. Our blessed God fills all the worlds and surrounds them. God is present within all the worlds. In that case He is closer to us than are those princes, who can only be in a single place and none other. **Has deities as close to it** refers to the angels above, who are close to us lower creatures. But it says that **Y-H-W-H our God**, though so highly elevated above us, is nevertheless even closer.

The strong pantheistic strain within Hasidism, especially in the school of the Maggid, is used as a way of emphasizing God's closeness to humans, even in a very personal way. The God who is everywhere, who indeed fills both world and self, is closer to us than any heavenly being we could imagine.

ME'OR 'EYNAYIM I (FROM *YITRO*)

> The mountain was burning in fire unto the heart of heaven.
>
> (DEUT. 4:11)

The two tablets that Moses brought down to Israel were really a heart, so that we might have "a heart toward our Father in heaven." The heart is called a tablet, as in "write them on the tablets of your heart" (Prov. 3:3). Our sages taught (*Zohar* 2:107b) that there are two chambers within the heart, the right ventricle being the dwelling of the good urge and the left the home of the will toward evil. These are the two tablets.

This is **The mountain was burning in fire**. "Are not my words like fire?" (Jer. 23:29). Israel attained the inner light **unto the heart of heaven**, until their hearts were indeed turned toward their heavenly Father. God is referred to as "heaven," as in "May You hear, O Heaven!" (1 Kings 8:34).

But after they made the Golden Calf, this heart was lost to them. Then began the praxis of *teshuvah*, return to God, which demands a broken heart. "O God, do not reject a broken and humbled heart" (Ps. 51:19). If we truly had hearts turned toward God we would not have sinned and we would have no need for *teshuvah*, the breaking of our hearts.

But so it was. On the seventeenth of Tammuz, the day they made the Calf, Moses came down from the mountain and the tablets were smashed. Since then we are in need of *teshuvah*, requiring the broken heart.

Religion is all about matters of the heart. "The merciful One seeks the heart," our sages tell us. We would do well to read Scripture's many references to the heart, including "hard-heartedness," the "heart of stone," the "heart of flesh," the "hollow heart," and the "new heart." Read them well and take them to heart.

Me'or 'Eynayim II

> You shall love Y-H-W-H your God with all your heart [*levavekha*]....
>
> (Deut. 6:5)

Our sages read this [the double *bet* of *levavekha*] to mean "with both your urges, the good urge and the evil urge" (b. Berakhot 54a). But how is it possible to love God with our evil urge?

Indeed, Y-H-W-H has commanded us to love Him. But how is this possible at all, since God's nature cannot be known? For this reason God gave us the counsel of the evil urge, creating a this-worldly reality that would serve as an example through which we could understand the truth behind it.

Regarding all the pleasures of this world, including eating, drinking, and sex, we come to ask ourselves, "Why do I love that thing?" It is, after all, just a broken form, derived from the World of Love, as we have taught repeatedly. How much more should I being loving the blessed Creator, the Source of all pleasure!

Of this King David said: "I have become a *mashal* ['parable' or 'example'] for them" (Ps. 69:12). They [the people] think that I am holding on to the *mashal* [earthly love or desire] alone, but do not get that to which it refers. But such is not the case [i.e., I truly love God].

There is an evil urge that blinds our eyes, not allowing us to see through to that which the *mashal* [earthly desire] comes to teach. The counsel for this is to study Torah. Our sages said [of the evil urge]: "If that ugly one attacks you, drag him to the house of study" (b. Kiddushin 30b). Why is he called the "ugly one" in this saying? Because all worldly pleasures are broken and unwhole forms, lasting only for a while, but then evaporating. In the end they turn out to be repulsive, just like that which we eat eventually turns into something that disgusts us. The same is true of the rest of our lusts. So if this "ugly one" draws you toward repulsive things, "drag him to the house of study." Torah is a seasoning [or "balm"] for the evil urge, as the sages go on to tell us: "I created the evil urge, but I also created Torah as a balm against it."

This is called "returning [to Y-H-W-H] out of love." By means of these very desires, you bring yourself to return to loving God. Then, we are taught, even intentional sins are transformed into merits (b. Yoma 86b). Every transgression becomes a way to love Y-H-W-H, as you take the message from this *mashal* and apply it to the reality [= God]. That is why the Torah is called a "seasoning" for the evil urge. The seasoning preserves the cooked dish itself. Torah turns the sins themselves into merits. Understand this.

This is an important text for understanding the debate about whether Hasidism negates this world, seeing it as transparent, or truly seeks to uplift it. There were divergent views on this in the Maggid's circle. The position of the *Me'or 'Eynayim* is clearly stated here. Torah, like the good spice, preserves the dish itself, making it worthy. Sin itself is uplifted and transformed into love of God.

Va-Ethanan Round Two

AG: They tell us so clearly here what it is that they are seeking to create: a Judaism of the heart, nothing less.

EL: Yes, and that helps us understand why the enemies of Hasidism found them so dangerous. Everything is in your heart. You can do a *mitsvah* without any real physical deed.

AM: What is it that they fear in this? Why should they find talk of the heart so threatening?

EL: This is a religion that can be used to easily justify the worst in people. It takes away all restraint, trusts only in the heart.

AM: But isn't that the internal and subjective religion that we too seek today? Why should people turn to Judaism if not in responding to the call of the heart?

EL: But listen to what they're saying. Maybe even your sins are ways to connect with God. What then is to keep you from sinning, both against God and against other people? Suppose King David was indeed thinking holy thoughts while sleeping with Bathsheba? What about her poor husband Uriah?

AG: I wish I could say that the anti-Hasidic forces were so concerned about Uriah and all the other innocents. I think what they really worried about was the challenge to their own power.

EL: Indeed they may have been focused on that. But I am concerned about the Uriahs. What kind of world will we have if there are no restraints?

AG: That's why I think we have to differentiate between sins "between person and person," where there really are victims, and those "between man and God," that are purely matters of the heart, and are there only to arouse the heart.

EL: It's not always easy to distinguish between these, especially once you enter the public realm as a religious figure.

AM: Another fear in this world of purely subjective religion is self-deception. With no external criteria, it is too easy to fool yourself. My "heart" can so easily be just what seems convenient or easy.

AG: Yes, but self-deception works the other way as well. You have worked so hard to say all the words or get the deed all properly done, you fool yourself into thinking that you've really come close to God, closer than the other guy.

EL: Which comes first? In their day, everyone still had the forms, so you could speak up for the deeper true religion of the heart. But for us? Most people today try to begin (and end!) with the heart.

AM: That's why all the Hasidic masters insist that *yir'ah* ["fear" or "awe"] has to precede *ahavah* ["love"]. Can we start with *ahavah*?

AG: Maybe we too can start with *yir'ah*, if we're careful to say that it really means awe and wonder, untinged by any memory of fear of punishment or old-fashioned religious guilt.

'Ekev

Tsemah ha-Shem li-Tsevi I

> ... For a person does not live by bread alone, but by all that comes forth from the mouth of Y-H-W-H.
> (Deut. 8:3)

Understand this through a parable: A servant is fed from the king's own food, taken right out of the ruler's mouth. More than that servant takes pleasure in the food itself, he rejoices that the king in all his glory gives it directly to him, from his own mouth. Even if the food is some great delicacy, this pleasure sustains him more fully than the food itself. This is the meaning of our verse, since we know that bread itself comes from the mouth of Y-H-W-H.

So too we can understand "Y-H-W-H gives wisdom from His mouth" (Prov. 2:6). "For wisdom gives life" (Eccles. 7:12). A person's vitality comes from God's own mouth. This is the sustenance of Torah, mentioned in the *Zohar* (2:62a). So too the Talmud: "Y-H-W-H gives wisdom from His mouth"—like a king who has a banquet and sends his loved ones some of the food that lies before him (b. Niddah 70b).

The same is true of the showbread (*lehem ha-panim*, lit. "the bread of the face"). It shines forth with the light of the living King's face. Thus "Mouth to mouth I speak to him" (Num. 12:8) and "Face to face Y-H-W-H addressed your whole assembly" (Deut. 5:4). Food is also called "bread from heaven" (Ex. 16:4).

Tsemah ha-Shem li-Tsevi II

> Eat, be sated, and bless Y-H-W-H your God.
> (Deut. 8:10)

The analogy is that of a flowing spring. The more you draw from it [by priming the pump], the more strongly its waters flow and offer their blessing. Our sages referred to a "river that grows from its own shores" (b. Nedarim 40a). If you don't draw from it, it recedes into its own source.

When Israel merit receiving the divine flow and draw it forth from God, the divine name itself is blessed. "You shall draw water in joy from the wellsprings of salvation" (Is. 12:3). Those wellsprings need to be saved! Their salvation comes about as you draw their water.

Our eating and being sated is a commandment to act: You shall **eat** and **be sated. And bless**: a commandment to speak.

These two short teachings, drawn together here, show the two sides of the divine-human relationship around the simple act of eating. We are given the most intimate of blessings, food from the King's own mouth. The shining face of God is present in the food we eat, a greater delight than any delicacy. At the same time, we give blessing and strength to God, and not only by our words of blessing. In eating and being sated we bless the One, the endless Spring of life, who thrives on giving without end.

Or ha-Emet

> What does Y-H-W-H your God ask of you, except that you fear Him…?
> (Deut. 10:12)

By way of parable: So long as the father walks together with his son, the son does not engage in childish behavior, since he fears his father. But once the father distanced himself from his son, and he then joined other children and played with them. He tripped and got hurt.

The pain was not so bad at first. But when his father came along and saw what had happened, he was very shaken. He saw there was an infection, one that could get worse and threaten the entire body, God forbid. He took firm hold of his son and pulled out the thorn that had caused the problem.

The son thought that his father was being awfully cruel, since the removal of the thorn hurt him much more than it had when it was still inside him. But really it was a great act of healing.

When that father later wanted to reprove his son, he said: "'Listen, my child, to your father's rebuke' [Prov. 1:8]. Don't hang on to your childish ways. Otherwise I will have to make you suffer, as I did when I was taking out that thorn."

The child's fear is completely unlike that of the father. The father fears for the real harm that might come about. Because of this, he frightens the child with what the child considers great pain, taking out that thorn. The child does not fear for the infection, but for the pain of the cure itself. If he had understanding, his fear would be the same as his father's.

This is the meaning of our verse: **What does Y-H-W-H your God ask of you, except that you fear** *et*—meaning "along with"—your God? Hold fast to the same fear that your Father in heaven has for you—that sin will cause you true harm. Then "the fear of heaven [i.e., that which heaven itself fears] will be upon you" (m. Avot 1:3).

Parables of father and child are found throughout the Maggid's teachings; he must have been a very loving father. But if the parable is to be taken seriously, a great question is left unanswered. Why does the Father "distance Himself" from the son in the first place, allowing him to be injured?

No'am Elimelekh

> Now Israel, what does Y-H-W-H ask of you? Only to fear God, to follow all God's ways, to love and serve God with all your heart and soul. To keep God's commandments and rules, which I have given you on this day, to your own good.
> (Deut. 10:12–13)

The question is obvious—after listing fear and love of God, and following all God's ways, what else could God have asked us to do? The only reason the blessed Creator created the world is to benefit the creatures. But this flow of good needs a vessel that can receive and contain it.

Imagine that you want to give a gift of wine or honey to a friend but do not have a beautiful container for it. You could borrow a beautiful silver vessel from the recipient and send it back full of wine or honey.

In the same way, every person is a vessel, a container. The means by which you prepare and fix your vessel so that it can contain the flow of goodness from God are the love and fear of God, following God's commandments and pathways. Through this you become a beautiful and appropriate vessel that God can borrow and return full of good.

What does Y-H-W-H ask [*sho'el,* "borrow"] **of you?**—meaning, under what conditions will God borrow the vessel that is you to fill it with good and blessing? **Only to fear God,** etc. This can only happen if you serve God in all the ways listed in the verse. Then you will be a beautiful vessel and an appropriate container....

To your own good, then God will be good to you, and through you all of Israel as well.

This is another call for divine-human partnership. God's deepest wish, to bring good and blessing to all creation, can only be fulfilled if you, the human, prepare your own vessel—your self as such a vessel—to contain that blessing.

Or Torah

> To love Y-H-W-H your God, to walk in all His ways, and to cleave to Him....
>
> (Deut. 11:22)

Our sages asked: Is it possible to cleave to the blessed Holy One? Is God not "a consuming fire" (Deut. 4:24)? Cleave rather to God's qualities, they taught. Just as God is compassionate, so you be compassionate, and so forth (b. Shabbat 133b).

They meant to say that it is impossible to serve God in fiery ecstasy—for that is what true "cleaving" is—in a constant manner. You can only do so in a way that both reaches and recedes, just like the flames of a fire. If you blow on a fire too soon, you will put it out. But the same blowing later will make the fire grow. The flame itself reaches up and down, in constant motion. So it is with the flame of ecstasy—it reaches and recedes—for constant joy would be no joy at all.

This is the Talmud's question: "Is God not a consuming fire?" Isn't it beyond us to cleave to God constantly in an ecstatic way? It responded: "Cleave to God's qualities." This refers to the garments of God, which are the letters. It is possible to think constantly of the letters of Torah, and Torah is God's garment. Even when in conversation with people, you should contemplate only the letters that compose those words being spoken. They too are derived from the twenty-two letters of Torah.

"Just as [*mah*] God is compassionate...." Note that the word *rahum* ("compassionate") has the same letters as *homer* ("physicality"). The blessed Holy One cannot have compassion on lowly matter. How can anything so coarse as the physical be present in the most subtle and refined thought of God? God has to become diminished in order to encompass matter and thus to have compassion for it. Whence does such diminishment (*tsimtsum*) come to God? It comes about when a person has compassion; that causes God to become dressed as well in the garment of compassion, reducing Himself, as it were, in order to have compassion upon us.

This is the meaning of "How is [*mah*] He compassionate?" "You be compassionate"—it is we who bring about divine compassion.

The Maggid has created a theological language for saying that we are the embodiment or concretization of the divine quality of compassion; it is only through human agency that God can come to embrace the physical world, including our own embodied selves. This is one of those moments where mysticism and religious humanism, seemingly distant from one another, reach the same conclusion. Humanity stands at the center.

'Ekev Round Two

AM: There is a common theme here around our giving or doing something for God.This is the Kabbalistic idea of *mitsvot tsorekh gavoha*, that we fulfill a divine need by doing the commandments, here reconceived in the Hasidic context.

AG: Yes, but there is a difference between the texts. The first piece is all about direct contact with God, the divine face shining upon us as we gaze at the showbread. But the *Or ha-Emet* piece has the letters stand as intermediaries, needed because we can't keep looking directly at God.

OR: In my own struggles with theism, this type of Hasidic text has become very important to me. I recognize the reality of divine energy but see us humans as the ones who need to seek it out and channel it. There is indeed something bigger than us, but the abstract language of Hasidism enables me to divorce that from personified pictures of God.

EL: But I find something attractively personal here. In the mutuality of giving to Y-H-W-H, I see God as *friend* here, something pretty rare in Jewish sources. This God even needs to *borrow* something from us, a vessel to be filled with divine light. I want to preserve the intimacy of that very human description.

OR: I understand and am touched by what you are saying, but I am (at least today!) drawn to the more abstract language that Hasidism offers. The non-personal picture of the wellspring that we help to replenish has the power of imagery without the overwhelming Person-in-the-Sky, an image that brings too much "baggage" with it.

AG: The Maggid sets up a strange dichotomy that runs throughout his disciples' writings: a very abstract theology, one about Being and Nothingness, fullness and contraction of divine light, and all the rest, but then he constantly illustrates it by touching little vignettes about Father and child.

EL: Either way, the real challenge is the question "Do I have anything to *offer* in this relationship?" Whether I am offering it to the cosmos or to a loving Father/King is a matter of metaphor. The issue is about human worthiness. What do I have to give?

AM: That challenge is very clear throughout these texts. It puts humanity at the center.

AG: Of course this understanding needs to be universalized to be useful for us. The Kabbalists understood it as applying only to Jews and our specific *mitsvot*. But these Hasidic texts are a bridge toward its universalization. It is the human being, the reflection of God's own image, that shines the divine light back into its Source.

Re'eh

Tsemah ha-Shem li-Tsevi I (from *Ki Tavo*)

> See, I place before you this day.... The blessing is if you listen to the commandments of Y-H-W-H your God, which I command you this day.
>
> (Deut. 11:26–27)

The *Zohar* (1:12a, 26b) quotes the verse "Know this day and set it upon your heart, that Y-H-W-H is God ..." (Deut. 4:39). We come to know that they are one, the name *elohim* ["God," signifying judgment] and the name Y-H-W-H [signifying compassion]. There is no separation between them. You may come to know this from the day itself, since each full day includes both night and daytime, "evening and morning, one day" (Gen. 1:5). This is the meaning of "Know this day." Know it from the day itself. Then "set it upon your heart [the word *levav* has a doubled *bet*]," including both your good and evil urges, which together are called "heart"; two that are one.

I place before you this day. Day and nighttime, right and left, from which are drawn forth blessing and curse. The blessing is if **you listen to the commandments of Y-H-W-H your God**. "Listen" here means to unify (b. Yoma 35b); joining together God's flow of blessing toward you and your gift to God, in "the commandment of Y-H-W-H your God," blessed Holy One and His *shekhinah* [within you]. **Which I command you this day:** By the power of unity that I offer you in the day, joining right and left....

The wholeness with which we need to meet God and accept the commandment is signified by the day itself. As it embraces both light and dark, the night serving as a pathway toward the bright sun of morning, so must we embrace our evil urge, finding within it a pathway toward the daylight of compassion. Then both we and God will see the works of that whole day to be "good."

Orah le-Hayyim I

> See, I place before you this day blessing and curse. The blessing is if you listen to the commandments of Y-H-W-H your God, which I command you this day. And the curse is if you do not listen to the commandments of Y-H-W-H your God and turn aside from the path I today command for you, going after other gods whom you have not known.
> (Deut. 11:26–28)

Why does it say **this day**? And why here are blessing and curse placed right next to each other, while later Moses says: "See, I place before you today life and goodness, death and evil; choose life ..." (Deut. 30:15)?

The *Shulhan 'Arukh* (*Orah Hayyim* 231) teaches that "Know Him in all your ways" (Prov. 3:6) means that "we should do all our deeds, even those where the choice is ours, for the sake of heaven. Eating, drinking, walking, sitting and rising, conjugal relations, all our bodily functions, should be done for the sake of serving our Creator, or in a way that leads to God's service...."

The teaching means that serving God is a matter of the heart's intentions. "The compassionate One seeks the heart" (RaSHI, b. Sanhedrin 106b). Even one who performs a *mitsvah*, but does so without intending to worship the Creator, is called a sinner. Our sages (b. Nazir 23a) talk about two people roasting their paschal lambs. One ate of it for the sake of the *mitsvah*, while the other just gorged himself. Of this, they said, Scripture speaks in "The righteous shall walk in [God's ways], but the wicked shall stumble in them" (Hos. 14:10).

Every person is given the choice to turn either right or left. You can intend in every deed to serve heaven, doing *mitsvot* always, or you can do the opposite. We humans have the capacity to discern the path of good from that of evil. Thus our sages said: "If there is no awareness, whence distinctions?" (y. Berakhot 5:2). This means that in all things, including the doing of *mitsvot*, in all loves or pleasures, there lie two paths: blessing and curse. If you intend them as ways of serving God, you draw forth blessing. If not, God forbid, the opposite. All loves and pleasures are called "day," as in "By day Y-H-W-H commands His love" (Ps. 42:9). Now Moses personified the awareness or mind of all Israel. Thus he could say, **See, I place before you**, the **I** referring to awareness. It is our awareness that places before us **this day**, the loves and pleasures, and they contain **blessing and curse**, together. The blessing lies within them if you listen.

The word "listen" (*shema'*) can also mean "to assemble" or "gather" (1 Sam. 15:4).... Gather things together, whether in doing a *mitsvah* or in permissible physical pleasures; they should all be **the commandments of Y-H-W-H your God**. This will be the case if you do them all with the intent of worship. The curse within them will be **if you do not listen to the commandments of Y-H-W-H your God**, if you do those physical things not for the sake of worship. In the end you will **turn aside from the path I today command for you** and will commit actual transgressions.

I place before you means that it lies within your hands to choose the good and wholesome life.

Awareness means that we have to learn to listen. There is a voice within every deed that comes before us, one that says: "There is something here to be gathered up for the sake of God." We have to make the choice to listen to that voice.

We see here an earlier Hasidic expression of the teachings later associated especially with the nineteenth-century teacher Mordechai Yosef of Izbica, who preached a *hasidut* entirely based on this concept of radical freedom and constant choices.

Me'or 'Eynayim

See, I place before you this day blessing and curse. The blessing is if you listen to the commandments of Y-H-W-H your God, which I command you this day. And the curse is if you do not listen to the commandments of Y-H-W-H your God and turn aside

> from the path I today command for you, going after other gods whom you have not known.
> (Deut. 11:26–28)

Why does the text say **See**, as though the matter were set out before the seer's eyes and someone was pointing with a finger? Further, why does the text use the particle *et* when outlining the blessing, but omit it when it comes to the curse?

First we need to bring in the verses from *Parashat Nitsavim* that say, "Behold I place before you today life and goodness, death and evil" and further "Choose life" (Deut. 30:15, 19).

It is well known that the worlds and all within them were created through Torah, consisting of the letters from *aleph* to *tav*. The blessed Creator concentrated Himself within the letters. In this process of emanation the intensity of divine presence was lessened, allowing for the flow of God's light into the world. This *tsimtsum* began with the letter *aleph*. From there on the presence was reduced further with each letter, the emanation of God's light proceeding from letter to letter on to *tav*, the lowest of rungs and the place of choice. Of this the sages spoke in saying *tav—tiheyeh* ("*tav*, you shall live") and *tav—tamut* ("*tav*, you shall die") [because the letter *tav* indicates the second person future, the choices that ever stand before you] (b. Shabbat 55a).

In each thing that you encounter, even if it is on the lowliest rung, far from the flowing light of the boundless One, you need to bring that lowly *tav*-rung near to the cosmic *aleph*, the "Prince" of the world. You have to raise and uplift everything to the Root of all, which is that *aleph* [the "place" where the divine process began]....

This is the meaning of "Choose life." Choose the force of life and goodness that lies within things, the concentrated presence of God, and not the evil within them. Ever since the first human sinned, all things that exist contain a mixture of good and evil. In everything our eyes see, we can find either good or evil. Each person is also mixed in this way. It is the good urge in us that is drawn after the good we see in things, while the evil urge is drawn to the bad that is within them....

This is the meaning of **See, I place before you this day blessing and curse**. In every thing you see in this world, know that **I** [*anokhi*] am there in it, placing **before you blessing and curse**, good and evil, mixed together in all. The blessing is preceded by *et*, referring to the uniting of *aleph* with *tav*, the lowest of all the rungs. By seeing the good in everything and raising it to the level of cosmic *aleph*, you bring about blessing in the world....

That is why the *et* is missing with regard to the curse. The main reason a curse exists in this world is the fact that *tav* has not been joined to *aleph*....

We see here the utter simplicity of mystical insight as it was taught in the school of the BeSHT. The author is seeking to address himself to the most ordinary, unlettered Jews who lived scattered in towns and villages throughout his region. I hear him answering the objection of a Jew who comes before him and says, "But how can I truly serve God, when all I know is the *aleph-bet*?" "The alphabet is plenty," the master replies. "All you have to do is reverse the process of Creation. As God went from *aleph* to *tav*, progressively reducing the intensity of light until the ordinary world, the domain of *tav*, appeared, so you need merely to rise up through the letters, bringing everything back to its source in *aleph*, in the One." What more does one need to teach?

TSEMAH HA-SHEM LI-TSEVI II

> If there be a poor person from among your brethren at one of your gates ... do not clench up your hand before your poor brother; open your hand wide [*patoah tiftah*] to him.
>
> (DEUT. 15:7–8)

The Midrash (*Shemot Rabbah* 25:3) comments on "You open Your hand and satisfy every living thing with favor" (Ps. 145:16): "Come and see, the ways of the blessed Holy One are not like those of flesh and blood. Among humans, so long as the sponge is in your hand and you keep it open, not a drop will come forth. Only when you squeeze your hand closed does the water flow. But the blessed Holy One holds the sponge in His hand, as Scripture says 'a godly stream filled with water' (Ps. 65:10), and if He squeezes it, the water stops flowing. 'He holds back the waters and they dry up' (Job 12:15) or 'He will hold back the heavens and there will be no rain' (Deut. 11:17). It is when He opens His hand that the rain falls. 'May Y-H-W-H open for you His treasure, the heavens' (Deut. 28:12)."

What is the basis of the distinction being made here? Among humans, the flow is not directly from its source. The person is just a sponge into whom the water, detached from its source, has been absorbed. The water remains in the sponge for as long as the hand is open, coming out only as it squeezes shut. But in God's case the water is directly attached to its Source; the "godly stream" is connected to God. So long as the hand is open, it flows out to the world from its Source. That Source is endless, and so the sponge operates in the opposite way. When God wants to keep it from flowing, He holds it back and absorbs it into the sponge. Thus Y-H-W-H teaches us His way is to give alms by opening the Source, unlike the way of people. We are to follow God's example.

The grammarians call the form *patoah* a *makor* ["source," the Hebrew term for the infinitive absolute], like *naton* in "surely give" (Deut. 15:10). It means that you are to open your hand and give by opening, rather than by squeezing a bit out of the sponge. In being open in generosity, you are giving from that Source of flow that indeed "satisfies every living thing with favor...."

The giver has to learn that the gift is not his, but God's. Our act of generosity is not just human kindness, but a direct link—for giver as well as receiver—back to the Source of all. We must give with a sense that the Source that stands behind us is endless.

Orah le-Hayyim II

> Take care lest there be an unworthy word within your heart that says: "The seventh year, the sabbatical, is coming close." Then you look with a wicked eye at your poor brother and do not give to him. He will call out to God about you, and you shall have a sin. Surely give to him; let your heart not feel bad as you do so, because for this thing Y-H-W-H your God will bless you in every deed to which you set your hand.
>
> (Deut. 15:9–10)

Couldn't the text simply have said "lest your heart be unworthy"? Why does it need to refer to a "word" here?

The evil urge comes to you in order to turn you off the path, keeping you from giving alms to one who is upright and needy. That wicked one uses words of Torah to convince you that you don't have to give, [like the

Torah's teaching that] "your life comes first" (b. Bava Metsia 62a). Especially in the sabbatical year, when we do no planting, the evil one will seek to prevent us from giving by saying, "Prepare for yourself what *you* will need to eat in the seventh year, since your own life comes first."

But if you have a good heart, you will have the faith that God will provide from heaven. Scripture speaks of this in saying: "Should you ask 'What will we eat in the seventh year? We are not planting and not gathering in our crops!' [It answers:] I will command My blessing for you in the sixth year, and it will provide sufficient produce for three years" (Lev. 25:20–21).

Now Torah is referred to as the "Word," as in "A word commanded to the thousandth generation" (1 Chron. 16:15). That is the meaning of **word** in our verse. Should you have words of Torah that release you from your obligation to give, things like "your life comes first," **within your heart**, this is unworthy, meaning that your heart is being unworthy. You are listening to the counsel of the wicked one, who is showing you these words of Torah, telling you that you don't have to give.

If you had a good heart, you would have the faith of which we have spoken. It is only because your heart is being unworthy that you sought out this Torah teaching, causing you to **look with a wicked eye at your poor brother** and to say "My life comes first...."

Here is a prime text for what we call "Jewish values." How loudly we of the so-called "first world" need to hear this voice, and how far beyond the sabbatical year context it extends! Think of our retirement accounts. How much more than we need do some of us have "put away"? Might it just be the evil urge that is saying, "Keep investing! You may need it," keeping us from being more generous with those who are truly in need?

Might countries as well as individuals find a lesson here?

Re'eh
Round Two

EL: We see here two different manifestations of the same tendency: to break through all boundaries. In the first two teachings, it applies to the devotional life. Take *everything* back up to the *aleph*; everything can be done with *kavvanah* and can thus be transformed. There are no limits. In the last two teachings, the same principle is applied to the interpersonal realm: give without limits; beware of anything that might restrict your generosity.

OR: Yes, but you can't read these texts in isolation. Remember the context of their very bounded and constricted lives, because of both *halakhah* and the narrowness of *shtetl* existence. We have to see these extreme statements as correctives, seeking to achieve some balance.

AG: Of course. But it's so interesting that here in *Parashat Re'eh*, where the Torah text is all about dichotomies and choosing, we find these statements that reach beyond dichotomy and seek a borderless oneness.

EL: Could we say that the Hasidic readers are reacting against the text they have before them? We usually don't read them that way.

OR: The first two texts are about awareness, a theme we see so often in these writers. You have to learn discernment, to know when you are really acting for God's sake. Once you do, you really can uplift everything.

AG: Then is there any place left for *havdalah*, making distinctions, and *hafrashah*, separating oneself from evil? Those too seem to be important Hasidic motifs.

AM: Discernment is also essential to the last piece, which I find very powerful. There are times when the Torah seems to be telling you the wrong thing. But how do you know? On what basis can we say, "This must be a wrong reading"? We need to have a clear inner moral barometer, itself based on a teaching from within Torah, that serves as a standard by which to judge our understanding of all the rest. We need to read Torah with a religious insight that comes from within.

Yes, distinctions are important and we need to work with them, but they ultimately all lead back to the single Source.

EL: It is we who need the distinctions and limits, not God. The limitations, you might say, are from our side.

AG: They are not ultimate, but that does not make them any less valid, both for living the moral life and for maintaining balance within the human mind.

Shoftim

Mevasser Tsedek

> When a Levite comes forth from one of your gates where he dwells amid all Israel, coming filled with desire to the place Y-H-W-H has chosen, he shall serve in the name of Y-H-W-H your God like all his brother Levites who stand before Y-H-W-H.
> (Deut. 18:6–7)

Elsewhere I have interpreted the Mishnah's statement "Pray for the welfare [*shalom*] of the government [*malkhut*]" (Avot 3:2) as "Pray for the wholeness of *malkhut* [the tenth *sefirah*]." There are two essential qualities in serving God: awe and love. The *Zohar* describes these as the two "wings" that allow prayer to fly upward (*Tikkuney Zohar* t. 10, 25b). This seems difficult to understand. Wouldn't it be best to serve God purely with love and passion? But the truth is that love alone can bring you to the dissolution of self, your own life-force swallowed up in the Root. You need awe in order to tamp down love's passion.

This is the meaning of "the life-force flows back and forth" (Ezek. 1:14). The person's life-energy exists in that state of back-and-forth movement. It flows back into you because of the awe. Without it you could be swallowed up in your attachment to the Root. This is the meaning of "You shall love Y-H-W-H your God" (Deut. 6:5). In the midst of your great love, hold fast also to awe, represented by "*Elohim*," **your God**.

Now we know that *malkhut* is composed of both love and awe. This is the meaning of "Pray for the wholeness [*shalom*] of *malkhut*," that it comprise both. "For without that fear," the Mishnah goes on to teach, "one person would devour his neighbor alive." "Neighbor" here refers to the blessed Holy One. Your life-force would be devoured by the Root! Therefore pray for awe, as we have taught. The more you are aware of God's greatness, the more you are in need of awe to hold you back from being consumed out of existence.

The angels, who are so powerfully aware of God's greatness, are granted an extra measure of awe and fear, so much so that a river of fire pours forth from their perspiration before the fear of God and divine grandeur, all this so that their existence [will] not be negated.... Angels are called the "brothers" of Israel ... they are also referred to as "standing," because they do not move from one rung to another....

This is the meaning of **When a Levite comes forth....** One who cleaves to the blessed Creator, for the word "Levite" means "to accompany," as in the verse "This time my husband will accompany [*yilveh*] me" (Gen. 29:34), referring to intimate union. **From one of your gates**, from within this world.... **Coming filled with desire**, coming only with love and passion **to the place Y-H-W-H has chosen**, to serve the Creator. **He shall serve in the name of Y-H-W-H your God** [the two names], referring to love and awe, both together. **He shall serve ... like all his brother Levites who stand before Y-H-W-H**. These are the angels, his brothers, who serve standing in great awe so they [will] not be consumed. He should do the same, for with love alone a person too could be wiped out of existence.

Your task as a devotee is to touch the moment of self-negation in your great love of God, but not to let it sweep you away. This is the classic stance of Hasidism, balancing an openness to mystical experience and a commitment to worldliness. These writers have been to that inner place where the self vanishes, but they understand that the more urgent task is that of return and living in the world. Awe is a valuable tool to keep your feet planted in this world, where you still have work to do.

Torat ha-Maggid (from *Bo*, from the Manuscript of R. Shmelke)

Be whole with Y-H-W-H your God.
(Deut. 18:13)

One who studies the Oral Torah (*Torah shebe-'al peh*) has to be aware that the entire Torah, indeed all of speech, is drawn from the primal Word, that of which it is said: "By the word of Y-H-W-H were the heavens made" (Ps. 33:6). The root of all is in the upper mouth (*peh*), that primal word; everything derives from it. That word is thus the "master" (*ba'al*), from whom all receive. This is the meaning of Torah *shebe-'al peh*: the upper mouth is the master.

When learning or speaking, we need to reach toward that primal Word, uniting everything with it. Then the true "fear of Y-H-W-H" dwells with us, since that fear is identified with *hokhmah*, the beginning of all ... the essence and root of all the worlds, the primal Word.

This is the meaning of "The Torah of Y-H-W-H is perfect, restoring the soul" (Ps. 19:8). When you study in this way, exposed to this perfect fear, your soul is indeed restored. It is no longer broken; even its lowest rung, referred to here as *nefesh*, sunk in its attachment to the lowliest rungs of existence, is restored by this indwelling of the fear of Y-H-W-H.

This is **Be whole with Y-H-W-H your God**. When you are at this rung of complete or perfect fear, you will be with your God. Note that the *tav* of the word *tamim* ("perfect") is written as an enlarged letter. There are letters in the Torah written in an extra large or extra small form. The reduced letters refer to *tsimtsum*, the reduction of divine presence; the large ones refer to the presence that did not have to be reduced. When you attain that whole or perfect fear, you have reached the "large letters," God's presence in its full, undiminished form.

"Fear of God" is a constant theme in Hasidism, as it is throughout Jewish piety. This passage and many others like it make it clear that we are talking about a kind of mystical awe, one that causes the person to "rejoice while trembling" (Ps. 2:11) as all things are restored to their source in Y-H-W-H. The promise of faith is that the person will emerge from this experience with a new wholeness, the personal self and the cosmic Self at once made whole.

Orah le-Hayyim

> Be whole with Y-H-W-H your God.
> (Deut. 18:13)

God created humans from above and below, the soul from above and the body from below. Our sages said (b. Berakhot 10a) that in the five occurrences of "Bless Y-H-W-H, O my soul" in the Psalms, King David was referring to [five parallels between] the blessed Holy One and the soul. "Just as God fills all the world, so does the soul fill all the body.... Let the one who has these five characteristics come forth to praise the One who has them as well."

I have interpreted the call "Y-H-W-H is God" (1 Kings 18:39) noting that *elohim* ("God") is numerically equivalent to *ha-teva'* ("nature"). This means that God conducts the physical world, that which runs by nature, according to His will and desire. "The whole earth is filled with His glory" (Is. 6:3); this is the God who "fills all the world." "Y-H-W-H is God," dwelling within nature and conducting it by His will. Nature is not something separate from God, but God, who dwells within [throughout] the natural world, leads it as He desires.

Strive to be like your Creator in this way. Let soul and body be fully united, with no separation. Let soul lead body. But do not do so like a camel or donkey driver, with the soul pulling in one direction and the body in the other. **Be whole with Y-H-W-H your God**. If you are whole, soul and body in harmony, without separation, soul leading the body, then you will be **with Y-H-W-H your God**, like unto God. God dwells within the natural world without separation, filling all the world and leading it in accord with the divine will. You be whole in the same way, your soul leading your body, which stems from the world of nature. Then you will be attached to Y-H-W-H your God.

The translation here is quite literal and complete. The author can almost be read as saying that nature is the will of God. Here we see Hasidic panentheism coming as close as it can to the pantheism of Spinoza, while remaining quite distinct from it. Nature is nothing other than an expression of divine harmony and inner oneness. Imitation of this is to be the basis of your own moral and spiritual life. But the God who dwells within nature also inhabits the mysterious beyond.

Or ha-Me'ir

> It shall be when you draw near to the war, the priest shall come forth and speak to the people, saying to them: Hear, O Israel; this day you draw near to war

> against your enemies. Let your hearts not be weak; do not fear, do not panic, do not cower before them. (DEUT. 20:2–3)

The term *ve-hayah* **(it shall be)** is usually an indication of joy (*Bereshit Rabbah* 42:3). What joy can there be here? They are coming close to war! Even seasoned veterans fear for their lives as they approach the battle, not knowing whether it will end in victory or defeat.... All this needs to be explained.

It appears that the hidden meaning here refers to study and prayer, which are the essential battles we face throughout life. "Happy is the man who fills his quiver with them" (Ps. 127:5), shooting arrows at [the wicked angel] Samael. Have sharply pointed "arrows" in your hand, arouse yourself with letters filled with love and fear. Then let your heart trust that you will come to victory and not defeat.

Most people, we see, come to the inner heart-work of prayer bearing "neither words nor speech; their voice is not heard" (Ps. 19:4). Only their bodies sway, like trees in the forest. The battle is heavily turned against these people; they have fear in their hearts before the enemy who dwells within. That foe, the evil urge, takes away their weapons of war, the letters, re-forming them into words that support the foe, confounding their minds with vain, worldly thoughts. Indeed they have no arrows to shoot into the darkness, to triumph in chasing this hidden one from their heart. This is indeed defeat. When they turn to study or prayer, they come away empty-handed.

All this happens because such people do not take to heart why they came into this world or what they are doing here. They [wrongly] infer that they exist in order to support themselves and their wives and children, and so many other needs that Jews have. They spend most of their years in pursuit of food and clothing. Service, the real reason they were created, is forgotten from their hearts.

The Torah hints at this directly. *Ve-hayah* represents joy. **It shall be when you draw near to *the* war.** Note the definite article. God is certainly joyous as Israel step forth to do battle against this well-known foe, the evil urge, in the war of study and prayer. They take heart to prepare themselves for all sorts of battle, shooting those sharp arrows. Scripture assures us that "if your arrows are sharp, nations will fall beneath you, by your heart [defeating] the enemies of the King" (Ps. 45:6).... Set upon your heart a firm awareness that those thoughts distracting you from prayer, the service of your Creator, are enemies of the cosmic King.... The enemy seeks to grab away your weapons, the letters, and lock them up within his "shells," so that you will have no way to fight this battle. But the veteran warrior, who knows the ways of service, is **the priest**, for it is their job to teach. They need to **speak to the people, saying to them: Hear, O Israel; this day you draw near to war against your enemies.** RaSHI comments: Even if they have no greater merit than that of reciting the *shema'*, it will suffice to save them. Clearly this is speaking of the battle of study and prayer. The essence of prayer, commanded within the Torah itself, is in reciting the *shema'*. That is the act of unifying God's name, as the mystics teach. That is why it demands your life and all your strength, clearing your mind of all distractions, no matter from which direction they come.

RaSHI was pointing deeply at this when he spoke of "merit." The word also means "purity" (*zekhut/zakkut*) or "clarity." Reciting the *shema'* with these truly does suffice to save you.

The reader familiar with Hasidism will find no surprise in such spiritualized readings of battle passages in the Torah text. These were indeed the "wars" described by Jews over many centuries of military disempowerment. The Talmudic tradition sees this mainly as intellectual battle, one fought out between peers in the house of study. In the Hasidic reading it is more the prayer-centered struggle to concentrate, and the enemy is the evil urge. But the great question being tested today is whether this spiritualized reading of the Torah can maintain its power in the face of a Jewish people that fights real battles, with weapons much swifter than sharpened arrows, against a deadly foe. Does that reality "take all the air" out of this inward struggle?

Daily recitation of the *shema'* would be an interesting new battle line for liberal Jews to draw.

Shoftim
Round Two

AG: The word *yir'ah*, "fear" of God, leaps out from these texts. We modern readers, even postmoderns, are always troubled by that word; we prefer "awe" to "fear" as a translation. But even the old-time Jewish moralists said that true *yir'ah* did not mean fear of punishment.

EL: What's wrong with fear of punishment, if we think about it in adult terms? People have to see the results of their actions, the way our ill-conceived deeds come back to punish us.

AG: Yes, it's interesting that here an impersonal notion of retribution seems to work better. If we see God as punishing parent, we recoil. That's even bad parenting, by our standards. But if we make it less personal, fear of punishment really means taking responsibility for one's way of living, knowing that there are consequences. Who could dispute that?

OR: Of course *yir'ah*, real fear, exists in our day. We look at our children and ask what sort of world—ecologically, politically, socially—they will inherit, and we are filled with fear. Each generation, but ours in particular, has to dread what we will (or won't!) leave behind.

EL: Yes, but the environmental movement really learned the great Jewish lesson of balancing fear and love. Preaching gloom and doom alone drives people away. Cultivating the love of nature is an important part of getting people to preserve it.

AG: How do we take that lesson back into the spiritual realm?

EL: It *is* the spiritual! That's what the *Orah le-Hayyim*, our second text, is trying to teach us. The presence of soul within the body, and its need to assert control, is just as real as the presence of the divine life-force within nature. They are one and the same.

OR: Jewish life often seems to be off balance. We are not motivated by fear of punishment, but by other sorts of fears. Will the Jews survive? Are there anti-Semites out to get us? Are critics of communal policy disloyal? Where is our love?

AM: I am dazzled by our first text, the one about love to the point of *bittul*, of utter loss of self. Are we capable of loving that much? Can we imagine love of God so intense that it wipes us out of existence? Love on that level has to be combined with fear. We love to the point of expiration, yet we fear that loss of self.

AG: That is the passion of the Song of Songs as a sacred text, the "Holy of Holies," as Rabbi Akiva called it. You need the personified figure of God the Lover to call it forth. So the side of love makes us need personal images of God, while the side of fear pulls us away from them.

EL: Maybe that's because they are so very powerful and fearsome. We moderns are just too afraid of fear.

Ki Tetse

Ma'amarey Admor ha-Zaken

> When you go forth to battle your enemy ... and capture his captivity....
> (Deut. 21:10)

A person's thoughts that stray into alien realms are called "a king caught up in the tresses [*rehatim*]" (Song 7:6). This refers to the rushing flow of thought (*rehit*) in the mind, where one can become caught up or imprisoned. They may be thoughts that you cannot bear, and you get caught up in them against your will. When you repent of them, your *teshuvah* "restores the letter *heh*" [= *malkhut*, kingdom; *tashuv heh* (*Tikkuney Zohar* t. 6, 21b)]. But how do you go about it?

"I abandoned you for a tiny moment, but with great compassion I will gather you in" (Is. 54:7). This verse seems strange. Our exile has already lasted seventeen hundred years! How can he call it "a tiny moment"?

Now we know that the blessed Holy One, Creator from the beginning, in each moment creates anew, being out of nothingness. The 1,080 seconds in each hour are really 1,080 breaths that a person takes, for the heart in each second takes life into it anew. "The life-force flows back and forth" (Ezek. 1:14). Above the hour stands the day, from which each hour derives its life. The day, as we know, is divided into twelve hours. But the weekdays get their life-force from the lowliest manifestation of Shabbat [the actual Shabbat in worldly time]. That Shabbat is animated by the one above it, and that one by a Shabbat still higher, until you reach the sublime Sabbath, where all is but a "tiny moment." This is "the ascent of Sabbath to its Sabbath and new month to its month" (Num. 28:10, 14). Each Shabbat rises to the Shabbat above it, and the same with months.

This is the meaning of "Your kingdom is a kingdom of all ages [worlds] and Your rule extends through all generations" (Ps. 145:13). The kingdom of God is above, but it extends downward until it reaches all ages. The same is true of generations. "A thousand years in your sight are as but yesterday" (Ps. 90:4). They are a thousand years below, in this world, but up above they are but a tiny moment.

"I abandoned you for a tiny moment, but with great compassion will I gather you in." I will bring you to that place of Great Compassion, where all harsh forces are sweetened. When you contemplate that all this world is but a tiny moment, you will be able to endure that moment for the sake of Great Compassion. Anyone would certainly be willing to take on a moment's suffering in order to reach Great Compassion.

This is also the way to serve God. Do not think that by serving in a certain way you will rid yourself of some bad quality, and then all will be good for you. Or the opposite, which will cause you great distress. This portrays you as a separate individual, denying Y-H-W-H your God as being entirely one. You need to come to see Y-H-W-H [= eternal Being] as your God, and not consider yourself. Then you will **capture his captivity**, the king who had been caught up in the rushing thoughts [of your mind]. You will be capturing His captivity.

R. Shne'ur Zalman, the great contemplative among the Maggid's disciples, is always working to implant a consciousness of mystical transcendence in his hearers. Here he sees God Himself taken captive in the rushing thoughts of our mind; it becomes our task to liberate Him. We can do that only as we leave the separate self behind.

Orah le-Hayyim

> No article of man's [clothing] shall be upon a woman, and no man shall wear a woman's dress; all who do these are despicable to Y-H-W-H your God.
> (Deut. 22:5)

We know that in the act of giving to a fellow person, the giver often receives more than the one who accepts the gift. Our sages said: "The pauper does more for the householder [who gives alms] than the householder does for the pauper" (*Va-Yikra Rabbah* 34:10). The same is true of giving Torah, as one of the sages said: "I learned much from my teachers ... but from my students most of all" (b. Ta'anit 7a).

This being the case, the one who gives must take care not to feel pride over the one who receives, saying in his heart, "I am the giver; this one needs me and is receiving from me." The fact is that you are receiving more than the other!

An **article of man's [clothing]** refers to such a giver. Although you are in the "male" [active] role, you must not think of yourself as superior to the passive "female" receiver in this interaction. Rather think, as you give either of thought or of money, that you are receiving more than you give.

No man shall wear a woman's dress. This seems to refer to acts of worship, whether Torah study or fulfilling the *mitsvot.* You should not be thinking of your own benefit or pleasure. If you do, you are dressing in the mental "garment" of a woman or one who receives. **No man shall wear a woman's dress** means that you should intend only to please your Creator. This puts you in the role of giver, one who brings about great pleasure above, as in "Give power to God" (Ps. 68:35). If you think of your own benefit, you are really serving yourself. That is a form of idolatry, God forbid.

Both that and taking pride over the one receiving are considered despicable, as our sages taught (*Mekhilta Yitro* 9), following the verse "Y-H-W-H despises all who are of haughty spirit" (Prov. 16:5). It is all who do *these* things that are **despicable to Y-H-W-H your God**.

This verse is obviously one that causes great discomfort to many a contemporary reader. We often wonder how one might go about reinterpreting such texts. Here is an example, one that takes the verse far out of the realm of cross-dressing. While still based on classic archetypes of man as giver and woman as receiver, the verse has been rendered in a way that offers moral teachings that reach completely beyond gender. The intent of many a Hasidic teaching is to make us all into "givers" in the ever-flowing cosmic stream of love and compassion. We, both male and female, receive God's blessing constantly. We need to turn that gift around and transform ourselves into givers.

Kedushat Levi (from *Balak*)

> If a bird's nest appears before you along the way, whether in any tree or on the ground, and there are chicks or eggs in it, with the mother bird perched over them, you may not take the mother along with her offspring. Send the mother forth; then you may take that which she has spawned. Doing so will be for your good; you will attain length of days.
> (Deut. 22:6–7)

The Talmud teaches that one who says [in prayer], "Your mercies reach even to a bird's nest!... Be as merciful with us" is to be silenced (b. Berakhot 33b). This person is attributing to God the character of mercy, when in truth this is the [inscrutable] decree of the King to His servants.

Yet the Tosafot note this claim for mercy is made also by the liturgical poet who wrote: "Be righteous by fulfilling: 'Parent and offspring do not slaughter [on the same day]' (Lev. 22:28). Your thoughts be merciful [also] towards us, Your actions to elevate us" (*Shaharit* of Second Day Pesah).

These objections can be resolved based on the sages' teaching: "Whoever is merciful upon creatures will receive the mercies of heaven" (b. Shabbat 151b). This is rooted in the *Zohar*'s teaching that the arousal above is in response to that which is awakened from below (1:77b). A person who has mercy for God's creatures serves to arouse the quality of mercy in God and then receives of that mercy.

We know that the compassion of God is not exhausted (Lam. 3:22); the blessed Holy One is constantly causing a goodly flow of mercy and compassion to come over us. If we are sometimes lacking in some good things, the obstacle is from our side; we are unworthy to receive that goodness. But the blessed Holy One can in great mercy transform our hearts, giving us the purity and strength of heart to serve God in truth. Then we would be ready to receive that good.

Thus we pray: "You O Y-H-W-H, do not hold back Your mercies from me!" (Ps. 40:12). May there be no blockage from my side, because "Your compassion and truth protect me [or 'create me'] forever." The blessed Holy One is creating you anew in each moment. Thus the Midrash (*Bereshit Rabbah* 14:9) says on the verse "All the soul praise YaH! Halleluyah!" (Ps. 150:6) that one should offer praise for each and every breath (*neshamah/neshimah*). You can create us anew in each moment, giving us a pure heart....

God's commandment that **You may not take the mother along with her offspring** does not reflect God's mercy [upon the bird]. If God wanted to be compassionate, He did not have to command us. God could protect the bird without us, for God surely has the capacity. God's intent was rather that *we* arouse our quality of mercy by being compassionate toward the bird. That's what the poet meant in saying, "Your thoughts be merciful [also] towards us, Your actions to elevate us." You gave us this commandment so that we would act mercifully, arousing Your mercy toward us.

This insightful reading of the verse and the Talmudic statement depicts a God who is ever aware of the mutual relationship between God and humanity. The blessed Holy One seeks to stir us to arouse the quality of mercy within our hearts, in order that our prayers allow the flow of divine mercy that God so longs to bestow upon us.

Or Torah

> When you build a new house, make a railing for your upper storey, so that blood-guilt not be held against your house should somebody fall from it.
> (Deut. 22:8)

This refers to one offering a new interpretation of Torah. **Make a railing for *your* upper storey.** If the verse were referring to a literal house, it would have said: "for *its* upper storey." As it is, the **upper storey** is on you, referring to the swelling of your pride at this new teaching. Do not let your head get turned by pride! Even though this is a bit of Torah that no ear has ever heard, it comes not from you, but from God.

Should somebody fall from it. You are all set for such a fall. You know that this has already happened, that the vessels were broken because of pride, when each one said "I will rule."

The Maggid exemplified and encouraged great creativity among his disciples. The whole point of Hasidic teaching is to bring forth new interpretations, readings of Torah "that no ear has ever heard." It should be no surprise that such encouragement needs to be accompanied over and over again with warnings against pride. Here the warning itself comes about in the form of a new and creative reading of Torah. In the classic Hasidic reading, the breaking of the vessels (*shevirat ha-kelim*) came about because of competition and pride.

No'am Elimelekh

> If a man in the camp becomes impure because of a nocturnal occurrence [emission], he should leave the camp and not enter it. As evening comes he should wash in water, and when the sun sets he can enter the camp.
>
> (Deut. 23:11–12)

This verse can be applied to the case of a righteous person who follows the way of God but has not yet completely purified his thoughts. In this context **nocturnal occurrence** alludes to the "night" of lowliness and sin that he has entered. He has not yet purified his body to the extent that it is protected from such impurity. His eyes are not protected from watching what they should not watch and from seeing evil. His ears still hear, and his mouth can still speak words not uttered in awe and in service of the blessed One.

The text offers this person advice—**he should leave the camp**. This means that when you find yourself outside the camp of the holy ones, you have to work on the basics. You cannot engage in the work of the holy *tsaddikim* who delve into supernal secrets. Their awe and love for God are perfect and not marred by sinful thoughts at all. You are not there yet. When your mind is not clear, and your limbs not prepared (for God's service) how could you enter the palace and go through the King's treasures? This is actually dangerous, as "the jealous ones attack him"—the forces of externality can grab you and push you deeper into sin.

You must therefore prepare your soul and body with practices that are "outside the camp" of supernal holiness. Take upon yourself some ascetic practice, regret and repent, and keep yourself away from the things that provoke that sin. Make a real effort to clear your mind, and pay attention to your actions—are you doing them wholeheartedly? Are you doing good deeds wholeheartedly? Do your deeds honestly without any mixture of "leaven," dross or corruption. Do not mix good with evil. Cleave to the holy Torah, study it in purity, and go to the *mikveh* when you should. Then approach *devekut* and enthusiasm, and your heart will ignite with the brightness of supernal holiness.

As evening comes (*lifnot 'erev*) means, when you have set aside (*le-fanot*) the evil that was mixed (*'erv*) in to you. **Wash in water**—water alludes to the Torah, which is called water, but also real water; immerse in the *mikveh* so you can study Torah in purity. Then, **when the sun sets** (*ke-vo*), meaning when you come (*yavo*) by clarity and enthusiasm, **he can enter the camp**—you can enter the inner camp of supernal secrets.

This is an interesting example of a teaching that still appreciates the ascetic practices that the Hasidism of the BeSHT deemphasized. Such practices are not "within the holy camp" and are not the innermost practices of *devekut* and enthusiasm, but they are essential for people who are struggling with sin. It is also interesting to note that while the homily clearly broadens the meaning of sin, it also preserves the basic biblical notion of the sinfulness and impurity caused by male emissions.

Ki Tetse Round Two

AG: There is a lot of the *tikkun ha-middot* side of Hasidism here, maybe best translated as "how to be a better person." Becoming more compassionate, avoiding pride, and remembering that you're not yet a *tsaddik* are all important parts of the Hasidic message.

EL: The *Orah le-Hayyim* text too, about remembering that you receive most when you're involved in giving, is part of that group.

AM: Yes, but here being a better person also has divine repercussions.

EL: Right. That's what distinguishes Hasidism from the *mussar* tradition. Here the ultimate concern is with affecting God and the cosmos, not just yourself.

OR: Is God vulnerable to human actions? This is an old conversation going back to the RaMBaM [Maimonides—God is the ever-perfect "unmoved Mover"] versus RaMBaN [Nahmanides—God *needs* us to do the *mitsvot*].

EL: Sure. Look at the *Admor ha-Zaken* text we started with. If it's just about you, you've missed the point.

OR: What a complicated choreography we have here! You affect God, who affects you as you reach toward affecting God.

EL: The point is that here we see people seriously working on themselves, yet realizing that this is not the ultimate goal.

AG: This all sounds very good, but what do we really mean today when we speak of "divine need" or "doing it for God"?

EL: "Divine need" means that it's not just about me; I am part of something larger than myself. If God is the evolving Self of the cosmos, present in each of us (as you have taught us!), each time I act a certain way I am leading a bit of that evolving God-Self in a certain direction, affecting the whole, since it is all one.

OR: Yes, but being "part of something larger" is not just about you and God. Remember the effect we have on other people and the world around us—they too are all part of that "evolving Self." And we do good or evil first and foremost by the way we treat others; let's not forget that "it is by deeds that a person is judged."

כי תבוא

Ki Tavo

Tif'eret 'Uziel

> Cursed is the one who does not fulfill the words of this Torah, to do them....
> (Deut. 27:26)

The sages say (b. Sanhedrin 111a) that the heretics tell us: "You are cursed by your God! Can anybody fulfill the entire Torah?"

Yet they speak vainly. R. Yehudah taught that the verse "She opened her gaping mouth for lack of law" (Is. 5:14) referred to the depths that would swallow up anyone who had not observed even a single one of God's laws, but that anyone who had followed even a single law was in the category of the "blessed."

Why is this? Because each of the commandments contains all 613 commandments within it. In doing a single *mitsvah*, you are doing all 613. But then one can object to God's statement, "If you do not listen to the voice of Y-H-W-H your God, actively observing all His commandments and statutes ... all these curses will come upon you ..." (Deut. 28:15). Everybody surely observes at least one commandment and thus fulfills the entire Torah! So why the reproach?

I have seen commentators say in the name of Maimonides that it is only when you perform the *mitsvah* in joy that all 613 are included within it, but this is not true without joy. "Prayer without inner direction is like a body without a soul." The letters of Torah and prayer, as well as the fulfilled commandment, are all the body; the soul is the inner direction and joyous thought you have in doing your Maker's will.

On the physical plane, each of the commandments is in fact distinct. *Tefillin* are made up of leather; *tsitsit* are of wool, and so forth, having no link with one another. But in the joyous thought of fulfilling God's commandment they are all one. They are united in the oneness of the Creator; hence all 613 are present. That is why the passage concludes "... because you did not serve Y-H-W-H your God in joy" (Deut. 28:47).

Because you did not serve in joy, the 613 commandments were not present in the single physical deed. Thus you have not fulfilled the entire Torah, and there is room for God's reproach.

The "heretics" being quoted in this rabbinic passage are not identified, but their claim sounds very much like the Pauline epistles' critique of emerging rabbinic law, a commitment to which would inevitably lead one to feel cursed by its unfulfillable burden. Here is the Hasidic answer: the commandments are all about joy. A single commandment has within it the entire Torah. Note how *simhah* (joy) and *kavvanah* (intention) are seen as identical here. There is no *kavvanah* without joy. What could be more essentially Hasidic?

Kedushat Levi

> In one path they will come out against you, but in seven paths they shall run from before you.
> (Deut. 28:7)

Israel are a holy people. This means that they have fear of God, love of God, godly glory, and all seven qualities that belong to our blessed Creator [adding triumph, gratitude, attachment, and kingship]. This establishes the flow of divine goodness to Israel, since they possess all these divine attributes.

But God has constructed this world in parallel form. There exist extraneous fears, false loves, and all the rest. The difference between these is that the holy versions can exist all together in simple unity. God save us from the parallel unholy qualities, which cannot exist all at once. If you live in fear [of someone], you are unable to love [that person], and so too for all the rest. Only in holiness can these diverse emotions coexist.

This is the meaning of **In one path they will come out against you**. The negative forces can use only one emotion at a time. They can make you afraid or cause you to fall in love, but not both. The same with all the other emotions. They can't arouse all of them in you at once.

But you are your truest self in holiness. You can serve our blessed Creator with all seven qualities at once. The enemy can attack you in only one way, but you possess all seven. Therefore **in seven paths they shall run from before you**.

Levi Yitshak encourages his hearers to fight back against the evil urge, assuring them that they possess seven times its strength as they rise up to serve God.

She'erit Yisra'el

> You have affirmed [*he'emarta*; lit. "caused to speak"] Y-H-W-H your God this day ... and Y-H-W-H your God has affirmed you....
> (Deut. 26:17–18)

The Song of Songs opens (1:2): "Let him kiss me with the kisses of his mouth." The word "mouth" is in the form *pihu*, rather than in the simpler *piv*. Why?

We in this world bring about divine speech. Y-H-W-H speaks in our name, as it were. It is we who cause that upper "mouth" to speak. Afterwards our own mouths are aroused to speech. All the blessing that flows upon us is first aroused by our own words. This is "Let him kiss me with the kisses of *pihu*." Those kisses first come about through *pi*, "my mouth." Afterwards He (*hu*) kisses me. It is we who cause the mouth above to speak, bringing our own words in its wake. This is the meaning of **You have affirmed Y-H-W-H your God this day**, really meaning speech. Afterwards Y-H-W-H causes you to speak.

The mutuality of the divine-human relationship receives its highest expression in the love language of the Song of Songs, the "Holy of Holies" within Scripture. This reading, attributed to R. Levi Yitshak of Berdichev, is a most dramatic expression of it. Just as we ask God to open our mouths in prayer (saying, "Lord, open my lips that my mouth might declare Your praise" before the *'amidah*), so do we, as it were, open the mouth of the One who seeks to bless us with the kisses of divine love.

Ki Tavo
Round Two

EL: The first two texts bear aspects of the same message: it is in being attached to God that you become whole.

AG: Which comes first? Don't you have to be whole in order to truly reach out to God? I learned that we take the four fringes of our *tallit* together before reciting the morning *shema'* because you can't proclaim God to be One until you are first a single unified self, taking in all your inner "corners."

EL: That's what our third text, the one on *pihu*, is saying: it's a cycle in which you are fully involved.

AM: That message is there in our first text as well. Joy enables you to see that all the *mitsvot* are one. That realization helps make you one as well.

OR: The inner wholeness, of the self and of all being, is always there. The only question is whether we see it. The question I need to address to myself is "How am I blocking it? How am I getting in the way?" Once we answer this, we can begin opening up the channel.

Nitsavim

Shemen ha-Tov (based on *Kedushat Levi, Be-shalah*)

> You are all standing today before Y-H-W-H your God. (Deut. 29:9)

"Behold I stand before you there on the rock at Horeb. Strike the rock that water may come out and the people will drink" (Ex. 17:6). There is a famous question about this verse. How can "I stand before you there" apply to Y-H-W-H? God's glory fills all the worlds! There is no place devoid of God! How can it be appropriate to say "I stand before you *there* on the rock?" It could not, God forbid, mean that Y-H-W-H stands there and nowhere else.

The root of the matter is thus. Our sages (b. Berakhot 6b) have taught that the word **standing** (*'amidah*) always refers to prayer, as in "Pinhas stood up and prayed" (Ps. 106:30). This is hard to understand. Do people really not stand up except to pray? This must be referring to some matter of the mind rather than what it seems to say. In fact our sages were not talking here about ordinary people, but only about those who have perfected the fear of God and Torah. Of these they properly said that all of their "standing" is prayer. Such people are always wandering in their minds, walking forward from one rung or world to a still higher one. A person who seeks God, wanting to serve truly and be attached to Him, has to be seeking day and night. You do this through Torah and *mitsvot*, by joining together holy letters and words, by [beseeching] the holy angels of each world and rung. You cannot stand in one perfect spot. That is why the righteous are called "walkers." One cannot imagine them standing still except in prayer. "Prayer" here means absolute cleaving and attachment to the blessed Creator.

[The same is true of our daily prayer.] We walk through all the worlds, singing and blessing our way through the verses of Psalms. We keep reaching higher levels [as we go through the service,] even though we are not yet speaking directly to the King and are not yet fully attached. [Only when we reach the *'amidah*] are we there with no interruption, curtain, or space, even of a holy sort, [between us and Y-H-W-H]. There is nothing but the simple endless Light. That is why this world is called *atsilut*, from *etsel*, or "next to." The person, as it were, stands truly next to Y-H-W-H. This refers to the eighteen benedictions, when you stand in the world of *atsilut*, with no curtain or space dividing you from your Maker. The endless Light surrounds you from all sides as you pour out your words before Y-H-W-H.... That is why this prayer is called the *'amidah*, because in it you stand directly before your Master.

As we sanctify ourselves from below in this manner, we awaken its likeness from above. When we reach such an *'amidah*, Y-H-W-H too stands directly before us, as it were. Just as we, in standing before God, attach our thoughts to the central point of divinity, the Root of all, the innermost point that is the Source of all life, so too does the blessed Holy One become concentrated and stand at the point of thinking of those who do [or "make"] God's will. It was for their sake that He created all the worlds! They are at the very core of God's thought, the foundation of all the world.

Now we can understand "Behold I stand before you there on the rock at Horeb." It is because of you that I *stand* there. Just as you stand in your thought, attached to Me, in just the same way I stand "on the rock" before you. Instead of *tsur* ("rock") read *tsiyyur*, "image." God is the image or reflection of those who do His will, seeking to have His goodness flow upon those for whom the world was made....

So too **You are all standing today before Y-H-W-H your God**. Moses looked upon Israel and saw that they were all truly standing still. He said to them: "Do not be concerned that you are standing [and not moving forward] this day. You are all on such a high rung that you are indeed **before Y-H-W-H your God**. You are cleaving to God face to face; no curtain separates you. You are so close to the King of kings that one can imagine no more walking, only standing."

In weaving back and forth between two biblical moments and the experience of the *'amidah*, the author of this passage given us a rare glimpse into his own innermost experience of prayer.

Mevasser Tsedek I

> Y-H-W-H your God will return as you return, and will be compassionate toward you, gathering you back from among all the peoples where Y-H-W-H your God has dispersed you.
>
> (Deut. 30:3)

We are subject to the yoke of exile because of the holy sparks that have fallen [there]. It is our task to separate them out. Each of us has to engage in this process of repair. When it is completed (speedily, in our day!), the blessed Holy One will gather us in from among the nations.

When you repent, see to it that your only intent be for the sake of those holy sparks that have fallen because of our sins. When we raise them up we will be redeemed. This is **Y-H-W-H your God will return as you return**; as you repent, God's blessed name, referring to the holy sparks, will, as it were, come along with you. Then God **will be compassionate toward you, gathering you back from among all the peoples**. That will be the redemption. But the verse goes on to say, **where Y-H-W-H your God has dispersed you**, meaning that our blessed Creator dispersed you among the nations because Y-H-W-H your God is [to be found] there; these are the holy sparks that have fallen. As soon as you raise them up by your own repentance, redemption will follow.

May the redeemer come to Zion speedily, in our own day. Amen. Selah.

This very simple, direct teaching captures the Hasidic understanding of *galut*. We are sent into exile to do the holy work of uplifting sparks, bits of divinity scattered throughout the world. But here this is depicted as a finite task, one that will lead directly to the much longed-for redemption of Israel.

Ma'amarey Admor ha-Zaken

> Even if your exile is at the farthest edge of heaven, from there Y-H-W-H your God will take you, from there will He gather you in.
> (Deut. 30:4)

How can it be that the community of Israel is spoken of here in the singular form? The same question is asked of "You shall love Y-H-W-H your God" (Deut. 6:5), also in the singular. There one may say that it applies to each Jew as an individual. But **from there will He gather you in**? How can "gather" apply to a single person?

But the truth is that a single person can be scattered and detached. No person is really whole, living up to full intellectual and emotional potential. Some people are lacking in a particular quality. If only they had that one thing, they could be whole. But without it, the person is like one lacking a limb. Sometimes that which you are lacking is found in another person, but with that person you could be whole. That person might be very far from you, but you cannot be whole without him.

So that is **Even if your exile**—in the singular—**from there will He gather you** [with the other whom you need], to become one. That is the nature of exile [being in the singular, isolated and alone]....

We usually see how one person can help fulfill another's lack in a life partner. But the same might apply to God's gift of a friend, a disciple, or a spiritual master.

Mevasser Tsedek II

> The *mitsvah* that I command you on this day is not too wondrous for you, it is not distant from you.
> (Deut. 30:11)

Rabbi Yehoshua ben Levi teaches: Why does Moses specify **on this day**? To teach that *mitsvot* should be done today, not tomorrow. Do them today even though you receive no immediate reward (b. Eruvin 22a). It is further taught that you should taste from the food cooking for Shabbat on Friday (*Shibboley ha-Leket* 82), ["tasting" a *mitsvah* as soon as possible].

To understand this, remember that this world is the Sabbath Eve that prepares for [the ultimate] Shabbat. When you fulfill any one of the commandments, you should do it with such clarity and purity [of intention] that you experience the pleasures of the world-to-come in the very act of the commandment. But even this pleasure is only a taste compared to the ultimate pleasure that "no eye has seen, but God alone" (Is. 64:3).

This is "you should taste" [this other-worldly pleasure] by your great love. This is the meaning of the teaching "enjoying the fruits of labor is better than the fear of heaven" (b. Berakhot 8a). Fulfilling the commandments with love and deriving pleasure from doing them is better than serving God from fear and not enjoying it.

That is the meaning of **the *mitsvah* that I command you on this day. This day** indeed means that although you must fulfill the commandments today, you will only benefit from them in the future. Still, it **is not too wondrous for you**, the reward is not hidden from you, and even in this world you can experience in fulfilling the commandment something of [the pleasure of] the world-to-come.

The verse continues: **it is not distant from you**. This pleasure from *mitsvot* is not unattainable. It can easily be attained by fulfilling the *mitsvot* with awe and love and with great longing. Then you will "enjoy the fruits of your labor."

In the Talmud, of course, the "fruits of labor" refers to making a living rather than being supported by others, but for the Hasidic master the only labor worth talking about is that of religious practice. The teaching is a rejection of asceticism in the tradition of the BeSHT. Strive to enjoy religious practice, not to suffer through it....

Nitsavim
Round Two

OR: I'm immediately struck by the *Admor ha-Zaken*'s picture of the scattered and detached individual, who can only be made whole by meeting someone else.

EL: That goes with the *Mevasser Tsedek* text, reading redemption in such a personal way. We've seen that in a lot of the Hasidic sources; God knows and reaches out toward your own individual need to be uplifted.

AG: Yes, but it's your need to meet another person. We might have expected that God or the religious life would fulfill the need. But God knows who it is you have to meet and arranges for that to happen.

OR: The inner work toward personal wholeness and the outer work toward the world's redemption need to go hand in hand for us. There is a danger that too much concentration on either of these leads toward ignoring the other.

AG: I'm also interested in our first text and its reading of *'amidah*. That's a moment of not being scattered, of being fully present in stillness.

OR: It stands out against the ethos of constant movement and growth that we usually see in the sources, where humans, as distinct from angels, have to keep moving.

EL: It feels to me like he is really talking about the very first moment of the *'amidah*, that silent bridge between *ge'ulah* and *tefillah*. That's when we say: "Lord, open my lips...." After that, the *'amidah* too is in motion, going from one *berakhah* to the next. But we driven human beings, always striving to conquer more, need that moment of absolute stillness.

Va-Yelekh

Kedushat Levi

> Moses went and spoke all these words.
> (Deut. 31:1)

When our sages describe a leader of prayer, sometimes they speak of "one who goes down in front of the ark" [think of ancient amphitheater-like synagogues; b. Shabbat 24b] and sometimes "one who passes before the ark" (b. Berakhot 34a).

The *tsaddik* who prays to God has to become attached to the words of prayer. It is the holy words themselves that take the lead. But there are some great *tsaddikim* who are on a higher rung than this: they lead the words. This was the rung of Moses, who was "husband" of the *shekhinah,* according to the holy *Zohar* [i.e., he was "higher" than *shekhinah,* the rung of divine word] (3:275b).

If one "goes down before the ark," it is the word [*tevah* means both "ark" and "word"] that is leading; the person praying stands beneath the word. But the one who "passes before the ark" is leading the word, standing above it.

These were Moses's last days. The font of wisdom was closing up for him, as the Midrash recounts (b. Sotah 13b). He was now on the lower level, the word leading him. That is why our text says that **Moses went and spoke**. He went to the word, which stood above him.

Anyone who has served as a prayer leader surely knows these two states. There are times when you need the words to carry you upward; it is only because of their beauty and magnetic power that you are able to lead. But at other times a strength from within takes hold. You are able to express what lies deep within you, and you bring the words along.

ME'OR 'EYNAYIM

... I am no longer able to go forth and enter....
(DEUT. 31:2)

Our sages (b. Sotah 13b) commented that "the wellsprings of wisdom became hidden to him." But what is this language of going forth and entering? Might this refer to matters of Torah?

We know that the *tsaddik* who moves from one level to another can only go higher if he first falls from his prior rung. He has to **go forth** from it entirely. Then, if he perseveres in his righteous way, from that place to which he has fallen he can reach yet a higher rung. The reason for this? "Greater light comes forth from darkness" (Eccles. 2:13). It is out of darkness that one can reach expanded light; privation has to precede existence. The same was true as the world was created; chaos and void had to come first. Then God "built worlds and destroyed them" (*Bereshit Rabbah* 3:9). Only afterwards could the [proper] worlds come into being. The same is true here.

It is known that forty-nine measures of wisdom were given to Moses; all the measures but one (b. Rosh ha-Shanah 21b). Of him Scripture says: "You made him a bit less than God" (Ps. 8:6). Moses attained all the forty-nine measures of wisdom that can be reached by any person. More than that it is impossible for any created being to attain. The fiftieth measure is the very essence of blessed godliness in its infinity, totally beyond even the angels' grasp, leaving them to call out, "Where is the place of His glory?" (*kedushah* of Shabbat *Musaf*).

Moses thus came to know everything a human being possibly can, excluding nothing. But surely as he proceeded from rung to rung he had to undergo a fall from his previous rung each time he reached higher. That is what he meant by saying, before he died, **I am no longer able to go forth and enter**. Until now I always have had to go forth from my prior rung in order to attain a higher one. But from the rung I am on now, there is no higher reach. Anything deeper is "the hidden of all hidings"; therefore "the wellsprings of wisdom were hidden from him."

Even Moses had to advance in knowledge through a series of falls. Finally, it seems, he reached a point where such falls no longer took him higher. Then he realized, as he now tells his people, that he could not go any higher.

This image of even the greatest prophet proceeding forward by a series of rises and falls contrasts sharply with R. Shne'ur Zalman of Lyady's image of the perfect *tsaddik*, one who is never even tempted by a thought of sin. One wonders whether he might not have been the one "across the table" when the Chernobyler offered this teaching, opening a door that was to be picked up so vigorously in the next generation by R. Nahman of Bratslav.

Dibrat Shelomoh

> Moses went and spoke all of these words to all Israel, and he said to them: "I am one hundred and twenty years old today."
> (Deut. 31:1–2)

At first glance the word **went** seems extraneous, as the *Or ha-Hayyim* pointed out. However, the *Zohar* teaches that Moses never became sullied with death (1:131b). [Rather at the end of his days] he cleaved to the *shekhinah* and thus entered into eternal life. This is considered living, [not death]. This the meaning of **Moses went**, like a person who goes from one room to another, without ever tasting death.

But there is another way of explaining our verse. It says in the *Zohar* (3:288a) that when Rabbi Shim'on ben Yohai gathered together all of his students before his death, he began by saying: "'I am my beloved's, and His desire is for me' (Song 7:11). Every day I spent in this world I have been attached to the blessed Holy One, and now 'his desire is for me.'" This is the meaning of **Moses went**; he left with all the parts of his soul, no longer being bound to this world in any way....

Now we know that love is a very special quality. It binds all of your actions and your vitality to God, no matter what you are doing. All the times you have studied Torah, performed good deeds, all the days you are alive, and all the words you have spoken are bound to our blessed Creator through this love ... this is the meaning of Moses **spoke all of these words to all Israel, and he said to them**. It might seem repetitious but fits well with our explanation. **All of these words** that he spoke on that day included everything he had ever spoken in his life. **I am one hundred and twenty years old today**, meaning that all **one hundred and twenty** of the years that I have lived thus far came together **today**.

R. Shelomoh reminds us that while death is the final step in our journey as physical beings, it need not be a terrifying event experienced only as a loss. One who has lived with vision and purpose approaches this transition with the confidence that his lifetime of connected moments will all come together on that day. Moses, like Rabbi Shim'on in the *Zohar*, lived each day as a devoted servant of God. His every deed expressed absolute love for the Creator, and this passion bound together every moment of his life into a single thread connecting him to God for one hundred and twenty years. The moments just before his death were no different.

But can it be that we too are called to rise to the impressive level of Moses and Rabbi Shim'on? What of those of us for whom such moments of intense love for God are present but fleeting? Living with God is no zero-sum game, but rather a struggle and a quest we engage in for all of our days. Perhaps when our time has drawn near as well, the One will recognize our devoted seeking and bring us home to the Source together with all of our years of longing.

Va-Yelekh
Round Two

AG: Moses's approaching death, as we near the end of the Torah cycle, is a screen onto which Jewish writers of all ages have projected their own thoughts about death.

EL: The last passage we have here reflects our idealized vision of death. All of life comes together in a great moment of wholeness, then leading to a wondrous passage from one life to another. Levi Yitshak's reading is much more realistic; he sees Moses as growing weaker, no longer ruling over the word as he once had.

AG: Yes, but he surprisingly contradicts the Torah itself that insists that Moses was in no way diminished by his hundred and twenty years.

AM: What does the *Dibrat Shelomoh* passage really mean? Was it that he had no more unfinished business left to do, therefore he was able to detach himself from the world? This is a retrospective view, looking back at life from its end. But the *Zohar* passage seems to depict Rabbi Shim'on as having lived his entire life that way, just barely attached to this world.

EL: The Tibetan Buddhists have a whole praxis around dying, spelled out in their *Book of the Dead*. Death is a great opportunity for the ultimate insight, a moment you do not want to miss.

AM: The *Zohar*'s *Idra Zuta*, the tale of Rabbi Shim'on's death, from which this passage is taken, is precisely that, but in Jewish terms.

AG: But how does this fit into the life-embracing character of Judaism, especially in the Hasidic mode? Isn't life all about engaging with this world in order to seek out holiness, raise up sparks, bring about redemption? Look at the *Me'or 'Eynayim*: Moses's last moment is one of enlightenment because he has kept on going, letting go only in order to rise from rung to rung of understanding.

AM: Yes, but that's the point made by the *Dibrat Shelomoh*: engagement is not for its own sake, but to join everything back to God. The moment finally comes when you are so fully joined to God that you can let go of all the rest, leaving the world behind.

Ha'azinu

Me'or 'Eynayim (from *Likkutim*)

> Listen, O heavens, and I shall speak;
> Let earth hear the words of my mouth.
> (Deut. 32:1)

... It is known that this world was created by the letter *heh*. Thus Torah refers to "heaven and earth as they were created" (Gen. 2:4), which the sages (b. Menahot 29b) read as "by *heh* they were created [*be-hibare'am/ be-heh bera'am*]." This *heh* [= 5] refers to divine speech, since speech is characterized by five groups of sounds that come out of the mouth. Together these constitute Torah [= language], through which everything came to be. "God looked into Torah and created the world" (*Zohar* 1:5a). By means of the entire Torah, as it is from beginning to end, God created everything that exists. As the blessed Holy One pronounced each group of letters, a particular world came to be. God then passed the Torah, which is that structure of the cosmos, on to us. When Scripture says, "On that day God rested from all the work that He had made *to do*" (Gen. 2:3), it tells us that something of Creation remains to be done. That completion is carried out by Israel in their study of Torah. When they do so with proper awe and love, they set aright the making of all the worlds. "Just as I by My word created heaven and earth, so do you" (*Zohar* 1:5a).

A person has to be completely humble. Just as the blessed Holy One became garbed in humility, reducing the intensity of His presence so that mortals might grasp Him, and thus was the world created, so too do we need to humble ourselves in order to attain the Torah wisdom by which we too will be able to create worlds. All the thirty-two paths of wisdom and fifty measures of understanding are contained within Torah, since *everything* is included within it. Each of us has to walk the path of our own distinct root, seeking out that aspect of Torah that fits us. That has to do with the particular imaginative capability that lies within our hearts. A person of heart (*lev*) will acquire that heart through the thirty-two [= *lev*] paths, heartily loving Y-H-W-H and cleaving to Him in heartfelt wisdom.

But should a person, God forbid, study Torah not for its own sake, heartlessly, our sages have taught (b. Yoma 72b) that Torah will become a poison for him. Torah is like rain, and we have both rains of blessing and rains that are a curse. If you learn properly, Torah is the fluid that gives life. But the opposite is true as well. Scripture tells us that "friends are listening to your voice" (Song 8:13). This refers to the angels, who gather together in desire to listen to whoever speaks words of Torah. Everything was created through Torah and derives its life from Torah's letters. Since Torah was passed on to Israel in order to complete Creation, the person who speaks words of Torah while cleaving to God sets things aright as though he had created them, causing life to flow into them. Thus they [the angels; all creatures] long to hear the voice of those who engage in Torah, since this is their very creation.

Thus **Listen, O heavens, and I shall speak**.... Engage in Torah in such a way that you cause the heavens and all the angels to listen to your voice. But how can this come to be? The answer lies in ***I* shall speak** [meaning that God speaks]. Come to know that your Torah speech is actually the word of God flowing through you in that very moment when "by the word of Y-H-W-H the heavens are made" (Ps. 33:6). This includes the person, for we are the purpose of Creation. Your words are the words of Y-H-W-H, and you too are building worlds.

Let earth hear the words of my mouth. We are taught (b. Zevahim 116a) that when the blessed Holy One spoke, "I am Y-H-W-H your God" (Ex. 20:2), the roaring sound of those words could be heard emerging from everywhere, even from inert stones in the wall. There was no place from which the sound of "I am" did not issue forth. The word of God, the "I am" of Y-H-W-H, fills all, since "the whole earth is filled with His glory" (Is. 6:3). God dwells within each thing, so indeed there was no place that did not proclaim, "I am."

From this we should understand that when you make yourself holy and speak Torah in holiness, even the ground around you resounds with that holiness. The greater your power to sanctify that place, the more fully *shekhinah* will come to inhabit it. This is the meaning of **Let earth** also **hear the words of my mouth....**

The sense of continuity between divine Creation and human creativity, here in the context of ongoing Torah, is a central theme throughout Jewish mystical thought, reaching back to the most ancient *Sefer Yetsirah* tradition. The creation of heaven and earth is a constant, rather than a onetime event. The human being has been invited by God to become a full partner in that process. That is why God gives us Torah, the ongoing font of divine-human creativity.

In our age, that notion wears a very different and ominous face. Humans have acted not as responsible partners, but rather as usurping masters, over God's Creation. Will teachings like this pull us back into partnership, a wisdom in which we can engage with such open hearts that we reassert our love for God's world and our devotion to preserving it? Religion—all religion—has no more urgent task in our age. Our Torah needs to serve as a beacon for this work.

Dibrat Shelomoh (from *Hukkat*)

The portion of Y-H-W-H is His people....
(Deut. 32:9)

All the worlds, the unifications of the holy names, and the upper realms were created only for the sake of Israel. The *Zohar* indeed teaches that no letter can refer to the blessed One, even the tip of the letter *yod* (*Zohar* 1:21a). God cannot even be grasped by thought, as we have learned in the *Tikkunim* (17a). Yet the letters and divine names, including the very letters of Y-H-W-H, were drawn forth on behalf of Israel. This is the meaning of **The portion of Y-H-W-H is His people**—God is *apportioned* into letters for our sake.

This will help us understand the Talmudic question: What is the meaning of the verse "Like an apple tree among the forest, so is my beloved among the youths" (Song 2:3)—why is Israel compared to an apple tree? [Because its fruit emerges before its leaves.] Tosafot challenge this question itself, saying the verse actually refers to the blessed Holy One, [the Lover throughout the

Song of Songs] (b. Shabbat 88a). But according to our explanation, *both* are correct. The blessed Holy One has no form, and not of even the tip of *yod* can refer to him. Rather, God is manifest according to the apprehension and the actions of Israel.

The Midrash says: "[Pour out your heart like water] in the presence of Y-H-W-H" (Lam. 2:19). We learn from this that when you study or pray, the blessed Holy One prays and studies facing you [like a reflection in the water] (*Tanna de-Vey Eliyahu* 18). This is the meaning of "At the Sea of Reeds He appeared to them as a youthful warrior, and when the Torah was given as an old man with white hair" (*Pesikta Rabbati* 21). The passage through the Sea of Reeds took place immediately after Israel left Egypt and emerged from the forty-nine gates of impurity, when they were like a baby just after it is born. Then they matured just a bit and could sing with divine inspiration, as our sages taught (*Shemot Rabbah* 23:2). Israel triumphed in difficult battles with their temptations, cravings, and negative thoughts. Therefore the blessed Holy One appeared to them [as a warrior].

But by the time the Torah was given they had grown up and begun to blossom. During the forty-nine days of the *'omer* they were cleansed and purified, entering into the forty-nine gates of holiness. On the fiftieth day they received the Torah, and God appeared to them as an old man with white hair. "Hair" (*se'ar*) can also be read as "gate" (*sha'ar*), referring to the fifty gates of holiness and understanding. In saying "we will do and we shall understand" (Ex. 24:7) we were likened to an apple whose fruit emerges before its leaves—thus God was conceived of as an apple as well.

The Hasidic master is here expanding an ancient Midrashic trope: God appears differently to people at different times, according to their needs. This realization comes within a hairsbreadth of what we today would call projection: we see God as we do in accord with our needs. In the context of a Hasidic theology, one would say that the God who fills all mental and emotional spaces also enters our minds as we try to imagine who God is. Thus an image that might seem like projection from our point of view may indeed be a manifestation of the true divine Self—if our souls are truly open and we are indeed seeking to know the One.

Maggid Devarav le-Ya'akov (#120)

> Rising like an eagle from its nest, hovering over its young.
> (Deut. 32:11)

There is divinity in everything, and that is what sustains all being. The core of life of every being comes from the connection it has to the Origin of Thought. The foundation of that connection is that nothing exists without that life and that all of existence is nothing but that life, which is united to the Origin of Thought, in an indivisible unity.

If you want to make it possible for divinity to rest upon you, the most important thing is to understand and internalize that nothing exists for you but the divinity that gives you life—you are really nothing without it. That is the preparation you must do to allow for divinity to rest upon you.

That alighting [of God] upon you is **like an eagle ... hovering over its young**, touching but not touching [at the same time]. It must be so that you can never really grasp it [God], for if you did, your existence would be totally negated.

But if you have even the tiniest bit of arrogance, as long as you have any awareness of self you are not attached and connected to God. You as yet have reached nothing....

In this teaching the biblical image of God as an eagle hovering over the nest serves the Maggid as a description of the peak moment of mystical experience. Only through total annihilation of self can you connect to the God who is your true reality, but we do not quite seek that annihilation. We and God live in a state "touching but not touching."

Likkutey Maharin (from *Va-Yelekh*)

> As an eagle arouses his nest, hovering over his young.
> (Deut. 32:11)

My father and teacher [Levi Yitshak of Berdichev] referred to RaSHI, who said: "He does not come down upon them heavily, but just hovers, touching and not touching them."

A person who serves God might say to himself: "I am so far from the blessed Holy One that my prayer, my good deeds, and my learning are not accepted by Y-H-W-H." God forbid that any Jew should say that about himself! God listens with compassion to the prayers of this folk so near to Him!

But there is another who says: "I have arrived. I understand the greatness of Y-H-W-H." Woe to the person who says this as well. Does Scripture not tell us: "Great is Y-H-W-H and highly praised; there is no attaining that greatness" (Ps. 145:3)? The higher the level on which you serve God, the more you come to know how that greatness can never be reached.

The struggle between despair and elation, between too much humility and too much grandeur, is well known to every person of faith. The realization that God hovers over us, touching and not touching, is something we have to learn over and over again.

Ha'azinu Round Two

EL: Here we see the mystical and moralistic sides of Hasidism beautifully juxtaposed: the Maggid and the *Kedushat Levi* are reading the same verse, one deriving a mystical truth and the other a guide to humility in prayer.

AG: Yes and no. There are a lot of texts that lie in the border area between these two. "Be so lowly ..." sounds like humility, but then goes on to say "... that you are really nothing," entering into the mystical space. The Maggid's disciples were trying to take his mystical teachings, sometimes pretty abstruse, and seeking to build a popular movement around them.

OR: But look at the *Me'or 'Eynayim*: God too acts humbly; *tsimtsum* is both a mystical event, allowing the non-God to exist, and a modeling of how we should act, making room for others in this world. The mystical cosmology itself bears a moral teaching.

EL: All of this comes out in practice, living the religious life. These are devotional teachings; everything the *tsaddik* says or does is meant to serve as an example. Of course they see God the same way.

AG: This has ancient Jewish roots, of course. The Midrash constantly sees God's actions as the source of moral and behavioral teaching: "Just as the blessed Holy One is compassionate, so you be compassionate ... just as God visits the sick, buries the dead ... so you too...."

OR: What we might see as projection of human social behavior onto God, they see as divine modeling for the way we should act.

EL: Can we hold on to both of those truths? Knowing with one part of our mind that it's projection, and yet still being moved by it and following it as divinely blessed moral teaching?

AG: Ah, that's what it must mean to be a postmodern Jew!

וזאת הברכה

Ve-Zot ha-Berakhah

Tif'eret 'Uziel I

> This [*zot*] is the blessing with which Moses, the man of God, blessed the Children of Israel before his death.
>
> (Deut. 33:1)

The Midrash asks, concerning the phrase "man of God": "If he was man, why "God"? If he was God, why "man"? (*Devarim Rabbah* 11:4). The passage also begins with **This is the blessing**, but then goes on to recount "Y-H-W-H came from Sinai ..." (Deut. 33:2). What blessing is that?

We may understand it in this way. The Hebrew word *zeh* means "this" in the masculine form; *zot* is the feminine.

Now Y-H-W-H is the One from whom all flows forth, the Source of all compassion. Nevertheless, God desires our prayers and receives our petition. You might be surprised that this "male" deity can become "female." The one who gives and flows forth toward others is usually depicted as "male"; the receiver is designated as "female."

Now God is the great Giver, surely "male." How does He become "female" enough to receive our prayers? King David considered this in saying: "From Y-H-W-H there has emerged *zot*; that is wondrous in our eyes" (Ps. 118:23).... How could "male" have become "female"? But "there is no fathoming His mind" (Ps. 147:5); even though He is "male," everything being in His hands, He is nonetheless also "female."

This is the meaning of ***Ve-zot ha-berakhah*** [***zot***] **is the blessing**: God blessed them so that God could also be "female," receiving the prayers of the righteous. And this is also **Moses, the man of God**.

Moses, being **man** in relationship to *elohim*, gave God the blessing of being addressed also in this female form....

The claim that God is both Giver and Receiver is the cornerstone of the Jewish mystical worldview. Our prayers are seen as gifts to God that help maintain the balance of the universe. We, created in God's image, are also both givers and receivers, "male" and "female." Many a mystical text supports the contemporary psychological insight that these "male" and "female" aspects of soul exist in each of us, whatever our biological gender.

Tif'eret 'Uziel II

> Moses commanded Torah to us, an inheritance of the community of Israel.
> (Deut. 33:4)

I heard from my master and teacher Dov Baer, whose soul is in Eden, concerning this verse: Our sages read it to say not *morashah* ("**inheritance**") but *me'orasah* ("betrothed"; b. Pesahim 49b).

We can come to understand this by a worldly analogy. The king has a beautiful daughter. How improper and disrespectful it would be to take hold of her and dance about like people do in a tavern! It would be inappropriate even to draw near to her, let alone to take her and go dancing!

All this is true except on her wedding day. Then the rules are loosened, and even the most ordinary person is permitted to approach her to dance.

This is the case with our holy Torah, the daughter of the King of kings, the blessed Holy One. It would seem improper even to approach her. Yet we are told that Torah is like water; just as water is owned by no one, so too is Torah accessible to all. How is this possible?

The answer is that Moses has given us a "betrothed" Torah. We are forever to approach Torah like the King's daughter on her wedding day. Everyone has permission to dance with her! All of us are welcome to study Torah!

He has in mind the "*mitzvah-tanz,*" a dance at the wedding during which even the poor (who were always given a special place of honor at the wedding feast) might have an opportunity to dance with a wealthy bride. In the usual image, Israel as a nation is the bridegroom of the Torah, at Sinai marrying the daughter of the King. But here we refer to the lowly individual, one who may not feel worthy to engage in Torah. This Jew too is invited to join in and dance with the bride.

MEVASSER TSEDEK

> Moses, the servant of Y-H-W-H, died there....
> (DEUT. 34:5)

This follows the Mishnah, "If I do not do for myself, who will do for me? If I am only for myself, what am I?" (m. Avot 1:14).

"The years of our lives are but seventy" (Ps. 90:10); how much can a person really serve God in a life so short and difficult? And after death, "the dead do not praise Yah" (Ps. 115:17), and we are all free from serving (b. Shabbat 30a).

But when a person goes about teaching Torah and raising up students, the students cause the teacher's lips to continue speaking even in the grave (b. Yevamot 97a). All the *mitsvot* the students do are to the credit of the teacher, who through them serves God even after death.

"If I do not do" only "for myself" but rather teach others, those "who" learned from me "will do for me" even after my death. But "when I am only for myself" and I do not create students, "what am I"? What is my life with regard to serving the great and awesome Creator?

Everyone knows that Moses acquired great merit for himself and shared merit with all of Israel. All of our merit comes about through him. Since he was the one who taught Israel how to serve God, whenever one of us worships God or fulfills a *mitsvah*, it is to Moses's credit, as though he were serving God.

Thus **Moses ... died there**, but even after his death he is still **the servant of Y-H-W-H**. He is still serving the blessed Creator through the Children of Israel, who are all his disciples.

Every step we take on the path of Torah is a continuation of Moses's service of God. We are forever repaying a debt of gratitude to the great teacher who started us all on this path.

Yesamah Lev (from *Yoma*)

> He buried him in a valley in the land of Moab, facing Bet Pe'or. No one know his burial place, until this day.
> (Deut. 34:6)

This burial refers to the hiding of *da'at* [mindfulness, awareness], symbolized by Moses. It is hidden in the Torah, as our sages taught [b. Hagigah 12b, referring to the "hidden light" of Creation]: "Seeing that the world was not worthy, God went and hid it until the time that is to come."

We will not be able to fathom the Torah with complete *da'at* until that time. Of this it says: **No one know his burial place**. This refers to *da'at*, hidden until this very day. However, each of us has some measure of that *da'at* hidden within Torah revealed to us, each in accord with the rung on which we stand and how well we act. It is all about our actions and our humility, for lowliness is essential in coming to it. Our teacher Moses merited to draw his own great *da'at* into all of Israel because he was so lowly and humble, "more humble than any person on the face of the earth" (Num. 12:3). Therefore the *da'at* he attained was also greater than that of any other person.... This *da'at* came to him because he turned his two-chambered heart (*levavo*) into two tablets, right and left, making them a dwelling-place for our blessed Creator. By drawing divinity into himself, he gave *da'at* to his heart as well. That too is God's presence, God's great name.

Now it is known that God causes *shekhinah* to dwell only with those of lowly spirit, as it says: "I shall dwell with the lowly and humble of spirit" (Is. 57:15). The concentration of divine dwelling within you is all in accord with the measure of your lowliness. By the same measure is *da'at*, the hidden light within the Torah, revealed to you.

Thus **He buried him in a valley**, a low place. The blessed Holy One hides *da'at* in those who are low, like a valley....

Da'at, long identified with Moses, is the key term in the theology of the *Me'or 'Eynayim*. It lies buried within us; we are the valley within which this Moses has been buried. Make yourself sufficiently humble and it will rise to the surface.

Ve-Zot ha-Berakhah
Round Two

AG: It's no surprise that the figure of Moses is more central than ever in the teachings on this final portion.

OR: We are told that we are all Moses's disciples; he is the *da'at*, the mind or awareness of Israel, and that passes on to us through the chain of tradition. But we also know that *da'at* has to be renewed in each generation.

AM: The mutual relationship of teachers and students is central to the whole enterprise of Judaism. We want to be faithful to our teachers, but we also need to teach a Torah that will work for those we teach.

AG: In that context, a major challenge for our generation is the fixed gender roles of these texts. Even when they are made more flexible, as in turning them from "male/female" to "giver/receiver," they are still alienating to many people in our day.

OR: Each generation, even each group of teachers and students, has its blind spots. I'm very aware that we are a study circle of four men editing this volume. We just don't hear how some of our teachings sound to female ears.

EL: All that is true. But we also have to give space to the warning of our last text. We need to approach this work with humility. That means deeply listening to our sources, not just coming at them with an agenda of change.

AG: Then will we be able to make changes at all? How can we be creative, responding to the needs of our own generation, if we are held back by humility?

EL: I only mean that we can't begin with a preconceived agenda of change from without. Our encounter with the text has to be an open one. That means that we take risks and are as willing to be reshaped by the text as we are willing to reshape it for the needs of those we teach.

OR: That's what we call covenant. To enter into relationship with the tradition means that we open ourselves to being challenged by it. But we also enter into that relationship bringing our whole selves, including our twenty-first-century questions and reservations. Humility for us means not knowing how our efforts will be seen a generation from now.

AM: Each of us already has experience in teaching texts included in this volume. Our selection and interpretation of the sources very much depend on the audience to whom we are presenting them.

AG: That is inevitably true. But we should also be careful of it. Tailoring the texts to the audience can be overdone. Yes, we want them to be attractive and acceptable. But we also want them to challenge the hearers, indeed as they have challenged us.

Shabbat and Holidays

Kedushat Levi (Hanukkah, Kedushah Sheniyyah)

This is the order of things. On holidays, because of the holiness of the day itself, the gates of light and compassion are opened above. But each of us has to fulfill the *mitsvot* designated for that day in order to draw those lights and blessings downward. On Pesah the gates of *hesed* are opened; on Shavu'ot, the gates of *tif'eret*, and so forth. Depending on us and the measure of our joy in fulfilling those prescribed commandments, we fill all the worlds, the palaces, the souls, and the angels with divine bounty....

This is like a king who opens his treasure-house on a certain day of the year, saying that anyone may come and take anything his soul desires from the king's treasury. Woe to the fool who pays no attention to those open gates and sleeps the day away. So on Sabbath or festival days we should take care to rejoice all day in serving God, not in worldly vanities....

It is possible that these lights are turned on by the Shabbat and festival candles. The lighting of candles is the first *mitsvah* of Shabbat, prior to the evening service or *Kiddush*, which follow them. It is in the lighting of the candles that the lights above are kindled as well....

Note the complicated interplay of divine and human action, especially in the teachings of R. Levi Yitshak. Y-H-W-H opens the gates at these special seasons; we are like invited guests coming into the King's treasure rooms. But then he adds another thought. Maybe it is our lighting of the candles that turns on the lights above as well.

Shabbat

Or ha-Me'ir (from *'Ekev*)

I was asked by my in-law, that faithful *hasid* the Rabbi of Chmielnik: In the *'amidah* prayer of Shabbat we say: "Grant us, Y-H-W-H our God, in loving grace, Your holy Sabbath." We recite these words four times, in each of the Sabbath prayer services.

Even as the holy day is passing away, we are still asking God to grant it to us! But we already received Shabbat on Friday, starting early so as to add to the holy day. We recited *Kabbalat Shabbat* and *Kiddush* [on Friday night], then the morning and additional prayers, followed by the daytime *Kiddush*! What more is a Jew supposed to do, that we are still asking: "Grant us ... Your holy Sabbath?" Whatever is done is done!

This is what I answered him: ... There is a great difference between our Sabbath, the one we observe here in this world, and the Sabbath of the blessed Holy One, among God's secret treasures. This is a light hidden from the eyes of all. So our prayer is one of asking, in which we say: "We have done what we have to. Now You do what You have to! Grant us, Y-H-W-H our God, *Your* holy Sabbath!" Give us such a pure heart that our mind might grasp the Sabbath that You Yourself observe in all Your glory!

For the Jewish mystical tradition, Shabbat is not just a particular time that appears on the calendar, set off with its own rules. It is rather a metaphysical entity, a state of being one enters that bears with it an increased sense of nearness to God. There are multiple, perhaps even infinite, levels of such an experience. But the ultimate Shabbat is God's own, the rest from labor that takes place within the divine Self. All our human Shabbatot are just the slightest taste of that Shabbat mystery, the one we call upon God to allow us to share.

Me'or 'Eynayim I (from *Va-Yakhel*)

Constructing the Tabernacle by means of the thirty-nine forms of labor represents perfect service, fulfilling the verse "Know Him in all your ways" (Prov. 3:6). Through this work we are building up all that has fallen into brokenness. We make a *mishkan* or "dwelling," through which God's presence dwells in lowly things, bringing them to their upper Root. This establishes the Creator's rule over the entire world and all creatures, proclaiming, "the whole earth is filled with His glory" (Is. 6:3).

This service exists in the realms of speech, thought, and deed. In each thing that you encounter [in the realm of "deed"], take notice of the life-force encased within it, though in a broken state. When that object comes into the hands of an Israelite person who is a "complete form," meaning that the divine part within you is attached to the Creator, you are to raise it up and make it whole. This is what is called "constructing the dwelling"; making a home for the Creator throughout the world by these forms of thirty-nine forms of labor, which together represent all of universal space.

The same is true of words and thoughts. When you speak in words, even concerning worldly and necessary matters, you should also not just be speaking for your own needs. Do not let yourself be separated from that upper life-force flowing through you, which gives you the power of speech. Here too you should be thinking "Know Him," [becoming attached to the letters *heh vav* of God's name Y-H-W-H]....

All this refers to the six weekdays, when we are constructing the Tabernacle through those thirty-nine forms of labor. But when Shabbat comes, all those activities are forbidden, for this is the time of erecting or uplifting the *mishkan*. [After the work was completed], "Moses erected the Tabernacle" (Ex. 40:18). Moses here represents the awareness that raises and uplifts *et ha-mishkan*, "the Tabernacle," [since *et* is written as *aleph tav*, the first and last letters of the alphabet], embracing every aspect of what has been constructed in the six days. All creatures are uplifted by the holiness of Shabbat that spreads through all the worlds and all existence.

That is why the construction of the Tabernacle did not supersede [the restrictions of] Shabbat. This service is on a high rung, higher than that of the world....

Our sacred labor during the week should have us fully engaged with the world, reaching throughout existence to find that which needs repair, always seeking to restore wholeness. This work has to embrace all creatures, including our entire human community but also reaching far beyond it. But on Shabbat we are to allow for a different point of view. This is a day of transcendence, a time when we look at the entire project of transformation somehow from without or "above." This glimpse of the divine perspective on our worldly efforts allows us to "uplift" rather than just "construct," taking the entire project to another level of contemplative existence.

Me'or 'Eynayim II (from *Ki Tissa*)

... The *Zohar* teaches: "Shabbat is the name of the blessed Holy One, perfect in all aspects" (2:88b). This means that nothing is lacking.

A person engages in work in response to a need. There is something lacking that will be completed through the work. Shabbat, being perfect in all aspects, lacks nothing, and needs no work to fulfill any need.

Therefore our sages taught that you should celebrate Shabbat as if all your work is done and you lack nothing (*Mekhilta Yitro*). On Shabbat, the completely perfect divinity spreads forth and reveals itself in the Israelite people. If you behave otherwise [i.e., implying that you still have needs], you demonstrate that you are not part of that community, and you act as though the divine presence did not rest upon you.

But it is not only regular work that is prohibited; even work on the Tabernacle is prohibited on Shabbat. The Tabernacle (*mishkan*) we are discussing is the one referred to in the verse "I shall dwell [*ve-shakhanti*] within the Children of Israel" (Ex. 29:45). The blessed Holy One dwells within the Israelite people, and you are to become a dwelling-place for the divine presence. But even if you are impure with sin, impeding the dwelling of the Divine within you, on Shabbat you should forget about this and not let it sadden you. Just keep Shabbat as it should be kept, and rejoice in the blessed One, who is total acceptance and joy.

Even the work of the Tabernacle, the work you need to do to become a dwelling-place for the Divine, should not be done on Shabbat....

Our spiritual lives also demand labor, the construction of our inner *mishkan*. That requires discipline, self-constriction, and precision. But on Shabbat this work too is to be set aside. We are instead to bask in the pleasure of being already fulfilled, to whatever degree we are. That should be a source of joy to the soul; Shabbat is given us to celebrate it. There will be time after *havdalah* to get to work on building that *mishkan*....

Me'or 'Eynayim III (from *Ki Tavo*)

... The Talmud teaches (b. Shabbat 118b) that "if Israel only kept two Sabbaths, they would immediately be redeemed." What are those two Sabbaths?

... Our blessed Creator is infinite, beyond all bounds. But human beings are finite and limited. How is it possible for these two opposite types to draw near to one another?

For this reason the Creator gave Israel the Sabbath, which serves as an intermediary between Israel and their Father in heaven, uniting and joining them to their Creator. It can do this because it has two parts, making it both like God and like Israel. Any intermediary, as we know, has to be similar to both of the things it links. The *Zohar* (2:88a) tells us that Shabbat is a name of God, perfect in every way. Shabbat [as *shekhinah*] represents the life-force of both the upper and the lower worlds, the flow of divine glory as it reduces itself and thus enters this world in the form of the seventh day.

That seventh day is what we call Shabbat. It serves as an embodiment and garbing of the upper Shabbat, the name of God. This upper Shabbat is the soul of the entire cosmos, ever passing through cycles of the six "days." The seventh day is Shabbat, in which that upper Shabbat concentrates itself, giving life to all the world.

That is why we are told, "Those who profane it will surely die" (Ex. 31:14). By profaning and not fulfilling the Sabbath, you are removing that upper life-force, the divine Shabbat, or cosmic soul, and are thus "killing" the world, taking its soul from it.

The word *mehalel* ("profane") is the same as *halal* ("corpse"), as in "If a *halal* is found on the ground" (Deut. 21:1). The term refers to the taking of the soul. That is why the punishment is also that of certain death.

When we fulfill both Sabbaths, the upper Shabbat, the soul of existence, and the lower, God's own name as cloaked in the seventh day, within the limitations of time, we allow Shabbat to serve as the intermediary between Israel and our Father in heaven. This is how we cleave to God.

Shabbat is described in the Midrash as the bride of Israel. But in identifying Shabbat with *shekhinah*, the cosmic "seventh day," the Kabbalists proclaimed Shabbat as the bride of God. Both are true; She is the bride who joins us together. It is around this mystery that the great Sabbath hymn *Lekha Dodi* is composed. Look at it in that light "and your eyes will behold wonders."

Me'or 'Eynayim IV (*Likkutim*, Prov. 3:19)

... In the future, "earth will be filled with knowledge of Y-H-W-H" (Is. 11:9). There will be complete and great awareness. Love and awe will be completely full; all of our limbs will be filled with awareness. Of this Scripture says: "Chambers will be filled with knowledge" (Prov. 24:4). Those chambers are the limbs, rooms to be filled with God's blessed presence that dwells within humans. They will all be filled up with awareness, unlike now, when awareness is only in the mind, a small part of the person. In the future, that awareness will spread forth broadly, filling all the earth. Even the lowest, most "earthy" realms will be filled up so that God can be known from them. This is the meaning of "with His knowledge the depths will be cleaved" (Prov. 3:19). Even those lowest rungs called "the depths" will be split open so that awareness can enter them.

But the blessed Holy One gave Israel the gift of Shabbat in advance of this great awareness and joy that we will attain in the future. If someone suddenly gives a great gift to a friend, without advance warning, the receiver can become too overwhelmed to accept it. That is why "one giving a gift to another must inform the receiver" (b. Shabbat 10b). The mind has to become settled so that the gift can be accepted. The future will culminate in "a day that is all Sabbath," constant joy. But such a gift cannot be absorbed all at once. That is why God gave us Shabbat, "a Sabbath day of rest, like the world-to-come." In this way we can accustom ourselves to the joy we are to receive.

This is the meaning of "I have a great gift in my treasure-house that I seek to give to Israel; it is called Shabbat—go and tell them" (ibid). This gift is hidden away until the future, "the day that is all Sabbath." I seek to give it to them at that future time. Therefore, "go and tell them." Through the Shabbat that I am giving them now they will be informed of what is to come, so the joy will not come upon them too suddenly, but by stages.

This is the true eschatology of Hasidism, a vision of a world where awareness of divine presence will flow forth from every being, absorbed by every pore of the human self.

Need we have any better reason than this to share our Shabbat with all humanity? It is our way of preparing for the ideal world that is to come. The way we live on Shabbat is a model for the world we dream will one day be shared by all. But then the rest of humanity needs to see and share in that mode. We all have to get ready to live together in that perfect world.

Yosher Divrey Emet #45–46

Now I will tell you some things about the holy Sabbath, even though we can't really even touch the edge of it or explain anything about it. Shabbat is the great tent-peg to which all the commandments are fastened, as we are taught (*Shemot Rabbah* 25:12): "Shabbat is of equal weight to all the [other] commandments."

.... Our sages (there, cf. RaSHI) asked concerning "God completed on the seventh day" (Gen. 2:2), "What was the world still lacking? It was lacking rest. When Shabbat came, rest came with it." I have in writing from our sublime teacher R. Baer an understanding of this matter according to our true faith. Our sages teach that the world was created for the sake of Israel (*Va-Yikra Rabbah* 36:4), meaning that the worlds exist so that there [will] be an Israel that will serve and be attached to God.... First the souls of Israel were created in divine thought. Afterwards, when God wanted those souls to become embodied, "He commanded and earth stood up" (Ps. 33:9). He spoke to each thing and said: "Be!" The firmaments, the luminaries, the earth sprouting forth grasses and trees....

Had Creation stopped after it was all finished on the sixth day, it could not have endured, because there was so little of the life-force within it. The life-force is present in the physical realm only in reduced measure. So after all was created, God shone forth a brilliant light from the most hidden aspect of Creation, from the very essence of divinity, where the spiritual entities had first arisen in God's mind. That light, coming from the most hidden root of divine thought, shone from one end of the world to the other, through all of Creation, but especially in humans, the choicest of God's creatures. This is the meaning of "The world was lacking rest"—"Rest" is a name of God, since the Divine does not move about from place to place, as do creatures....

The term Shabbat derives from "returning [*hashavah*]," the return of all creatures to their Source. They all exist only through the will of God ... and God's desire in creating them is the delight that comes about when they cleave to their Source by their own desire. This attachment to God is what allows them to endure, since God is eternal [and the life-force thus endures in them] and also because they are fulfilling God's will....

By the fact of their physical creation itself, they had become distanced from their Source, separated from the single spirit that is their Root. So after Creation was completed, God shone that bright light ... and they were filled with longing for Him. This is like a child who follows some youthful pursuits and forgets his father. But then, when he sees his father, he longs for him so greatly that he puts everything else aside, running to him and holding onto him. He is, after all, a very part of him!

So it was, as it were, when God shone His light upon all His creations, and their faces turned toward Him in great desire. That was His hope; this is why they exist, for both of the reasons mentioned. This is the matter of Shabbat, returning to our Root. The Root gives light [or vitality] to the branches; the branches in turn are filled with delight and with longing for their Root. This is what it means to be one with God.

This profoundly mystical explanation of Shabbat captures some of the passionate love that the Jewish soul has for this most basic form of our religious life. It is not only the person who has a *neshamah yeterah*, an "extra soul," on Shabbat. It is as though all of Creation is filled with a new radiance, one that the "extra soul" just allows us to see.

Kedushat Levi (from *Ki Tissa*)

> Y-H-W-H said to Moses: "You speak to the Children of Israel and say to them: 'Moreover, keep My Sabbaths....'"
> (Ex. 31:12–13)

From here the rabbis derived that one who is giving someone a gift has to inform the recipient: "The blessed Holy One said to Israel: 'I have a goodly gift in My treasure-house; it is called Shabbat'" (b. Shabbat 10b).

Surely Shabbat is indeed a goodly gift. This refers to the light and holiness that come down from above, bringing a spirit of sanctity and a new awareness to the human heart. This spiritual recharging derives from an upper realm known as *'aravot* (the "plains" but also the "pleasantness" of heaven), the treasure-source of life and joy.

A person should really live all week long in anticipation of this gift of Shabbat, with its holy renewal of life. But Shabbat also demands great preparation throughout the week. The better your preparation, the more you derive from Shabbat. On the verse "they shall prepare what they bring" (Ex. 16:5), the sages said that you indeed have to make an effort during the week so that you have what you need for Shabbat, and "one who prepares on the eve of Sabbath shall eat on the Sabbath" (b. 'Avodah Zarah 3a).

Even though you work at preparing yourself, Shabbat remains a goodly gift. Even if we prepared ourselves in all sorts of ways, we would not be deserving of the holiness and bounty that God gives us on Shabbat. It remains an unearned gift. But the preparation is there so that we make ourselves into a vessel, giving us the strength to receive that gift.

There is a delicate balance between the need to work at one's spiritual life and understanding that it ultimately is a gift that comes from beyond. Both are completely true, and not only regarding Shabbat. All the ritual forms of religion may be seen as vessels in which to catch the divine light that shines upon us.

The comment that the vessel gives us the "strength to receive" God's gift is also worthy of note. Receiving itself can be a struggle. Often we are too closed to be able to receive the many gifts we are given.

Tsemah ha-Shem li-Tsevi (from *Yitro*)

In the Shabbat evening *Kiddush*, we recite: "God has granted us Shabbat as a memorial of the act of Creation ... a holy calling in memory of the Exodus from Egypt."

The RaMBaN already noted that the second version of the tablets (Deut. 5:14) says regarding Shabbat: "Remember that you were a slave in the land of Egypt ... therefore Y-H-W-H has commanded you to fulfill the Sabbath day." How does one of these things relate to the other? In the first tablets it said: "For in six days Y-H-W-H made heaven and earth.... Therefore God blessed the seventh day and made it holy" (Ex. 20:10). He replied that Shabbat is indeed a memorial of Creation.... But who really remembers Creation? When we came forth from Egypt, God's divinity was revealed [to us], including the faith that Y-H-W-H had created the world. Thus you are to "remember that you were a slave in the land of Egypt and Y-H-W-H brought you forth," through which you will have the faith that "in six days Y-H-W-H made heaven and earth...."

"Memorial [*zikkaron*]" is used referring to Creation. This is like telling a person of a new thing, something neither known nor seen. But something that you have seen yourself does not need a "memorial"; you just need a reminder (*zekher*) that you saw it and know it. This is the memory (*zekher*) of coming out of Egypt.

The Exodus from Egypt is still a palpable memory among Jews. Our long history of oppression, combined with our so widely observed annual *seder* ritual, keeps that memory alive from one generation to the next. Our memory of having been reborn into freedom points to a world filled with God's presence, leading us back to Creation.

But is it so clear that we do not somehow "remember" Creation well? The DNA within us contains traces that go all the way back through our most ancient ancestry, linking us to all creatures in an extended family of extant beings. Becoming aware of that aspect of our own inner selves might build the bridge toward restoring that memory as well, one so urgently needed in our day.

Rosh Hodesh

Hayyim va-Hesed

> At the heads of your months [*uve-rashey hodsheykhem*], offer a burnt-offering to Y-H-W-H.
> (Num. 28:11)

Offerings are called *korbanot* because through them you draw yourself upward and near (*karov*) to God. That is why the sacrifice is also called *'olah la-Y-H-W-H,* "an ascending to God." This means that through it you raise your corporeal self up to its Root. A sin-offering has to do with fear of God, establishing a place in your heart for that fear. The "whole-offering" is about attachment, becoming bound to God. Each of them has a particular human quality that is being raised up to the Root. As they are offered, their parallel roots are awakened above. Thus by your quality of love, you awaken God's love as well. So too with them all. This process brings about a renewal of life and reenergizes our own qualities.

Now we no longer have those sacrifices actually offered. But we can fulfill them by acts of speech, reciting the passage about each sacrifice. Raising up the inner core of the letters that compose those passages can awaken those qualities above. If you only offer up the letters themselves, the outer garb, this will have no effect. That [empty] garment will have to fall back down, since it exists only for the sake of the physical world. That is why you have to raise up the innermost core. This is "The secret things are for Y-H-W-H our God" (Deut. 29:28), referring to the inner core of our emotions.

But "the revealed," referring to the outer garb, the letters themselves, are only "for us and our children," the physical world.

In raising up the innermost, you can bring about renewal (*hithaddeshut*) of the mind, called the head (*rosh*).

Do you get it? He's reading the verse to mean: *uve-rashey hodsheykhem*, "to renew your minds," *takrivu*, "come close, *'olah la-shem*, "go up to God!"—the rest is all scaffolding.

Kedushat Levi I (from *Bo*)

> This month is for you as the first of months;
> it is the first for you of the months of the year.
> (Ex. 12:2)

Our sages taught that [in the *Musaf 'amidah* of *Shabbat/Rosh Hodesh*] one should say, "the One who sanctifies the Sabbath, Israel, and the New Moon," since it is Israel who declare Rosh Hodesh holy [by fixing its date], while Shabbat is established and eternal (b. Betsah 17a, *Shemot Rabbah* 15:24). They also said that everything about [to take place in] a certain month depends on Israel, because all is set in place when they sanctify the month. For example, on Rosh Hashanah the seats of judgment stand by and wait until Israel have sanctified the day (b. Rosh ha-Shanah 8b) ... everything depends on when Israel set the date of the month.

This month is for you, for I have placed it in your hands. The holiness of the month depends on Israel. **It is the first for you**. "First" here alludes to the blessed One, who is referred to as the "First" (Is. 44:6). **For you**—the one who is called the First belongs to you, since the month is given to Israel to sanctify as they wish. This shows us that even God is **for you**; it is in our hands to direct God's conduct [of the world] as we wish. Everything depends on when Israel sanctify the month, since God's actions and judgment will follow suit. **The months** [*hodshey*] **of the year**, the renewal (*hithaddeshut*) for the entire year lies in our hands....

Playing on the well-known theme that it is Israel who set the date of the New Moon, and therefore the holidays, Levi Yitshak finds an opening for what is really a rather radical theological view. In some passages in *Kedushat Levi* it appears that *everything*, including the divine will, is in human hands, that Y-H-W-H has, as it were, retreated from the scene and left everything to humanity.

This is the theological concomitant to Levi Yitshak's endless love for people. God loves them the same way he does (or the *tsaddik* loves them as God does!), placing everything in their trusted hands.

KEDUSHAT LEVI II (FROM *SHABBAT SHEKALIM*)

Why do we recite Psalm 104, *barkhi nafshi et Y-H-W-H*, on Rosh Hodesh?

We call this day Rosh Hodesh for the following reason. Our mental processes begin with desire, and then proceed, in accord with our will, to bring forth a [mental] construct (*boneh*). To this we then add love, awe, glory, and the rest of the *middot*. Desire is the very beginning (*reshit*). On each Rosh Hodesh a new (*hadash*) desire, a new way to serve the Creator, is revealed for the Jewish people. Therefore it is called day *Rosh Hodesh*, a new beginning.

The word "soul" (*nefesh*) can also refer to desire, as it is written, "if it be your will [*nafshekhem*]" (Gen. 23:8). This is why we say *barkhi nafshi et Y-H-W-H* on Rosh Hodesh. A new pond, a *bereykhah*, is formed, from which desire is drawn from Y-H-W-H, the Source of all energy and life.

The associative nature of the Hebrew language gives birth to a richness of imagery that is often hard to convey in translation. Every blessing (*berakhah*) is also a pond (*bereykhah*) from which the flow of divine blessing is drawn forth. Our *nefesh* (here meaning "desire") longs to draw forth that flow of blessing in ever new (*hadash*) ways. So *of course* we recite this psalm on the new month (*hodesh*). Isn't that obvious?

Rosh Hashanah

OR HA-EMET

> Do not come into judgment with us, since no living being can be found righteous before You.
> (*SELIHOT* FOR 'EREV ROSH HASHANAH)

Whoever judges Israel judges God as well, as it were, since God is one with us.

No living being can be found righteous before You, since You are all; all life comes from You. How can one judge God?

We have a dispute about the meaning of this enigmatic little statement. One reading is as follows: we ask God to step away from us, as it were, in this season when we need to be judged. It is our fallible human selves, somehow separate from the overwhelming divine presence within us, that needs to stand in judgment. We recognize the artifice of this separation, but still ask that it at least seem real for the upcoming drama of these Awesome Days.

But the passage may also be read simply as a last-minute plea to avoid judgment.

We ask God: "How can You judge us when You are always inside us?" There is no setting aside the flow of God's presence that is our very life. Judgment is therefore impossible.

SHEMU'AH TOVAH

Regarding the *shofar* blasts, a fine parable partly by my holy teacher R. Berish [= Dov Baer, the Maggid]:

There was a king who sent his only son away to a distant land, for some reason known only to him. As time passed, the son became accustomed to the ways of the villagers among whom he lived. He became a coarse fellow, forgetting the niceties of life with the king. Even his mind and his most intimate nature grew coarse. In his mind he came to think ill of the kingdom.

One day the son heard that the king was going to visit the province where he lived. When the king arrived, the son entered the palace where he was staying and began to shout out in a strange voice. His shout was in wordless sound, since he had forgotten the king's language. When the king heard his son's voice and realized that he had even forgotten how to speak, his heart was filled with compassion. This is the meaning of sounding the *shofar*.

But once he told it this way: One of the king's servants had a family member of whom the king thought very highly. In fact he loved him so much that he had his image engraved (*toke'a*) on his throne. That way he could constantly look at his lovely form and take pleasure in remembering him. On the day when the king's servants were to be judged, they shouted out to the king: "Just look at that form carved on your throne, and you will be filled with compassion because of your love for us."

This is the meaning of sounding (*teki'ah*) the *shofar*. "The image of Jacob our Father is engraved beneath the Throne of Glory" (*Tikkuney Zohar* t. 22, 65b).

The two versions of this touching parable are about God's love for Israel, and our ability, even from a distance, to arouse His compassion. The first parable is based on a well-known Midrashic motif of the wayward son who has wandered far away from his father's palace. The second version, however, is strikingly original, based on a rare use of the root *taka'* to mean "engrave." This too is based on an ancient Midrash. God so loves Israel that He is seduced by the wordless sound of the *shofar*, which reminds Him of the image of the one He loves.

Or ha-Me'ir

I heard from the Maggid a parable he offered before the *shofar* sounding:

A king sent his beloved children to a far-off country. They spent long years there, exiled from their father's table. But they were constantly concerned with how to get back, how to come to dwell again in the restful home of their father's innermost royal court. How happy they had been when sharing in their father's joy! How much better things were then than now!

They began to send affectionate messages to their father, hoping he would take pity on them and bring them back. But once they got close enough to the royal court, they saw that their father's countenance was not the same as it had once been. They kept calling out and begging for his mercy, but they were met with silence.

After a long period of receiving no reply, the king's children began to wonder what they might yet do to reawaken their father's former love. "Why is it that we call out and receive no answer? Surely our father has no lack of mercy! There must be some reason for this."

They decided that maybe over the course of their years in that distant land they had forgotten the king's language. "We became so mixed up with other nations that we took on their ways and started speaking their language. We have no way to communicate with the king. That's why our words are not heard in his palace!"

So they decided to stop calling out in words or language. They would just let out a simple cry to arouse his mercy, since a cry without words can be understood by anyone.

Levi Yitshak and Ze'ev Wolf are both recalling a parable they heard from the Maggid in their youth. Their differing versions of it show us something about the process of how oral teachings are preserved and transformed by the time they reach us in documents often written down only years later and by third parties, the disciples of those who heard them.

There is a truth behind this parable, however it is told. What is the heart's forgotten language? Is there a language of God, once known to us, but now forgotten? What do we do when we realize we've lost the words of our heart's most native tongue?

Kedushat Levi

> Sing to God, O sing! Sing to our King, O sing!
> (Ps. 47:7)

[This psalm is recited seven times before the *shofar* is sounded.] Rosh Hashanah and Yom Kippur are the times when judgment is sweetened. We need to cut away the judging forces and serve with true compassion. God judges His people compassionately as a parent would a child.

The name *elohim* ("God") refers to the forces of strict judgment. The word *zamru* ("sing") can also mean "to cut." We are being told to cut down the quality of stern justice.

Let God judge us as a parent does. Then we will be saved from all harm.

This assertive transformation of a verse that has powerful resonance in the liturgy reflects Levi Yitshak's view of his role as *tsaddik.* He is to defend Israel before God, especially in this dangerous season of judgment. "Cut down the God of judgment," he hears the Psalmist say. "Cut down 'our King'!" Leave only our loving Father to judge us.

Orah le-Hayyim

> The blessed Holy One said: "On Rosh Hashanah, recite before Me kingship verses, remembrance verses, and *shofar* verses. Kingship verses so that you make Me King over you, remembrance verses so that memory of you arise before Me. How? Through the *shofar.*"
> (B. Rosh ha-Shanah 16a; Rosh Hashanah *Musaf* Service)

On Rosh Hashanah the entire world is judged. Is it worthy enough to stand? The judgment is about whether Creation fulfills its purpose, that of revealing divine kingship, the awesomeness of God. Therefore: **the blessed Holy One said: "... Recite before Me kingship verses ... so that you make Me King over you,"** thus fulfilling the intent of Creation. **Remembrance verses so that memory of you arise before Me:** even if we are entirely undeserving, we remind God of the original love in which He created all the worlds. God sought to do good for Israel, not in response to their worthiness, but just out of a generous desire to bless. By reminding God of this primal love, we call forth that desire for goodness today as well, the will to shower blessing upon us, even if we have no merit....

How? Through the *shofar*. We arouse that primal love by means of the *shofar*.

This follows what I heard in the name of that holy lamp Dov Baer, who interpreted "Raise up your voice like a *shofar*" (Is. 58:1) this way. You have to consider yourself as nothing, having no merit, having done nothing good at all. Even though you have performed some good deeds and commandments, it was really only by God's power that you were able to do so. It was the intellect, the love, and goodness that God bestowed upon you.... You are just like a *shofar*, having no sound except that which someone blows through you....

In this way we awaken and draw down upon ourselves that first love. **How?**

Through the *shofar*: by considering ourselves to be a mere trumpet, having no merits that might obligate God to be good to us. It all comes from God....

The beautiful simplicity of this metaphor undercuts all the counting up of sins and merits that so trivializes the experience of the Days of Awe. Look at the big picture: God created, and continues to create, the world out of love. When we stop trying to compete with that love and accept that we are just one echo of it, we will feel its spirit blow right through us.

Torey Zahav

In the Midrash (*Va-Yikra Rabbah* 29:3): Rabbi Berekhiah opened with "Blast the *shofar* on the New Moon" (Ps. 81:4).... In this month [*hodesh*], do new [*hadash*] good deeds. The word *shofar* means "improve"; do better deeds this month. Said the blessed Holy One to Israel: If you improve [*shapper*] your conduct, I will act

> like a *shofar* toward you. Just as you blow into one end and the sound comes out the other, I will rise from the throne of judgment and be seated on the throne of mercy. In this seventh month I will turn from My judging self toward My merciful self.

We need to explain the views of Rabbi Berekhiah. What is the difference between these "new" deeds and the "improved" deeds? Don't they both point to better acting? How does the metaphor make any sense? [Is God's movement from one throne to the other really like blowing sound out of a *shofar*?]....

We know that the meaning of the *shofar* has to do with "Out of the narrow straits I called unto God; He answered me in the broad, open places" (Ps. 118:5). The end where you place your mouth on the *shofar* is narrow, and the sound comes out of the wide end. The *shofar* points to the penitent, who turns to God out of the narrow straits.... We know that the forces of judgment are a narrowing or constriction of love. The love-force itself is more broad and free-flowing.

The penitent has to first admit the sin and resolve to leave it behind. When you repent, you should see yourself as a newborn child and begin to act in new ways. Afterwards you may afflict yourself and do what you need to kill off the old behaviors. If you do so with love, you may even transform them into merits. That is why Rabbi Berekhiah spoke first of "new" deeds and afterwards of "improvements.".... God promises that if you improve your deeds, I will act like a *shofar* toward you.... I will arise from the throne of judgment, a place of narrowness (since every judgment is a constriction), and I will be seated on the throne of mercy, a place where the forces of compassion flow. I will turn My quality of judgment into that of mercy because you have improved (*shippartem*; read as "*shofar*ed"). The sins have thus turned into merits, and there is no longer a case against you. The Accuser turns around and defends.

The metaphor thus works nicely. Just as the narrow end of the *shofar* broadens out as you reach the other end, so does divine judgment itself go forth and widen itself until it is all mercy. When does this take place? In this seventh month. "His left hand is beneath my head as his right hand embraces me" (Song 2:6)....

The shape and sounding of the *shofar* are here taken as a powerful symbol of the inner movement that has to take place in this holy season. We have to move from our narrow, constricted places into a realm of greater breadth and open-heartedness. As we do so, we understand that God does the same with regard to us.

ME'OR 'EYNAYIM (*LIKKUTIM*)

> From afar Y-H-W-H appears to me. I have loved you with an eternal love; therefore I have drawn grace upon you.
>
> (JER. 31:2)

Our sages said (b. Rosh ha-Shanah 10b) that "in [the month of] Tishrey the world was [or 'is'] created." They did not say: "In Tishrey God created the world." The truth is that every Rosh Hashanah the world is created. The blessed Holy One created the world in such a way that there remained something "to do" (Gen. 2:3). He placed this in the hands of Israel, their actions having an impact above. If they are unworthy, the world deserves to return to its original chaos.

Rosh Hashanah is the Day of Judgment; everyone shakes in fear and returns to God. As each person goes back to his Source, God's mercies are aroused and the world is created. "On Rosh Hashanah the world *is* created," constantly.

The *Zohar* (*Tikkuney Zohar* 16) reads the word *bereshit* of "In the beginning God created" as consonantally *ba tishrey*, "Tishrey has come." *Elohim* ("God"), the aspect of judgment, creates. This means that because of all the fear of judgment people return to God, awakening mercy, and that re-creates the world. The word *Tishrey* represents the returning of light to God, since its first three letters are the end of the alphabet, the return of all things, the power of judgment and limitation. Since this brings about Creation, judgment itself is really the ultimate compassion. **From afar Y-H-W-H appears to me.** From the "afar" of judgment, where God appears far off, Y-H-W-H, the aspect of mercy, is revealed....

That mercy was at first hidden ... but now comes to be revealed. That is why we say, "This day the world was conceived." It was like a pregnancy; mercy was hidden away, like an unborn child in the womb. Now the sound of the *shofar* awakens it, bringing it into a revealed state. So too do we say that "the patriarchs were born in Tishrey" (b. Rosh ha-Shanah 10b). The compassion they represent was in a latent state and now was born into reality. That is why "In Tishrey the world is created," ever being made anew....

Here the two key themes of Rosh Hashanah, judgment and renewal or rebirth, are joined together on the cosmic plane, just as they are linked in the life of the individual.

We should recall that early Judaism went through a transformative shift in moving from a spring New Year celebration to one in the fall. The rabbis recall this in arguing about whether "the world was created" in Nissan or Tishrey. The triumph of the fall New Year means that we are in fact celebrating what the Kabbalists call *or hozer*, the light that we radiate back to God. Both the name *Tishrey* and the sounding of the *shofar* point in that direction. The "pregnancy" described here is the process that leads to our birth as beings capable of giving light back to its Source.

Yom Kippur

Mevasser Tsedek (from *Va-Yera'*)

> Who is a God like You, bearing iniquity and remitting transgression, who has not maintained His wrath forever against the remnant of His own people, because He loves graciousness! He will take us back out of love; He will cover up our iniquities, You will hurl all our sins into the depths of the sea.
> (Mic. 7:18–19)

R. Levi Yitshak of Berdichev explained the verse in this manner: The sages taught (b. Sukkah 52b) that the blessed Holy One regrets having made four things—[exile, the Chaldeans, Ishmaelites, and the evil inclination], as it is written: "as I have done wrong" (Mic. 4:6). According to this, when a person sins, God forbid, the Holy Blessed One takes responsibility for the mess created. With abundant mercy and infinite kindness He takes the sin upon Himself, as it were, saying that He caused it by having created such a powerful evil inclination. This is the meaning of **bearing iniquity**.

I heard it said in the name of his student Reb Arush [Aharon of Zhytomir] that he explained the verse as follows: **He will take us back out of love; He will cover up our iniquities**—we know that when a person returns to God out of love, sins are transformed into merits (b. Yoma 86b). However, if God truly bears the sin, the penitent no longer possesses any transgressions that may be turned into merits! Yet since God is exceedingly merciful, "like a father who favors his son" (Prov. 3:12), God forgives the sin and returns it at the moment that we turn to Him out of love, so that it may accrue to our positive merit. This is the meaning of **He will take us back**—when a person returns [to the Almighty] **out of love**, then God responds with compassion. **He will cover up our iniquities**—God sets the iniquity down upon the penitent, in order for it to be transformed into a merit. These are the words of Reb Arush.

It is taught that the evil inclination is referred to as a real "thing" (RaSHI on Hab. 3:5), and that which a person creates by his sin is also called a real "thing." These two are actually one and the same. Just how may a person convert his sins into merits? Through what means is this possible? This is the answer: In committing a transgression, you generate a destructive spirit. At the time you return to God out of love, recognizing His blessed greatness and realizing that there is no place devoid of Him, everything is once more filled with His glory. There is no room for destructiveness, no empty space where it can stand. Even it is uplifted and transformed into a proper angel! Because it has no place to stand as it was, it has to be turned into a servant of God. It then draws you to return to God with fiery enthusiasm, as you bring positive energy into the body of the sin and cast forth the unclean. As you affirm God's kingship in each and every place, impurity is nullified and the life-force of holiness is extended.

There are two distinct themes in this teaching. In the first, God so loves us that He takes on the burden of our sins, but then returns them to us as they are turned into merits. In the second, we see a panentheist seeking an approach to evil. Sin or evil can only exist in a place from which God is absent. Find God everywhere, even in the place of your own evil thoughts, and you will be transformed by that vision.

Orah le-Hayyim (from *Emor*)

> Moreover, on the tenth day of that seventh month is the Day of Atonement, a holy convocation [*mikra*] shall it be for you, on which you shall afflict [*ve-'initem*] your souls.
>
> (Lev. 23:27)

The *Shulhan 'Arukh* (*Orah Hayyim* 619:2) tells us that "On the evening and day of Yom Kippur one is to recite 'Blessed is the name of His glorious kingdom forever' [following the *shema'* and ordinarily whispered] out loud...." The reason for this is given by the [commentary] *Magen Avraham*: "We say it in a whisper during all the year because Moses stole this formula from the angels. But on Yom Kippur Israel are themselves like angels [so they may recite it aloud]."

Our sages claim that "there is nothing that is not alluded to in Scripture" (cf. b. Ta'anit 9a). This tradition may be hinted at by our verse. It is known that this formula "Blessed is the name ..." refers to *malkhut* ["His kingdom"], which represents the [lowest] soul level called *nefesh*.

Wherever Scripture refers to "responding," it means responding out loud. In *Parashat Ki Tavo* (Deut. 27:14) it says, "The Levites shall respond," and they were to do so aloud.

There too, concerning the bringing of first fruits, Scripture (Deut. 26:5) says, "You shall respond, saying ...," and RaSHI comments that "respond" refers to raising one's voice.

This is the point here as well. **The Day of Atonement** [is] **a holy convocation [*mikra*] ... on which you shall afflict [respond with *ve-'initem*/*'anitem*] your souls.** This too is a matter of raising one's voice. Read *et* to mean "with"; raise up your voice with your soul! That refers to "Blessed is the name of His glorious kingdom ...," identified with both *malkhut* and *nefesh*. On Yom Kippur you should raise the voice of your soul and call it out aloud!

This is a very Hasidic rereading of Judaism's best-known ascetic prescription.

"*Ve-'initem et nafshotekhem*" here means "Make your souls responsive!" This witnesses the Hasidic transformation of asceticism.

The whispering of *Barukh shem* ("Blessed is the name ...") is a powerful evocation of the worship as it was practiced in Temple times. When the people heard the high priest utter the name of God from within the Holy of Holies, they fell on their faces and called out this phrase in response. It was then placed in the liturgy as a response to especially holy names. It follows the *shema'* because reciting the *shema'* is tantamount to calling out the name of God. This may recall an ancient memory of a time when Jews actually pronounced the name at this moment in the service.

Dibrat Shelomoh (from *Devarim*)

I heard from my teacher [the Maggid]: Why is it that in the confessional (*viddui*) we have to mention each sin? Isn't it enough to leave the sin behind and to heartfully regret having done it? Isn't that the essence of *teshuvah*? After all, everything we have done is revealed to God.

He said that when we transgress we do so using our strength and vitality. We actually draw the energy of the letters of that act we commit into the deed itself: "Theft," "cheating," "harlotry," and the like. Therefore when we repent, we have to speak them out with those same letters, reciting them with a broken heart and in tears. We have to follow them down to the low place called "sadness" and "weeping," raising those letters up by reciting them in both fear and love, with great devotion, before the world's Creator. This allows them to fly upward, as the *Zohar* teaches (*Tikkuney Zohar* t. 10, 25b).

Afterwards I heard from the late and great *hasid* R. Shelomoh of Karlin that he also heard our teacher explain the word *viddui* ("confession") in this way. *Viddui* has the spelled-out letter *yod* within it. You are raising all those letters back up to their root in *yod*, the root of all the letters, [reading *viddui* as "remaking into a *yod*"].

Human deeds make a difference; that is an essential part of Hasidic teaching. As this is true of good deeds, so is it true of transgressions. Therefore, regret in the heart does not suffice to undo them. But we have been given the gift of language, the very tool by which God created the world. Saying the words aloud permits the letters, building blocks of reality, to re-form themselves into the *yod*, the starting point for new directions, for reshaping the creative energies within us.

Such a teaching could easily be rewritten for the "talking cure" of the post-Freudian age. We need to engage in an act of *yiddui*, allowing our blocked inner silence to become a *yod*, taking ourselves through a primal point of language, allowing the silent self to pour forth in words.

Me'or 'Eynayim (from *Emor*)

> ...You shall afflict your souls on the ninth of the month....
>
> (Lev. 23:32)

But do we fast on the ninth? It is on the tenth that we fast! This is to teach you that whoever eats and drinks on the ninth, Scripture considers it as though you had fasted on both the ninth and the tenth (b. Yoma 81b)....

Eating is called a sacrificial offering, as our sages taught (b. Hagigah 27a): "A person's table stands in place of the altar." Since the Temple was destroyed, it is a person's [conduct at] table that atones. But we also find that fasting is considered a sacrifice, one in which you offer of your own fat and blood (b. Berakhot 17a). How is it possible that these two opposite things could be seen as one and the same?...

There is a way of attaching oneself to the Root of all by approaching it from below. You bring up all the lower rungs, raising holy sparks out of things that have fallen. As you tie them to the Creator, you too become linked to the Creator along with them. This is the way in which eating is considered a *korban* ("offering"), which literally means a "drawing near." You bring forth all the sparks within that thing, all the sublime life-energy that has been "garbed" within it. This is the taste that you encounter in the food, for taste is a spiritual, not a physical, quality. It is that holy sublime life-energy garbed within the physical food. When you consume it, that life-force enters into you; it is added and bound to your own life-force, the portion of God that dwells within you. You may then serve Y-H-W-H with that added strength and life-force, speaking words or fulfilling *mitsvot* in an attached and devoted way. All this has come about through the energy you derived from that food. In rising up and being attached to God by its power, you have given ascent to the holy sparks that lay within that food. The externals have been pushed aside once the life-energy has been separated from them. The beauty that made it so attractive previously was due to the life-force. Once it is gone, the rest remains dead and rotting....

The secret of fasting is that divine part within you being drawn close to its Root by a movement reaching downward from above. Movement in the other direction cannot take place, since you are not eating on the fast day [and therefore are not raising anything up]. But the broken heart with which you submit to God during that fast causes the Root of Holiness itself to be aroused toward you and draw you near.

Now not every person can reach the level where eating is considered a sacrifice, a way of becoming linked to God along with the life-energy being uplifted. They may not have the awareness needed to do this; they eat only to fulfill their desires. Thus they remain below, along with the new life-energy derived from that eating.... But Y-H-W-H desires compassion and thinks of ways to keep the lost from being utterly abandoned. Therefore God seeks a way to have all the ordinary eating of all Israel raised up to Him. So He decreed that there be one day in the year, the eve of Yom Kippur, when feasting and drinking were themselves commanded, even if done in a superficial way. On that day, even if we eat to fulfill our desires, it is considered to be a *mitsvah*, just like that of fasting. This single day when eating is commanded allows for the raising up of all our non-conscious eating throughout the year, drawing it all near to holiness by means of the *mitsvah*....

Afterwards, on Yom Kippur itself, we have our annual fast. According to the Torah itself, only this single day is declared for fasting. This Day of Atonement is the time when *teshuvah* in its highest sense [*binah*] shines down upon all of Israel. This happens even to those who cannot awaken any *teshuvah* from within themselves without help from above....

Now the approach that reaches upward from below has already been repaired on the preceding day, the eve of Yom Kippur. Had this not already taken place, the reaching from above could not happen. But since the eve of Yom Kippur has done its work, the upper *teshuvah* can flow forth and shine. Now the two parts of the offering can be joined together: that which rises up from the eating of Yom Kippur eve, bearing with it all the eating done without consciousness throughout the year, is joined to the holy intimacy that comes down from above because of the fast.... In this way Israel are made holy and drawn near to our Creator. That is why the day is called *Yom ha-Kippurim* [in the plural], for it atones for all their sins by joining together the parts of holiness that constitute the secret souls of Israel, [separating them from that which is] external.

This text, like so many others, is written in the language of the vertical metaphor, energy being raised up from below or sent down from above. But suppose we placed this text on an internal/external axis instead. In eating, we bring energy into ourselves from without. That act is one of ingesting and thus releasing (or discovering) holy sparks (the presence of God within material things, within the world that surrounds us). When fasting, we take nothing in. The discovery of holiness therefore has to take place from deep within us. Like the high priest, on this day we have to enter our Holy of Holies, and bring the sparks outward.

We are capable of doing that, however, only because of God's grace. We are given a "free" day of eating on the ninth, when even the least of us can experience the process of discovering the light from without. That opens a channel for us, enabling us to seek out light from within as well.

סוכות Sukkot

Or ha-Emet

The meaning of *lulav*, from the viewpoint of the receptive self.

You begin each wave of the *lulav* from your chest, the locus of the heart. It is in our hearts that we proclaim God's kingship.

Waving the *lulav* means this. We are a microcosmic representation of the divine form, "Israel in whom I am glorified" (Is. 49:3) (i.e., within each of us). But sometimes we have bad love in our hearts. [As we raise up the *lulav*,] we raise those loves from heart to mind. There the love becomes purified. [In my mind I say:] "Why should I love corporeal things? It is better to love worshipping God, to proclaim Y-H-W-H King over all." I come to accept this higher love from each of the three chambers within the mind. Then I bring the *lulav* and other species back down to the chest, allowing that love to flow into my [heart, or] receptive self. That is how one can accept God's kingship in true love. You can do the same with loving the awe of God, or the glory. Bring each of them back to your chest, the place of your heart, your receptive self where you serve God.

Hasidic teaching has long recognized the distinction between mind and heart.

Often we know what is right in our minds but remain unable to convince our emotional selves to live in accord with that truth. Here the very physical act of waving the *lulav*, where it is brought back to the chest after it moves in each direction, is taken as a symbolic expression of the need to bring awareness, especially that of love, into our heart.

Or ha-Me'ir (from *Emor*)

> Take for yourselves on the first day the fruit of the lovely tree, branches of the palm....
> (Lev. 23:40)

This verse instructs us to take up the *middot*, which are alluded to by these weapons of spiritual struggle: the *lulav*, *etrog*, and other two species. The *middot* are also called the "seven days of building." We must accept upon ourselves on the **first day**, meaning Rosh Hashanah, a day of spiritual battle, that the goal of our prayers and the *shofar* is to arrive at awareness (*da'at*) of divine kingship. We build it up and give it a new form ... but simply accepting the divine kingship is like when *da'at* was brought out of exile in Egypt. The *middot* remain stuck there! That is why we are commanded to dwell in a *sukkah* for the "seven days" right after Rosh Hashanah and Yom Kippur ... completing the process with physical deeds. We pick up the *lulav* and the *etrog* with our hands, and by waving them we infuse the *da'at* attained on Rosh Hashanah into the six *middot*, the six directions....

This helps us understand what we recite every day in *sim shalom*, the last blessing of the *'amidah*: "Bless us as one, our Father, with the light of Your countenance...." But how can it be that our sages arranged the words of the prayer thus? The needs of Israel are so many! Each person asks for the particular things that his soul is lacking, since that which one person is missing someone else may not need, and so forth. Therefore, how can we ask, "Bless us as one, our Father," with a single blessing?

We can explain it in this way. The primary goal of worship is to attain the illuminating light that refracts through the different colors, which are the "seven days of building." These are differentiated from one another. But this is not true of the illuminating light that shines through them. It contains no distinctions whatsoever. All of the individual elements that we find in this world of division exist there in absolute unity. This is what we ask of God: "Bless us as one, our Father...." If you wonder how all of our needs can be fulfilled by a single blessing, the answer comes along with the request: we ask for the deepest illuminating light that holds the blessings for all of our various needs. This is why we say "with the light of Your countenance [*panim*]." After succeeding in awakening that shining interior (*bi-fenim/penimi*) light, then "You grant us, Y-H-W-H, our God, the Torah of life and loving-kindness, righteousness, blessing, compassion, life, and peace." All of the blessings enumerated here are contained within that total unity....

Thus we see there is a difference between Rosh Hashanah and Sukkot, even though they are part of the same process. On Rosh Hashanah we resolve in our hearts to build up the *shekhinah*, which is the meaning of *da'at*. During Sukkot we now bring this awareness into realization in all the six directions through our physical acts....

The blessing of God is one and undifferentiated. The divine light shines forth upon and through all creatures. We absorb that light as love; as that love radiates through us, it is the source of our human love as well, in all of its endless varieties. But trees, stretching in the forest to catch rays of light, turn it into chlorophyll, their own life-giving substance. We stand in awe, both at the oneness of divine blessing and the infinitely different prisms through which it is received.

Kedushat Levi (from *Ha'azinu*)

> Take unto yourselves on the first day the fruit of the lovely tree....
> (Lev. 23:40)

The sages ask (*Tanhuma* Emor 22): "Is this [fifteenth of the seventh month] really the first day?" Their answer: yes, it is the first day when sins are counted. This statement remains unexplained, despite the best efforts of our early interpreters.

This seems to be the meaning. On the days from Rosh Hashanah until Yom Kippur, every Jew goes about with open eyes, surveys his deeds, and prepares to return to God. Each of us, according to our own mind and our own level of piety, fears Y-H-W-H and His glorious majesty as God rises to judge the earth. The "day of God" is near, and who can ever feel righteous in judgment? Who can but fear and be humbled in coming before the Judge of all the world? If you tremble before God in this way, you will rise in the heights of your mind to set aright whatever has gone wrong. Such a return to God is called "repentance from fear."

But after Yom Kippur we are involved with such *mitsvot* as *sukkah* and *lulav*. We give to the needy as generously as God has blessed us. We love serving God in this joyous and good-hearted way. This is repentance out of love.

Our sages taught that when one repents out of fear, intentional transgressions are reduced to the status of unintended misdeeds (b. Yoma 86b). But when one repents out of love, the same transgressions are transformed into actual merits. Now God, in His great mercy and compassion, wants the penitent to return in true love. "You do not seek the death of mortals, but that they return from their way and live" (*u-netaneh tokef* from the Yom Kippur liturgy, based on Ezek. 18:32).

So on this holiday, when we come to rest in God's shade, performing *mitsvot* and good deeds out of the love of Y-H-W-H, God begins counting our sins. He wants to know how many merits we are earning in the process of exchange! He doesn't count them prior to Sukkot, when only fear is in the air....

This is the meaning of "the first day when sins are counted...." God gives us all this goodness and blessing, just as God always wants to do. "More than the calf wants to nurse, the cow wants to be suckled" (b. Pesahim 112a).

Levi Yitshak's God, like the teacher himself, loves people and seeks to find only the best in them. Or should we say this in reverse? Levi Yitshak, like God above, loves people and seeks only the best in them. His God, like the *rebbe* himself, would never think of counting people's sins—until they are ready to be turned into merits.

Tsemah ha-Shem li-Tsevi (from *Emor*)

Take unto yourselves on the first day....
(Lev. 23:40)

Our sages called this "the first day in the account of sins" (*Tanhuma* Emor 22). I read this in accord with the verse "Happy is the person to whom Y-H-W-H accounts [*yahashov*] no sin; [there is not deceit in his spirit]" (Ps. 32:2). The pious books read this to mean that such a person considers just not thinking (*yahashov*) about God to be itself a sin, even though there is nothing deceitful about him.

The book *Duties of the Hearts* mentions that when you are working at preparing your *sukkah* and *lulav*, even if you are not thinking of God because you are so preoccupied with those activities, they are considered *mitsvot* nonetheless.

This is the meaning of "the first day in the account of sins," following the verse "Great deeds have You done, Y-H-W-H my God; Your wonders and thoughts are toward us. Though there is none like You, I will declare and speak of that which is beyond telling" (Ps. 40:6). Every person is obliged to serve God in thought, since Israel arose in divine thought [before Creation]. God was thinking of us even when making and establishing the cosmos. But "there is none like You"; we cannot imitate God in this matter [of concentrating in thought while involved in detailed preparation].

The Midrash reads this word "thoughts" as "accountings" (*Pesikta Rabbati* 15).

The two words are related; without "thought" there is no "account." ...

So in these four days between Yom Kippur and Sukkot, when we are so busy preparing for the *mitsvot,* the sin of not thinking about God does not apply. Therefore [without thought] there is no counting even of other transgressions, [and the first day of Sukkot indeed begins a new account].

This is true except for the one who tries to count on it by saying in advance, "I will sin and Yom Kippur will atone" (b. Yoma 85b)....

The oft-repeated claim that "Israel arose in God's thought before Creation" or "The world was created for the sake of Israel" can best be understood in our day through a literal reading of the word "Israel": "one who struggles with God." The world thus exists for the sake of all of those, within any tradition or outside them, who strive to make meaning of life, who seek to understand why we are here and what we need to do about it. It is they who will stretch themselves to carry forward the great process of existence, the ongoing evolutionary journey in which Y-H-W-H is ever present. Our particular "Israel," the Jewish path, is our own refraction of this unbounded light.

Shemini 'Atseret—Simhat Torah

Ma'amarey Admor ha-Zaken

> The eighth day will be a gathering for you....
> (Num. 29:35)

... Why do we begin to recite "the One who makes the wind blow and the rain to fall" on Shemini 'Atseret?

... Dew represents love, and rain represents awe or fear. Both are crucial, since with love alone your personal existence would be totally annihilated, [for love would reabsorb you back into the divine self]. Fear is necessary, because it represents drawing back. Love and fear together are called the two wings [by which prayer flies upward].

The Torah has qualities of both dew and rain. Dew is the thought of Torah, and rain is its words and letters. Each word of the Torah exists on its own, like the falling drops of rain. But the thought within it is totally undifferentiated, like the appearance of dew. Rain sustains the world, and the quality of fear that it represents prevents the [overwhelming] love from being revealed all at once; it appears one drop at a time.

Therefore we mention rain in the blessing that describes God's power (*gevurot*, associated with "fear"). Rainfall is actually an expression of divine restraint, since it descends drop by drop [rather than all at once]. On the eighth day of Shemini 'Atseret, [God's] love [for Israel] is revealed without any limits, and therefore we must mention the rain in order to hold it back (*la-'atsor/'atseret*). This allows the world to maintain its existence....

Rain and dew are ancient biblical symbols often invoked by the mystical tradition to describe the flow of God's energy into the physical world. Rain is offered as one model: it can be fierce and powerful, but rain has life-giving and nourishing aspects as well. The same is true of the divine life-force, for without it comes spiritual drought. Like the independent words of the Torah, raindrops represent our personal existence infused with God's vitality. The sublime dew, on the other hand, alludes to the divine element that binds together all of existence. This is like a pool of deeper ideas that exists beyond the literal meaning of the biblical text. Yet too much of this sublime unity, an overabundance of God's love, surely would drown out our individual identity.

After the holiday season and the intimate moments with God it hopefully brings, we ready ourselves for the long period until Hanukkah by praying that God hold back some of that "dew," showering us instead with the divine "rain" we need in order to continue seeking in the months to come.

Me'or 'Eynayim (from *Emor*)

... By means of the sublime *teshuvah* undertaken on Rosh Hashanah and Yom Kippur, all parts of holiness, all parts of Israel, come near to Torah, where the souls of Israel are rooted. Each one of us has a letter in the Torah in which we are rooted. When we stray far from our blessed Creator, we are cut off from that root in Torah. But the repair brought about in this season causes that part within every Jew to return to Torah.

We each have an *'aliyah*, an "ascent" to Torah.

Yom Kippur is followed by Sukkot, called "the shade of faith," sheltering and protecting Israel because of the repair wrought on Yom Kippur. The last day of this festival is Simhat Torah, "the joy of Torah." Sublime Torah Herself rejoices as all the parts of Israel's soul-root come near to Her and unite with Her. Each of us returns to our soul-root in Torah through the repairs we effect at this season.

That is why it is customary for everyone to go up to the Torah on Simhat Torah.

We really have "gone up" to Torah in a spiritual sense as well, bringing our soul-root and the divine portion within it back to Torah.... It is known that there are six hundred thousand letters in Torah, the same number as the soul-roots within Israel. That is why we read the portion "This is the blessing" (Deut. 33:1) on Simhat Torah. After the repairs of this season, in which all of our soul parts come together, we link our soul-roots to Torah and to our blessed Creator, and blessing flows from above to every one of Israel.

The word *'aliyah* (lit. "ascent"), well known to Jews as referring to the call to recite Torah blessings in the synagogue, in modern times has also been adopted to mean an "ascent" to settle in the Land of Israel, long considered "higher" than other lands. It is worth recalling that in Jewish spiritual language it also refers to an ascent of the soul, a climb "up" to a higher spiritual state. On a *yortseyt* [anniversary of a death], *hasidim* lift a glass to the memory of the departed and say: *Di neshamah zol hobn an aliyah*, "May the soul have an ascent!"

Hanukkah

Me'or 'Eynayim I

> Our sages taught: "What is Hanukkah?"
> (b. Shabbat 21b)

... In fact the word *Hanukkah* is composed of *hanu koh*, "they dwelt in 'thus.'" There is an aspect of divinity that is called "thus"; this is *malkhut*, the seat of divine rule. The king commands: "Thus will it be! Thus will it be!" It is this aspect that issues commands through all the worlds, by which the universe is ruled. This is why the *tsaddikim* have it within their power to rule over all the worlds: they bear within themselves this aspect of divine kingship. So the rabbis (b. Mo'ed Katan 16b) have taught us on the verse "The righteous one rules the fear of God" (2 Sam. 23:3). On this verse they said: "Who rules over Me? The *tsaddik*. The blessed Holy One issues a decree, but the righteous one may cancel it."

The *Zohar* (1:45b) objected: "Does the *tsaddik* then control God?" In fact it is God Himself who cancels the decree. Several times we have taught that "in all their suffering, He suffers" (Is. 63:9), referring to the *shekhinah* in exile. *Shekhinah*—so called because She dwells (*shokhenet*) everywhere—is identical with this aspect of divine rule. She is also called *kenesset yisra'el*, "Assemblage of Israel," gathering all of Israel within Her, since all of them are derived from Her. Thus our sages (b. Shabbat 128a) taught: "All Israel are children of kings" (i.e., of *malkhut*). All sufferings that Israel undergoes, God forbid, secretly belong to the fall of *shekhinah*. Scripture refers to this in "You weaken the Rock that bore you" (Deut. 32:18). The righteous, by their good deeds, raise up the *shekhinah*, as it were, as in "Give strength to God!" (Ps. 68:35). The rabbis (*Eikhah Rabbah* 1:33) add: "Israel add power to the upper 'family.'" *Malkhut* is called "family" because She gathers into Herself all the divine potencies that stand above Her. All of their powers flow into *shekhinah*. As She is uplifted, all decrees and judgments are negated...

This is an important articulation of the Maggid's view of the *tsaddik* and his powers. It is not that he is a magician who can arbitrarily control fate and overrule the divine will. It is rather that the exiled *shekhinah* so fully partakes of Israel's suffering that She falls and rises with them. Harsh judgments are due to the eclipse of light shining through *shekhinah* in Her exilic state. When the *tsaddik* does good, She is uplifted; then the evil decrees will "naturally" fall away. The *tsaddik* in fact prays for the sake of the *shekhinah*.

Me'or 'Eynayim II

... Y-H-W-H has given us the commandment to light the Hanukkah candles. As the season for each of the *mitsvot* comes along, the very power that was present in that onetime event is reawakened.... Hanukkah is the time for a person to draw near to God by means of Torah, just as it was way back in the days of Mattathias the high priest. The Hellenists had defiled all the oil, meaning that all wisdom had been corrupted. There remained but a single container of [pure] wisdom, and that was Torah. There too there was only a drop, hardly enough to last for a single day, yet it burned for eight. The world is constructed around cycles of seven "days"; once one passes, another begins. These are referred to as "the seven structural days" (= seven lower *sefirot*). Now Mattathias served God on a very high contemplative level: he was indeed a "high priest." He was able to bring forth the light of an eighth day, reaching beyond the seven into the realm of *binah*, so that eight candles would be lit.

This is why the Hanukkah candles have to be elevated from the ground by at least three handbreadths, so as not to appear set into the ground, but remain lower than ten handbreadths, for "*shekhinah* has never come down lower than ten" (b. Sukkah 5a). God searches for ways that we not be utterly cut off from Him; He miraculously brings the divine presence down lower than ten handbreadths, right to where we stand, so that He might restore us and bring us back to Y-H-W-H. The oil of the candles refers to wisdom, as in "God grants wisdom from His own mouth, knowledge and understanding" (Prov. 2:6), teaching us with higher mind, enabling us to serve God in a more mindful and contemplative way. All this takes place through the *mitsvah* of lighting the Hanukkah candles. Just as it was then, so it is in every generation when the time for this commandment arrives....

The eight days of Hanukkah stretch beyond the normative seven-day week, cosmologically referring to *binah*, the eighth *sefirah* from below, representing the contemplative mind that is the source of the lower seven qualities. This breaking of the cycle to reach back into a place of higher or deeper origins is also found in homilies for Shemini 'Atseret and for the placing of circumcision on the eighth day.

The claim that "*shekhinah* has never come down lower than ten" is offered in the Talmud to explain why a proper *sukkah* must be at least ten handbreadths high. Here Hanukkah, which is often described as a second Sukkot, offers the special "worldly" miracle of the *shekhinah* coming down even lower.

Kedushat Levi (*Kedushat Hanukkah* #5)

The Talmud teaches that the commandment of lighting Hanukkah candles should be performed "between sunset and the time when feet disappear from the marketplace" (b. Shabbat 21b).

... Know that the miracles our Creator has performed for us are divisible into three categories. There are hidden miracles and revealed ones. The revealed miracle, like those that took place for our ancestors in Egypt, including the ten plagues and the splitting of the Reed Sea, involved a change in the natural order. Everybody witnessed these miracles. But then there are hidden miracles, like those that took place in the days of Mordecai and Esther, things that appeared natural. First [the king] raised up Haman. Then, because he loved his wife, he had his friend killed for her sake. So too the [Hanukkah] miracle as mentioned in the *'al ha-nissim* prayer, "He handed over the many to the few, the defiled to the holy ..." etc., is a hidden miracle. It came about partly through battle; the same is true of the story of Judith. These really were miracles, not natural occurrences, but they happened in a secret way. This was noted by [Rabbi Loew of Prague,] the author of *Or*

Hadash, who said that the miracle of Hanukkah came about partly through natural means. Our teacher R. Dov Baer taught that the revealed miracle is called "day" and the hidden miracle, like that of Purim and Hanukkah, is "night." It is something that is not known to all, like the night in which not everyone can see.

Now the hidden miracles themselves may be divided into two categories. The first includes Purim, when the Cause of Causes Himself brought things about without any activity on the part of those below. He foiled Haman's intent, brought retribution on his head, and saved us from the hands of all our oppressors. No one down here did anything.... But on Hanukkah the Hasmonean and his sons did act and fight God's battles. God only intervened by "handing over the many to the few and the strong to the weak," but He did so with human help.

There are thus three levels of miracle. The great miracle called "day" is that of the Exodus from Egypt, where nature is changed. Less than that is Purim, which seems partly natural, called "night" by our master and teacher, a hidden miracle without human aid.

And the third level, less than Purim, is that of Hanukkah, a hidden miracle in which there is human participation.

That is why, following the [fall festival season], Hanukkah comes first, then Purim, and then Pesah. "We go up in holiness, and not down" (b. Shabbat 21b). We draw forth the lights and grace of Hanukkah, which are not so great, since this was a hidden miracle accomplished with human help.... Then we rise up to Purim, a hidden miracle in which humans did not act ... and then we rise again to the holy state when we can receive the great lights of Pesah, the revealed "daytime" miracle that is seen by all....

If a person has no faith, God forbid, in hidden miracles, but thinks that the sun simply rises every day and the moon each night, that at night he sleeps and wakes by day, or that whoever does much business will get rich, or that the one who travels far will profit, or that medicine aids the sick—such a person sees all this as just ordinary. But when he sees the hidden miracles that the Creator has wrought, placing the strong in the hands of the weak, or the fall of Haman, and even more so the revealed miracles, he will come to see that there is nothing ordinary about the way the world works. It is God who releases the bound and raises up the fallen, who rolls away light before darkness, creating both light and dark; it is God who brings healing to the sick....

This is why the *mitsvah* is to be performed "between sunset and the time when feet [*regel*] disappear from the marketplace." The setting sun refers to the hidden miracles, those that are not so easily seen. "Until the *regel* disappears from the marketplace"—you have to contemplate the Hanukkah candles until you overcome your sense that the world is conducted by the ordinary (*hergel*) force of nature. Such an idea comes to you from forces that lurk without, the evil urge, the "marketplace." When you kindle Hanukkah lights, this thought disappears from you, and you no longer see the world as ordinary....

In this way you come to the faith that the hidden miracle is not merely natural, but that God is constantly re-creating the world, in every hour and moment. Sometimes He re-creates the natural order set into motion in the six days of Creation, and sometimes He changes something, like a revealed miracle. But once you accept that there are hidden miracles, you realize that all is constantly being re-created, even the established natural order....

Levi Yitshak has got it right. The purpose of faith in miracles is to teach us that all of life is miraculous, that there is nothing ordinary, even in the plainest day.

But we need to question his understanding of Purim. Was there in fact no human action that was important in bringing about that hidden miracle? How can we ignore Esther's bravery? And what of all the slaughter of our enemies in the last chapters of the Megillah? Is that embarrassing part of the holiday just to be swept under the rug?

Siddur ha-Rav

A *mezuzah* is placed on the right side of the entranceway; Hanukkah candles are kindled on the left. This distinction is rooted in the difference between Torah and *mitsvot.*

While both bring about the upper unity, one does so from above, the higher entity reaching downward, while the other moves in the opposite direction, the receiver rising up from below toward the Source of blessing's flow....

This is the root distinction between Torah and *mitsvot.* Torah represents the drawing forth of light from the Endless, reaching far downward from above. "Y-H-W-H descended upon Mount Sinai.... And God spoke ..." (Ex. 19:20–20:1). That is why Torah is composed of *halakhot* (lit. "walkings"), based on "He walks in cosmic ways" (Hab. 3:6) and "walking toward me, my holy King" (Ps. 68:25). This is the light's journey downward from the very Endless, through the wisdom (*hokhmah*) contained in Torah, as is known.

Mitsvot are rooted in the act of walking upward from below. The essence of the commandments, 365 negative and 248 positive, is the raising up of lower (lit. "female") waters, transforming darkness into light. This is the meaning of "the commandment is a candle and Torah is light" (Prov. 6:23). Torah is called light because it represents the divine flow from above. The *mitsvah* is a candle, a vessel to contain that light....

Through the physical act of fulfilling the commandment, the corporeal comes to be included within the spiritual, raising it up to the highest rung. This is the case with the wool of *tsitsit* or the leather used in *tefillin*. It applies also to the sacrifices, where the physical animal is drawn into the spiritual realm, rising from world to world up to the highest Root, the Source of emanation. That is why they are called "a sweet-smelling savor unto Y-H-W-H" (Lev. 1:17). In such acts as *tsitsit* and *tefillin* we rise up to the Source of the divine will that is cloaked in those commandments. This is the meaning of the blessing formula "... who has made us holy through His commandments." It is through this ascent that the light of Torah is drawn forth from the Emanator. This is manifest as the revelation of spiritual Torah light in each of the *mitsvot*....

This divine light shines forth even into this world of separate beings, transforming darkness into light. "Even darkness is not dark before You" (Ps. 139:12). This is why we have Hanukkah lights, the word *Hanukkah* meaning "dwell in 'thus.'" "Thus" (*koh*) refers to *malkhut*, which is given extra light so that she may light up those external realms known as "darkness." "For You light my candle; Y-H-W-H my God brightens my darkness" (Ps. 18:29).

This is the opposite of that "guarding" [of the entranceway] offered by the *mezuzah*, keeping the external (or "demonic") forces from entering or seeing the light. The Hanukkah candles offer such an abundance of light that those forces are obliterated, "as wax melts before fire" (Ps. 68:3). That is due to the intensity with which divinity is revealed, so much so that darkness itself can no longer be dark. Unlike the case of a guard standing outside a closed door, here he gets up and opens that doorway. But the dark forces flee in awe before the power of revelation. This is a higher form of guarding, the protection offered by the light that lights up darkness itself, no longer requiring a closed door.

That is why the Hanukkah lights are on the left side of the doorway, while *mezuzah* is on the right. The *mezuzah* represents the commandment whose light will rise up to *keter*, the highest place. But it can bring forth with it only the light surrounding divine *hesed* [the right side] that has already been revealed but is waiting to be coaxed forth from below. It does not have the power to light up the darkness. But the light of Torah comes from the place where light is most hidden. Torah represents the primal atmosphere, that of which Scripture says: "He sets His secret in darkness" (Ps. 18:12) and "Revealing the depths from within darkness" (Job 12:22). When this light of Torah shines forth from within the darkest hidden recesses of divinity, brought about by the rising up of the *mitsvot*, a new and more exalted light begins to shine....

Therefore they taught that the Hanukkah lights are to be placed on the left, the side of *gevurah* ("power"), so that they break through the darkness above. Great power is required for this; "Y-H-W-H lights up my darkness" (2 Sam. 22:29). But this cannot take place unless the *mezuzah* is on the right side. Without it, the Hanukkah candles on the left would not be effective. "The commandment is a candle" is what allows for the increase of hidden light, manifest in the light of Torah.

The complementary nature of these two types of sacred activity, Torah study and fulfillment of commandments, is a key theme in the teachings of R. Shne'ur Zalman and throughout HaBaD thought. Most powerful here is the notion that wisdom's light, manifest in Torah, comes from within the uttermost dark, unknowable recesses of divinity. Because of that, it has the power to light up darkness below as well. These two entirely different types of darkness are thus remarkably linked.

Shabbat Zakhor

MA'AYAN HA-HOKHMAH (FROM *MATTOT*)

> Y-H-W-H said to Moses: "Write this [*zot*] down in a book, so that you remember, and place it in Joshua's ears. I will surely erase [*maho emheh*] the memory of Amalek from beneath the heavens."
>
> (Ex. 17:14)

The Torah is referred to as *zot*, as in *zot torat*, "this is the teaching of," [which appears frequently]. God seeks to teach us that we should not hold fast to our holy Torah only in its obvious meaning. We hold onto the *peshat* because through it we can find our way to Torah's inner self. This is the intent of our verse: ***Zot***, this holy Torah as written down, is only **so that you remember** the innermost Torah.

Therefore **place it in Joshua's ears.** The word "ears" (*oznayim*) can also refer to the handles of a vessel. If you hold on to this [innermost] rung, you will overpower the evil urge [Amalek]. But if you ask: How can I overpower it? It is entirely spiritual, without a body! The answer is: by the "handles" of Joshua, for that name means "God will save you [*YaH yoshi'akha*]" (b. Sotah 34b). Hold fast to that handle and trust.

This is ***maho emheh***. If you seek to **wipe out [*mahoh*]** the evil urge in order to fulfill Torah and *mitsvot* in their innermost sense, God promises **I will surely erase [*emheh*] the memory of Amalek**, which is the evil urge....

All this shows that our gaze at Torah should be directed toward its innermost self.

Here we see a strong example of the Hasidic attempt to spiritualize the entire tradition. The enmity of Israel and Amalek is only the surface meaning of Torah, itself pointing to the deeper and eternal struggle of the righteous with the evil urge.

Teshu'ot Hen

> Remember what Amalek did to you along your way out of Egypt, when they came upon you along the way.... You were tired and exhausted and did not fear God. When God gives you rest ... blot out the memory of Amalek from beneath the heavens. Do not forget.
>
> (Deut. 25:17–19)

The word *karekha* **(came upon)** has no clear meaning. Nor do we understand why the repetition of **Do not forget** after we are told **Remember**. And how are we to fulfill the commandment of blotting out Amalek today?

Scientists tell us that memory and forgetfulness are related to human temperament. The more cool-minded person is likely to be forgetful, while the more heated mind is one that remembers. Our master the Reprover [R. Yehudah Leib of Polonnoye] reported in the name of the Ba'al Shem Tov that Amalek is a name for forgetfulness.

The hearts of Israel were filled with flame when they saw the wonders the blessed Holy One performed in bringing them forth from Egypt. The Egyptians were struck down by miracles, the ten plagues and the splitting of the sea. Seeing all those things that happened to our ancestors, even a brick in the wall would cry out to praise God's great name. But wicked Amalek dressed those miracles up in ordinariness ("It's all nature"), thus cooling off the intensity of Israel's faith. Then they too became forgetful of God's loving-kindness.

This is the meaning of **Remember what Amalek did to you ... when they** *karekha* ["cooled you off"] **along the way**. They turned down your boiling passion for God, until you too began to forget. **You were tired and exhausted and did not fear God**; you gave rest to your intensity like an exhausted person. You did not maintain the piety of gratitude for God's loving-kindness. Therefore **When God gives you rest ... blot out the memory of Amalek.** Do not believe things are merely the happenstance of nature. Then you will **not forget**.

The Hasidic master seems to foresee the coolness and detachment of the scientific mind coming around the bend of history. He is not wrong in seeing it as the enemy of faith. But we stand on the other end of that great struggle and have learned that warming science with a sense of wonder makes more sense than doing pitched battle against its truth.

Purim

Or ha-Emet

> There was a certain Jew in the capital of Shushan....
> (Esth. 2:5)

The Midrash tells of a traveler who came to a tower (*birah*) and asked one of the residents, "To whom does this tower belong?" The reply: "It is mine." So it was with Abraham—God appeared to him and said, "All the worlds belong to Me" (*Bereshit Rabbah* 39:1). Everything, including this lowly world, comes from God. This is the meaning of **There was a certain Jew in the capital** [*birah*] **of Shushan**. He served the Creator even through the corporeal world, since God is the Source of all.

Perhaps this is the meaning of "Mordecai knew everything that was done" (Esth. 4:1). "Knowing" refers to connection, and he connected everything to the Creator, even the world of deeds, the corporeal realm.

Therefore [in the blessing upon reading the scroll of Esther we say], "and commanded us to read the scroll [*megillah*]," since the divine light is revealed (*mitgalah*) in words.

> One is required to become inebriated on Purim, that the difference between "cursed is Haman" and "blessed is Mordecai" is no longer clear.
> (b. Megillah 7b)

Become drunk with Purim's love, and then you can lift up everything to God—even the corporeal world, which also comes from God. This is what it means: everything is equal before you, and thus you can serve God even through the **cursed** ... **Haman**, representing the physical realm.

Here we see the Maggid's "Purim Torah"—playful, but still contemplative and concerned with the deepest theological questions. Even amid the seeming absurdity of the mundane world we are told to seek divine unity, but on this day we are assisted in our quest by the exuberance of the high-spirited festivities. Purim offers a temporary (if extreme) window of what it means to uplift and sanctify the physical world!

Tif'eret 'Uziel

> Esther was a sallow color, but a thread of divine grace was drawn down upon her.
>
> (b. Megillah 13a)

This teaches us about fulfilling the *mitsvot*. The blessed One has hidden their light from us, and therefore we see *tefillin* only as physical objects. The same is true of *tsitsit*, the *lulav*, and all of the other commandments. Thus the sages asked (b. Hullin 139b), "Where is Esther alluded to in the Torah? It is written, 'And I will surely hide [*haster astir*] My face' (Deut. 31:18)." In the Temple the light of the commandments was fully revealed to us, but during our exile their light has become obscured (*haster/esther*) and **sallow**. Yet even so, **a thread of divine grace was drawn down**. The *mitsvot* still draw down the light, even if it is invisible to us.

Purim is all about having faith in God's hidden presence in the world, even in the most seemingly arbitrary or natural processes. The same is true for our entire spiritual lives: our religious acts have deep significance even when we ourselves don't see the fullness of their light. This is an important voice for an age in which so much of religion has been reduced to the question, "What does it do for *me*?" Part of the spiritual quest is indeed finding personal meaning, but we must remember that we fulfill the *mitsvot* because God needs us to bring more light into the world, even if we cannot directly see it.

Kedushat Levi I (*Kedushat Purim* 1)

> The Jews fulfilled and accepted upon themselves to observe these two days of Purim.
> (Esth. 9:27)

Our sages learned from the words **fulfilled and accepted** that Israel re-accepted the Torah during the reign of Ahasuerus (b. Shabbat 88a). But the Talmud uses this same verse to prove that the book of Esther was composed in the holy spirit (b. Megillah 7a). These two views seem interconnected.

RaSHI on the passage in Shabbat says that Israel re-accepted the Torah "due to loving the miracle." But why should this miracle of Mordecai and Esther have been more beloved to them than all the others? Hadn't they already seen the ten plagues and the splitting of the sea and lots more during the Exodus?

... There are two types of miracles, the revealed and the hidden.... A hidden miracle is the sort that took place for Mordecai and Esther, in which the forces of nature went on undisturbed; the miraculous took place within the realm of nature. Our teacher the holy lamp R. Dov Baer taught that she was named Esther because of *hester* ("hiddenness"), the hiding of the miracle within nature....

Now we can understand why this miracle was so great that their love allowed them to accept the Torah. It took place within nature, where God's kingship is hidden. That made it all the greater. It is no great surprise when the king comes along with a vast army and wins the battle. But what if the king is alone in the forest, without either weapons or troops, and wins by his courage alone? Or imagine the fear and submission that overwhelm you when you come into the king's palace and see all his grandeur.... But suppose you met that same king alone in the forest, without any soldiers and dressed like an ordinary person, yet you were still overcome by fear and shame? Wouldn't that be a much greater wonder? The blessed Holy One can transform nature and make His heavenly kingdom appear. The one who created everything can change things as well.

That is not so great a miracle as when He works through nature, with His kingship hidden, and yet does wonders. That was what happened at the time of Mordecai and Esther, and it was so wondrous that it caused Israel to re-accept God's Torah.

But let us look at this in a more inward way. First we should note that the term *Megillah* [used especially for the "scroll" of Esther], when God's kingship was hidden within nature ... [derives from the word *megalleh*, "reveals"], since God was revealed to be present in the natural world and still to defeat evil....

Why then did they come to accept the Torah?... They read the Megillah in that first year ... and through it they saw clearly God's active presence within the natural, physical realm. They then accepted the Torah out of love....

The point of this (somewhat excerpted) teaching is that the supernaturally revealed Torah could only be lovingly accepted once Israel had seen that in fact there exists no real boundary between the natural and the supernatural realms. Since we live within nature, we need a God and a Torah that are active and present in that dimension. This is the truth we learn at Purim.

Kedushat Levi II (*Kedushat Purim 1*)

The holy *Zohar* teaches that the Day of Atonement is called *Yom Kippurim* (*ke-Purim*), "a day like Purim" (*Tikkuney Zohar* t. 21, 57b). The light of Yom Kippur is like that of Purim. As of Yom Kippur, that which has passed is all negated; now you are pure and the accounting begins anew. That is why the Midrash teaches on "Take unto yourselves on the first day [the branches and citron of Sukkot] (Lev. 23:40)," that this is the first day for the account of sins (*Tanhuma* Emor 22). The true illumination of Yom Kippur is that of acquiring a new heart to serve God, "so that we cease the oppression of our hands and return to do the decrees of Your will." So too on Purim, the past is negated and now we accept anew the yoke of God's Torah and commandments.

We have taught that on Purim the natural world itself is purified as we read the Megillah, since its light shines directly into this world.... That is because these events took place within nature, and Israel "fulfilled what they had already accepted" (b. Shabbat 88a). But we know that this world is the dwelling-place of demonic forces, indeed it is mostly composed of such forces. They are purified, however, by human actions. Now on Purim, when this world, that of nature, is made pure by the reading of the Megillah and our true acceptance of Torah, all those demonic forces are purified as well. The same is true on Yom Kippur, when all those powers are rendered pure. The casting of lots on Purim is parallel to the selecting and sending forth of the scapegoat on the Day of Atonement.

Therefore burn with ecstatic fire when you hear the Megillah read; prepare to accept anew the burden of Torah and *mitsvot.* Let your youth [i.e., your youthful faith] be renewed like that of a soaring eagle as you rejoice in receiving the Torah. As you read the Megillah, intend that all the worlds become pure, including this lowly world of nature.

Take great joy in all this purity, as you see fulfilled "May Y-H-W-H rejoice in His works" (Ps. 104:31).

The parallel between these two very different days of spiritual intensity is a well-known trope of Hasidic exegesis. Both are times of transformation, opportunities to begin anew. But Purim has a special role in Jewish life as an embodiment of very this-worldly spirituality.

Pesah

Dibrat Shelomoh (from *Emor*)

> Y-H-W-H spoke to Moses, saying: "... These are festivals of Y-H-W-H.... Six days shall work be done, but the seventh day is a Sabbath of Sabbaths.... He shall wave the barley-measure before Y-H-W-H as you will it; on the day following the Sabbath shall the priest wave it...."
>
> (Lev. 23:1–3, 11)

RaSHI interprets **the day following the Sabbath** to refer to the day following the first day of Pesah.... But RaSHI was troubled by the question of why the Sabbath is mentioned here along with the festivals [having already been commanded elsewhere].

Why, in fact, should Pesah have been referred to here as Shabbat?

... To resolve all this, we should note that Maimonides lists belief in the resurrection of the dead as one of the thirteen principles of faith. Everyone considered a Jew has to have that faith. We are also obligated to believe that this resurrection is hinted at in the Torah. Thus our sages taught: "All Israel have a place in the world-to-come.

"Who are those who have no such place? One who says there is no resurrection of the dead to be derived from the Torah" (m. Sanhedrin 10:1)....

There must be a reason why this should be considered an essential principle of our religion. It seems to be because this is a great proof of God's oneness and infinity. Since God is truly one and without limit, all else flows from that oneness. This applies in a special way to His people Israel, who are considered God's own portion. It must then be that they cannot be utterly destroyed, even physically. Our sages referred to a single bone within the body called the *niskhoi* that survives and is never lost. It is from this that the entire body will be rebuilt at the time of the resurrection (*Bereshit Rabbah* 28:3). But all creatures contain the power of the blessed Infinite One within them. By that power God can overturn all the systems and replace nature with miracle any time God desires.

... All creatures are dependent on the divine word and life-force that willfully flows through them constantly. The only exceptions are those who cut themselves off from God's blessed life-force. They are truly destroyed, as though they did not exist at all, not to be considered.

That power of the blessed Infinite flowed into God's creatures after all of Creation had taken place. Creation appeared to be complete in the six days of action, but it was not. It was not whole until Shabbat came, as our sages have taught: "What was the world still lacking? Rest. When Shabbat came, there was rest" (RaSHI on Gen. 2:2). This "rest" is the power of the blessed Infinite. Thus I have heard from my teacher, of blessed memory: "The notion of movement cannot be applied to *eyn sof*, the Infinite. To where could it move?" Therefore it is called "rest."

In the *Kiddush* for Shabbat we [also] mention that it is in memory of the Exodus from Egypt. It was because of Shabbat [the presence of infinity within being] that all the miracles and suspensions of nature could come about, beginning with the Exodus from Egypt. This is why the festival of Pesah, the first of those miracles wrought by Shabbat, is itself called by that name....

Although R. Shelomoh begins with a quotation from Maimonides, the essence of his teaching is drawn from Kabbalah. The Hasidic message here is that the natural rhythms of life are only an outer shell that contains within it the full presence of the mysterious Infinite. In such a universe, miracles should come as no surprise.

We also see here the complex interplay of Jewish exclusivism and a vision that embraces all of being. He knows that the received tradition of resurrection is said to apply only to Israel. But his understanding of it places it into a framework that embraces all creatures. This "awkwardness" is a very regular feature of Hasidic teachings.

Kedushat Levi (from *Bo*)

> What does the wise child ask? "What are these testimonies, statutes, and judgments that Y-H-W-H our God has commanded for you?"
> (Passover Haggadah)

... There are two ways of serving our blessed Creator. One comes about as we behold miracles and wonders, the transformation of nature. When God makes natural forces do His bidding, we understand that God rules over all and that all His creatures are obliged to serve Him in awe.

The second path is that of true awareness, knowing that He has created all things by the word of His mouth. Because of that, He is able to transform them. This is the better way; it makes awareness based on miracles unimportant.... Such a person already has the wisdom to understand that the Creator can change nature ... and the miracle is not surprising to him....

This is the wise child's question: "**What are these testimonies, statutes, and judgments that Y-H-W-H our God has commanded for you?**" He knows that the wonders are not really wondrous from God's point of view, that the Creator can change anything He wants. But the acts of [eating] *pesah* and *matsah* point toward worshipping God because of the miracles. That is his question. "Why should this be? Don't we already have true recognition of Y-H-W-H, knowing that nothing is too wondrous for Him?" To this question we give the answer "We do not follow the *pesah* with dessert."

Matsah and *pesah* refer to the miracles and wonders. It is this sort of service that endures forever.... This is why the Talmud says that you must taste *matsah* last, and the same was true of the *pesah* sacrifice when the Temple stood (b. Pesahim 119b). This taste of worshipping God because of the miracles had to remain, because this is the sort of worship that lasts forever. Of this we say: "May it never depart from us or from our descendants."

This is not the case with the true awareness. This is present only among the great, and only so long as they remain in a state of attachment to God and have not fallen. That is why we answer the wise son in this way, so that the service in response to miracles not be something he sets aside.

Here we see a strong current of anti-elitism that is frequently found in Levi Yitshak's teachings. Indeed he knows which sort of religion is the higher or more refined; that is "true awareness." But he also knows that it is simple faith in the miraculous that will last from one generation to the next.

Our own age is so different from his; "simple faith," as he understood it, is harder in our day. But does that mean there is nothing to be learned from this insight? In what ways do we still feel this same tension between the faith of a spiritual elite and the real needs of the community?

Peri Hayyim

> What does the wise child say? "What are these testimonies, statutes, and judgments that Y-H-W-H our God has commanded you?" [Deut. 6:20]. Answer him according to all the practices of Passover, [including] "One does not conclude [*maftirin*] the Pesah meal with *afikoman*."
>
> (Passover Haggadah)

Is this really **all the practices** and laws of Passover? This refers only to the conclusion of the meal!.... In the Siddur of Rabbi Isaac Luria it is taught that the word *pesah*, which means "skipping," refers to the fact that [Israel at the Exodus] reached the highest state of mind (*gadlut*) before going through [hence "skipping over"] the lesser stages (*katnut*)....

I heard from that holy lamp R. Avraham, the son of our teacher the Maggid R. Dov Baer, that a person needs to repair all of the seven qualities, beginning with love, awe, and glory. Each has to be turned toward God alone, so that we love only God and so that we do not make use of these attributes for our own bodily benefit, but only for the sake of Y-H-W-H. Each of these qualities contains all seven within it, thus adding up to forty-nine. Only after all of these does the fiftieth gate, *binah*, come to dwell with us.

But at the Exodus from Egypt, they came immediately to the fiftieth gate. Thus Scripture says: "Israel came forth from Egypt *hamushim*" (Ex. 13:18), read as "fifty-fold." It was through *binah* that the miracle took place. But afterwards this enlightenment was taken away from them and they were commanded to count out the forty-nine *'omer* days, in which each quality would be specifically addressed. Then, on Shavu'ot, they reached the fiftieth gate. So [at the Exodus] there was *gadlut* before *katnut.* Thus far his teaching....

Now it is taught that the patriarchs fulfilled the Torah before it was given. Jacob effected *tefillin* through the setting out of sticks, and so forth. This means that they fulfilled the inner Torah through different acts of worship, less constricted than the Torah is for us, [filled with] restrictions and measures.

This is the meaning of the wise child's question. **"What are these testimonies, statutes, and judgments that Y-H-W-H our God has commanded you?"** He experiences himself as in *gadlut,* having attained this state of expanded mind on Pesah. So from there he objects: "What are these testimonies and statutes?" Why is the Torah so constricted into rules and regulations commanded by God? It should be possible to fulfill the inward Torah through other acts of devotion, just as our ancestors did before the Torah was given.

Then you have to answer the child by laying out the full practice of Passover. Explain fully the reason why it is called Pesah, because of that great enlightenment that took place without the prior *katnut* stages. And that is why *eyn maftirin,* "you cannot be released from the obligation," of carrying out all the commandments and statutes that Y-H-W-H has given us in such constricted form. Why? Because after the Pesah comes *afikoman,* namely the taking away of that great first revelation of expanded consciousness. *Afiko* [in Aramaic] means "going out" or removal of the *man,* the manna or "bread that comes down from heaven." Right after Pesah this is taken away from us and we enter the stages of *katnut,* needing to fulfill the commandments in their present constricted state.

This is the question of the wise son, seeing himself with this expanded mind.

This is a classic statement of the great tension felt throughout these early Hasidic teachings between the grand inward moment of transformed insight and the hard struggle to improve one's moral life, step by difficult step. The wise son has indeed reached a great spiritual "high" during the *seder,* somehow reexperiencing that which happened at the original Exodus moment. Such events within the spirit are indeed possible. They may inspire us greatly, but they do not release us from the obligation of the other part of what religious life is all about.

Tif'eret 'Uziel

> This *matsah* that we eat.... These bitter herbs....
> (Passover Haggadah)

Why is *matsah* explained before *maror*? The bitter herbs recall the exile of Egypt, while *matsah* recalls the liberation that came afterwards.... Shouldn't the order be reversed? Indeed there are some sources that do so.

Yet our version seems to have it right. When you are in the midst of bondage and engaged in backbreaking labor, you do not realize how much your body is broken. Only when you rest do you feel the toll that your labor has taken.

As long as Israel were in Egypt, hard at labor, they did not feel the pain of their toil or the damage it was doing to their limbs. They were working day and night, with no chance to rest at all. Only when their labors ceased did they realize the price they had paid, how their limbs were broken. The arranger of the Haggadah understood this, placing *matsah* first and *maror* after it....

A bit of wisdom that is well confirmed by tales of American slavery, in the memory of Holocaust survivors, and by many others.

Me'or 'Eynayim (Adapted from *Va-Era* in *Haggadah shel Pesah im Perush Arba'ah Ofaney ha-Kodesh*)

> In every generation you should see yourself as though you personally had come out of Egypt ... not only our ancestors were redeemed from Egypt, but we with them.
> (Passover Haggadah)

Every year there is an exodus from Egypt. Every person has to go through certain trials. Even after you have accepted God intellectually, you still need to be tried ten times. This process is first recorded with Abraham, who withstood them all (m. Avot 5:3). The trial means that your sense of personal connection to God, which had been based on intellect, is taken away from you. In the moment of trial all you have left is the power to choose. Without this removal of awareness, there would be no test, for surely the righteous, maintaining this connection, would hold fast to their ways. But in the trial their awareness is diminished, though not removed entirely. If you withstand your trials, it is due to what was fixed in your heart beforehand, when your awareness was strong.

When Israel were in Egypt, awareness itself was in exile. The shell, which preceded the fruit, served to cover it. This is the hard shell of the nut spoken of by Scripture in "I went down into the garden of nuts" (Song 6:11), referring to the exile in Egypt. The nut has a hard outer shell and several finer membranes inside it, hiding the meat within. The hard outer shell was broken in Egypt, so that we can see the food inside. The thin membranes are still there, until our messiah comes (speedily, in our day!). But the essential fact of hiding has been revealed.

The word *mitsrayim*, "Egypt," is made up of *metsar yam*, "the narrow strait of the sea." "Sea" refers to the Sea of Wisdom, whence our awareness comes. Even today, a person who has no awareness [of Y-H-W-H] still dwells in the straits, not yet having entered into the Sea of Wisdom.

That is why the Haggadah says: **Not only our ancestors were redeemed from Egypt, but we with them**. Every year we go forth from Egypt. But the "wicked," those who have no awareness, have not yet left Egypt. That is why the wicked son says: "'What is this service to you?' To you, but not to him." Because he has no awareness, he objects to the service of Y-H-W-H. "And you are to say to him ... for had he been there, he would not have been redeemed." Even today he lives in an "Egypt" of the mind.

Here, as so frequently in the Hasidic sources, exodus from Egypt is depicted as a challenge, rather than a fact to be taken for granted. Pesah is thus both a joyous holiday, rejoicing in the reality of our liberation, and a question put to each of us. "Have you really come out of your own trials, your own Egypt of the mind?" Has your awareness of Y-H-W-H served to make you free?

Shavu'ot

Torat ha-Maggid (from the Manuscript of R. Shmelke)

> Everyone agrees that the Torah was given on Shabbat....
>
> (b. Shabbat 86b)

Our sages taught: "Torah was given only to those who eat the manna" (*Tanhuma Be-Shalah* 20).

Moses received the Torah. In the great clarity of his mind he indeed took it all in within those forty days. Our sages said that he kept learning and forgetting it until it was finally given to him as a gift. They also said that it takes forty years for a student to truly understand his teacher's mind.

This was why God had to rain food down on us from heaven. He makes Shabbat flow down upon us, giving us spiritual sustenance as a gift. Understanding of Torah comes to us as "food" as well. The *Zohar* says (2:60b) that even now food that is consumed by a true sage is not just corporeal, but includes a subtle spiritual essence. That spirit derives from Torah, since "man does not live by bread alone, but by all that comes forth from the mouth of Y-H-W-H" (Deut. 8:3). This refers to the divine word by which the food itself was created. That word is the Torah, which flows on to us all; we are nourished by the spirit of Torah.

This is the meaning of "Three who sit at the table and speak over it words of Torah, it as though they ate at the table of the Everpresent" (m. Avot 3:3).... Everything contains Torah ... the true sage can attain Torah through his food; the eating itself is engaging with Torah. The word *shulhan* ("table") can be derived from "sends fifty" (*shole'ah nun*) the fifty measures of wisdom that God sends to awaken us to purify ourselves....

This is also the meaning of "Had He fed us the manna but not brought us to Mount Sinai, it would have been enough" (Passover Haggadah). We would have acquired Torah as we ate the manna. Just being fed the manna would have been enough.

On our own, we are not truly able to grasp Torah. It would take us decades to sharpen our minds; only Moses was able to receive it in the course of a forty-day fast. For the rest of us, God has to bestow it upon us like a gift, coming down like the *sukkah* of peace that flows over us on Shabbat or the food we ingest at a holy table.

It is worth recalling here that most of the texts in this volume are *Tischreden*, talks given at the table in the course of a meal. The two great activities of our highly oral Jewish culture are thus deeply linked to one another. Here is a rare articulation of that truth. But it is hard for a reader living amid a Christian culture (as did the Maggid!) not to compare this sort of insight to the experience of Eucharistic theology. As Jews we will never understand what a Christian experiences in the act of ingesting "the body of Christ." But here it is claimed that *all* the food taken in by the person of true spiritual insight is in fact a way of ingesting God's spirit, that ever-present creative word of Torah. This can be seen as an authentic "incarnational theology" within Judaism.

Or ha-Me'ir

> Y-H-W-H said to Moses: "Behold I will come to you in a thick cloud, so that the people will listen when I speak to you."
> (Ex. 19:9)

In *Parashat Va-Ethanan* it says: Face to face Y-H-W-H spoke to you from amidst the fire. "I stood between Y-H-W-H and you at that time to tell you the word of Y-H-W-H, for you feared the fire and did not ascend the mountain—(Y-H-W-H spoke) saying: I am Y-H-W-H your God ..." (Deut. 5:4–6).

This means as follows: Moses our Teacher had so purified and clarified his own bodily self that God could have shown him the power of Torah with full clarity, without any "garbing" or diminution of intensity. Our sages were stirred to comment on the verse "He is the most faithful of all My house" (Num. 12:7, referring to Moses) that he knew the permutations of letters by which heaven and earth had been created. He had the ability within his hands to create worlds, but nevertheless "he was the most faithful of all My house" [i.e., he did not use his potentially magical powers].

But if that is the case, why did the blessed Holy One dress up the brilliant light of Torah in stories, until it became something like tales one person would tell another?

Elsewhere I have commented on the verse "Y-H-W-H spoke to Moses face to face, like one [person] would speak to another" (Ex. 33:11). This means that God garbed the powerful light of Torah in "face" after "face." There are in fact seventy "faces" of Torah.

In its original state it was just a clear light, comprising holy names, all of them none other than the single blessed name Y-H-W-H. That is why Torah is referred to as "the keepings [*pekudey*] of Y-H-W-H" (Ps. 19:9), because all the teachings and narratives are really kept and hidden within that single name. But God dressed them up in face after face, so that they now appear to be the sort of tales one person would tell another. But in truth the *opening* of her words would shine a brilliant light....

Sometimes a marvelous bit of wisdom falls into an intelligent person's mind, something that contains a real insight into understanding God. But when you try to share that thought with another person, you are unable to reveal the wisdom that lies buried deep within your own heart. It would just be too subtle for them to understand. You therefore have to dress it up as a comment on a biblical verse or some saying of the sages. For this purpose one can employ any of the four ways of reading Scripture: the obvious, the allegorical, the homiletical, or the esoteric. Those people in any case will not be able to grasp the depth of your thoughts, however they are garbed. They therefore pay attention only to the garments themselves. "How well this one preaches! How nicely this one speaks!" They are just too unaware to pay attention to that wonderful inner wisdom and the good counsel for serving God that they could be finding in the multiple levels of his preaching.

Our holy Torah herself is in the same situation. Her words as open in their own setting indeed shine a high and lofty light, but one so subtle that "thought cannot grasp it at all." But when the time came for the [ten] words [or "commandments"] to be revealed in the holy event at Sinai, they had to be garbed in the outer meanings and narrative tales of Torah....

This is true even of the prophets, of whom we are told that "they had the great merit of depicting the human form to be like its Maker" (*Bereshit Rabbah* 27:1). They still did not have the power to see Torah clearly, without its being dressed up in visual forms and images. Moses alone, "most faithful of all My house," was greater than the rest and could look directly into the shining light.... He "heard the voice speaking to him" (Num. 7:89), in a spiritual manner that needed no covering up ... in stories.

But this was to be "the Torah that Moses placed before the Children of Israel" (Deut. 4:44), and the whole people did not have the strength to perceive in their learning the light of Torah in its own intensely spiritual core. God nevertheless sought their good and wanted to give this precious vessel to the entire people. That is why Scripture tells us: **Behold I will come to you in a thick cloud**. The whole Torah, with its point of departure of the word *anokhi* ("I am"), will come to you ... clothed and with reduced intensity, all for the sake of this holy people in its entirety, since they are not prepared to receive Torah in its clear state. **So that the people will listen when I speak to you**. They will hear and understand the Ten Commandments, each in accord with their own levels of personal purity and the ability of each soul to hold fast to the letters of Torah.

This bittersweet comment on the revelation to Moses is also a statement of the Hasidic *tsaddik*'s own role as mystic and communal leader. The *Or ha-Me'ir*, one of the most intellectually rarified thinkers within this circle, might have preferred to seek out the Torah of pure light and permutations of letters. But the Torah he needs to receive is one that he can "place before the people," a Torah dressed up in attractive parables and stories, one that every Jew could find a way to absorb.

The notion that "the Torah herself" has this same problem is quite a stunning formulation of the ongoing tension between the inward heart of Torah's teaching and the outer garb, including both narrative and ritual, that fills so much of the Torah text itself.

We too, as teachers within Judaism, have the same tension. So much of our energy has to go to just passing on the forms and seeing that they are preserved! How much of our attention are we free to devote to the heart of our message, one of personal uplifting and spiritual transformation? How might we right that balance?

Kedushat Levi I

> Our rabbis of blessed memory taught, "The Torah was given as black fire on white fire."
> (Devarim Rabbah 3:13)

One might say that this alludes to the fact that on account of *mattan Torah* ("the giving of the Torah") Israel possesses [great] power, as in the saying of our sages, "You decreed from below and the blessed Holy One will fulfill it from above" (b. Ta'anit 23a).

Now the color white includes all colors, for it absorbs all colors. This alludes to Y-H-W-H, who is inclusive of all.

This is not the case, however, with the color black, for it does not include the other colors—it is simply black [and excludes all light and color]. This alludes to the human being.

This is what it means that through *mattan Torah* the Children of Israel merited that the black fire would be "on"—that is to say, *above*—the white fire; Israel would be above [God], so to speak. The words of Israel would be more operative than the words of the Divine; as in the saying of the rabbis, "The blessed Holy One makes a decree, and the *tsaddik* annuls it" (b. Mo'ed Katan 16b).

To celebrate Shavu'ot fully means that we recognize the great power we have to shape God's Torah in this world. While God's teaching is forever greater and more glorious than ours—containing the full color spectrum—the Divine wishes for us to take ownership of it. Every year on this festival, we renew our commitment to the covenant by thanking God for this loving and awesome gift and recommitting ourselves to the great responsibility it implies, that of fashioning lives of Torah, knowing that our attempts are always imperfect.

We of the "black fire" keep out much of the divine radiance, allowing ourselves to survive by hiding the great light, but also creating a Torah appropriate to the dimly lit world in which real people live.

Kedushat Levi II

I was asked in the province of Lithuania why the holiday of Shavu'ot is also called 'Atseret (Assembly). Is it not the case that only the holiday of Shemini 'Atseret [following Sukkot] is called by this name (Num. 29:35)?

... This follows the words of Nahmanides (Jacob bar Sheshet, *Sefer ha-Emunah ve'-ha-Bitahon*, ch. 19), who commented on the verse "Do not arouse or awaken love until it so desires" (Song 2:7). He said that when you are aroused by the love or fear of the blessed Creator, you should be careful to immediately create a vessel. That is, as soon as possible, carry out a *mitsvah*—give charity, sit and study, etc. For it is known that an arousal that comes to one suddenly is a light emanating from above as is called "soul." You must clothe it in a "body" so that it has strength and a foundation so that it [will] not be misdirected, heaven forbid, as is known to those of spiritual understanding.

Now this is the meaning of the verse "Do not arouse or awaken love until it so desires." The word *hefets* can be read as "desire" or as "vessel." Meaning, the arousal that comes upon you needs to immediately become [be placed in] a vessel—this is the [alternative] meaning of "until it so desires [*'ad she-tehpats*]." Here I conclude my paraphrase of Nahmanides's interpretation.

Now at the time of the giving of the Torah, when Israel certainly experienced a great arousal, they did not have a single *mitsvah* to serve as a vessel. Therefore, we must say that they carried out the *mitsvah* of *hagbalah*, setting limits around the mountain, which Moses had warned them not to touch (Ex. 19:12). They stopped themselves (*ne'etsarim*) from touching it, and by enacting this *mitsvah* they created a vessel for the arousal. It is for this reason that Shavu'ot is also called by the name 'Atseret (Assembly or "Stoppage").

The Berdichever here reminds us of the importance of channeling our spiritual impulses into concrete acts of goodness and righteousness. We need to be mindful in moments of arousal to direct these surges of energy appropriately. Using a teaching attributed to one of his favorite medieval commentators, Nahmanides, R. Levi Yitshak explains that even in the moment of the great revelation at Sinai—before the Israelites were given the *mitsvot*—they sought to create a holy vessel for themselves by adhering to Moses's instruction to set a limit around the mountain. In so doing, they shaped a space into which God's great flow could be contained and actualized.

'Avodat Yisra'el I

> In the third month after the Children of Israel had left Egypt, on that day they came to the wilderness of Sinai.
>
> (Ex. 19:1)

The third "month" (*hodesh*) can also be read as "the third renewal [*hithadshut*]." First God took them forth from the iron furnace of Egypt, and they ate those *matsah* loaves they had brought out of Egypt, tasting in them the taste of manna. Then they rose higher, and God actually brought both bread and meat down from heaven for them. Now they were at their third renewal, moving still higher, and they drew near to Mount Sinai to receive the holy Torah.

The zodiac sign of this month is Gemini, the twins. This indicates that the blessed Holy One and those who do His will are like twins, as it were. Scientists tell us that if one twin falls ill, the other feels it as well. If one improves, so does the other, since they stand under the same sign, having been born at the same time.

The same is true of our blessed Creator and those who do His will, as it were. They too are twins. That is why we are called *yisra'el*, which can be read as *yashar el*, "straight with God," meaning equal with God. [The letters of *yisra'el* may also be read as] *rosh li*, "I have a head."

Thus they drew near to Mount Sinai in the third month. The blessed Holy One was revealed and spoke to them the way a man speaks to his brother, for they were together under the sign of twins.

Astrological symbolism has a long history among Jewish thinkers and is occasionally found in Hasidic sources. One major Hasidic work of the generation following the teachings recorded here (*Beney Yissakhar* by R. Tsevi Elimelekh of Dynow) is entirely based on this heritage.

The description of God and Israel as "twins" may seem surprising, but it too has an ancient history. The prohibition of leaving the corpse of an executed convict hanging overnight (Deut. 21:23) is explained by a parable of a king whose twin brother became a bandit and was executed. The sight of the degraded corpse would be an insult to the king's image, because every human being—even the worst among us—is made in the image of God.

'Avodat Yisra'el II

> Moses took the people forth toward God [*elohim*] from the camp, and they stood at the base of the mountain.
>
> (Ex. 19:17)

The Midrash says that on the day the Torah was given the people sought to doze off in the morning (*Pirkey de-Rabbi Eliezer* 40). They were sleeping sweetly until Moses awakened them to receive the Torah.

The *tsaddik* R. Levi Yitshak taught: God forbid that we should think the holy people were just lazy and fell asleep on that glorious day when they knew that God was about to give them His Torah! Surely their intent was for the sake of heaven. Ever since the second day of Sivan (four days earlier) they had been preparing to receive the Torah. They put so much effort into their holy thoughts that they had simply become exhausted. Now they feared that they would not be able to receive the Torah with the proper clear mind. They gave their eyes some rest so that their minds would be refreshed and they would regain the strength and clarity needed to accept the holy Torah. Thus far his words.

Reading the Torah simply, we are told that **Moses took the people forth**. "People" generally refers to the ordinary folk. It is indeed imaginable that they were sleeping until Moses woke them up in order to take them forth toward God. Even if that *hasid* was right in saying that their intentions were good, it is still clear that these folks were not on a very high level. One who truly trusts in God does not need such preparation. Such a person goes forth strongly, based on trust, toward the service of God. You trust that heaven's mercies will grant you the strength and clarity you need. But if you are not closely attached to God, you lack that trust. Then you need to rely on the way of nature. You preserve your mental powers, being sure to get proper sleep and all the rest, instead of casting your entire burden on Y-H-W-H and paying no attention to your own physical welfare.

We know that whatever a person thinks, says, or does down here arouses those same qualities above. Therefore we read that **Moses took the *people* forth**. These were the ones who remained on a lower rung. They wanted take care of their minds and get enough sleep, all in a natural way. Moses awakened them and took them forth **toward *elohim***. The word *elohim* has the same numerical value as "the nature." Since their path was that of nature, it was the name *elohim* that was aroused in response.

This is the meaning of **they stood at the base of the mountain**—on a low rung.

The Hasidic masters, fully engaged in the work of reaching out to “the people,” understand full well that it is not an easy task. You want to bring them along to the top of your mountain, but they are simply not prepared to go there. They are in fact “asleep” at a moment when you are more than wide awake. The best you can do is to bring them forth to a level of religious awareness that fits with their state of mind, one in which nature reveals itself to be identical with the divine presence within it. For them that “low rung” is itself quite a climb.

Tish'ah be-Av

Or ha-Me'ir (from *Devarim*)

The sages taught, "Align your heart [during prayer] toward the Holy of Holies" (m. Berakhot 4:5). Their intent was to teach us that a person's form and its limbs correspond to the structure of the Tabernacle and the number of its holy vessels.

It follows that you must put your *middot* (moral qualities) in order and build yourself up as a complete structure from head to toe, in order to align yourself with the Temple. Then doing something repugnant won't even occur to you, since you have become mindful of the great sanctity of the Holy of Holies. No impure forces may come into that space. Even the high priest entered it only once a year to perform the service [of Yom Kippur]. This is how you sanctify your heart, which corresponds to the Holy of Holies. Your heart is indeed a *mishkan*, a dwelling-place for holiness....

Now you will see the insight in the sages' teaching: "If the Temple is not rebuilt in your days, it is as if it were destroyed in your days" (y. Yoma 1:1) ... you should see the Temple rebuilt in your improved actions and upright qualities, the way you should act all of your days, thus building up your form and constructing the *mishkan* with all of its vessels. If not, it is as though your wicked ways have razed the seat of God's holiness.

You have destroyed *your* Temple, composed of your body and limbs.

A person has both interior [organs] and exterior limbs. So too were there vessels for the inner and outer areas of the Temple. All of these allude to lights above, both inner and outer, as is obvious to all those who know the holy books. The works of Creation allude to these lights as well. These three parallel structures are really one: the works of Creation, the structure of the Tabernacle, and the form of a person. Through their single form the divine presence is revealed in the physical world....

If you are fickle, taking no notice of your deeds, and do not contemplate mending your ways and realizing God through each of your limbs and physical senses, you will have an improper number of limbs ... if you diminish one limb of your own form, you will also be denying its parallel the structure of world, and the Temple will lack one vessel or have one too many ... this is the reason that [the] Temple was destroyed by Israel's sins—as long as their flaws remained, the structure of the Temple had to be destroyed and some of its sacred vessels were missing....

The threefold parallel between self, world, and Tabernacle goes back to Midrashic sources and was a favorite of such medieval preachers as Rabbi Bahya of Barcelona, one surely read by the Hasidic authors. For the *Or ha-Me'ir*, the force of this analogy was that of self and Temple, referring to the "Temple" of the cosmic structure above. To our ears, however, the soul/world parallel is one we ignore at our peril. The selfishness or unconcern of my inner life certainly has implications for the planet, especially if I am part of a society so fully engaged in overconsumption and destruction as is ours.

Me'or 'Eynayim (from *Ha'azinu*)

> After the destruction of the Temple Rabbi Yohanan ben Zakkai instituted that the *lulav* be taken all seven days—a way of remembering the Temple.
>
> (B. Sukkah 41a)

> To speak Your kindness in the morning, and Your faithfulness at night.
>
> (Ps. 92:3)

It is a *mitsvah* to do things to remember the Temple, even if today it lies in ruins. The idea is thus: When you are uplifted and on a very high rung, utterly connected to the blessed One, you are referred to as the "Temple," as it says, "*they* are the Temple" (Jer. 7:4), and it says, "He set His tent within man" (Ps. 78:60). Falling from this level is called the "destruction" of the Temple. Yet even when you fall from your rung, you must be strong and keep striving for God where you are right now, just as you did when you were on a higher level. This is the meaning of **a way of remembering the Temple**—having faith that God is present on this lower rung as well, since there is no place devoid of Y-H-W-H.

This is the meaning of "From the rising [of the sun to its setting, the name of Y-H-W-H is praised]" (Ps. 113:3). "Rising" refers to the illuminated consciousness of a *tsaddik*, called the sun. "To its setting" describes the fall [from this level]. And yet through all this "the name Y-H-W-H is praised," by means of faith....

This is [the] meaning of **To speak**, which can also mean "to draw forth"; **in the morning**, at the time of illuminated consciousness, we can drawn forth God's kindness. **And Your faithfulness at night**, in the moments of darkness you must have faith. If you do so, you will be able to reach an even higher level afterward.

The BeSHT, whose soul is in Eden, used to give the following parable: A parent will sometimes teach a child to walk by walking ahead and calling out. When the child approaches, the parent continues on and walks a little farther away—then the child falls!

Why does the parent do this? If he didn't, the child would only be able to walk a short distance, but this way he grows sturdy on his legs and he continues to come closer and closer. The meaning of this is clear.

That we must continue to serve God from each and every spiritual rung, even the lower ones, is among of the *Me'or 'Eynayim*'s core ideas. His parable of the parent teaching his child to walk by strolling ahead of him is common in Hasidic texts, but this version has a rare additional detail: the child actually falls down. How fitting for Tish'ah be-Av, the day upon which the Temples were destroyed! The meaning is indeed clear: God is teaching us to walk, and falling down sometimes is a necessary part of becoming confident on our own two feet. This is true for us both as individuals and as a people.

'Avodat Yisra'el (from *Devarim*)

> Y-H-W-H builds Jerusalem....
> (Ps. 147:2)

It is odd that this verse is in the present tense. Had God said, "Jerusalem is to be rebuilt," surely "the counsel of Y-H-W-H would come to pass" (Prov. 19:21). The fact that it has not yet been built means that God has not yet brought this about for good. But how is the present tense appropriate?

It is known from holy books that the word *Yerushalayim* really means "complete awe [*yir'ah shalem*]." ... There in Jerusalem awe was indeed perfect, all of us together performing our Creator's will in a most mighty and awe-filled manner. But now that we are distanced from our land, we are unable to go up and regularly behold the face of Y-H-W-H. Due to our many sins, the evil urge hides from us the awesome light of Y-H-W-H. Therefore every one of us has to rise up against our own urge, strengthening the bonds of love and awe, binding us to Jerusalem the holy city. This is the reason we pray facing east, focusing on Jerusalem, as the sages taught (b. Berakhot 30a). When we all manage to awaken that love and properly weave the threads of grace into the ropes of perfect awe, we will merit to witness the rebuilding of our city of holiness and glory.

This is what King David meant in saying: "Rebuilt Jerusalem is like a city drawn together" (Ps. 122:3). It will be the drawing together of Israel and their reawakening of love and awe that will rebuild Jerusalem. [He goes on to say:] "Where the tribes [*shevatim*, also can mean 'staffs'] went up." It is the bonds of love and awe, linked [as staffs to one another] in our hearts that form the Jerusalem of the heart. Those links bind us also to Jerusalem the holy city....

"Y-H-W-H your God has blessed you in all the work of your hands, knowing how you have walked across this great desert" (Deut. 2:7). This portion is always read in the nine days between the New Moon of Av and Tish'ah be-Av. It reminds us in several ways of how we have wandered from place to place, Y-H-W-H our God always having been with us. Even as we walk through the "straits" that mark this period, Y-H-W-H will not abandon His people and His inheritance. As Y-H-W-H led us through that desert, a place no person had ever crossed, Scripture saying, "Y-H-W-H walked before them (Ex. 13:21)," so too in these days, which are also considered a desert, the valley of death's shadow. Of this the psalm says: "Even as I walk through the valley of death's shadow, I will fear no evil, for You are with me" (Ps. 23:4)....

This teaching is a strong statement of Judaism's faith. Indeed the true Jerusalem is that of the heart, and it is by our own inner processes of love and awe that it must come together. But it is also the reawakened unity of Israel that is part of this process, our tribes or "staffs" joined together as one. When that fullest expression of renewed bonds of love takes place, the real this-worldly Jerusalem—which we have never abandoned—will be rebuilt as well.

The second section of this teaching applies in a different way to the long journey we four have taken together in the composing of this book. As we come to its end, there is a postpartum moment of seeing the emptiness, a "valley" crossed by death's shadow, before us. We too have faith that Y-H-W-H is with us there, too, and will yet bring us before another mountain.

Sources and Authors

'Avodat Yisra'el (1842). **Yisrael Hopstein "the Maggid" of Kozhnits** (Kozienice 1733–1814).

As a young man he met the Maggid, later studying with both Levi Yitshak of Berdyczow and Elimelekh of Lezajsk. He was an erudite scholar of traditional rabbinics and Kabbalah (both theoretical and practical), as well as a prolific author and collector of manuscripts. Founded one of the most important Polish Hasidic dynasties.

Beit Aharon (1875). **Aharon "the Great" of Karlin** (1736–1772).

First of the Maggid's students to bring Hasidism to northern Belorussia and Lithuania, where he established himself as a leader in the early 1760s. Early documents from that region refer to all *hasidim* as "Karliner." *Beit Aharon* was written and published by Aharon II of Karlin (1802–1872), the grandson of Aharon "the Great," and the work contains teachings from the leaders of the first three generations of Karliner Hasidism. The dynasty has continued to this day.

Beit Rabbi (1902). **Hayyim Meir Heilman.**

Work of internal HaBaD historiography that chronicles the first three generations of the movement's leadership. While sometimes considered tendentious by scholars, it records much early memory from sources otherwise lost.

Dibrat Shelomoh (1848). Shelomoh of Lutsk (d. 1813).

Close disciple of the Maggid, whom he quotes frequently throughout this work. He did not have a circle of disciples, but he played an important role in the spread of Hasidism and the birth of Hasidic literature as an editor and printer of early Hasidic books, including *Maggid Devarav le-Ya'akov. Dibrat Shelomoh* was edited within the author's lifetime and printed after his death.

Divrey Emet (1831). Ya'akov Yitshak Horowitz, the "Hozeh (Seer) of Lublin" (1745–1815).

Important figure in the spread of Hasidism to Poland. He began as a disciple of the Maggid and then later studied with Elimelekh of Lezajsk, continuing to lead the circle of disciples after his death. His teachings highlight the role of the *tsaddik* as a miracle worker and intermediary capable of using material wealth in the service of God. This work was written by the Seer himself and printed after his death.

Ginzey Yosef (1792). Yosef Bloch.

Little is known about his life other than that he served as a rabbi and preacher in the communities of Olesk and Satinov and was a student of the Maggid as well as a halakhic scholar. His work received a large number of approbations from both Hasidic and non-Hasidic leaders.

Haggadah shel Pesah im Perush Arba'ah Ofaney ha-Kodesh (1938).

Collection of teachings adapted for the Haggadah from the works of four important leaders of the Chernobyl Hasidic dynasty, including its founders Menahem Nahum Twersky (see *Me'or 'Eynayim*) and his son Mordecai (Mottel).

Hayyim va-Hesed (1891). Hayyim Hayka of Amdur (d. 1787).

Known for being an ascetic, this disciple of the Maggid inherited the more radically mystical and spiritual aspects of his teacher's thought. He was among the early Hasidic leaders in Lithuania, where he remained despite the intense protestations and excommunications levied by the *mitnaggedim*. This book also includes some of the Maggid's *hanhagot* (religious instructions) held in manuscript by Hayyim Hayka.

Hesed le-Avraham ha-Malakh (1851). **Avraham ben Dov Baer of Miedzyrzec** (1741–1776).

Small collection of teachings attributed to the Maggid's son, who was an intensely ascetic, pietistic, and retreating individual. Often printed together with *Hesed le-Avraham Kalisker*.

Hesed le-Avraham Kalisker (1851). **Avraham of Kalisk** (1741–1810).

Controversial figure whose group of disciples were reputedly boisterous and raucous during prayer, inciting the wrath of *mitnaggedim*. He accompanied Menahem Mendel of Vitebsk on his immigration to the Land of Israel in 1777, where he took over as leader of the small Hasidic community in 1787. He was a fierce opponent of Shne'ur Zalman of Lyady's *Likkutey Amarim/Tanya*, which he condemned as an improper mix of Kabbalistic and Hasidic spirituality. *Hesed le-Avraham Kalisker* is often printed together with *Hesed le-Avraham ha-Malakh*.

Kedushat Levi (1798, 1811). **Levi Yitshak of Berdyczow** (1740–1809).

Rabbi of Ryczwol, Zelichow, Pinsk, and Berdyczow. A leading figure in the spread of Hasidism and the struggle with the *mitnaggedim*, he was known as an advocate for ordinary Jews and for responding to their needs. He was possibly the editor of some recensions of the Maggid's writings.

Likkutey Maharin (1811). **Yisrael ben Levi Yitshak** (d. 1818).

Teachings from the son of Levi Yitshak of Berdyczow, who often quotes teachings in the name of his father (see *Kedushat Levi*).

Likkutim Yekarim (1792).

Early collection of Hasidic teachings from the Ba'al Shem Tov, the Maggid, Menahem Mendel of Premyshlan, and Yehiel Mikhel of Zloczow. Edited by Meshulam Feibush Heller of Zbararz (see *Yosher Divrey*

Emet). Though most of the material is unattributed to any particular master, the majority of the book reflects the thought of the Maggid.

Ma'amarey Admor ha-Zaken (1981). Shne'ur Zalman of Lyady (see _Torah Or_).

Short teachings from earlier in the author's career; recently printed from an early manuscript.

Ma'ayan ha-Hokhmah (1817). Asher Tsevi of Ostrog (d. 1817).

Rabbi and preacher in communities of Barzdov, Ostrog, and later Korzec. This volume was printed within the author's lifetime.

Maggid Devarav le-Ya'akov (1781). Dov Baer Friedman of Miedzyrzec (1704–1772).

The first and most important collection of the Maggid's teachings. It was assembled from manuscripts by Shelomoh of Lutsk and was the third Hasidic book ever printed.

Me'or 'Eynayim (1798). Menahem Nahum Twersky of Chernobyl (1730–1797).

Founded one of the most important Ukrainian Hasidic dynasties. He was a disciple of the Ba'al Shem Tov as well as the Maggid, and his teachings fuse the Maggid's mystical, contemplative approach with the BeSHT's embrace of the physical world as an avenue for divine service.

Mevasser Tsedek (1798). Yissakhar Dov of Zloczow (d. 1795).

Influenced by both the Ba'al Shem Tov and the Maggid, he quotes frequently from the Maggid's other students as well. He moved to Safed shortly before he died. His book *Bat 'Ayni*, on selected parts of the Talmud and *Shulhan 'Arukh,* was published in 1798 as well.

No'am Elimelekh **(1788). Elimelekh of Lizhensk (1717–1787).**

Brother of the famous Zusya of Hanipoli. Though the author died rather early in the history of Hasidism, his teachings were extremely influential, particularly regarding the figure of the *tsaddik*. He believed that the *tsaddik* is not inherently different from others but arrives at that high level by intense spiritual work. Many of the leaders of the fourth generation of Hasidism emerged from his circle. This classic work is considered a veritable "handbook for *tsaddikim.*"

Or ha-Emet **(1899). Dov Baer Friedman of Miedzyrzec (see *Maggid Devarav le-Ya'akov*).**

Printed from an early manuscript of the Maggid's teachings copied from one held by Levi Yitshak of Berdichev.

Or ha-Ganuz la-Tsaddikim **(1800). Aharon ha-Kohen of Apta (c. 1803).**

Student of 'Uziel Meizels and leader of the community in Zelichow nearly thirty-five years after Levi Yitshak was expelled. He was a devoted student of the Ba'al Shem Tov's spiritual path and often quotes in his name teachings that are elsewhere attributed to the Maggid. As the editor of a number of early Hasidic books, including the popular anthology *Keter Shem Tov* (1796), he played an important role in the emergence of Hasidic texts.

Or ha-Me'ir **(1798). Ze'ev Wolf of Zhytomir (d. 1797).**

One of the senior figures in the Maggid's circle. His was a voice that bore both a strong mystical message and a note of dissent. He was fiercely critical of sham piety and populist styles of leadership that catered to the masses, favoring a more elitist approach to the spread of Hasidic faith.

Or Peney Mosheh (1810, 1904). **Mosheh Sofer of Przeworsk** (d. 1806).

A professional scribe (*sofer*) whose ritual articles were highly prized by Hasidic masters. This work has the greatest number of appropriations of any early Hasidic book.

Or Torah (1804). **Dov Baer Friedman of Miedzyrzec** (see *Maggid Devarav le-Ya'akov*).

Collection of the Maggid's teaching arranged according to the order of the Torah readings. It has significant overlap with *Maggid Devarav le-Ya'akov*, but this text includes original material from the Maggid found nowhere else.

Orah le-Hayyim (1816). **Avraham Hayyim of Zloczow** (1750–1816).

Disciple of Yehiel Mikhel of Zloczow and Shmu'el Shmelke as well as the Maggid. He married the daughter of Yissakhar Dov of Zloczow after the death of his first wife, the daughter of Pinhas Horowitz. He served as a rabbi in Zeburov before assuming the rabbinate of Zloczow after his father-in-law emigrated to the Land of Israel. He himself prepared his manuscript for printing.

Panim Yafot (1825). **Pinhas Horowitz** (1730–1805).

Brother of Shmu'el Shmelke and one of the earliest students of the Maggid, whose influence on his thought is clear even when not cited by name. He served as rabbi of Vitkov, Lekhovits, and Frankfurt. The important anti-reformist leader Mosheh Sofer, known as the Hatam Sofer, was one of his students. This work is the third and final section of a larger work known as *Ha-Fla'ah*, which includes *Ha-Ketuvah* (on Tractate Ketubot) and *Ha-Makneh* (on Tractate Kiddushin).

Peri ha-Arets (1814). **Menahem Mendel of Vitebsk** (1730–1787).

Leader of Hasidism in White Russia, he led the Hasidic immigration to Tiberias in 1777 in the wake of persecution by the *mitnaggedim*. His teachings as preserved are quite complicated and emphasize *devekut* as the ultimate goal of religious life. He was the teacher of Avraham of Kalisk and Shne'ur Zalman of Lyady. This volume includes a substantial number of letters sent to his followers who had remained in Eastern Europe, through which he attempted to remain leader of Belorussian Hasidism even from a distance.

Peri Hayyim (1873). **Avraham Hayyim of Zloczow** (see *Orah le-Hayyim*).

Commentary on the Passover Haggadah.

Rav Yeevi (1792). **Ya'akov Yosef of Ostrog** (1738–1790).

Close student of the Maggid and others who had been associated with the BeSHT. He became the preacher and rabbi of Ostrog after his father died in 1766. He was deeply critical of rabbinic leadership and the empty casuistic style of learning. He did not emphasize the role of *tsaddik*. This popular book is filled with quotations of early proto-Hasidic masters, including the BeSHT, Menahem Mendel of Bar, and Nahman of Kossov.

She'erit Yisra'el (1955). **Levi Yitshak of Berdyczow** (see *Kedushat Levi*).

Published in the twentieth century from an early manuscript passed down within Hasidic families. Excerpts are reprinted in *Yalkut Kedushat Levi* (2004).

Shemen ha-Tov (1925). **Shmu'el Shmelke Horowitz of Nikolsburg** (1726–1778).

Brother of Pinhas Horowitz. He studied in Lithuanian *yeshivot* and was brought to the Maggid by Avraham of Kalisk. He served as rabbi of Ryczywol, where he established a yeshivah, and later of Sienewa. In 1773 he became the leader of the Jewish community in Nikolsburg, Moravia, a city far to the west of the Hasidic heartland. He was responsible for attracting many students to the Maggid's table, including Levi Yitshak of Berdyczow. This work is a late compendium of stories and teachings passed down both orally and in manuscript.

Shemu'ah Tovah (1938).

Published very late from an early manuscript, this text represents the teachings of the Maggid as they were transcribed by either Levi Yitshak of Berdyczow or one of his students. While many of these have parallels in other collections of the Maggid's thought, the work also includes a significant amount of original material never before printed.

Siddur ha-Rav (*Tefillot mi-Kol ha-Shanah,* 1816). **Shne'ur Zalman of Lyady** (see *Torah Or*).

Mystical commentary on the liturgy for the entire year, including lengthy essays on many aspects of the daily and yearly liturgical calendar. It was printed with Shne'ur Zalman's unique version of the prayerbook text and liturgical practice, according to the Kabbalistic teachings of Rabbi Isaac Luria (*Nusah ha-ARI*).

Siftey Tsaddikim (1864). **Pinhas Lerner of Dinovitz.**

Selected teachings of early Hasidic masters, including R. Abraham Joshua Heschel of Apt. Written in the 1820s but published much later. Not to be confused with two later collections of Hasidic tales bearing the same title.

Teshu'ot Hen (1816). **Gedaliyah Rabinovits of Linits** (1738–1804).

Disciple of the Ba'al Shem Tov as well as the Maggid. He took his first rabbinic job in Ostropol when he was eighteen, then moved on to Mariapol and Linits. This volume is an important source for the material in *Shivhey ha-BeSHT.*

Tif'eret 'Uziel (1863). **'Uziel Meizels** (1744–1785).

One of the first leaders of Hasidism in Poland. He first met the Ba'al Shem Tov in his youth, then studied with the Maggid for many years. He served as a rabbi in Neustadt, Ostrowtsa, and Ryczywol. His work quotes a number of the Maggid's other students. He is well known as a Talmudic scholar and author of several halakhic works.

Torah Or (1836). **Shne'ur Zalman of Lyady** (1747–1812).

Compilation of lengthy, rather involved sermons by the founder of the HaBaD Hasidic dynasty in White Russia. A student of the Maggid and subsequently Menahem Mendel of Vitebsk, he was the most important leader in that area in the 1790s and first decade of the nineteenth century. His most famous work is *Likkutey Amarim/Tanya* (1796), the first book of systematic Hasidic theology, but he also wrote a compendium of Jewish law known as *Shulhan 'Arukh ha-Rav* (1814). Other sermons on the Torah and holidays are found in *Likkutey Torah* (1848) and in the manuscripts published in the recent series *Ma'amarey Admor ha-Zaken* (1958).

Torat ha-Maggid (1968). **Dov Baer Friedman of Miedzyrzec** (see *Maggid Devarav le-Ya'akov*).

Teachings of the Maggid as quoted in the writings attributed to him and works of his disciples. Collected and printed by Israel Klapholts, it includes texts in manuscript held by Hayyim Hayka of Amdur (see *Hayyim va-Hesed*) and Shmu'el Shmelke of Nikolsburg (see *Shemen ha-Tov*).

Torey Zahav (1816). **Binyamin ben Aharon of Zalocze** (d. 1791).

Preacher and prolific writer. While he does not seem to have taken an active role in spreading Hasidism, he often quotes from the early Hasidic masters and especially from his teacher the Maggid. He was the author of a number of other works, including *Amtahat Binyamin* (on Ecclesiastes, 1796), *Helkat Binyamin* (on the Passover Haggadah, 1794), and *Ahavat Dodim* (on Song of Songs, 1793).

Tsemah ha-Shem li-Tsevi (1818). **Tsevi Hirsh of Nadvorna** (c. 1740–1802).

Student of Yehiel Mikhel of Zloczow and Meshulam Feibush of Zbararz as well as the Maggid. He served as a rabbi and preacher in Dolina before moving to Nadvorna. His students included Tsevi Hirsh of Zydachov and Menahem Mendel of Kossov. He also wrote the enormously popular *Alpha Beta* (1790), a short moralistic tract that became one of the most frequently reprinted early Hasidic books.

Yesamah Lev (1798). Menahem Nahum of Chernobyl (see *Me'or 'Eynayim*).

Short commentary on Talmudic *aggadah* printed with *Me'or 'Eynayim.*

Yosher Divrey Emet (1800). Meshulam Feibush Heller of Zbarash (1740–1795).

Studied under Menahem Mendel of Premyshlan and Yehiel Mikhel of Zloczow in addition to the Maggid. The main body of the work consists of two lengthy, theologically rich letters written by Meshulam Feibush, and it is generally printed along with *Likkutim Yekarim.* His students included Ze'ev Wolf of Charny-Ostrog and Menahem Mendel of Kossov.

Afterword

As this project reaches completion, I find myself filled with both wonder and gratitude. I stand in awe at the marvelously rich quality and variety of Hasidic *derashot* that we were able to find and include in these volumes. Having loved and studied these materials over the course of half a century, I still felt excited and uplifted by many a new discovery as we set about seeking materials for this volume. Having restricted ourselves here to the Maggid's circle (slightly expanded), I continue to look forward to new discoveries as I examine other corners of the Hasidic imagination.

My gratitude is directed first to the One who has given me the health and vigor to complete this project. May I be granted the grace to continue with several more. I am grateful to my colleagues and students at Hebrew College, who have both given me the time to work on these sources and served on many occasions as "first readers" or listeners in formal and informal class settings.

I have been blessed with the gift of wonderful students over the course of my lifetime, none more dear to me than the three partners with whom I have worked on *Speaking Torah*. Ebn Leader and Or Rose were my students at Brandeis University and came with me to found the Hebrew College Rabbinical School. Many of the *Kedushat Levi* texts in this volume were translated by Or, and most of the *No'am Elimelekh* texts by Ebn. The three of us have grown together and learned much from one another, as well as from the sources (and the Source!) in the course of our weekly meetings to review and discuss every text presented here.

The newest member of our circle is Ariel Evan Mayse, a Harvard doctoral candidate working under my supervision. Although the youngest and the newest reader of these texts, he has impressed us all with his wisdom and devotion to the work. In addition to working as a translator, Ariel has been responsible for the preparation of the Hebrew texts and much of the final editing and formatting of the project. I cannot overstate how grateful I am to him; it is hard to imagine this work having come to fruition without him.

I am grateful to several friends for having offered material help to support this project. These include Neal Twersky (a direct descendant of one of the key teachers represented here), Max and Esther Ticktin of the Rita Paretsky Memorial Fund, Rabbi Matthew Gewirtz of Temple Bnai Jeshurun, and Douglas Cohen.

This work is dedicated, as you may have noticed, to my students' children and my own grandchildren. They are growing up in a world unimaginably different from that in which these *derashot* were created. We have worked hard here at trying to build a bridge between those worlds. It is our fervent hope that they, and many others of their generation, will choose to walk across it.

Avraham Yitzhak ben Etl
Arthur Green

תשואות חן

ע' קיח צו - ... זאת תורת העולה היא העולה על מוקדה על המזבח... (ויקרא ו:א-ב).

קכו תזריע

ח"ב

לד בלק - ויען בלעם ויאמר אל עבדי בלק... (במדבר כב:יח); מי מנה עפר יעקב... (במדבר כג:י).

קלג שבת זכור - זכור את אשר עשה לך עמלק... (דברים כה:יז-יט).

תורה אור

ע׳ ד בראשית - ...יובל... היה אבי כל תופש כנור ועוגב (בראשית ד:כ-א).

תורי זהב

קלו אחרי מות - וכל אדם לא יהיה באהל מועד... (ויקרא טז:יז).
קמז בהר - ... ושבתה הארץ שבת לה׳: שש שנים תזרע שדך... (ויקרא כה:ב-ג).

ח״ב

יב בהעלותך - וכי תבאו מלחמה בארצכם... (במדבר י:ט).
כה חקת - זאת התורה אדם כי ימות באהל... (במדבר יט:יד).
מג פנחס - ... את קרבני לחמי לאשי... את הכבש אחד תעשה בבקר ואת הכבש השני תעשה בין הערבים (במדבר כח:ב-ד).
נו דברים - רב לכם סוב את ההר הזה פנו לכם צפונה (דברים ב:ג).
קיב ראש השנה - ... בחדש הזה שפרו מעשיכם... (ויקרא רבה כט:ג).

תורת המגיד

ח״ב

נח ואתחנן - כי מי גוי גדול אשר לו אלהים... (דברים ד:ז).
עב שופטים - תמים תהיה עם ה׳ אלהיך (דברים יח:יג).
קמד שבועות - דכולי עלמא בשבת ניתנה תורה (שבת פו:).

תפארת עוזיאל

פ יתרו
קא כי תשא - ... לוחות כתובים משני עבריהם... (שמות לב:טו).
קמב קדושים - ... והדרת פני זקן ויראת מאלהיך אני ה׳ (ויקרא יט:לב).
קנד בחוקותי - וזכרתי את בריתי יעקוב... והארץ אזכור (ויקרא כו:מב).

ח״ב

פב כי תבוא - ארור האיש אשר לא יקים את דברי התורה הזאת... (דברים כז:כו).
צו וזאת הברכה - וזאת הברכה אשר ברך משה... (דברים לג:א).
צז - תורה צוה לנו משה מורשה קהילת יעקב (דברים לג:ד).
קלד פורים - אסתר ירקרוקת היתה וחוט של חסד משוך עליה (מגילה יג.).
קמא פסח - מצה זו שאנו אוכלים... מרור זה... (הגדה של פסח).

ע׳ קז ראש חודש - החדש הזה לכם ראש חדשים... (שמות יב:ב).
קח - ברכי נפשי את ה׳׳ (תהלים קד).
קיא ראש השנה - זמרו אלהים זמרו זמרו למלכנו זמרו (תהלים מז:ז).
קכב סוכות - ולקחתם לכם ביום הראשון פרי עץ הדר... (ויקרא כג:מ).
קכז חנוכה
קלה-ו פורים
קלט פסח - חכם מה הוא אומר... (הגדה של פסח).
קמז שבועות

רב ייבי

קח פקודי - אלה פקודי המשכן משכן העדות... (שמות לח:כא).
קכב שמיני - ויהי ביום השמיני קרא משה לאהרן... (ויקרא ט:א-ב).
קמג אמור - אמור אל הכהנים... לנפש לא יטמא בעמיו (ויקרא כא:א).
ח״ב
ב במדבר - וידבר ה׳ אל משה במדבר סיני... (במדבר א:א).

שארית ישראל

ח״ב
פג כי תבוא - את ה׳ האמרת היום להיות לך לאלהים... וה׳ האמירך היום להיות לו לעם סגולה (דברים כו:יז-יח).

שמועה טובה

ח״ב
קט ראש השנה

שמן הטוב

קמא קדושים - ... ואהבת לרעך כמוך אני ה׳ (ויקרא יט:יח).
ח״ב
פה נצבים - אתם נצבים היום כולכם לפני ה׳ אלהיכם (דברים כט:ט).

שפתי חכמים

הקדמה

ע׳ כה	חיי שרה	- הנה אנכי נצב על עין המים ...והנה רבקה יוצאת אשר ילדה לבתואל... (בראשית כד:יג-טו).
לג	ויצא	- וירא והנה באר בשדה... (בראשית כט:ב-ג,י).
לז	וישלח	- הצילני נא מיד אחי מיד עשו...(בראשית לב:יב).
לח		- ... כי יפגשך עשו אחי... (בראשית לב:יח-יט).
מב	וישב	- וישב יעקב בארץ מגורי אביו בארץ כנען (בראשית לז:א).
מז		- ויבאו אחי יוסף וישתחוו לו... (בראשית מב:ו-ז).
נד	ויגש	- ויאסור יוסף מרכבתו... (בראשית מו:כט).
נז	ויחי	- מאשר שמנה לחמו והוא יתן מעדני מלך (בראשית מט:כ).
נח		- ויאמר אליהם יוסף אל תיראו... (בראשית נ:יט).
סא	שמות	- ... ראה ראיתי את עני עמי אשר במצרים... (שמות ג:ז).
עא	בא	- החודש הזה לכם ראש חדשים... (שמות יב:ב).
עג	בשלח	- וישב הים לפנות בוקר לאיתנו... (שמות יד:כז).
פא	יתרו	- ... ויתיצבו בתחתית ההר (שמות יט:יז).
פג		- אנכי ה׳ אלהיך... (שמות כ:ב).
פט	משפטים	- ומראה כבוד ה׳ כאש אוכלת... (שמות כד:יז).
צד	תרומה	- ככל אשר אני מראה אותך... וכן תעשו (שמות כה:ט).
צח	תצוה	- ...ומלאת יד אהרן ויד בניו (שמות כט:ט).
קג	כי תשא	- ... וראית את אחורי ופני לא יראו (שמות לג:כג).
קה	ויקהל	- והמלאכה היתה דים לכל המלאכה... (שמות לו:ז).
קיד	ויקרא	- ונפש כי תחטא ועשתה אחת מכל מצוות ה׳ אשר לא תעשינה ואשם (ויקרא ד:כז).
קכה	תזריע	- ...אשה כי תזריע וילדה זכר... (ויקרא יב:ב).
ח״ב		
ג	במדבר	- כאשר צוה ה׳ את משה ויפקדם במדבר... (במדבר א:יט).
כט	חקת	- ... ודברתם אל הסלע לעיניהם... (במדבר כ:ח,יב).
לג	בלק	- ויגר מואב מפני העם מאוד... (במדבר כב:ג).
מב	פנחס	- יפקוד ה׳ אלהי הרוחות... (במדבר כז:טז).
מג		- ...אל אלהי הרוחות לכל בשר... (במדבר טז:כב).
נ	מסעי	- ויכתב משה את מוצאיהם למסעיהם... (במדבר לג:ב).
נח	ואתחנן	- ראה למדתי אתכם חוקים ומשפטים... (דברים ד:ה).
עח	כי תצא	- כי יקרא קן צפור לפניך בדרך... (דברים כב:ו-ז).
פג	כי תבוא	- ... בדרך אחד יצאו אליך ובשבעה דרכים ינוסו לפניך (דברים כח:ז).
פט	וילך	- וילך משה וידבר את הדברים האלה... (דברים לא:א).
קה	שבת	- ... אך את שבתותי תשמורו... (שמות לא:יא-יב).

פרי הארץ

ע׳ נא ויגש - ויגש אליו יהודה ויאמר בי אדני... (בראשית מד:יח).

פרי חיים

ח״ב

קמ פסח - חכם מה הוא אומר... (הגדה של פסח).

צמח ה׳ לצבי

עד בשלח - אז ישיר משה ובני ישראל... (שמות טו:א).

קא כי תשא - ועתה אם תשא חטאתם... (שמות לב:לב)

קה ויקהל - וכל אשה חכמת לב בידיה... (שמות לה:כה-ו).

קכג שמיני - ...וידום אהרן (ויקרא י:ד).

ח״ב

יז שלח לך - ... וימלא כבוד ה׳ את כל הארץ (במדבר יד:כא).

יח - ... ועשו להם ציצית על כנפי בגדיהם...(במדבר טו:לח-ט).

יט - והיה לכם לציצית וראיתם אותו... (במדבר טו:לט).

כג קרח - ... עבודת מתנה אתן את כהונתכם... (במדבר יח:ז).

כח חקת - ...ודברתם אל הסלע לעיניהם... (במדבר כ:ח).

לז פנחס - פינחס בן אלעזר בן אהרן הכהן השיב את חמתי...
(במדבר כה:יא-יב).

נא מסעי - ויכתב משה את מוצאיהם למסעיהם... (במדבר לג:ב).

סא עקב - כי לא על הלחם לבדו יחיה האדם... (דברים ח:ג).

סא - ואכלת ושבעת וברכת את ה׳ אלהיך... (דברים ח:י).

סה ראה - ראה אנכי נותן לפניכם היום... (דברים יא:כו-כז).

סח - כי יהיה בך אביון מאחד אחיך... (דברים טו:ז-ח).

קו שבת

קכג סוכות - ולקחתם לכם ביום הראשון פרי עץ הדר... (ויקרא כג:מ).

קדושת לוי

ג, ד בראשית - בראשית ברא אלהים... (בראשית א:א).

- אלה תולדות השמים והארץ בהבראם... (בראשית ב:ד).

ח נח - ... נח איש צדיק תמים היה בדורותיו (בראשית ו:ט).

יג לך לך - ... והיה ברכה (בראשית יב:ב).

טו - ומלכי צדק מלך שלם הוציא לחם ויין... (בראשית יד:יח).

יט וירא - וה׳ אמר המכסה אני מאברהם אשר אני עושה...
(בראשית יח:יז-יט).

ע' צג תרומה - ... ויקחו לי תרומה... (שמות כה:ב).
ק כי תשא - כי תשא את ראש בני ישראל לפקודיהם... (שמות ל:יב).
קיא ויקרא - ויקרא אל משה וידבר ה' אליו... (ויקרא א:א).
קיד - או כי יגע בטומאת אדם... (ויקרא ה:ג).
קכ צו - ולבש הכהן מדו בד... (ויקרא ו:ג-ד).
קכג שמיני - ויאמר משה אל אהרן קרב אל המזבח... (ויקרא ט:ז-ח).
קכז תזריע - בכל קודש לא תגע ואל המקדש לא תבוא... (ויקרא יב:ד).
קכח - אדם כי יהיה בעור בשרו שאת או ספחת...(ויקרא יג:ב-ג).
קלב מצורע - זאת תהיה תורת המצורע... (ויקרא יד:ב).
קלה אחרי מות - בזאת יבא אהרן אל הקודש... (ויקרא טז:ג-ד).
ח"ב
א במדבר - וידבר ה' אל משה במדבר סיני... (במדבר א:א).
ז נשא - ולבני קהת לא נתן כי עבודת הקודש עליהם (במדבר ז:ט).
י בהעלותך - ...ויעשו בני ישראל את הפסח במועדו...(במדבר ט:א-ה).
יז שלח לך - ועבדי כלב עקב היתה רוח אחרת עמו... (במדבר יד:כד).
ל חקת - וירם משה את ידו ויך את הסלע... (במדבר כ:יא).
מה מטות - וידבר משה אל ראשי המטות לבני ישראל...(במדבר ל:ב).
נה דברים - ותקרבון אלי כולכם ותאמרו נשלחה אנשים לפנינו... (דברים א:כב,כט-ל,לב-ג).
סג עקב - ועתה ישראל מה ה' אלהיך שואל מעמך...(דברים י:יב-ג).
פ כי תצא - כי יהיה בך איש אשר לא יהיה טהור... (דברים כג:יא-יב).

סידור הרב

קכט חנוכה

עבודת ישראל

צח תצוה - ואתה תצוה את בני ישראל... (שמות כז:כ).
ח"ב
קמח שבועות - בחודש השלישי לצאת בני ישראל מארץ מצרים ביום הזה באו מדבר סיני (שמות יט:א).
קמט - ויוצא משה את העם לקראת האלהים... (שמות יט:יז).
קנב תשעה באב - בונה ירושלם ה'... (תהלים קמז:ב).

פנים יפות

עה בשלח - ... ולא יכלו לשתות מים ממרה כי מרים הם... (שמות טו:כג).

ע' פז נצבים - ושב ה' אלהיך את שבותך... (דברים ל:ג).
פח נצבים -... נפלאת היא ממך ולא רחוקה היא (דברים ל:יא).
צז וזאת הברכה - וימת שם משה עבד ה'... (דברים לד:ה).
קטו יום הכפורים - מי אל כמוך נושא עון ועובר על פשע...(מיכה ז:יח-ט).

מגיד דבריו ליעקב

יח וירא - ... והשענו תחת העץ (בראשית יח:ד).
מ וישב - וישב יעקב בארץ מגורי אביו בארץ כנען (בראשית לז:א).
מד - ותתפשהו בבגדו לאמר שכבה עמי... (בראשית לט:יב).
מח מקץ - ואת הארץ תסחרו (בראשית מב:לד).
קיג ויקרא - ...אשה ריח ניחוח לה' (ויקרא א:ט).
ח"ב
צה האזינו - כנשר יעיר קנו על גוזליו ירחף... (דברים לב:יא).

מעיין החכמה

ס שמות - ואלה שמות בני ישראל הבאים מצרימה...(שמות א:א).
סז וארא - וארא אל אברהם אל יצחק ואל יעקב... (שמות ו:ג).
פה משפטים - כי תקנה עבד עברי שש שנים יעבוד... (שמות כא:ב).
קלא מצורע - ... זאת תהיה תורת המצורע... (ויקרא יד:א-ב).
ח"ב
קלב שבת זכור - ... כתוב זאת זכרון בספר ושים באזני יהושע כי מחה אמחה את זכר עמלק מתחת השמים (שמות יז:יד).

נועם אלימלך

ז נח - ... נח איש צדיק תמים היה בדורותיו... (בראשית ו:ט).
יג לך לך - ... לך לך מארצך... (בראשית יב:א).
יד - ויהי רעב בארץ וירד אברם מצרימה... (בראשית יב:י).
יז וירא - וירא אליו ה' באלוני ממרא... (בראשית יח:א).
יח - ואקחה פת לחם וסעדו לבכם... (בראשית יח:ה).
כג חיי שרה - ואברהם זקן בא בימים... (בראשית כד:א).
כט תולדות - ורבקה אמרה... הנה שמעתי את אביך ... (בראשית כז:ו).
לו וישלח - וישלח יעקב מלאכים לפניו... (בראשית לב:ד).
מא וישב - וישב יעקב בארץ מגורי אביו בארץ כנען (בראשית לז:א).
סא שמות - וירא מלאך ה' אליו בלבת אש... (שמות ג:ב).
סח בא - ויאמר משה בנערינו ובזקנינו נלך... (שמות י:ט).
פו משפטים - וכי יפתח איש בור... ונפל שמה שור... (שמות כא:לג-ד).

ח״ב

ע׳ כד חקת - ... זאת חקת התורה... פרה אדומה... (במדבר יט:א-ב).

לח פנחס - ... אמור הנני נותן לו את בריתי שלום (במדבר כה:יא-ב).

מה מטות - איש כי ידור נדר לה׳... (במדבר ל:ב-ג)

נג דברים - ... הואיל משה באר את התורה הזאת לאמר (דברים א:ה).

נט ואתחנן - ...וההר בוער באש עד לב השמים... (דברים ד:יא).

ס - ואהבת את ה׳ אלהיך בכל לבבך... (דברים ו:ה).

סז ראה - ראה אנכי נותן לפניכם היום... (דברים יא:כו-כח).

פט וילך - ... לא אוכל עוד לצאת ולבוא... (דברים לא:ב).

צב האזינו - האזינו השמים ואדברה... (דברים לב:א).

ק-קג שבת

קיג ראש השנה - מרחוק ה׳ נראה לי... (ירמיה לא:ב).

קיז יום הכפורים - ... ועניתם את נפשותיכם... (ויקרא כג:לב).

קכד שמחת תורה

קכו-ז חנוכה - ... מאי חנוכה? דתנו רבנן בכ״ה בכסלו... (שבת כא:).

קמב פסח - בכל דור ודור חייב אדם לראות את עצמו... (הגדה).

קנא תשעה באב - משחרב בית המקדש התקין רבי יוחנן בן זכאי שיהא לולב ניטל במדינה כל שבעה זכר למקדש (סוכה מא.).

מאמרי אדמו״ר הזקן

ח״ב

כג קרח - ועבד הלוי הוא... (במדבר יח:כג).

עו כי תצא - כי תצא למלחמה... (דברים כא:י).

פז נצבים - אם יהיה נדחך בקצה השמים... (דברים ל:ד).

קכד שמיני עצרת - ביום השמיני עצרת תהיה לכם... (במדבר כט:לה).

מבשר צדק

מ וישב - וישב יעקב בארץ מגורי אביו בארץ כנען (בראשית לז:א).

נג ויגש - ונאמר לא נוכל לרדת אם יש אחינו הקטן אתנו... (בראשית מד:כו).

פו משפטים - אם כסף תלוה את עמי את העני עמך... (שמות כב:כד).

קכט תזריע - וראה הכהן אותו ביום השביעי שנית (ויקרא יג:ו).

ח״ב

כז חקת - ... קח את המטה והקהל את העדה... (במדבר כ:ז-יב).

נז דברים - אוכל תשברו מאתם בכסף ואכלתם... (דברים ב:ו).

עא שופטים - וכי יבא הלוי מאחד שעריך... (דברים יח:ו-ז).

יושר דברי אמת

ע׳ קלז אחרי מות - ערות אחותך... לא תגלה ערותן (ויקרא יח:ט).

ח״ב

כא קרח - ... ומדוע תתנשאו על קהל ה׳ (במדבר טז:ג).

ישמח לב

ח״ב

צח וזאת הברכה - ויקבור אותו בגיא... (דברים לד:ו).

ליקוטי מהרי״ן

ח״ב

צה האזינו - כנשר יעיר קנו על גוזליו ירחף... (דברים לב:יא).

לקוטים יקרים

עח יתרו - ומשה עלה אל האלהים... (שמות יט:ג).

קנג בחוקותי - אם בחוקותי תלכו... ונתתי גשמיכם... (ויקרא כו:ג-ד).

ח״ב

לד שבת

מאור עינים

א,ב בראשית - בראשית ברא אלהים... (בראשית א:א-ב).

ו נח - ... נח איש צדיק תמים היה בדורותיו... (בראשית ו:ט).

י, יא לך לך - ... לך לך מארצך... (בראשית יב:א).

כח תולדות - וישב יצחק ויחפור את בארות המים...(בראשית כו:יח-ט).

לא ויצא - ויצא יעקב מבאר שבע וילך חרנה (בראשית כח:יא).

נט שמות

סד וארא

פח משפטים - ... כל אשר דבר ה׳ נעשה ונשמע (שמות כד:ז).

קד ויקהל - ויקהל משה את כל עדת בני ישראל... (שמות לה:א-ב).

קיא ויקרא - ויקרא אל משה וידבר ה׳ אליו... (ויקרא א:א).

קטז צו - ... זאת תורת העולה היא העולה...(ויקרא ו:א-ב,ו).

קלד אחרי מות - ... בזאת יבא אהרן אל הקודש... (ויקרא טז:א-ג).

קמד אמור -...אמור אל הכהנים...לנפש לא יטמא בעמיו (ויקרא כא:א).

קנב בחוקותי - אם בחוקותי תלכו...ונתתי גשמיכם... (ויקרא כו:ג-ד).

דברי אמת

ח"ב

ע' ו נשא -... כה תברכו את בני ישראל אמור להם (במדבר ו:כג).

נ מסעי - ויכתב משה את מוצאיהם למסעיהם... (במדבר לג:ב).

דברת שלמה

צא תרומה - ... ויקחו לי תרומה... (שמות כה:ב).

ח"ב

יג בהעלותך - והמן... ועינו כעין הבדלח (במדבר יא:ז).

לה בלק - מה אקוב לא קבה אל... (במדבר כג:ח-ט).

מ פנחס -... כן בנות צלפחד דוברות נתון תתן... (במדבר כז:ו-ז).

צ וילך - וילך משה... בן מאה ועשרים שנה... (דברים לא:א-ב).

צד האזינו - כי חלק ה' עמו... (דברים לב:ט).

קיז יום הכפורים

קלח פסח - ... מועדי ה' אשר תקראו אותם... (ויקרא כג:א-ג,יא).

חיים וחסד

ל תולדות - ... יצוא יצא יעקב ועשו אחיו בא מצֵידו (בראשית כז:ל).

עא בא - החודש הזה לכם ראש חדשים... (שמות יב:ב).

פד יתרו - ... אל תיראו כי לבעבור נסות אתכם בא האלהים... (שמות כ:טז).

קו ויקהל - ויעש בצלאל את הארון עצי שטים... (שמות לז:א-ב).

קמ קדושים - איש אמו ואביו תיראו... (ויקרא יט:ג).

ח"ב

ז נשא - ישא ה' פניו אליך וישם לך שלום (במדבר ו:כו).

קז ראש חודש - ובראשי חדשיכם תקריבו עולה לה'... (במדבר כח:יא).

חסד לאברהם המלאך

ח"ב

כב קרח - ויחר למשה מאוד ויאמר ... לא חמור אחד מהם נשאתי... (במדבר טז:טו).

חסד לאברהם מקאליסק

קט פקודי - אלה פקודי המשכן משכן העדות... (שמות לח:כא).

אורח לחיים

ע' מו מקץ - ויצבר יוסף בר כחול הים... (בראשית מא:מט).
ע בא - וגם מקננו ילך עמנו לא תשאר פרסה... (שמות י:כו).
עג בשלח - וירא ישראל את מצרים מת... (שמות יד:ל-לא).
פז משפטים - כי תראה חמור שונאך רובץ תחת משאו (שמות כג:ה).
צה תרומה - ונתת על השולחן לחם פנים לפני תמיד (שמות כה:ל).
צח תצוה - ואתה תצוה את בני ישראל...(שמות כז:כ).
קי פקודי - ותכל כל עבודת משכן... (שמות לט:לב).
קכב שמיני - ויהי ביום השמיני קרא משה לאהרן... (ויקרא ט:א)

ח"ב

ה נשא - ... כה תברכו את בני ישראל אמור להם (במדבר ו:כב-ג).
סו ראה - ראה אנכי נותן לפניכם היום... (דברים יא:כו-כז).
סט - השמר לך פן יהיה דבר עם לבבך בליעל..(דברים טו:ט-י).
עג שופטים - תמים תהיה עם ה' אלהיך (דברים יח:יג).
עז כי תצא - לא יהיה כלי גבר על אשה...(דברים כב:ה).
קיא ראש השנה - ואמרו לפני בראש השנה מלכיות זכרונות ושופרות. (ראש השנה טז.).
קטז יום הכפורים - אך בעשור לחודש השביעי לכם ועניתם את נפשותיכם... (ויקרא כג:כז).

בית אהרן

מח מקץ - וכסף משנה קחו בידכם... (בראשית מג:יב,יד).
פג יתרו - ויהי קול השופר הולך וחזק מאד... (שמות יט:יט).

בית רבי

הקדמה

גנזי יוסף

כ וירא - אולי יש חמשים צדיקים בתוך העיר...(בראשית יח:כד).
מג וישב - ויראו אותו... ויתנכלו אותו להמיתו (בראשית לז:יח).

ח"ב

ב במדבר - ...שאו את ראש כל עדת בני ישראל... (במדבר א:א-ב).
לב בלק - וירא בלק בן ציפור... (במדבר כב:ב).
מז מטות - ואשה כי תדור נדר לה'... (במדבר ל:ד-ה).

ח"ב

ע' ד נשא - ובאו המים המאררים האלה במעיך... (במדבר ה:כב).

טו שלח לך - ויספרו לו ויאמרו באנו אל הארץ (במדבר יג:כז-ח,ל).

עד שופטים - והיה כקרבכם אל המלחמה... (דברים כ:ב-ג).

ק שבת

קי ראש השנה

קכ סוכות - ולקחתם לכם ביום הראשון פרי עץ הדר... (ויקרא כג:מ).

קמה שבועות - ... הנה אנכי בא אליך בעב הענן... (שמות יט:ט); אנכי עומד בין ה' וביניכם... (דברים ה:ה-ו).

קנ תשעה באב

אור פני משה

ח"ב

מא פנחס - יפקוד ה' אלהי הרוחות... ולא תהיה עדת ה' כצאן אשר אין להם רועה (במדבר כז:טז-יז).

אור תורה

כו תולדות - ואלה תולדות יצחק בן אברהם... (בראשית כה:יט).

נ ויגש - ויגש אליו יהודה ויאמר בי אדני... (בראשית מד:יח).

נה ויחי - ... המלאך הגואל אותי מכל רע... (בראשית מח:טו-טז).

סב שמות - ... וילך ויפגשהו בהר האלהים וישק לו (שמות ד:כז).

סה וארא - ... וארא אל אברהם אל יצחק ואל יעקב... (שמות ו:ב-ג).

צז תצוה - ואתה תצוה את בני ישראל... (שמות כז:כ).

קב כי תשא - ... וחנותי את אשר אחון (שמות לג:יט).

קטו צו - ... זאת תורת העולה... (ויקרא ו:א-ב,ו).

קלח קדושים - ... קדושים תהיו כי קדוש אני ה' אלהיכם (ויקרא יט:ב).

קנא בחוקותי - אם בחוקותי תלכו... ונתתי גשמיכם... (ויקרא כו:ג-ד).

ח"ב

י בהעלותך - ... בהעלותך את הנרות... (במדבר ח:ב).

יא - עשה לך שתי חצוצרות כסף... (במדבר י:ב).

טז שלח לך - ...ארץ אוכלת יושביה היא... (במדבר יג:לב).

לו בלק - וישא בלעם את עיניו וירא את ישראל... (במדבר כד:ב).

נב מסעי - ויסעו ממרה ויבואו אלימה... (במדבר לג:ט).

סד עקב - ... לאהבה את ה' אלהיכם... ולדבקה בו (דברים יא:כב).

עט כי תצא - כי תבנה בית חדש ועשית מעקה לגגך... (דברים כב:ח).

רשימת הספרים המובאים בספר הזה

אור האמת

ח"ב

ע' סב עקב - ... מה ה' אלהיך שואל מעמך... (דברים י:יב).

קט ראש השנה - אל תבוא במשפט עמנו (סליחות לערב ראש השנה).

קכ סוכות

קלד פורים - איש יהודי היה בשושן הבירה... (אסתר ב:ה).

אור הגנוז לצדיקים

קלג מצורע - וצוה הכהן ולקח למטהר שתי צפרים... (ויקרא יד:ד).

קמה אמור - ומן המקדש לא יצא... (ויקרא כא:יב).

ח"ב

מט מסעי - אלה מסעי בני ישראל... (במדבר לג:א-ב).

אור המאיר

ט נח - ואתה קח לך מכל מאכל אשר יאכל (בראשית ו:כא-כב).

כב חיי שרה - ואברהם זקן בא בימים... (בראשית כד:א).

כד - ... וה' ברך את אברהם בכל (בראשית כד:א).

לב ויצא - ויצא יעקב... ויפגע במקום (בראשית כח:י-יא).

לד -... והיה העטופים ללבן והקשורים ליעקב (בראשית ל:מב).

לח וישלח - ויקרא יעקב שם המקום פניאל... (בראשית לב:לא).

מה מקץ - והנה מן היאר עולות שבע פרות... (בראשית מא:יח-כה).

נב ויגש - ויגש אליו יהודה ויאמר בי אדני... (בראשית מד:יח).

נה ויחי - ויקרא יעקב אל בניו ויאמר... (בראשית מט:א).

סט בא - ... ויהי חושך אפלה בכל ארץ מצרים... (שמות י:כב-כג).

ע בשלח - ... הנני ממטיר לכם לחם מן השמים... (שמות טז:ד-ה).

עט יתרו - אתם ראיתם אשר עשיתי למצרים... (שמות יט:ד).

צב תרומה - ... ויקחו לי תרומה... ועצי שטים (שמות כה:ב,ה).

קלט קדושים - ... קדושים תהיו כי קדוש אני ה' אלהיכם (ויקרא יט:א-ב).

קמח בהר - ובכל ארץ אחזותכם גאולה תתנו לארץ (ויקרא כה:כד).

קמט - כי ימוך אחיך ומכר מאחוזתו ובא גואלו...(ויקרא כה:כה).

עבודת ישראל

בונה ירושלם ה׳... (תהלים קמז:ב).

וקשה גם כן לשון הווה, דממה נפשך אם יאמר ה׳ שיבנה ירושלים ״עצת ה׳ היא תקום״ (משלי יט:כא), ומה שלא נבנית עדיין הוא מפני שלא פקדה לטובה, ואיך שייך לשון הווה.

ונראה לומר דהנה ירושלים בצירופו נודע מספרים קדושים ״ירו שלם״ כי ירו עולה יראה, ושם בירושלים היתה היראה בשלימות, כולנו יחד עושים באימה וביראה רצון קוננו. אכן מפני שנתרחקנו מעל אדמתנו אין אנו יכולים לעלות ולראות תמיד פני ה׳, רק שבעוונותינו הרבים היצר הרע מסתיר מפנינו אור ה׳ ויראתו. לכן צריך כל אדם להתעורר בקרבו ולעמוד נגד יצרו ולהתחזק בעבותות אהבה ויראה עד שיקושר בירושלים עיר הקודש. ולכן הטעם שאנחנו מתפללין למזרח ומכוונים לירושלים כנודע מאמר חז״ל (ברכות ל.). וכאשר נזכה כולנו להתעורר באהבה וחוטי חסד לעבותות היראה כראוי בשלימות אז נזכה לבנין עיר קודשנו ותפארתנו.

וזה שאמר דוד המלך ע״ה ״ירושלים הבנויה כעיר שחוברה לה יחדיו״ (תהלים קכב:ג), פירוש לפי התחברות בני ישראל והתעוררותם באהבה ויראה נבנה ירושלים. ״ששם עלו שבטים״ (שם קכב:ד), פירוש כי מוסרות אהבה ויראה הנקשרים בלב ונעשה ירושלים בלב הם נקשרים עד ירושלים עיר הקודש...

״כי ה׳ אלהיך ברכך בכל מעשה ידיך ידע לכתך את המדבר הגדול הזה...״ (דברים ב:ז). הנה הפרשה הזאת קריאתה תמיד בתשעה ימים שאחר ראש חודש אב עד תשעה בו. ומרמז הפרשה בכמה ענינים להזכיר את אשר עברנו ממקום למקום וה׳ אלהינו היה עמנו, להורות הגם שכשאנו עוברים בין המצרים ומראש חודש אב עד תשעה בו לא יטוש ה׳ את עמו ונחלתו, וכמו שהוליכנו במדבר בארץ לא עבר איש ״וה׳ הולך לפניהם וכו׳״ (שמות יג:כא), כן בימים הללו אשר נקראים גם כן מדבר וגיא צלמות. וכמו שכתבתי פירוש הפסוק ״גם כי אלך בגיא צלמות לא אירא רע כי אתה עמדי״ (תהלים כג:ד)...

בנינו, מכחש דוגמתו איזה ציור עובדא דבראשית, וגם בבית המקדש חסר כלי אחד או יתיר כלי אחד... וזהו סבת שנחרב בית המקדש בשביל עוונותיהם של ישראל, כי כל עוד שפגמו בבנין קומתם, מוכרח להיות הריסה בבנין הבית, וחסרון במנין הכלים.

מאור עינים

(*מפרשת האזינו*)

משחרב בית המקדש התקין רבי יוחנן בן זכאי שיהא לולב ניטל במדינה כל שבעה זכר למקדש (סוכה מא.).

להגיד בבוקר חסדך ואמונתך בלילות (תהלים צב:ג).

הרי שמצוה לעשות זכר למקדש אף שכהיום חרב בית המקדש. והענין הוא כשהאדם מוגבה ומנושא במדריגתו ודבוק בה' יתברך, הוא נקרא בחינת מקדש כאמור "היכל ה' המה" (ירמיה ז:ד), וכתיב "אוהל שִׁיכֵּן באדם" (תהלים עח:ס), וכשנופל ממדריגתו נקרא חורבן בית המקדש. וצריך האדם גם בנפלו ממדריגתו להתחזק ולילך אל ה' יתברך באותה מדריגה שהוא עכשיו כמו בהיותו במדריגה העליונה. וזהו נקרא זכר למקדש, והיינו בהאמינו שבמדריגה שהוא עכשיו יש גם כן ה' יתברך כי לית אתר פנוי מיניה.

וזהו "ממזרח שמש עד מבואו מהולל שם ה'" (תהלים קיג:ג), היינו בעת בהירות המוחין של הצדיק הנקרא "שמש", "עד מבואו" היינו בנפלו. בין כך ובין כך צריך להיות "מהולל שם ה'", והיינו על ידי האמונה... וזהו **להגיד** הוא לשון המשכה, **בבוקר** היינו בעת בהירות המוחין יכול להמשיך חסדים. **ואמונתך בלילות**, היינו בעת חשכות המוחין צריך להיות על ידי האמונה כזנכר לעיל, ואם עושה כן אז הוא בא אחר כך למדריגה יותר גבוהה.

והיה אומר הבעל שם טוב נ"ע משל האב המלמד את בנו לילך עומד רחוק מעט וקורא אותו לבא, ובבואו קרוב לאב נמשך האב להלאה ומתרחק יותר מהבן, והבן נופל. ולמה עושה האב כן? היינו שלולא זה לא היה יכול הבן לילך רק אותו מעט, אבל עתה מתחזק הבן על רגליו והולך ומתקרב אצלו יותר, והנמשל מובן.

- קנ"א -

תשעה באב

אור המאיר
(מפרשת דברים)

חכמים הגידו: יכוין את לבו נגד קדשי קדשים [קדש הקדשים] (מ׳ ברכות ד:ה), והכוונה כלפי דברים הנאמרים שהאדם שוה בבנין קומתו ותכונת אבריו לתכונת ומנין בנין וכלי המשכן. וממילא צריך להשוות מידותיו, לבנות תחילה בנין מלא קומתו מראש עד עקב, בכדי שיוכל לכוין ולהשוות עצמו לבנין המקדש. ואז לא יעלה על הלב לעשות זר מעשהו, כי בשׂם על לב קדושת בית קדשי קדשים שלא רשאי לבוא לשם זר ושום טומאה, כי אם אחת בשנה כהן גדול בשעת עבודה, וככה יקדש את לבו המכוון נגד קדש הקדשים שבמקדש. ישנה באדם בחינת הלב משכן השראת כללות הקדושה השורה בקרב לבו...

ולזה תאיר עינך בדבריהם שנתעוררו "כל מי שלא נבנה בית המקדש בימיו, כאילו נחרב בימיו" (ירושלמי יומא א:א). והכוונה... כל מי שלא נבנה בית המקדש בימיו, ירצה באמצעות כושר דרכו מידות ישרות שנוהג בימיו, לבנות מלא קומתו לכוונו לבנין המשכן עם כל כליו כנזכר, יכוין את לבו כנגד קדשי הקדשים, כאילו נחרב בימיו, כלומר באמצעות דרכו ומידותיו המגונות שנוהג בימיו נחרב ודאי בית מקדשו, מוסב על בנין ומנין כלי גופו ופרטי אבריו עושה הריסה בהם.

והנה כמו שיש באדם אברים חיצונים ופנימיים, כמו כן היה בבית המקדש כלים חיצונים ופנימים, והכל לרמז על אורות עליונים פנימים וחצונים, כידוע להמבין בספרים. ועובדא דמעשה בראשית מרמז גם כן לאורות אלו, ובאמצעות שלוש אלה, עובדא דבראשית וציורא דמשכנא וציורא דאדם, נתגלה ונתפרסם התפשטות אלהותו יתברך שציורם חד.

... ואיש הפכפך במעשיו ואינו מתבונן על דרכיו וכושר מידותיו, להשיג את הקדוש ברוך הוא בכל פרטי אבריו והרגשת חושיו, אזי הוא או חסר או יתיר אבר, ואינו דומה כלל לתכונתם... כמו שפוגם איזה אבר מתכונת

עבודת ישראל ב׳

ויוצא משה את העם לקראת האלהים מן המחנה ויתיצבו בתחתית ההר... (שמות יט:יז).

דהנה איתא במדרש (פרקי דרבי אליעזר פ׳ מ) שביום מתן תורה ביקשו להתנמנם בבוקר ושנתם ערבה להם עד שעוררן משה רבינו ע״ה לקבל את התורה.

ואמר הצדיק הגאון מורנו הרב לוי יצחק זצ״ל חלילה לחשוב על עם קודש שנפלו בתדרמת העצלות והשינה ביום הנכבד שידעו שיתן הקדוש ברוך הוא את תורתו להם! אלא יש לומר דכוונתם היה לשם שמים, שמיום שני בסיון שהתחילו לעשות הכנה לקבלת התורה ועבדו בכל כוחם ובמחשבותם הקדושים עד שנפל עליהם לאות ועייפות והיו מתייראים פן לא יוכלו לקבל את התורה במחשבה צלולה כראוי, על כן נתנו שינה לעיניהם ולעפעפם תנומה בכדי שיתחדשו מוחותיהם ויתחזקו עשתונותיהם בבהירות לקבלת תורה הקדושה - עד כאן לשונו.

והנה מפשוטו של מקרא דכתיב **ויוצא משה את העם**, וכל מקום דכתיב ״עם״ הם פשוטי בני אדם כנודע. ולכן ניחא לומר עליהם שהיו ישנים ונרדמים עד שהקיצן משה, ויוצא אותם לקראת האלהים. ואף גם לפי מה שאמר החסיד הנזכר לעיל דכוונתם היתה לשם שמים, מכל מקום מוכרע שלא היו אותם האנשים במדריגה גדולה, כי מי שנכון לבו בטוח בה׳ אינו צריך להכנה ומתחזק בבטחונו להלוך אל ה׳ ולעבודתו ומן השמים ירחמו לחזק מוחו ולתת לו בהירות. אמנם מי שאינו דבוק בבוראו בדביקות כראוי אינו בטוח בו כראוי ומתנהג על פי דרך הטבע ושומר מוחותיו ומחשבתו וישן בשעת שינה וכן שאר ענינים. הגם שגם זה לשם שמים, מכל מקום אינו במדריגה גדולה כמשליך על ה׳ יהבו ואינו משגיח על עצמו לשמור נפשו על פי דרך הטבע.

והנה ידוע כי כל מה שהאדם מחשב ומדבר ועושה למטה מעורר מידה כזאת למעלה, ולכן כתיב **ויוצא משה את העם** דייקא שהיו במדריגה קטנה ובקשו לשמור מוחותם על פי דרך הטבע ושינה, והקיצן משה והוציאן **לקראת האלהים**, כי אלהים גימטריא הטבע, כי על ידי דרך הטבע שדרכו בו נתעורר שם אלהים. וזה **ויתיצבו בתחתית ההר** במדריגה קטנה.

- קמ״ט -

תיכף ומיד כלי. וזהו **עד שתחפץ**, עד כאן לשונו אף שאין זה לשונו ממש.

והנה בשעת מתן תורה שהיה בוודאי לישראל אז התעוררות גדולה, ולא היה להם עדיין שום מצוה לעשות להתעוררות כלי, מוכרח לומר שהיו מקיימים מצות הגבלה שהזהיר משה רבינו ע"ה שלא ליגע בהר (שמות יט:יב), והם היו נעצרים מליגע, וממצוה הזאת היו עושים כלי להתעוררות, ועל שם זה נקרא בשם עצרת.

עבודת ישראל א'

בחודש השלישי לצאת בני ישראל מארץ מצרים ביום הזה באו מדבר סיני (שמות יט:א).

בחודש השלישי, היינו בהתחדשות, שמקודם הוציא אותם מכור הברזל ממצרים ואכלו העוגות שהוציאו ממצרים וטעמו בהם טעם מן. ואחר כך עלו למעלה יותר והוריד להם הקדוש ברוך הוא לחם מן השמים ובשר מן השמים, וזהו התחדשות השלישי שבאו למעלה יותר וקרבו לפני הר סיני לקבל התורה הקדושה.

וזה החודש הוא מזל תאומים, שמורה שהקדוש ברוך הוא עם עושי רצונו הם כתאומים כביכול. וכמו שכתבו המחקרים שהתאומים אם לאחד ח"ו לא טוב גם להשני כן, ואם טוב לאחד טוב להשני דבר מזליה הוא שנבראו בשעה אחת.

כן הבורא ב"ה כביכול עם עושי רצונו כתאומים. ולזה נקראו ישראל שהוא ישר אל, ששוים לאל וגם הוא ראש לי. ולזה קרבו לפני הר סיני בחודש השלישי ונתגלה להם הקדוש ברוך הוא ודיבר עמהם כאיש אל אחיו, לפי שהוא מזל תאומים...

קדושת לוי א'

רז"ל אמרו: התורה ניתנה באש שחורה על גבי אש לבנה (דברים רבה ג:יב). אפשר לומר דהרמז דעל ידי מתן תורה יש כח בישראל, כמאמר רז"ל: אתה גזרת מלמטה והקדוש ברוך הוא מקיים [מאמרך מלמעלה] (תענית כג.).

והנה גוון לבן כולל כל הגוונין, שמקבל כל הגוונין, וזה מרומז על ה' יתברך שכולל הכל.

ושחור אינו כן, שאינו כולל כל גוונין רק גוון שחור שיש בו, זה מרומז על בן אדם.

וזהו שעל ידי נתינת התורה זכו ישראל שהאש שחורה יהיה על גבי, רוצה לומר למעלה, מאש לבנה, דהיינו שישראל יהיו למעלה, כביכול יהיה יותר פועל דברי ישראל מדברי הקדוש ברוך הוא, כמאמר רז"ל: הקדוש ברוך הוא גוזר גזירה וצדיק מבטל (מועד קטן טז:).

קדושת לוי ב'

נשאלתי במדינת ליטא מפני מה נקרא חג שבועות בשם עצרת, והלא לא נזכר בתורה שם עצרת רק בשמיני עצרת (במדבר כט:לה)...

הוא על פי דברי הרמב"ן (ספר האמונה והבטחון פ' יט) שפירש על פסוק **אם תעירו ואם תעוררו את האהבה עד שתחפץ** (שיר השירים ב:ז), ופירש כשמגיע לאדם איזה התעוררות של יראה ואהבה להבורא ב"ה אזי תיכף ומיד יראה לעשות לה כלי, היינו שיעשה תיכף איזה מצוה, דהיינו שיתן צדקה או ישב תיכף ללמוד וכדומה. כי ידוע שהתעוררות הבאה אל האדם בפתע פתאום הוא אור הנשפע עליו מלמעלה, ונקרא בחינת נשמה, אזי צריך האדם להלבישה בגוף, בכדי שיהיה לה חיזוק ובסיס שלא יהיה מוטה ח"ו, כידוע למביני מדע.

וזה פירוש הפסוק **אם תעירו ומה תעוררו את האהבה עד שתחפץ**, כי חפץ הוא מלשון "כלי," דהיינו ההתעוררות ההוא שבא אל האדם צריך

וגנוזה בפשט או רמז או דרוש או סוד, אזי אינם נותנים עיניהם כי אם על בחינת ההלבשה, לומר כמה זה נאה דורש ונאה אומר! ונבערים מדעת להשגיח על פנימיות חכמה נפלאה ועצה לעבודת הבורא המלובשות שם בארבע בחינות פרד"ס.

ודומה לזה תורתנו הקדושה. פתח דבריה במקומה יאיר גבוה ורמה לרוב דקותה, לית מחשבה תפיסא כלל, וכאשר באה אל בחינת הדברות במעמד הקדוש על הר סיני, הוכרחה להתלבש ולהצטמצם פנים אל פנים, חכמה נפלאה וסודות נוראים ועמוקים נתלבשו בפשוטי תורה כמו ספורי מעשיות...

ואפילו הנביאים ש"גדול כחם לדמות צורה ליוצרה" (בראשית רבה כז:א), עם כל זה אין כחם יפה לקבל בהירות התורה בלי התלבשות ציורים ודמיונות. יתיר עליהם משה רבינו נאמן ביתו, אשר כחו יפה להסתכל באספקלריא המאירה... כי אם "וישמע את הקול מדבר אליו" (במדבר ז:פט), ברוחני בלי שום התכסות הענין [ב]ספורי מעשיות.

אמנם להיות "זאת התורה אשר שם משה לפני בני ישראל" (דברים ד:מד) וכללות עם אין כוחם יפה לשמוע בלימודים אור התורה כאשר היה במקומה לעוצם רוחניותה. ובאמת "ה' חפץ למען צדקו" (ישעיה מב:כא) ליתן להם כלי חמדה לכללות בני ישראל. מול זה בא הרמז בתורה **ויאמר ה' אל משה הנה אנכי בא אליך בעב הענן**, ירצה כללות התורה אשר פתח דבריה יאיר באנכי, כל זה בא גם אליך... בבחינת התלבשות וצמצומים, והכל לתועלת כללות עם קדוש ישראל שאין זכות גופם מוכן ומוכשר לקבלת התורה כאשר היא בבהירותה. וזהו **בעבור ישמע העם בדברי עמך** את עשרת הדברות, ישמעו ויבינו גם הם לערך בחינתם וזכות גופם כל אחד ואחד לפי בחינתו ואחיזת נשמתו באותיות התורה.

אור המאיר

ויאמר ה' אל משה הנה אנכי בא אליך בעב הענן בעבור ישמע העם בדברי עמך... (שמות יט:ט).

אנכי עומד בין ה' וביניכם בעת ההוא להגיד לכם את דבר ה' כי יראתם מפני האש ולא עליתם בהר לאמר: אנכי ה' אלהיך אשר הוצאתיך מארץ מצרים... (דברים ה:ה-ו).

והכוונה כי הנה בודאי נגד זיכוך ובהירות גופו של משה רבינו, בודאי היה יכול הקדוש ברוך הוא להראות עוצם בהירות התורה בלי שום בחינת התלבשות וצמצומים, וכאשר מצינו לרז"ל שנתעוררו על פסוק "בכל ביתי נאמן הוא" (במדבר יב:ז), שמשה רבינו ע"ה ידע אותן הצירופים שעמהם נבראו שמים וארץ. ויכולת בידו לברוא כל העולמות, ועם כל זה "בכל ביתי נאמן הוא."

ואם כן למה הלביש הקדוש ברוך הוא אור בהירות התורה בספורי מעשיות, עד שנעשה עתה כאשר ידבר איש אל רעהו? וכמו שכתבתי לעיל פירוש הפסוק "ודבר ה' אל משה פנים אל פנים כאשר ידבר איש אל רעהו" (שמות לד:יא), והכוונה עוצם בהירות התורה הלביש הקדוש ברוך הוא "פנים אל פנים". ובאמת יש שבעים פנים לתורה, ושם במקומה היה אור בהיר רק שמות קדושים, וכללותם אינה רק שם הגדול וקדוש הוי"ה ב"ה. ולכן נקרא "פקודי ה'" (תהילים יט:ט), שכללות וסיפורים פקודה וגנוזה בשם הוי"ה ב"ה, והלביש אותה כל כך "פנים אל פנים" עד שנראה עתה ספורי מעשיות "כאשר ידבר איש אל רעהו," ובאמת פתח דבריה יאיר אור בהיר...

כי הנה אנו רואין לפעמים נופלת לאדם המשכיל חכמה נפלאה בפנימיות מחשבתו בהשגת רוממות אלהות, וכאשר עלה ברצונו לגלות זאת המחשבה לזולתו, בוודאי בלתי אפשרי לגלות פנימיות מחשבתו עם החכמה כאשר היא שם בנקודת הלב, כי לא ידעו ולא יבינו השומעים מרוב דקותה. ואזי מוכרח להלביש פנימיות דקות מחשבתו באיזה פסוק או מאמר מדבריהם, באמצעות ארבע בחינות פרד"ס כפי הצורך. והשומעים אין השגתם חזקה להבין ולהשכיל עומק מחשבתו הפקודה

שבועות

תורת המגיד

(מכתב יד של ר׳ שמעלקי)

דכולי עלמא בשבת ניתנה תורה (שבת פו:).

... אמרו רז״ל: לא נתנה תורה אלא לאוכלי המן (תנחומא בשלח ס׳ כ).

הענין כי משה קיבל תורה, ובבהירות שכלו קיבל הכל בזמן הארבעים יום, כמאמר רז״ל שהיה לומד ושוכח עד שניתן לו במתנה (תנחומא כי תשא ס׳ טז). ואמרו רז״ל: אין אדם עומד על דעת רבו עד ארבעים שנה (עבודה זרה ה:).

ולכן הוצרך להמטיר להם לחם מן השמים, שהוא השפיע להם השפעות השבת, שזה היה מזון רוחני; השגת התורה נשתלשלה למזונות, וכן מבואר בזהר שגם מזונות בזמן הזה של תלמיד חכם לאו מגשמיות אינון, אלא משפע שנשפע בו מזון דק ורוחני (ח״ב סא:). והוא בחינה מן רוחניות התורה, ״כי לא על הלחם לבדו [יחיה האדם], כי על כל מוצא פי ה׳ יחיה האדם״ (דברים ח:ג), שהוא הדיבור של הקדוש ברוך הוא שבו נברא. ודיבורו הוא התורה המשפיעה לכל, נמצא מאכלו הוא רוחניות התורה.

וזהו: שלשה שאכלו על שולחן אחד ואמרו עליו דברי תורה כאילו אכלו משולחנו של מקום (אבות ג:ג)... שהכל הוא תורה... שנשתלשל לאדם תלמיד חכם השפעות התורה במאכלו, ועל ידי מאכלו משיג התורה, ומאכלו הוא עסק התורה. ולכן נקרא שולחן, שולח נ׳ [חמשים] שערי בינה, שהקדוש ברוך הוא שולח לאדם התעוררות המעורר ומזכך עצמו החמשים שערי בינה של התורה...

וזהו: אלו האכילנו את המן ולא נתן לנו את התורה דיינו (הגדה של פסח), שהיינו משיגים עם אכילת המן התורה. ואילו היה מאכיל את המן בלבד, היה די בזה - ודי למבין.

- קמ״ד -

הגם שנשארו עדיין הקליפות הדקות עד שיבוא משיחנו, במהרה בימינו, שיתגלה הפנימיות לגמרי - מכל מקום עיקר ההתכסות נתגלה.

כי מצרים אותיות "מצר ים", כי יש ים החכמה שהוא הדעת שבא משם, ומי שאין לו דעת כלל הוא גם היום במצר ים, שלא נכנס עדיין בים החכמה. על כן אמר בעל ההגדה: **לא את אבותינו בלבד גאל הקדוש ברוך הוא, אלא אף אותנו גאל עמהם**. כי בכל שנה יש יציאת מצרים באופן הנזכר לעיל. והרשעים שאין להם דעת עדיין לא יצאו ממצרים. על כן אמר: "רשע - מה הוא אומר? 'מה העבודה הזאת לכם'?" מאחר שאין לו דעת, קשה לו על העבודה. "ואף אתה אמור לו... 'לי ולא לו. אילו היה שם לא היה נגאל'." מאחר שגם היום הוא במצרים, דהיינו הדעת שלו.

ונראה שגירסתנו היא נכונה. שידוע שאם אדם עובד עבודת פרך אינו מרגיש שבירת אבריו, וכשנח מעבודתו אז הוא מרגיש שבירת אבריו. והדוגמא היא כן כשישראל היו במצרים והיו עובדין עבודת פרך, לא היו מרגישין שבירת אבריהם וצער של עבודתם שהיו עובדים יומם ולילה ולא היו נחים כלל. וכשיצאו מעבודת הפרך שהיו עובדין, אז הרגישו את שבירת אבריהם וצער עבודתם. וזה הרמז שמסדר בעל ההגדה: מצה זו... ואחר כך מרור זה...

מאור עינים

(*מהגדה של פסח של ארבעה אופני הקודש, על פי מאור עינים פרשת וארא*)

בכל דור ודור חייב אדם לראות את עצמו כאילו הוא יצא ממצרים... שלא את אבותינו בלבד גאל הקדוש ברוך הוא, אלא אף אותנו גאל עמהם... (הגדה של פסח).

כי בכל שנה יש יציאת מצרים, שצריך כל אחד ואחד לבוא לידי נסיונות. אף שמקבל אלהותו במחשבתו, מכל מקום מנסין את כל אחד בעשר נסיונות, כמו שנאמר באברהם אבינו ע"ה: בעשרה נסיונות נתנסה אברהם אבינו ועמד בכולן (מ' אבות ה:ג). והנסיון הוא שמסלקין ממנו ההתקשרות, שהיה קשור בה' יתברך על ידי הדעת בעת שבא לידי נסיון, ונשאר אצלו רק הבחירה. כי לולא זה לא היה נקרא נסיון, כי בוודאי על ידי התקשרות יאחז צדיק דרכו, ועל ידי זה [על כן] נתמעט הדעת אצלו, לא סילק הדעת ממש. ואם עומד בנסיון, על ידי שנקבע בלבו מקודם כשהיה לו דעת רחבה.

והנה כשהיו ישראל במצרים היתה הדעת בגלות, כי קליפה קדמה לפרי, כי הדעת היתה מכוסה בקליפה כמו קליפת האגוז, כמו שנאמר "אל גנת אגוז ירדתי" (שיר השירים ו:יא), שהוא על גלות מצרים. ובאגוז יש קליפה חיצונה היותר קשה ומכסה את האוכל, ותחתיה קליפות דקות זה על זה. וביציאת מצרים נשברה קליפה הקשה כדי שיוכלו לראות האוכל,

כמו שנאמר בזהר. ותיכף ממחרת הפסח נלקח מהם הארה זו וציוה אותם לספור ספירת העומר מ"ט יום כדי לתקן כל מידה ומידה בפרטות ויבואו בחג שבועות לחמשים שערי בינה ונמצא היה ביציאת מצרים גדלות קודם לקטנות - עד כאן דבריו ודברי פי חכם חן...

והנה איתא שאבות קיימו התורה עד שלא ניתנה, ויעקב אבינו היה מניח תפילין במקלות וכו'. רוצה לומר שקיימו פנימיות התורה בעובדות אחרים ואינם מצמצמין כך כאשר התורה אצלינו בצמצומים ושיעורים.

וזה שנאמר **חכם מה הוא אומר: מה העדות והחוקים והמשפטים אשר ציוה ה' אלהינו אתכם?** רוצה לומר שרואה עצמו בגדלות גדולה ובמוחין גדולים בפסח ועל כן הקשה מה העדות והחוקים וכו', רוצה לומר למה נצטמצם התורה כל כך בחוקים ומשפטים אשר ציוה ה' כי יכולין לקיים פנימיות התורה בעובדות אחרים כמו האבות שקיימו התורה עד שלא ניתנה.

ואף אתה אמור לו כהלכות הפסח, רוצה לומר אמור לו הלכות וטעם של פסח, שלמה נקרא פסח על שם הארת גדלות קודם לקטנות. ועל כן **אין מפטירין**, רוצה לומר לשון פטור, רוצה לומר אין אנו מפטירים ממעשה המצוות והחוקים כאשר ציונו ה' יתברך בצמצומים משום **שאחר הפסח אפיקומן**, רוצה לומר לאחר הפסח תלקח התגלות הארה ראשונה דגדלות. וזהו אפיקו מן, כי הלחם היורד מן השמים נקרא מן, ותיכף אחר הפסח תלקח הארה זו דגדלות ותהיה כקטנות השכל ונצטרך למעשה המצוות וחוקים כמו שהם עתה מצומצמין.

וזהו שאלת החכם שרואה עצמו בגדלות השכל.

תפארת עוזיאל

מצה זו שאנו אוכלים... מרור זה... (הגדה של פסח).

והקשו על מה נקט מצה קודם מרור, הא מתחילה מרור הוא זכר גלות שמררו חייהם, ואחר כך היא מצה זכר לגאולה שלא הספיק [בצקם של אבותינו להחמיץ]. ויש שגרסו להיפך - מרור קודם מצה.

- קמ"א -

יתברך הכרה אמיתית ולא יפלא ממנו דבר לעשות. על זאת השאלה באה התשובה "אין מפטירין [אחר הפסח אפיקומן]."

... המצה והפסח מורים על הניסים ונפלאות, וזאת העבודה העומדת לעד... וזה הרמז ממה שאמרו רז"ל (פסחים קיט:): צריך שיטעום טעם מצה באחרונה, ובזמן המקדש פסח באחרונה כדי שיהא נשאר הטעם, שמורה על עבודת ההכרה מצד ניסים ונפלאות. הרמז שהעבודה הזאת היא עומדת לעד, ומשום הכי צריכה העבודה הזאת למען אשר לא תמוש מפינו ומפי זרעינו עבודתו יתברך.

מה שאין כן הכרה האמיתית הנזכרת לעיל שאינה אלא לגדולים אשר בארץ המה, ובהיותם דבקים בעבודתו יתברך ולא נפלו ממדריגתם. וזהו התשובה לחכם "אין מפטירין אחר הפסח אפיקומן" כדי שישאר טעמו בפיו, והוא רמז שהעבודה שהיא מכח ניסים ונפלאות לא תבצר...

פרי חיים

חכם מה הוא אומר: מה העדות והחוקים והמשפטים אשר ציוה ה' אלהינו אתכם? אף אתה אמור לו כהלכות הפסח: אין מפטירין אחר הפסח אפיקומן (הגדה של פסח).

צריך להבין וכי זה כל הלכות פסח ודיני הפסח, הלא זה הדין אחר אכילת הפסח... איתא בסידור האר"י זלה"ה למה נקרא פסח לשון דילוג וקפיצה שהיה אז גדלות קודם לקטנות - עד כאן...

ושמעתי מהרב בוצינא קדישא מורנו הרב אברהם ז"ל בן הרב בוצינא קדישא הרב המגיד מורנו הרב דוב בער זלה"ה דהנה האדם צריך לתקן שבע מידותיו אהבה יראה והתפארת וכל מידה ומידה ופרטותיה שיהיה לה' לבדו, שלא יאהב רק לה' יתברך לבדו ודומיהן שלא ישתמש לשום הנאת הגוף בשום מידה רק לה' יתברך לבדו. וכל מידה כלולה משבע, והם מ"ט [49] פרטיות ואחר כך שורה עליו שער הנ' - חמשים שערי בינה.

וביציאת מצרים באו תיכף לשער החמשים שערי בינה, כמו שנאמר "וחמושים עלו בני ישראל מארץ מצרים" (שמות יג:יח), ובו היה הנס

- ק"מ -

... כל הנבראים תלוים במאמרו וחיותו יתברך שמו השופע בתוכם תמיד, חוץ מאותן שמפרידין עצמן מן חיותו יתברך, הם כלים ונפסדים שהוא בחינת ההעדר וכלא נחשבים.

ואותו כח האין סוף ב"ה נשפע בנבראים אחר גמר כל מעשה בראשית, שלפי הנראה נגמר בששת ימי המעשה, אבל באמת לא נגמר עדיין עד בוא יום השבת, כמו שאמרו חז"ל: מה היה העולם חסר? מנוחה - באת שבת באת מנוחה (רש"י על בראשית ב:ב). והוא כח האין סוף ב"ה שנקרא מנוחה, כמו ששמעתי ממורי זללה"ה דבאין סוף לא שייך שום תנועה, כי להיכן יתנועע? עד כאן [דבריו]. ועל כן נקרא מנוחה.

ולכן אנו אומרים בקדושת שבת גם כן "זכר ליציאת מצרים," כי על ידי שבת נעשו כל הניסים ושינוי הטבע, שתחילת כולם היתה יציאת מצרים. ולכן חג הפסח שהיה תחילת הניסים הנעשה על ידי שבת, ולכן נקרא גם הוא שבת...

קדושת לוי

(*מפרשת בא*)

חכם מה הוא אומר: מה העדות והחוקים והמשפטים אשר ציוה ה' אלהינו אתכם? (הגדה של פסח).

... יש שתי בחינות בעבדות הבורא יתברך: בחינה אחת כשאנו רואים ניסים ונפלאות שמשנה דברים הטבעיים ועושה בהם כרצונו, מכח זה ניכר שהוא יתברך מושל בכל ומחויבים כל ברואיו לעבדו ביראה. והדרך השני הכרה אמיתית במה שהוא יתברך ברא כל הברואים במאמר פיו, משום הכי בידו לשנותן. וזהו הדרך היותר טוב, ומכח זה אין חשוב אצלו הידיעה מצד הנס... מאחר שיש לו השגה אמיתית שהבורא ב"ה ברא כל הנמצאים... ומשום הכי אין הנס בעיניו פלא כלל...

וזהו שאלת החכם: **מה העדות**, רצה לומר כיון שהוא יודע שאין הנפלאות פלאים מצד הבורא ב"ה, שזהו פשוט שיכול לשנותן למה שירצה, כי הוא בורא הכל. והנה מעשה פסח ומצה מורים על עבודת ה' מצד ניסים ונפלאות, על זה הוא שאלת החכם למה הוא כך, הלא אנחנו מכירים אותו

- קל"ט -

פסח

דברת שלמה

(*מפרשת אמור*)

וידבר ה' אל משה לאמר... מועדי ה' אשר תקראו אותם... ששת ימים תעשה מלאכה וביום השביעי שבת שבתון... והניף את העומר לפני ה' לרצונכם ממחרת השבת יניפנו הכהן (ויקרא כג:א-ג,יא).

ופירש רש"י ממחרת יום טוב ראשון של פסח... הרגיש רש"י ז"ל: מה ענין שבת אצל מועדות? גם באמת למה נקרא יום טוב של פסח שבת?

... ולתרץ כל זה, דהנה הרמב"ם מנה תחיית המתים אחד משלוש-עשרה עיקרים שצריך להאמין כל אשר בשם ישראל יכונה. וגם צריך להאמין שתחיית המתים מרומז בתורה, כמו שאמרו חז"ל: כל [ישראל יש להם חלק לעולם הבא. ואלו שאין להם חלק בעולם הבא:] האומר אין תחיית המתים [מן התורה...] (מ' סנהדרין י:א).

וטעמא בעי שיהיה זה עיקר גדול מעיקרי הדת. והנראה בזה על שהוא ראיה גדולה על אחדותו יתברך שמו האין סוף, כי מאחר שה' יתברך הוא אחד אמת ואין סוף וממנו נשתלשל הכל, ובפרט עמו ישראל הקדושים שהם חלקו ונחלתו, כמו שכתוב "כי חלק ה' עמו" (דברים לב:ט), מוכרח הוא שלא יהיה להם הפסד וכליון לגמרי אפילו בבחינה גופנית. כמו שאמרו חז"ל על עצם אחד יש באדם הנקרא נסכוי [או לוז] שנשאר ואינו כלה (בראשית רבה כח:ג), וממנו יחזור ויבנה את הגוף לעת התחיה. וכן בכל הנבראים יש כח האין סוף ב"ה בתוכם, ועל ידי הכח ההוא יכול הקדוש ברוך הוא לשדד ולשנות המערכות ולעשות ניסים בשינוי הטבע בחפצו ורצונו בכל עת וזמן.

לכן יתלהב האדם בקריאת המגילה, ובשמעו יכין את עצמו לקבל עליו מאותו יום עול תורה ומצוות, ויתחדש כנשר נעוריו וישמח בעול קבלת תורה. ויכוין בקריאת המגילה שיזדככו כל העולמות, ואפילו העולם הזה הוא עולם הטבע יזדככו על ידי קריאת המגילה, וישמח מאוד שיזדככו כל העולמות ויקוים מקרא שכתוב "ישמח ה' במעשיו" (תהלים קד:לא)...

כן עושה פלאים, כמו בימי מרדכי ואסתר, הוא פלא גדול. ולכן גדלה הנס כל כך בעיני ישראל עד שקבלו את התורה.

ונראה מפנימיות הדבר, שלכן קבלו את התורה מאהבה בימי מרדכי ואסתר. ומקודם נבאר כי לפי דברינו יתכן שנקראת מגילה בשם מגילה כי בדברים הטבעיים, מלכותו בהסתר ומכוסה הנהגתו יתברך שמו... עכשיו על פי הנס של מרדכי ואסתר נתגלה שגם בתוך הטבעים הוא משבר ומכלה ומכרית זרוע רשעים...

למה קבלו התורה? ... על ידי מצות קריאת המגילה שקראו בשנה ראשונה את המגילה... כן קיבלו עליהם מאהבה את התורה, שראו שאפילו בתוך הטבעים הוא מושל בכל...

קדושת לוי ב׳

(*קדושות לפורים א׳*)

... אמרו בזהר הקדוש (תיקוני זהר ת׳ כא נז:): יום כפורים שהוא כמו פורים, כלומר שהארת יום כפורים הוא כְּפוּרים, עבור שביום כיפור מה שחלף ועבר אין, מעתה הוא מטוהר. וחושבנא מכאן ולהלאה, כמו שאמרו במדרש: "ולקחתם לכם ביום הראשון" (ויקרא כג:מ) - ראשון לחשבון עוונות (תנחומא אמור ס׳ כב). כי העיקר הארות יום הכפורים לקנות לב חדש לעבוד אותו, כמו שתיקנו "למען נחדל מעושק ידינו ונשוב לעשות חקי רצונך" (תפילת נעילה). כך בפורים, מה שחלף ועבר אין, ומעתה מקבלין עלינו עול תורה ומצוות יתברך שמו.

וגם כי בפורים ביארנו שהטבעים נזדככו על ידי קריאת המגילה שמאיר בעולם הזה... ולכן נעשה בתוך הטבעים, ו"קימו מה שקבלו כבר" (שבת פח.). והנה ידוע שמושב חיצונים הוא בעולם הזה, ובעולם הזה הוא רובו חיצונים, רק שנזדככו על ידי מעשה בני אדם. ונמצא בפורים שנזדכך העולם הזה, הוא עולם הטבע, על ידי קריאת המגילה ומקבלים עול תורה ומצוות נזדככו כל החיצונים. כן הוא ביום הכפורים שנזדככו כל החיצונים, ומטילין גורל הוא פורים - השעיר לעזאזל.

- קל"ו -

של חסד משוך עליה, דהיינו האורות נמשכין על המצוות אף על פי שאין נגלות לנו.

קדושת לוי א׳

(*קדושות לפורים א׳*)

למדו חז״ל דהדר קיבלו [את התורה] בימי אחשורוש **מקימו וקבלו** (שבת פח.), ובו[מסכת] מגילה למדו **מקימו וקבלו** דאסתר ברוח הקודש נאמרה (מגילה ז.). והנראה דהא בהא תליא.

דהנה צריכין להבין דרש״י (שם בשבת) פירש דהדר קיבלוה בימי אחשורוש מאהבת הנס, למה היה זה הנס של מרדכי ואסתר חביב עליהם מכל הניסים שנעשו להם לישראל, והלא ביציאת מצרים ראו קריעת ים סוף ועשר מכות וכל הניסים והנפלאות?

... יש שני מיני ניסים. אחד ניסים נגלים, ואחד ניסים נסתרים... נסים נסתרים כמו בימי מרדכי ואסתר שלא היה שינוי הטבעים, רק הנס היה בתוך הטבעים. ואמר אדוננו מורנו הגאון בוצינא קדישא הרב דוב בעריש זצ״ל שלכן נקראת אסתר, שהיה הנס בהסתר בתוך הטבעים, עד כאן אמר מורי ורבי זלה״ה.

... לכן היה הנס גדול אשר מאהבתם קבלו את התורה הקדושה, כיון שהנס היה בטבעים אשר בה מלכותו מכוסה, לכן הוא נס גדול. כי דרך משל הוא, למלך אשר בא ברוב חייליו ומנצח את המלחמה, אין כל כך פלא כמו שהמלך בא לפעמים ביער יחידי בלא כלי מלחמתו וחיילותיו אינם עמו, והוא מנצח בגבורתו לבדו. וגם דומה למלך כשבאין לפלטרין שלו ורואין גדולתו והאיך משרתיו ועבדיו עושין רצונו ומפחדים ממנו ובושין מפניו, ואין כל כך חידוש כמו שהמלך ביער יחידי ואיננו לבוש בלבושי מלכות וחייליו אינם עמו ומפחדים ומתביישין ממנו - זה פלא גדול. כן הדבר הזה כשהקדוש ברוך הוא משנה הטבעים ונראה מלכותו אשר הוא עושה משמי שמים וכל צבאם אינו כל כך פלא, כי מי שברא יכול לשנותם. אבל אם עושה נסים בטבעים ומלכותו בהסתר, ואף על פי

פורים

אור האמת

איש יהודי היה בשושן הבירה... (אסתר ב:ה).

כתיב במדרש (בראשית רבה לט:א): משל לאחד שבא לבירה ושאל לאחד של מי זה הבירה, אמר אחד שלי הוא. כך אברהם נגלה אליו ה' ואמר לו כל העולמות שלי הם - אפילו עולם השפל הכל הוא מהבורא. וזה פירוש **איש יהודי היה בשושן הבירה**, אפילו בגשמיות היה עובד להבורא יתברך, כי הכל מהבורא יתברך. ואפשר לומר שזה פירוש **ומרדכי ידע את כל אשר נעשה** (אסתר ד:א), **ידע** הוא לשון התחברות, שהיה מחבר הכל להבורא יתברך, אפילו עולם העשיה שהוא עולם הגשמיות. [ומברכים על המגילה] "על מקרא מגילה," פירוש על ידי הדיבורים מתגלה ההארה.

חייב אינש לבסומי בפוריא עד דלא ידע בין ארור המן לברוך מרדכי (מגילה ז:). פירוש צריך שיהיה מבוסם באהבה של פורים, ויעלה הכל להבורא יתברך אפילו הגשמיות, כי הכל הוא מהבורא. וזה הוא **דלא ידע**, שיהיה הכל שוה בעיניו שיהיה עובד לבורא אפילו **בארור המן** שהוא הגשמיות.

תפארת עוזיאל

אסתר ירקרוקת היתה וחוט של חסד משוך עליה (מגילה יג.).

הכוונה על מעשה המצוות, שהוא יתברך מסתיר האורות מאתנו, שאין אנו רואין התפילין רק בגשמיותם, וכן הציצית והלולב וכדומה ביתר מצוות. וזה מאמרם ז"ל (חולין קלט:): אסתר מן התורה מנין, שנאמר "ואנכי הסתר אסתיר פני" (דברים לא:יח). ובמקדש היתה לנו התגלות אורות התפילין וכדומה, ובגלות **אסתר ירקרוקת**. אבל מכל מקום **חוט**

זכור את אשר עשה לך עמלק בדרך בצאתכם ממצרים: אשר קרך בדרך... ואתה עיף ויגע ולא ירא אלהים... והיה בהניח ה'... תמחה את זכר עמלק מתחת השמים לא תשכח (דברים כה:יז-יט).

מלת **קרך** אין לו הבנה כפשוטו, גם כפל אומרו **לא תשכח** אחר אמרו כבר **זכור**, גם איך מצות מחיית עמלק גם עתה.

נראה דהנה על פי חכמי הטבע תלוי הזכרון והשכחה בהמזגת תולדת האדם קר או חם, הקרירות מביא לידי שכחה והחמימות מביא הזכירה. וקבלתי מפי הרב המוכיח [אריה לייב מפולנאה] ז"ל בשם הבעש"ט שבחינת השכחה מכונה בשם עמלק.

והענין הוא על שבני ישראל התלהב לבבם בראותם האיך הקדוש ברוך הוא הפליא נסיו בהוציאם ממצרים על ידי מכות המופלאות ובקריעת ים סוף ועשרה נסים שנעשו לאבותינו על הים אשר לענינים אלו אבן מקיר תזעק לשבח להודות ולהלל לשמו הגדול. ועמלק הרשע הלביש הנסים בטבעיות ובזה צינן וקירר את לב בני ישראל מאמונתם, ובאו לידי שכחה מחסדי המקום ב"ה.

וזהו **זכור את אשר עשה לך עמלק... אשר קרך בדרך**, שצינך והפשירך מרתיחתך להקדוש ברוך הוא, ובאת על ידי זה לידי שכחה. ועל ידי זה **ואתה עיף ויגע ולא ירא אלהים**, שנחת מרתיחתך כאיש עיף ויגע ולא יראת אלהים להודות ולהזכיר חסדי המקום. וזהו **והיה בהניח ה' לך... תמחה את זכר עמלק**, שלא תאמין בטבעיות - **לא תשכח**, שלא תבוא שוב לבחינת השכחה.

שבת זכור

מעיין החכמה
(מפרשת מטות)

ויאמר ה' אל משה כתוב זאת זכרון בספר ושים באזני יהושע כי מחה אמחה את זכר עמלק מתחת השמים (שמות יז:יד).

זה ידוע שהתורה נקראת זאת, כמאמר הכתוב "זאת תורת..." ולומד לנו ה' יתברך בתורתו שלא להחזיק ידנו בתורתנו הקדושה על דרך הפשוט לבד, אלא שצריך להחזיק הדרך הפשוט בכדי שעל ידי פשט תורתנו נבוא בפנימיות שבה. וזה **כתוב זאת**, רוצה לומר מה שכתוב בתורתנו הקדושה אינו אלא **זכרון בספר** כדי להזכיר את פנימיות התורה.

וזה **ושים באזני יהושע**. אזני הוא לשון "אוזן הכלי", רוצה לומר שתאחז בזאת המדריגה ותגבר על היצר הרע. ואם תאמר איך אני יכול להגביר [להתגבר] עליו, הלא הוא קשה לפי שהוא כולו רוחניות בלא גוף, על זה אמר הכתוב **באזני יהושע**, רוצה לומר שתחזיק ידך בזה ותבטיח ש"יה יושיעך" (סוטה לד:).

וזה **מחה**, רוצה לומר אם תרצה למחוק את היצר הרע בכדי שתקיים את התורה והמצוות בפנימיות שלהם, מבטיח לנו ה' יתברך **אמחה את זכר עמלק**, שהוא היצר הרע...

והיוצא לנו מזה שכל הסתכלות שלנו בתורתנו צריך להיות אל הפנימיות שבתורה...

- קל"ב -

וזהו ענין נר חנוכה משמאל דווקא אחר שהמזוזה מימין. כי הנה המזוזה מימין הוא בחינת נר מצוה שעולה עד הכתר כנזכר לעיל, אבל אינו נמשך רק בחינת מקיף דחסד עליון שכבר בא בגילוי אור רק שצריך התעוררות, ועל כן אין ביכולתו להאיר את החושך. אבל בחינת מקיף דאור דתורה בא מבחינת העלם האור דתורה הנקראת אויר קדמון הוא שנאמר "ישת חושך סתרו" (תהלים יח:יב) וכתיב "מגלה עמוקות מני חושך" (איוב יב:כב). וכאשר מבחינת החושך והעלם עצמות המאציל יאיר אור דתורה בסיבת העלאת המצוות כנ"ל, אזי יאיר אור חדש ונעלה יותר...

וזהו שאמרו דנר חנוכה משמאל דווקא שהוא בחינת הגבורות שכדי שיהיה בוקע ומאיר את החושך העליון צריך לו בחינות תגבורת גדולה, כמו שנאמר "וה' אלהי יגיה חשכי". אמנם אף על פי כן אם לא על ידי מזוזה שמימין לא היה מועיל נר חנוכה משמאל כמובן מענין הנזכר לעיל בפירוש "כי נר מצוה" גורם בחינת תוספת אור הנעלם באור דתורה.

שנאמר "וירד ה' על הר סיני... וידבר אלהים..." (שמות יט:כ-כ:א). ועל כן נקרא הלכות, כמו שנאמר "הליכות עולם לו" (חבקוק ג:ו) ו"הליכות אלי [מלכי בקדש]" (תהלים סח:כה), שהוא בחינת ההליכה מלמעלה למטה מעצמות אור אין סוף בחכמה שבתורה כו' כידוע.

ושורש המצוות הוא בחינת ההליכה מלמטה למעלה כידוע דעיקר המצוות בשס"ה [365] לא תעשה ורמ"ח [248] מצוות עשה הוא בחינת העלאת מיין נוקבין לאהפכא חשוכא לנהורא כו'. וזהו שנאמר "כי נר מצוה ותורה אור" (משלי ו:כג), שהתורה נקראת אור להיותה בחינת אור ושפע האלקי מלמעלה למטה. והמצוה נקראת נר בחינת כלי לאור הזה...

על ידי המצוות הגשמיות יש התכללות הגשמיות ברוחניות עד רום המעלות, כמו מצות ציצית מצמר גשמי ומצות תפלין מקלף גשמי או הקרבנות שנעשין מבהמות גשמיות ונכללים בבחינת הרוחניות מעולם לעולם כנ"ל עד רום המעלות בשורש הראשון שהוא עצמות המאציל כמו על ידי הקרבנות שנקרא "אשה ריח ניחוח לה'" (ויקרא א:יז), ועל ידי ציצית ותפלין נתעלה עד בחינת שורש הראשון בעצמות רצון הפשוט המלובש במצוות הללו, וכמו שנאמר "אשר קדשנו במצותיו." וכידוע הנה על ידי העלאה זאת נמשך מעצמות המאציל אור דתורה להיות תורה אור והוא להיות בחינת גילוי אור דתורה הרוחניות שבכל מצוה...

גם במקום עולם הפירוד ממש יאיר אור האלהי לאהפכא חשוכא לנהורא כו' משום ד"גם חושך לא יחשיך [ממך]" (תהלים קלט:יב). הנה לזה הוא מצות הדלקת נר חנוכה, פירוש "חנו כה" להאיר תוספת אור ביותר במלכות שנקראת "כה" כידוע עד שתאיר גם את בחינת חושך של החיצונים, וכמו שנאמר "כי אתה תאיר נרי וה' אלהי יגיה חשכי" (תהלים יח:כט).

ואם כן הרי זה היפך השמירה דמזוזה שלא יקרבו החיצונים ולא יראו אור כו' ובמצות נר חנוכה נמשך תוספת גילוי אור גם בהם עד שנתבטלו כמו שנאמר "כהמס דונג מפני אש" (תהלים סח:ג), והוא מפני עוצם הגילוי אלהות עד דגם חושך לא יחשיך כו'. ואין זה כמו השומר שעומד מבחוץ לפתח הסגור אלא אדרבה עומד ופותח הפתח אבל יתרחקו החיצונים מפני היראה ועוצם הגלוי, והוא שומר יותר מעולה. וזהו ענין השמירה דאור התורה שמאיר גם את החשך ואינו צריך לסגור הפתח.

- ק"ל -

והנה אם אדם ח״ו אינו מאמין בנסים נסתרים, אזי הוא במחשבתו שכך הוא ההרגל שביום מאיר החמה ובלילה מאיר הלבנה, ובלילה הוא ישן וביום הוא נעור, והמרבה בסחורה הוא מעשיר וההולך למרחקים הוא מרויח, וכשהוא חולה ליקח רפואה, והוא סבור שכך ההרגל. אמנם כשרואה נסים נסתרים אשר מסר האל הבורא ב״ה גבורים ביד חלשים וכמו מפלת המן, וכל שכן נסים נגלים, הוא רואה שאין העולם מתנהג בהרגל, רק שה׳ יתברך הוא מתיר אסורים והוא הזוקף כפופים והוא הגולל אור מפני חושך והוא היוצר אור והחושך, וה׳ יתברך הוא הרופא חולים...

וזה מצותה משתשקע החמה ועד שתכלה רגל מן השוק, כלומר מצותה משתשקע החמה, נסים נסתרים אשר המה מרומזים בשקיעת החמה שאינו מאיר כל כך, ועד שתכלה רגל מן השוק, כלומר שצריך אתה לחשוב במחשבתך בהדלקת נר חנוכה שתכלה רגל מן השוק, שתכלה ממחשבותיך שהעולם מתנהג על פי הרגל הטבע. וזה המחשבה היא מעשה חיצונים ומחשבת יצר הרע, אשר המה רמוזים בתיבת שוק. ובהדלקת נר חנוכה תכלה זה המחשבה, לילך ממך זה המחשבה שהעולם מתנהג על פי ההרגל...

ובזה מאמין שהנסים נסתרים אינם טבעים, רק שהוא מחדש את העולם תמיד בכל עת ובכל שעה, רק לפעמים מחדש את הטבע כמו כשקבע בהעולם בששת ימי בראשית, ולפעמים מחדש דבר חדש כגון נס נגלה. רק המודה בנס נסתר אזי הוא מודה שהוא מחדש תמיד ואפילו הטבע הקבוע בעולם...

סידור הרב

להבין שורש ענין מזוזה מימין ונר חנוכה משמאל כו׳. הנה שורש ההפרש אשר בין תורה למצות הוא בבחינת היחוד העליון מפני שיש בסיבת היחוד העליון שני דברים. האחד שהעליון ירד למטה אל המקבל, והשני שהתחתון יעלה למעלה אל המשפיע...

וכך יובן הענין בשורש ענין התורה והמצוות. הנה שורש בחינת התורה הוא בחינת המשכות וירידת אור אין סוף מלמעלה למטה מטה, כמו

- קכ"ט -

בימי מרדכי ואסתר שהיה כמדומה שהוא טבעיית. שבתחילה גדל את המן ואחר כך אהב את אשתו והרג אוהבו בשביל אשתו. וגם הנס הנזכר ב[תפילת] על הנסים "שמסר רבים ביד מעטים וטמאים ביד טהורים כו'" - והנה נס נסתר, שהמה בדרך מלחמה, וגם מעשה יהודית היה קצת בטבעים. אמנם באמת מעשה נסים ולא טבעיית, אבל נס נסתר היה ולא נס נגלה. וכן מבואר באור חדש שחיבר בעל גור אריה [מהר"ל], שנס חנוכה היה קצת טבעיית. גם אדוננו מורנו בוצינא קדישא הרב דוב בער ז"ל אמר שנס נגלה כמו במצרים נקרא יום, שמאיר לכל, ונס נסתר כמו חנוכה ופורים נקרא לילה, שאינו ידוע לכל כמו לילה שהוא חושך ואינו מאיר לכל.

והנה הנסים נסתרים נחלקו לשני בחינות: בחינה אחת כמו פורים, שה' יתברך עילת כל העילות הוא סבב הסיבה בעצמו ובכבודו בלי שום פעולה מהתחתונים, עד שהפר עצת המן הרשע והשיב לו גמולו בראשו והציל אותנו מכף כל העריצים, והתחתונים לא עשו כלום שום פעולה... אבל בחנוכה עשו תחתונים איזה פעולה, כי חשמונאי ובניו נלחמו מלחמות ה' ועשו פעולה, רק שה' יתברך עשה שלא כדרך הטבע ומסר גבורים ביד חלשים, אבל היה באיזה סיוע תחתונים.

נמצא הם שלשה מדריגות. נס דיציאת מצרים היה שינוי טבעיית והוא נקרא יום, והוא נס גדול. וקטן ממצרים הוא פורים, שהיה בטבעיית קצת, נס נסתר, והוא נקרא לילה כאשר כתבתי בשם אדוננו ומורנו ז"ל, אבל לא היו בסיוע התחתונים. וקטן מפורים נס חנוכה, שהיה נס נסתר וגם סיוע מתחתונים.

לכן אחר ראש השנה ויום הכפורים ושמיני עצרת... בתחילה חנוכה, ואחר כך פורים, ואחר כך פסח, כי "מעלין בקודש ולא מורידין" (שבת כא:). כי אנו ממשיכין ההארה של הנסים והחסדים של חנוכה, שהמה אינם כל כך גדולים, שהוא נס נסתר בסיוע התחתונים... ואחר כך מעלין בקודש ומקבלין ההארה מחסדים ומנסים דפורים שהוא נס נסתר אבל לא היה בו סיוע תחתונים... ואחר כך מעלין בקודש ומקבלין ההארה יותר גדולה בנסים וחסדים דפסח, שהיה בו נס נגלה שהוא דומה ליום שמאיר לכל...

- קכ"ח -

מאור עינים ב׳

... נתן לנו ה׳ מצות הדלקת נר חנוכה כי כל המצוות שנצטווינו בבוא עת וזמן של כל מצוה ומצוה נתעורר הדבר שהיה בעת זמן המצוה כמאז ומקדם...

ובחנוכה הוא עת לקרב האדם אל ה׳ על ידי התורה, כמו מאז ומקדם בימי מתתיהו בן יוחנן כהן גדול. שהיוונים טמאו כל השמנים הם כל החכמות ולא נשאר כי אם פך אחד של שמן - היא התורה. ולא נשאר כי אם מעט מזעיר, ונעשה נס שלא היה כי אם מעט על יום אחד ודלקו שמונה ימים. כי העולם הוא נבנה על ידי שבעה ימים, ואחר כלות השבעה מתחילין עוד שבעה ימים אחרים, וזהו הנקרא שבעת ימי הבנין. ומתתיהו בן יוחנן היה עובד את ה׳ בשכל גדול, וזהו כהן גדול, והמשיך בעבודתו להאיר שמונה ימים, היינו מעולם הבינה, להאיר שמונה הנרות.

ולכן נר חנוכה הוא למעלה משלושה [טפחים], שלא תהא כארעא סמיכתא, ולמטה מעשרה, כי מעולם לא ירדה שכינה למטה מעשרה (סוכה ה.). רק שה׳ חושב מחשבות "לבלתי ידח ממנו נדח" (שמואל ב יד:יד) היה על ידי נס שה׳ כביכול מוריד למטה מעשרה ומתקרב אל האדם להשיבו ולהחזירו אליו. היינו שהשמן מרמז על חכמה, ו"ה׳ יתן חכמה מפיו דעת ותבונה" (משלי ב:ו), ומלמד את האדם שכל איך לעבוד את ה׳ יתברך בשכל ותבונה. וכל זה הוא על ידי מצות הדלקת נרות חנוכה, וכאז כן עתה בכל דור בבוא עת וזמן מצוה זו...

קדושת לוי

(*קדושות לחנוכה ה׳*)

ועתה אבאר על מאמר חז"ל: מצות נר חנוכה משתשקע החמה עד שתכלה רגל מן השוק (שבת כא:)...

דע כי הנסים אשר עשה לנו הבורא ב"ה מתחלקים על שלשה אופנים. כי הנה יש נסים נסתרים, ויש נסים נגלים. הנסים הנגלים, כמו שנעשו לאבותינו במצרים, כמו דצ"ך עד"ש באח"ב (עשר המכות) וקריעת ים סוף, שהם שנוי טבעיים, והכל ראו באלו הנסים. ויש נסים נסתרים, כמו

חנוכה

מאור עינים א'

תנו רבנן מאי חנוכה? דתנו רבנן בכ"ה בכסלו... כשנכנסו יוונים להיכל... (שבת כא:).

הנה לכאורה על כרחך כוונת קושיתו הוא למה נקראת "חנוכה," ומה תירץ לו על זה? אך האמת היא שמלת חנוכה הוא "חנו כה".

שיש מידה הנקראת כה והיא מידת מלכות, שהמלך הוא מצוה כה יהיה וכה יהיה, כמו כן המידה זו מצוה בכל העולמות ועל ידה מתנהגים כל העולמות. ומפני זה הצדיקים יש בכחם למשול בכל העולמות מפני שיש בתוכם המידה מלכות של הבורא יתברך, וכמאמר רז"ל על פסוק "צדיק מושל יראת אלהים" (שמואל ב כג:ג): ומי מושל בי? צדיק - שהקדוש ברוך הוא גוזר גזירה וצדיק מבטלה (מועד קטן טז:).

והקשו בזהר הקדוש: וכי צדיקא קטרוגא דמאריה הוא [האם הצדיק הוא קטגור של רבונו] (ח"א מה:)? אך האמת הוא שהקדוש ברוך הוא בעצמו מבטלן. וכמבואר אצלנו כמה פעמים מזה כי "בכל צרתם לו צר" (ישעיה סג:ט), והוא בסוד גלות השכינה - שמידת מלכות הנזכרת לעיל נקראת שכינה מפני ששוכנת בכל מקום. והיא נקראת גם כן כנסת ישראל שהיא כונסת בתוכה כביכול שכולם נלקחו ממידה זו, וכמאמר רז"ל: כל ישראל בני מלכים הם (שבת קכח.). וכל הצרות שיש לישראל רחמנא לצלן הוא בסוד נפילת השכינה, כביכול, שהיא מידת מלכות, כמו שנאמר "צור ילדך תשי" (דברים לב:יח), והצדיקים על ידי מעשיהם הטובים מעלים כביכול השכינה, כמו שנאמר "תנו עוז לאלהים" (תהלים סח:לה), שישראל מוסיפין כח בפמליא של מעלה (איכה רבה א:לג). שהמידה הנזכרת לעיל נקראת פמליא של מעלה שכונסת בתוכה כל המידות העליונות, שכולם משפיעים בתוכה, וכשמידת מלכות נתעלית אז נתבטלו כל הגזירות וכל הדינים...

הבורא ב"ה נפסק חלקו משורש התורה. ועל ידי תיקון ראש השנה וביום הכפורים שב החלק של כל אחד מישראל אל התורה, ויש לו אז בחינת עלייה אל התורה.

שעל כן אחר יום הכפורים חג הסוכות, שהוא צילא דמהימנותא החופה ומגן על ישראל על ידי תיקון שהיה להם ביום הכפורים. ונקרא יום אחרון של חג שמחת תורה, שהוא שמחה לתורה עילאה ששבו ועלו אצלה ונתקרבו כל חלקי שרשי נשמות ישראל ונתאחדו בה, כי כל אחד שב על ידי תיקון הזמן של המועדים להתורה שמשם שורש נשמתן.

ועל כן המנהג שכל ישראל עולין לתורה ביום שמחת תורה, שבאמת אז עולין להתורה ברוחניות גם כן שמקרבין שורש נשמתן וחלק אלהי שבהן להתורה שמשם שורש נשמתן כמבואר, כנודע שיש ששים רבוא אותיות לתורה כמספר שרשי נשמות ישראל. ולכך קורין בפרשת וזאת הברכה שאחר תיקון שנעשה בזמנים הללו נשפע ברכה מלמעלה לכל אחד מישראל על ידי שנתיחדו בתורה ובבורא ב"ה כל שרשי חלקי נשמות ישראל.

שמיני עצרת ושמחת תורה

מאמרי אדמו"ר הזקן

ביום השמיני עצרת תהיה לכם... (במדבר כט:לה).

... למה מתחילין גבורות גשמים בשמיני עצרת?

והנה יש בחינת טל ובחינת מטר - טל הוא אהבה, ומטר הוא היראה. והוצרך שתי בחינות כי מחמת האהבה היה יכול יתבטל במציאות לגמרי, ולכן הוצרך היראה כי מחמת היראָה הוא נסוג אחור. ולכן נקראים אהבה ויראה גדפין, ודי למבין.

ובתורה יש גם כן בחינת טל ובחינת מטר. בחינת טל הוא המחשבה - טל תורה. ובחינת מטר הוא הדיבורים והאותיות, שהדיבורים הוא כל דיבור בפני עצמו כמו מטר שהן טיפין טיפין, אבל המחשבה היא אחדות כמו טל. ובחינת מטר הוא מעמיד העולם... כי מחמת מטר שהוא היראה אינו יורד התגלות האהבה ביחד אלא טיפין טיפין. לכן נקרא גבורות גשמים לפי שיורדים בגבורה, דהיינו מחמת יראה אינן יורדין רק טיפין טיפין. ובשמיני עצרת התגלות האהבה היא בלי גבול, ולכן אנו אומרים [מזכירים] גשמים כדי לעצור האהבה הנזכרת לעיל ויהיה העולם יכול להתקיים...

מאור עינים

(*מפרשת אמור*)

... על ידי התשובה עילאה [בראש השנה וביום הכפורים] מתקרבין כל חלקי הקדושה, חלקי ישראל, אל התורה, כי כל חלקי נשמות ישראל הן מושרשין בתורה. כנודע שכל אחד יש לו אות בתורה, ובהתרחקו מן

צמח ה' לצבי

(*מפרשת אמור*)

ולקחתם לכם ביום הראשון פרי עץ הדר... (ויקרא כג:מ).

ראשון לחשבון עוונות (תנחומא אמור כב). ונראה לי על דרך "אשרי אדם לא יחשוב ה' לו עון, [ואין ברוחו רמיה]" (תהלים לב:ב), וכמו שכתוב בספרי יראים פירושו שמה שלא יחשוב יראת ה' לו עון, ואין כו' אף על פי שלא היה ברוחו רמיה, ועיין בשל"ה (עשרה מאמרות מאמר תשיעי).

וזה ידוע מספר חובות הלבבות (שער חשבון הנפש פ' ג) דבעת שאדם עוסק במצות סוכה ולולב בעשייתן ותקונן, אף שאינו חושב בה' יתברך באותו עת מפני טרדת תקון המצוה ומכשיריה, מכל מקום למצוה יחשב, עיין שם.

וזהו שאמרו ראשון לחשבון עוונות, ועל דרך הפסוק "רבות עשית אתה ה' אלהי נפלאתיך ומחשבותיך אלינו אין [ערוך אליך אגידה ואדברה עצמו מספר]" (תהלים מ:ו). דהנה כל איש מחויב לעבוד את ה' יתברך במחשבה, כיון שישראל עלו במחשבה אצלו יתברך מחויב להיות העבודה נגד זה. והנה כשישראל עלו במחשבה, היה מחשב בהם אפילו בעת עשיית ותיקון העולם. וזה שנאמר "רבות עשית... ומחשבותיך אלינו," כי "אין ערוך אליך" ולא נתדמה אנחנו אליך בזה הדבר.

ובמדרש (פסיקתא רבתי ט"ו): "מחשבותיך" - חשבונותיך אלינו כו' עיין שם. והטעם כי החשבון הוא לפי המחשבה, ואם אין מחשבה אין חשבון, כמו שאמרו המקובלים מחשבה - חשב מה (תקוני זהר ת' סט קיב:).

ולכן בארבעה ימים שבין יום כפור לסוכות שטרודין בתיקון המצוות, אין עון המחשבה חל כנזכר לעיל. ולכן אין חשבון כלל אפילו על שאר עוונות שאינם נכנסין תחת החשבון, אם לא שסומך על זה כמו שאמרו חז"ל (יומא פה:): [האומר] אחטא ויום כפורים מכפר...

קדושת לוי

(*מפרשת האזינו*)

ולקחתם לכם ביום הראשון פרי עץ הדר... (ויקרא כג:מ).

איתא בגמרא (תנחומא אמור ס׳ כב): וכי ראשון הוא? אלא ראשון לחשבון עוונות. שלכאורה אין לו באור, כאשר האריכו... המפרשים הקדמונים.

והנראה כי באמת נכון הדבר שבימים האלו, מראש השנה עד יום הכפורים - כל איש ואיש בוודאי עיניו פקוחות על כל דרכיו לשוב אל ה׳, איש לפי שכלו יהלל ולפי מדריגתו מפחד ה׳ ומהדר גאונו בקומו לשפוט הארץ. כי קרוב יום ה׳ ומי יכול להצטדק בדין, ומי הגבר אשר לא יירא?! ואיזהו נפש אשר לא תענה כי יבוא להיות נשפט לפני שופט כל הארץ על כל מעשיו?! הלא החרד על דבר ה׳ יעשה במרום הר שכלו לתקן את אשר עיות, והתשובה נקראת תשובה מיראה.

ואחר יום הכפורים, כשעוסקין במצות סוכה ולולב וארבעה מינים וצדקה כיד ה׳ הטובה בנדבה וחיבה לעבוד את עבודת ה׳ בשמחה וטוב לב, אזי התשובה הזאת תשובה מאהבה.

וידוע מאמר חז״ל שעל ידי תשובה מיראה הזדונות נהפכו לשגגות, ועל ידי תשובה מאהבה הזדונות נהפכו לזכויות, כאשר איתא שם (יומא פו:). והקדוש ברוך הוא ברב רחמיו וחסדיו, הרוצה בתקנת השבים לפניו באמת ובאהבה, כאמור ״כי לא תחפוץ במות המת כי אם בשובו מחטאתו [מדרכו] והחיה״ (ונתנה תוקף מתפילת יום כפור, על פי יחזקאל יח:לב).

על כן בחג הזה שאנו באים לחסות בצל שדי על ידי מצוות ומעשים טובים מאהבת ה׳ יתברך, אז מונה העוונות לידע כמה מצוות יהיה חילוף עוונות. מה שאין כן עד סוכות, דהוא מיראה, אזי לא ימנה כלל...

זהו פירוש ״ראשון הוא [לחשבון עוונות]״... ואזי הוא משפיע לנו טובה וברכה כאשר רצונו יתברך להשפיע תמיד, כי יותר ממה שהעגל רוצה לינוק, פרה רוצה להניק (פסחים קיב.).

- קכ"ב -

ויום כיפור, לישב בסוכה שבעת ימים הידועים... לגמור הענין ממש בעובדא, שאנו לוקחים הלולב ואתרוג ביד, ומנענעים אותו הדעת שקבלנו עלינו בראש השנה, להכניסו בהמידות, להמליך מלכותו בשית סטרין, מורה שש קצוות...

ובזה בארתי מה שאנו אומרים בכל יום בשמונה עשרה בברכת שים שלום: "ברכנו אבינו כולנו כאחד באור פניך, כי באור פניך נתת לנו ה' אלהינו תורת חיים ואהבת חסד, וצדקה וברכה ורחמים וחיים ושלום." ולכאורה יש להבין איך תקנו לנו קדמונינו לומר ברכנו אבינו כולנו כאחד, והלא צרכי כללות עמך ישראל מרובים, וכל אחד מישראל שואל צרכיו הפרטיים מה שחסר לנפשו, ומה שחסר לזה אינו חסר לזולתו, ואיך יתכן לומר ברכנו אבינו כולנו כאחד בברכה אחת?

ובאמת על פי הדברים הנאמרים יובן, כי עיקר מגמת נפשנו לזכות לאור המאיר אל בחינת הגוונים, המה שבעת ימי הבנין, אשר בכאן יש בחינת התחלקות, מה שאין כן באור המאיר אליהם, אין שם שום התחלקות כלל, וכל פרטיות שיש בעולם הפירוד שם כלולים באחדות גמורה. ולזה אנו שואלים ומתחננים לפניו יתברך, "ברכנו אבינו כולנו כאחד," ונפשך לדעת איך יתכן שיתברכו כללות עם בברכה אחת, לזה באה התשובה בצד השאלה: הכוונה שנזכה כולנו שתברכנו באור המאיר לפנים ושם כללות הברכות לערך צרכי הפרטים. ולזה אנו אומרים "כי באור פניך," כלומר כיון שזכה לעורר אור המאיר בפנים, "נתת לנו ה' אלהינו תורת חיים ואהבת חסד, וצדקה וברכה ורחמים וחיים ושלום," כלומר כללות הברכות והטובות שמונה והולך, כלולים שם באחדות גמורה.

ונחזור לענין ההפרש של ראש השנה משל עתה, הגם שכוונתם עולה בקנה אחד כמבואר. אמנם החילוק בראש השנה אינו רק בסוד קבלת הלב לבנות קומת השכינה בסוד הדעת, ועתה בחג מכניס הדעת בשית סטרין בעובדא ממש...

סוכות

אור האמת

כוונת הלולב פרצוף נוקבא: מתחיל מהחזה כי שם הלב, ובלב ממליכין אותו יתברך.

וכוונת הנענועים היא כי זעיר אנפין הם "ישראל אשר בך אתפאר" (ישעיה מט:ג). ואשר היתה להם אהבת גרועים בלבם, ועל ידי הנענוע מעלה האהבות רעות בהשכל, ושם מתברר ומיישב בדעתו: מה לי לאהוב דברים גשמיים, טוב לו [לי] לאהוב עבודת הבורא להמליכו. ומקבל זה אהבה משלושה מוחין. ואחר כך מחזיר הארבעה מינים להחזה, פירוש משפיע זה האהבה לנוקבא, דהיינו שמקבל על עצמו להמליך להבורא יתברך בזה האהבה. וכן באהבת היראה ואהבת התפארת, ומחזיר כולם להנוקבא, פירוש ללב לעבודת הבורא יתברך בזה.

אור המאיר

(*מפרשת אמור*)

ולקחתם לכם ביום הראשון פרי עץ הדר כפת תמרים... (ויקרא כג:מ).

והכוונה להורות בא הכתוב שצריך האדם ליקח אלו המידות המרומזים בכלי קרב, האתרוג ולולב עם מיניו, מורים לשבעת ימי הבנין, צריך האדם לקבל עליו **מיום הראשון** ראש השנה, שהיא גם כן יום המלחמה, וזאת עיקר מגמת נפשנו עם סדר התפילות וכוונת שופר, עצם הכוונה לקבל עלינו בסוד הדעת מלכותו יתברך, לבנות אותה ולסעדה קומה חדשה...

ומהות קבלת עול מלכות שמים בראש השנה, כמו יציאת הדעת מגלות בפסח, ועדיין המידות המה בגלות. לכן מצוה עלינו תיכף אחר ראש השנה

ואחר זה הוא יום הכפורים שהוא סוד התענית פעם אחת בשנה, כי מן התורה אין תענית קבוע יותר בשנה כי אם יום הכפורים... כי ביום הכפורים הוא התעוררות והופעת התשובה עילאה [ספירת בינה] על כל ישראל, אפילו אותן שאין להן כח להתעורר תשובה בתוכן מצד עצמן בלא אתערותא דלעילא...

ובחינת תיקון התקרבות מתתא לעילא כבר נתקן מיום אתמול בערב יום הכפורים, שאם לא היה נתקן מקודם בחינת התקרבות מתתא לעילא לא היה אפשר להיות קירוב מעילא לתתא כנודע. ועל ידי כן שנתקן מקודם בערב יום הכפורים נשפעת ומאירה התשובה עילאה מעילא לתתא, ונתאחדו התקרבות חלקי הקרבן: העולה מתתא לעילא מאכילות ערב יום הכפורים תיקון כל אכילות חיצוניות של כל השנה, נתאחדו עם התקרבות הקדושה היורד מעילא לתתא ביום הכפורים מבחינת התענית, ונעשין אחדות אחת כל חלקי הקדושה שעושין מתתא והיורדין מלמעלה. ועל ידי זה נתקדשו ישראל ונתקרבו לבוראן, ועל כן הוא יום הכפורים שמכפר עוונותיהם על ידי שהתקרבו כל חלקי הקדושה שהן סוד נשמות ישראל מן החצוניות...

- קי"ט -

שמקריב חלבו ודמו כנודע (ברכות יז.). ולהבין זה איך אפשר ששני הפכים בנושא אחד יחשבו דבר אחד?

... יש בחינת דביקות בשורש הכל מתתא, שהוא לקרב כל המדריגות תחתונות והניצוצות הקדושים מדברים נפולים ולקשרם בבורא יתברך. ועל ידי זה דבוק בבורא יתברך הוא עם אותן המדריגות הנפולות, שהוא סוד האכילה שנחשב כקרבן על ידי שמקרב כל הניצוצות והחיות העליון המלובשת במאכל ההוא, שהוא הטעם שטועם במאכל ההוא. שהטעם הוא רוחני ולא ממשי, שהוא החיות הקודש העליון המלובשת תוך המאכל הגשמי ההוא. ובאכלו ממנו נשאר החיות בתוך האדם ונתוסף ונקשר בחיות ההוא שהוא החלק אלהי השוכן בתוכו, ועם אותו הכח והחיות הנתוסף בו עובד את ה' ומדבר דיבורים בדביקות ועושה מצוות בדביקות. וכל זה על ידי הכח וחיות מן המאכל שנתוסף בו ועל ידי שעולה ונדבק בבורא יתברך עם זה הכח יש עלייה לניצוץ הקדוש ההוא שהיה מלובש בגשמיות המאכל, והחצוניות נדחה לחוץ אחר שנפרש ממנו החיות, ויופיו שהיה מתחילה יפה ומהודר מחמת החיות ומעתה בהעדר החיות ממנו נשאר דבר מת ומוסרח...

וסוד התענית הוא התקרבות החלק אלהי בשרשו מעילא לתתא, כי מתתא לעילא אין בו על ידי שאינו אוכל ביום התענית. ועל ידי שיש לו אז לב נשבר ונכנע לו יתברך, אזי מתעורר אליו שורש הקדושה העליונה לקרבו אליו יתברך.

והנה לא כל האדם זוכה לזה להיות במדריגה זו להיות אכילתו נחשב קרבן שידבק את עצמו עם חיות המאכל. והוא על ידי שאין לו דעת כאמור, כי אינו אוכל רק למלאות תאותו ונשאר עם חיותו ועם חיות שנתוסף בו מן המאכל למטה... ומפני שה' יתברך חפץ חסד וחושב מחשבות "לבלתי ידח ממנו נדח" (שמואל ב יד:יד) שתהיה עלייה בצד מה לכל האכילות החצוניות של כל ישראל. על כן קבע יום אחד בשנה והוא ערב יום הכפורים שמצוה לאכול ולשתות בו, אפילו כשאוכל בבחינת חיצוניות שהוא למלאות תאותו בערב יום הכפורים נחשב לו גם כן למצוה וכאילו התענה. ועל ידי זה שיש פעם אחת מצוה באכילה חצונית ההיא על ידי זה יש עלייה לכל אכילות חיצוניות לכל השנה מאחר שגם בבחינה זו יש פעם אחת קירוב לקדושה על ידי הכח של מצוה...

דברת שלמה

(*מפרשת דברים*)

שמעתי ממורי זללה"ה על ענין הוידוי שצריך להזכיר מה שחטא. וצריך להבין למה לא די בעזיבת החטא וחרטה בלב, שזהו עיקר התשובה, והלא לפניו יתברך הכל גלוי מה שעשה.

ואמר כשאדם עושה עבירה הוא עושה בכחו וחיותו וממשיך ונותן חיות, שהם אותיות, בדבר ההוא שעושה, גניבה או גזילה או זנות וכדומה. ולכן כשעושה תשובה כדת צריך לומר הוידוי שהם האותיות של החטא, ואומר אותם בלב נשבר ובבכי. כי צריך לירד אחריהם למקום שהם שם במדריגה התחתונה ומצומצמת הנקראת עצבות ובכי, ולהעלות אותם אותיות משם על ידי שאומרים אותם בדחילו ורחימו לפני בורא העולם יתברך שמו. ועל ידי זה פורחין לעילא, כמו שכתוב בזהר הקדוש (תקוני זהר ת' י כה:)...

ואחר כך שמעתי מהמנוח הרב המאה"ג הקדוש החסיד המפורסם מורנו הרב שלמה קארלינר זללה"ה שאמר ששמע עוד ממורי זללה"ה על הדברים הנזכרים לעיל, שזה לשון וידוי שיש בהן אותיות י' ו' ד', שמביא האותיות לשרשן, שהוא הי' שהוא שורש כל האותיות...

מאור עינים

(*מפרשת אמור*)

... ועניתם את נפשותיכם בתשעה לחודש... (ויקרא כג:לב).

... וכי בתשיעי מתענין? והלא בעשירי מתענין! אלא לומר לך כל האוכל ושותה בתשיעי מעלה עליו הכתוב כאילו התענה תשיעי ועשירי (יומא פא:)...

והנה נודע שהאכילה נקראת קרבן - כמו שנאמר שהשולחן של אדם הוא במקום מזבח, וכמו שנאמר: משחרב בית המקדש, שולחנו של אדם מכפר עליו (חגיגה כז.). והנה מצינו גם כן שהתענית נקראת קרבן, על שם

- קי"ז -

מלאך כשר. כי אין לו מקום פנוי שיהיה בעמדו, וצריך להיות גם כן מעבדי ה', וממשיך האדם הבעל תשובה בגודל התלהבותו באש לעשות תשובה חיות לגוף העון ומוציא ממנו חיות הטומאה. על ידי שממליך לקודשא בריך הוא בכל אתר ואתר, נתבטל חיות מהטומאה, ונתמשך לו חיות הקדושה.

אורח לחיים

(*מפרשת אמור*)

אך בעשור לחודש השביעי הזה יום הכפורים הוא מקרא קודש יהיה לכם ועניתם את נפשותיכם... (ויקרא כג:כז).

איתא בשולחן ערוך (אורח חיים ס' תריט:ב) וזה לשונו: בליל יום הכפורים ומחרתו אומרים "ברוך שם כבוד מלכותו לעולם ועד" בקול רם... והביא במגן אברהם הטעם וזה לשונו: משום דכל השנה אומרים אותו בלחש מפני שמשה גנבה מהמלאכים, אבל ביום הכפורים גם ישראל דומין למלאכים - עד כאן לשונו.

והנה אמרו רז"ל: לית לך מידי דלא רמיזי באורייתא (תענית ט.). ואפשר לומר שנרמז בכאן בפסוק זה דהנה ידוע דברוך שם כבוד מלכותו הוא בחינת מלכות - נפש, וכל מקום שנאמר לשון "ענייה" הוא בקול רם, כמו שנאמר בפרשת כי תבא "וענו הלוים" (דברים כז:יד) קול רם, וכן בפרשת הבאת בכורים כתיב "וענית ואמרת לפני ה' אלהיך 'ארמי אובד אבי' וכו'" (דברים כו:ה), ופירש רש"י ז"ל "וענית" לשון הרמת קול - עד כאן לשונו.

וזהו הרמז בכאן: **יום הכפורים הוא מקרא קודש... ועניתם את נפשותיכם** הוא גם כן הרמת קול, כלומר **ועניתם** בקול רם **את נפשותיכם. ואת** פירושו עם כלומר עם נפשותיכם, היינו ברוך שם כבוד מלכותו לעולם ועד שהוא בחינת מלכות - נפש. וביום הכפורים תרימו קול עם נפשותיכם ותאמרו ברוך שם כבוד מלכותו לעולם ועד בקול רם.

יום הכפורים

מבשר צדק
(*מפרשת וירא*)

מי אל כמוך נושא עון ועובר על פשע לשארית נחלתו לא החזיק לעד אפו כי חפץ חסד הוא: ישוב ירחמנו יכבוש עונתינו ותשליך במצולות ים כל חטאותם (מיכה ז:יח-יט).

לפרש זה אקדים לפרש בשביל הרב הגאון המפורסם מורנו הרב לוי יצחק אב"ד דק"ק בארדיטשוב פירוש נושא עון דאיתא (סוכה נב:): על שלשה [ארבעה] הקדוש ברוך הוא מתחרט בכל יום [- גלות כשדים וישמעאלים ויצר הרע], שנאמר "ואשר הרעותי" (מיכה ד:ו). ולכן כשהאדם עובר ח"ו עבירה, אזי הקדוש ברוך הוא ברוב רחמיו וחסדיו הגדולים לאין קץ תולה בעצמו כביכול הסרחון, ונושא העון על עצמו באמרו שהוא כביכול הגורם שברא היצר הרע הגדול. וזהו **נושא עון**.

ושמעתי בשם ר' ארוש תלמידו שפירש **ישוב ירחמנו [יכבוש עונתינו]** דאיתא כששב מאהבה נעשו מעבירות זכויות (יומא פו:). ונמצא אם ה' ב"ה נושא העון, שוב אין לו לבעל תשובה העון שיהיו לו זכויות על ידו. רק שה' יתברך הוא רחמן גדול, "וכאב את בן ירצה סלה" (משלי ג:יב), ומחזיר העון להאדם בעת שעושה תשובה מאהבה כדי שיהיה לזכויות. וזהו **ישוב**, כשהאדם עושה תשובה, **ירחמנו**, אז ה' יתברך מרחם עליו. **יכבוש עונתינו**, היינו שכובש העון למטה על הבעל תשובה כדי שיהיה לו זכויות - עד כאן דבריו.

ואיתא דהיצר הרע נקרא "דבר" (רש"י על חבקוק ג:ה), ומה שהאדם בורא ח"ו בעבירתו נקרא גם כן דבר, כי הוא הוא. ואקדים להבינך מפני מה יכול האדם לעשות מעבירותיו זכויות? באיזה כח הוא? זה הוא כי האדם כשעובר ח"ו איזה עבירה בורא בזה מחבל. וכשהאדם עושה תשובה מאהבה, והוא על ידי שמכיר גדולתו יתברך ויודע שלית [אתר] פנוי מיניה, נמצא שוב אין מקום פנוי בלעדי ה' ואף המחבל נתעלה ונעשה

ולכן על ידי זה נברא העולם ונמצא הדין הוא תכלית החסד. וזהו **מרחוק ה' נראה לי**, רוצה לומר מבחינת רחוק שהוא מידת הדין שהוא מתדמה לבחינת רחוק מתוך זה נראה לי ה' שהוא הרחמים...

והנה תחילה היתה הרחמים גנוזה בהעלם... ו[אחר כך] נתגלה הרחמנות בפועל. לכן נקרא היום הרת עולם שהיה בבחינת הריון, שהרחמנות היתה בהעלם גנוז כמו עובר בהריון, ועתה צריך לעורר על ידי שופר שיתגלו בפועל. וזהו בתשרי נולדו האבות (ראש השנה י:), רוצה לומר הרחמנות שיהיו בבחינת הריון ועתה נולדו בהתגלות, וכן בתשרי נברא העולם שתמיד הוא כן התחדשות הבריאה...

- קי"ד -

הקליפות של העבירות, ושיעשה מהם זכויות כשיעשה מאהבה. וזהו אמרו בחודש זה "תחדשו מעשיכם," רוצה לומר שיעשו מעשים טובים. ואחר כך אומר "שפרו מעשיכם"... ואמר הקדוש ברוך הוא אם תשפרו מעשיכם כנזכר לעיל אהיה לכם כשופר - מה שופר זה מכניס בזו ומוציא בזו... רוצה לומר שמכניס במקום צר ומוציא במקום רחב, כך אני אעמוד מכסא דין שהוא מקום צר, דהיינו צמצום כי כל דין הוא צמצום, ואשב על כסא רחמים שהוא התפשטות החסדים. והופך לכם מידת הדין למידת הרחמים, כי מכח זה ששפרתם מעשיכם ומעוונות נעשו זכויות, ממילא לא נשאר לכם שום דין והמקטרג נעשה סניגור.

ושפיר המשל דומה לנמשל שהמקום צר של שופר הולך ומתרחב, כך מידת הדין עצמו יהיה הולך ומתרחב עד שיעשה כולו רחמים. אימתי? בחודש השביעי שהוא עת דין, "שמאלו תחת לראשי" (שיר השירים ב:ו)...

מאור עינים

מרחוק ה' נראה לי ואהבת עולם אהבתיך על כן משכתיך חסד (ירמיה לא:ב).

הענין הוא דאמרו רז"ל: בתשרי נברא העולם (ראש השנה יא.), ולא אמר ברא. כי באמת בכל ראש השנה הוא בריאת העולם כמבואר שהקדוש ברוך הוא ברא העולם ונשאר עדיין "לעשות" (בראשית ב:ג). וזהו מסר ביד ישראל, והנה כפי מעשיהם כן גורמים למעלה, ואם הם אינם זכאין הרי ראוי העולם להיות תוהו ובוהו.

ולפי שבראש השנה יום הדין כולם רועדים ופוחדים ושבים אל ה', וחוזרים כל אחד לשרשם מעוררים הרחמנות של הבורא ב"ה ונעשה בריאת עולם... ולכן אמר בראש השנה נברא העולם תמיד הוא כן.

וזהו "בראשית ברא אלהים" ואמר בתיקונים (הקדמה טז): בראשית - "בא תשרי", כאשר בא תשרי נעשה בריאה על ידי האלהים שהיא מידת הדין, מחמת פחד הדין חוזרים אל ה' ומעוררין הרחמנות לברוא העולם. ותשרי הוא אור חוזר בסוד תשר"ק שהוא חזרת כל הדברים בסוד הדין,

שעושה מצוות ומעשים טובים הוא אינו עושה. כי עושה בכח ה' יתברך, ובשכלו ובחסדו ובטובו שהיטיב לו... הוא כשופר שאין בו שום קול, רק מה שתוקעין...

ובזה אנו מעוררין וממשיכין עלינו אהבה ראשונה, וזהו במה? בשופר. רוצה לומר במה שאנו מחזיקים עצמנו כשופר שאין בו שום קול רק מה שתוקעין בו האדם בכחו, כך אין בנו שום זכות שיתחייב להיטיב לנו, כי הכל מאתו יתברך...

תורי זהב

במדרש פרשת אמור (ויקרא רבה כט:ג) רבי ברכיה פתח: "תקעו בחודש שופר [בכסה ליום חגנו]" (תהלים פא:ד)... בחודש זה תחדשו מעשיכם בשופר: בחודש הזה שפרו מעשיכם. אמר להן הקדוש ברוך הוא לישראל אם שפרתם מעשיכם הריני נעשה לכם כשופר הזה - מה שופר זה מכניס בזו ומוציא בזו, כך אני עומד מכסא הדין ויושב על כסא רחמים והופך לכם מידת הדין למידת הרחמים. אימתי? בחודש השביעי.

ומקודם נפרש לדברי ר' ברכיה: אחד, מהו החילוק בין תחדשו מעשיכם לשפרו מעשיכם, הא שניהם כאחד מורים על חידוש מעשים טובים. שני, קשה היאך דומה המשל לנמשל?...

וידוע דכוונות דשופר הוא "מן המצר קראתי יה ענני במרחב יה" (תהלים קיח:ה), דבמקום הנחת הפה הוא צר ומקום הוצאת קול הוא רחב, ושופר מרמז על בעל תשובה צריך לעייל לקדוש ברוך הוא ממקום צר... וידוע דהדינים הוא צמצום החסדים, והחסדים הוא מרמז להתרחבות והתפשטות.

ולפי זה נבוא אל הביאור דידוע דהבעל תשובה צריך להיות מקודם מודה ועוזב, ומיום ההוא והלאה יחשוב שהוא כקטן שנולד ויתחיל לעשות מעשים טובים. ואחר כך יעשה סיגופים וכל התשובות הצריכים לו להרוג

קדושת לוי ב'

זמרו אלהים זמרו זמרו למלכנו זמרו (תהלים מז:ז).

לבאר כי בראש השנה וביום הכפורים שאז הוא המתקת הדין, צריך האדם לחתוך את הדינים, ולעבוד את הבורא במידת הרחמים, ולא במידת דין ששופט את עמו, רק לאחוז במידת הרחמים, וכמו האב ששופט את בנו.

והנה ידוע ש[שם] אלהים מרמז על דין. וזהו **זמרו**, כלומר תראו לחתוך זו המידה, שלא ישב במידת דין שופט את עמו, רק כאב את הבן, והוא יציל אותנו מכל דופי.

אורח לחיים

(מפרשת האזינו)

ואמרו לפני בראש השנה מלכיות זכרונות ושופרות. מלכיות כדי שתמליכוני עליכם, זכרונות כדי שיעלה זכרונכם לפני לטובה. ובמה? בשופר (ראש השנה טז.).

והנה בראש השנה דנין את כל העולם, עם ראוי והגון לעמוד, ורואין ודנין אם נתמלא כוונת הבריאה שברא את העולם כדי שיתגלה מלכותו - היא מידת יראתו. על כן אמר הקדוש ברוך הוא: **אִמרו לפני מלכיות כדי שתמליכוני עליכם** ונמצא נתקיימה כוונת הבריאה. **זכרונות כדי שתבוא [שיעלה] זכרונכם לפני לטובה**, רוצה לומר אף על פי שאין בנו שום זכות אנו מזכירין לפני ה' יתברך אהבה ראשונה שברא כל העולמות להיטיב לישראל, לא בזכותם רק ברצון ברכה ונדבה. ובזה שאנו מזכירין אהבה ראשונה, אנו מעוררין אהבה ראשונה להיטיב גם עתה ברצון ברכה ונדבה אף על פי שאין בנו שום זכות...

ובמה? בשופר. רוצה לומר במה אנו מעוררין אהבה ראשונה? בשופר. כי שמעתי בשם הרב בוצינא קדישא מורנו הרב דוב בער זללה"ה פירוש הפסוק "כשופר הרם קולך" (ישעיה נח:א): רוצה לומר האדם צריך לחשוב את עצמו כאין, ואין בו שום זכות ומעשים טובים, ואף על פי

ועל דרך זה הוא ענין תקיעות שופר, על דרך הגמרא: צורת יעקב אבינו חקוקה תחת כסא כבודו (תיקוני זהר ת' כב סה:).

אור המאיר

ושמעתי מהמגיד זצלה"ה משל נאה לפני התקיעות: למלך ששלח בניו ידידיו למרחקים למדינה אחרת, ונשתהו שם ימים ושנים, ונתגרשו מעל שולחן אביהם. ודאג לבם בקרבם ליתן עצות לנפשם באיזה אופן נאות להם להשיב אל מנוחתם ומדינתם, אשר היה שם אהלם מתחילה בחצר המלך פנימה, לשמוח ולהשתעשע בתענוג אביהם כראות פני אלהים, אשר טוב להם אז מעתה.

והתחילו לשלוח דיבורים של רחמנות אל המלך, אולי יכמרו רחמיו להשיבם אליו. ויהי כאשר שבו ונתקרבו לחצר המלך ויראו את פני אביהם, והנה איננו אליהם כתמול שלשום ומימים ימימה טרם שנתרחקו מעליו. והנה כל עוד שהרבו דבריהם בהתחננם בדברי תפילה ותחנונים, אולי יכמרו רחמיו כאב רחמן על בניו הנעימים, ואין קול ואין עונה.

ויהי כאשר ארכו הימים ואין מענה בפיהם, התחילו הבנים להתבונן ליתן עצה וגבורה כדת מה לעשות, לעורר רחמי האב אהבתו הישנה, ומה הגיע על ככה שצועקים ואינם נענים, הלא רחמי האב גדולה, ובודאי לא על חנם. והשיבו אל לבם פן ואולי שכחנו בארץ מרחקים לשון אבינו המלך, ונתערבנו בגוים ולמדנו מעשיהם ולשונם ודיבור אין לנו אל המלך, ולכן לא נשמע דברינו בהיכל אבינו המלך.

ונתנו עצה לנפשם, למה לנו לזעוק ולצעוק בחיתוך דיבורים, כי אם נשמיע קול פשוט לעורר רחמנותו סתם בקול הפשוט, כי קול פשוט שוה לכל, והנמשל מובן...

ראש השנה

אור האמת

אל תבוא במשפט עמנו כי לא יצדק לפניך כל חי (סליחות לערב ראש השנה).

פירוש כל הדנין את ישראל דנין כביכול אותו יתברך, דהוא אחדות עמנו. כי לא יצדק לפניך כל חי, שהוא הכל חיות מאתך. והיאך ידין אותך?

שמועה טובה

בענין התקיעות משל נאה והוא קצת מהאיש אלקי קדוש מורנו בעריש זללה"ה: מלך אחד ששלח בנו יחידו לארץ מרחקים על איזה טעם כמוס שהיה אתו. והנה הבן הזה ברוב הימים שהורגל בין אנשי הכפרים נעשה איש שובב ושכח בנימוס המלך, ונתעבה שכלו גם נתעבה טבע טבעותיו הדקים ומזגיו הטובים. וגם שכלו השלם של המלכות.

ביום אחד שמע הבן שיבוא המלך למדינה זו שהבן בתוכה. והנה כשבא המלך אז בא הבן בתוך אפלטר המלך וצעק בקול גדול ומשונה, ורק בצעקת קול כי שכח הדיבור של המלך. ואז כששמע המלך קולו וראה ששכח אפילו הדיבור נתמלא רחמים על בנו. וזה ענין הקול של שופר.

ופעם אחת אמר המשל בסגנון זה: שהיה לעבדי המלך קרוב אחד מבני משפחתו שהיה גדול מאוד בעיני המלך. ומחמת גודל האהבה שהיה לו היה תוקע צורתו על הכסא שלו להסתכל תמיד על הוד יפיו ותענוגי שפע עליו מידי זכרו אותו.

והנה ביום המשפט של עבדי המלך היו צועקין למלך רק שיסתכל על הצורה החקוקה על הכסא שלו, ויתמלא רחמים בעבור אהבתו אליהם.

- ק"ט -

שבת קביעא וקיימא (ביצה יז.; שמות רבה טו:כד). וידוע מאמר חז"ל שכל הדברים השייכים לחודש תלוים בישראל, כי כפי הזמן שמקדשין ישראל החודש כן נגמרים כל הדברים השייכים ל[אותו] חודש, כמו שאמרו רז"ל לענין ראש השנה שכל הכסאות למשפט כולם תלוים ועומדים וממתינים עד שיקדשו ישראל ראש השנה (ראש השנה ח:)... נמצא שהכל תלוין בישראל כפי הזמן שמקדשין את החודש.

וזהו **החדש הזה לכם**, היינו שמסרתיו **לכם**, כי קדושת החודש תלויה בישראל. וזהו **ראשון הוא לכם**, "ראשון" הוא מרומז עליו יתברך שמו (ישעיה מד:ו), כי הוא ראשון. **לכם**, היינו שה' יתברך הוא שנקרא **ראשון** הוא **לכם**, כי בזה החודש מסור לישראל לקדש אותו בזמן שירצו, בזה רואים שאפילו ה' יתברך כביכול **הוא לכם**, כי בידכם להנהיג הנהגתו כפי רצונכם, כי הכל תלוים כפי הזמן שישראל מקדשים החודש כן הוא יתברך מנהיג הנהגתו ומשפטו. וזהו "חדשי השנה," שכל התחדשות השנה הכל מתנהג על ידכם...

קדושת לוי ב'

(*מפרשת שקלים*)

והטעם שאומרים בכל ראש חודש "ברכי נפשי את ה'" (תהלים קד), דיש לומר הטעם שנקרא "ראש חודש" משום דידוע דמכל השכליות הראשית הוא הרצון, ואחר כך כשרוצה בדבר אז בונה הדבר, אחר כך ניתוסף אהבה והיראה והתפארות, ואם כן רצון נקרא ראשית. והנה בכל ראש חודש נתגלה רצון חדש על ישראל האיך לעבוד את הבורא יתברך. ולכך נקרא "ראש חודש." והנה נפש הוא מלשון "רצון," כמו "אם יש את נפשכם" (בראשית כג:ח). ולזה אומרים בראש חודש "ברכי נפשי את ה'," רוצה לומר נעשה בריכה והמשכת רצון בראש חודש מן ה', דהוא המקור של כל ההשפעות והחיים.

ראש חודש

חיים וחסד

ובראשי חדשיכם תקריבו עולה לה׳... (במדבר כח:יא).

כי זה ידוע שענין הקרבנות היה שהיה מקריב ומעלה נפשו לה׳ יתברך, ועל כן נקרא קרבן עולה לה׳, רוצה לומר עליית הארציות לשרשו. וקרבן חטאת הוא היראה שיעשה בלבו יסוד ליראה, וקרבן שלמים הוא התקשרות, וכן כל המידות היה מעלה לשרש, ובזה היה מעורר שרשם למעלה. במידת אהבה שלו היה מעורר מידת האהבה של ה׳ יתברך, וכן כולם, ועל ידי זה היה נמשך להם חיות חדשה ושכל חדש מידותיהם.

ועכשיו אף שאין לנו זה בעובדא אך יכול לפעול זאת בדיבורים פרשת הקרבנות, ומי שמעלה הפנימיות מהאותיות על ידי זה מעורר מידות עליונות. ומי שמעלה רק הלבוש, הם האותיות לבד, אין לו קיום כי הלבוש סופו ליפול כי הלבוש הוא רק קיום עולם הגשמי. על כן צריך להעלות הפנימיות מהאותיות. וזהו ״הנסתרות לה׳ אלהינו,״ הוא פנימיות המידות, אבל ״הנגלות,״ הוא הלבוש הם האותיות, הוא רק ״לנו ולבנינו״ (דברים כט:כח) - קיום העולם הגשמי. וכשיעלה הפנימיות הנזכרת לעיל אז יכול לעורר התחדשות השכל שנקראת **ראש**...

קדושת לוי א׳

(*מפרשת בא*)

החדש הזה לכם ראש חדשים ראשון הוא לכם לחדשי השנה (שמות יב:ב).

כי אמרו רז״ל שצריך לאמר [בתפילת העמידה] ״מקדש השבת וישראל וראש חודש [ראשי חדשים]״, כי ראש חודש ישראל מקדשין ליה, אבל

דבוודאי שבת היא מתנה טובה, רוצה לומר האור והקדושה הבאים מלמעלה לתוך לבות בני אדם ורוח קדושה ושכל חדש וחיות רוחניות הבאה מעולם עליון הנקרא ערבות, אשר שם תענוג וחיות שבו גנזי חיים.

והנה באמת יש לאדם לצפות כל ימי החול על מתנת השבת, על קדושה וחיות זו הבאה לאדם, ובוודאי בעי הכנה רבה כל ששת ימי המעשה על שבת. וכפי אשר יעשה הכנתו כן תהיה השגתו, והכתוב אומר "והכינו את אשר יביאו" (שמות טז:ה), שאדם צריך להטריח את עצמו בחול שיהא לו בשבת, ומי שטרח [בערב שבת יאכל בשבת] (עבודה זרה ג.).

ואף על פי שאדם מכין את עצמו, מכל מקום מתנה טובה היא. כי אף אם יכין אדם את עצמו בכל מיני הכנות שונות, אינו ראוי לקדושה ושום שפע לו מה' יתברך ביום השבת, ובוודאי הוא מתנת חנם. אך דהכנה צריך להיות, להכין את עצמו האדם להיות לו לבית קבול וכח לקבל.

צמח ה' לצבי

(*מפרשת יתרו*)

בקידוש ליל שבת: "הנחילנו... זכרון למעשה בראשית... [תחילה] למקראי קודש זכר ליציאת מצרים."

הענין על דרך שכתב הרמב"ן שבדברות שניות כתיב אצל שבת "וזכרת כי עבד היית בארץ מצרים [ויוציאך]... על כן צוך ה' אלהיך לעשות את יום השבת" (דברים ה:יד), היאך תלוי זה בזה? ועוד שבדברות הראשונות נאמר "כי ששת ימים עשה [ה' את] השמים ואת הארץ... על כן [ברך ה' את יום השבת ויקדשהו]" (שמות כ:י). ותירץ שבאמת השבת היא בכדי לזכור חידוש עולם... ומי יודע מחידוש העולם? רק על ידי יציאת מצרים נתגלו אלהותו ואמונתו שהוא ברא העולם, וזהו "וזכרת כי עבד היית בארץ מצרים ויוציאך, ועל ידי זה תאמין טעם שנאמר "כי ששת ימים..."

נמצא הזכרון במעשה בראשית הוא כמו שאומרים לאדם דבר חדש שלא ידע מעולם ולא ראהו, וזה נקרא "זכרון למעשה בראשית." אבל דבר שראה בעצמו אין צריך רק להזכירו מה שראה וידע, וזה נקרא זכר, וזה שאומרים "זכר ליציאת מצרים."

רוחניות מאד, והיא ממש עצם אלהות, והבהיק זיו הדרו מסוף העולם ועד סופו בכל מעשה בראשית, ועיקר בהאדם שהוא מובחר ברואי ה׳ יתברך הבהיק אליו בהירות משרשו הנעלם שבמחשבת ה׳ יתברך ב״ה. וזהו ענין ״מה היה העולם חסר? מנוחה.״ רוצה לומר ה׳ יתברך נקרא מנוחה, שאין שייך בו תנועה ממקום למקום כמו בברואים...

ולזה נקראת שבת, לשון ״השבה,״ ששבו הברואים לשרשם. ורוצה לומר ענין זה הוא כי אין קיום לשום נברא בעולם זולת ברצון ה׳ יתברך... ורצונו בברואים הוא התענוג מהם כשיתדבקו לשרשם על ידי תשוקתם. ועל ידי זה יהיו קיימים מפני שיתדבקו בו והוא נצחי וקיים, ועוד שימלאו רצונו שרצה מהם ויהיה רצונו במקומו...

על ידי הבריאה נתרחקו מהשורש, מחמת התהוות הגופניות של בני אדם, ונתפרדו על ידי זה מהשורש שהוא רוחניות ואחדות אחת. לזאת אחר הבריאה שרצה ה׳ יתברך שיתקיימו ולא יכלו מחמת התרחקם ממנו, לזה הבהיק בהירות הווייתם הנעלם... ואז נתמלאו חשק ורצון אליו, כמו התינוק שהולך אחר מעשה נערות ושוכח באביו. ואחר כך כשרואה את אביו מחמת חשקו אליו משליך הכל ומתדבק בו ורץ אליו מחמת שהוא נתח מנתחיו.

כן כביכול כשה׳ יתברך מבהיק זיו הדרו אל הברואים, אז מגמת פניהם אליו בתשוקה גדולה. וזה רצונו שמקוה מהם, וזה סיבת קיומם משני טעמים כנזכר לעיל. וזהו ענין השבת שהוא השבה אל השורש, רוצה לומר השורש מאיר על הענפים והענפים חושקים ומתענגים בו ונכספים אליו, והוא אחדות עם ה׳ יתברך.

קדושת לוי
(*מפרשת כי תשא*)

ויאמר ה׳ אל משה לאמר: ואתה דבר אל בני ישראל לאמר אך את שבתותי תשמורו... (שמות לא:יא-יב).

והנה חז״ל למדו מכאן דהנותן מתנה לחבירו צריך להודיעו. אמר הקדוש ברוך הוא לישראל, ״מתנה טובה יש לי בבית גנזי ושבת שמה״ (שבת י:).

- ק"ה -

שהוא מעין עולם הבא, יום שבת מנוחה שירגילו עצמם לקבל התענוג אחר כך.

וזהו (שם): "מתנה טובה יש לי בבית גנזי" [ושבת שמה ואני מבקש ליתנה לישראל לך והודיעם], רוצה לומר שגנוזה המתנה עד לעתיד. "ושבת שמה", הוא יום שכולו שבת. "ואני מבקש ליתנה לישראל" לעתיד, לכן "לך והודיעם", רוצה לומר על ידי השבת שאתן להם הוא הודעה למה שיהיה אחר כך, שלא יהיה התענוג פתאום אלא בהדרגה...

לקוטים יקרים

(יושר דברי *אמת* ס' מה-מו)

ועתה אתחיל לכתוב איזה דברים מענין יום השבת קודש, אף על פי שאי אפשר ליגע אפילו בקצהו ולבאר ממנו דבר, כי הוא היתד הגדול שבכל המצות כמו שאמרו רז"ל: שקולה שבת [כנגד כל המצוות] (שמות רבה כה:יב)...

נודע מה שאמרו חז"ל על הפסוק "ויכל אלהים ביום השביעי" (בראשית ב:ב), מה היה העולם חסר? מנוחה. באת שבת באת מנוחה (רש"י שם על פי בראשית רבה י:ט). וכתוב אצלי בשם קדוש עליון רבי בער זלה"ה הענין כפי אמיתת אמונתנו, שבריאת העולמות היתה בשביל ישראל, כמו שאמרו רז"ל: בראשית - בשביל ישראל (ויקרא רבה לו:ד). והענין שעלה במחשבה לפניו שיהיו העולמות כדי שיבראו ישראל בתוכם ויעבדוהו ויתדבקו בו...

בראשונה נבראו נשמות ישראל במחשבתו של ה' יתברך ואחר כך כשרצה ה' שיהיו הנשמות בגשמיות, "צוה ויעמוד" (תהלים לג:ט). רוצה לומר דיבר על הכל: "יהי כן" - "יהי רקיע, יהי מאורות, תדשא הארץ תוצא הארץ..."

ואחר שנגמר הכל ביום ששי אילו היה העולם נשאר בזה, לא תוכל הבריאה להתקיים מחמת מיעוט החיות אשר בה, כי החיות שבגשמיות היא בצמצום. לזאת אחר גמר כל מעשה בראשית הבהיק ה' יתברך בהירות מבריאה הנעלמה, דהיינו ממה שנתהוו הברואים במחשבתו הויה

השביעי הוא שבת שהשבת עילאה מצטמצמת בזה היום והוא חיות כל העולם.

שעל כן נאמר "מחלליה מות יומת" (שמות לא:יד). כי בזה שהוא מחלל את השבת ואינו מקיימו מסלק החיות העליון, שבת עילאה שהוא בחינת נשמת העולם, מן העולם. ונמצא הורג את העולם שמסלק נשמתו ממנו, ולשון "מחלל" הוא מלשון "כי ימצא חלל" (דברים כא:א) שהוא לשון נטילת נשמה - ועל כן ענשו גם כן כך מות יומת.

ועל ידי השבת שמקיימים את השבת שהוא בחינת שתי שבתות, שבת עילאה ושבת תתאה, שהוא בנשמה וחיות כבוד שמו יתברך המלובש ביום השביעי שהוא בזמן וגבול, יש כח להשבת להיות ממוצע בין ישראל לאביהם שבשמים לדבקה בו יתברך...

מאור עינים ד'

(*מפרשת כי תבוא*)

לעתיד "ומלאה הארץ דעה [את ה']" (ישעיה יא:ט), שיהיה דעת שלמה וגדולה ותהיה האהבה ויראה בתכלית השלימות. כי באמת כל האברים יתמלאו דעת כדכתיב "ובדעת חדרים ימלאון" (משלי כד:ד), שכל החדרים, הם האברים שהם חדרים להכניס בהם שכינתו יתברך השורה באדם, יתמלאון על ידי הדעת השלמה שתהיה. מה שאין כן עתה שהדעת אינה רק במוח והוא מיעוט, ולעתיד יתפשט ויתרחב ויתמלא כל הארץ, אפילו במדריגות תחתונות שהם ארציות יתמלא לדעת בהם ה'. וזהו "בדעתו תהומות נבקעו" (תהלים ג:יט), אפילו במדריגות התחתונות הנקראות בלשון "תהומות" נבקעו - יהיה בהם בקיעה ופתיחה לכנוס [להכנס] בהם הדעת.

אמנם הקדים הקדוש ברוך הוא לישראל מתן שבת לפי שהדעת הגדולה ישיגו לעתיד, והוא תענוג גדול. ודרך משל: הנותן מתנה גדולה לחבירו אם לא הודיעו תחילה אלא יתן לו פתאום, יתבהל דעתו מלקבל. ולכן הנותן מתנה לחבירו צריך להודיעו תחילה (שבת י:), שיתיישב דעתו בקבלתו אחר כך. כן הוא על דרך משל לעתיד יהיה יום שכולו שבת תענוג תמידי, ואי אפשר לקבל פתאום מתנה גדולה כזאת. לכן נתן השבת

ולכן אמרו רז"ל: שיהא בעיניך כאילו כל מלאכתך עשויה ואין מחסור דבר (מכילתא יתרו). שהרי בשבת אלהותו יתברך מתפשטת ומתגלה בבני ישראל, ואיהו שלים בכל סטרוי בכל מיני שלימות. ואם מורה היפך ח"ו מראה שאינו מהם ואין בו השראתו כביכול.

ואמנם לא לבד מלאכת הדיוט אסורה בשבת, אך אפילו מלאכת המשכן. רוצה לומר משכן נקרא על שם "ושכנתי בתוך בני ישראל" (שמות כט:מה), שהקדוש ברוך הוא שוכן בתוך בני ישראל והאדם צריך להיות משכן אליו. ואם לא טהור הוא מחלאת עוונותיו ומעכב השראת שכינתו ב"ה, בשבת יסיר מלבו גם דבר זה שלא יעצב על זה. רק ישמור שבת כהלכתו, וישמח בה' יתברך שלפניו הוא רעוא דרעוין ושמחה.

ונמצא אפילו מלאכת המשכן שיעשה דבר הצריך אליו שיהיה משכן לה' גם זה ממעט בשבת...

מאור עינים ג'

(*מפרשת כי תבוא*)

... נודע מה שנאמר בש"ס: "אלמלא שמרו ישראל שתי שבתות מיד היו נגאלין (שבת קיח:)". ולהבין מה הן השתי שבתות?

... הבורא ב"ה הוא בלתי בעל תכלית וגבול, והאדם הוא בעל גבול ותכלית. והאיך אפשר לשני הפכים להתקרב [זה] לזה? נתן הבורא ב"ה לישראל את השבת שהוא ממוצע בין ישראל לאביהם שבשמים ומאחדן ומקשרן בבורא ב"ה, על ידי שיש בו שני החלקים מתדמין בין לישראל ובין לקדוש ברוך הוא.

כנודע שכל דבר הממוצע בין שני הפכים צריך להיות דומה לשתי הבחינות דנודע מה שנאמר בזהר (ח"ב פח.): שבת שמא דקודשא בריך הוא שלים מכל סטרין. שהשבת הוא חיות עולם העליון וחיות זה העולם, שהוא אצילות כבודו יתברך שמשתלשל ומצטמצם בזה יום השביעי שהוא בזה העולם. והיום השביעי שנקרא שבת אצלנו הוא כמו גוף ולבוש ליום השבת עילאה דאיהו שמא דקודשא בריך הוא כאמור לעיל. ובחינת שבת עילאה הוא נשמת כל העולם שחוזר חלילה תמיד בששת ימים, ויום

להמליך הבורא על כל העולם והנבראים לקיים "מלא כל הארץ כבודו" (ישעיה ו:ג).

ובחינת עבודה זו כוללת הן בדיבור הן במחשבה הן במעשה כאמור לעיל, שבכל דבר שעושה יראה על החיות המלובשת בדבר ההוא שהוא בשבירה. ובבוא הדבר ההוא ליד האדם הישראלי השלם, שהוא קומה שלימה ודבוק החלק אלהי שבקרבו אל הבורא ב"ה, אזי יש עלייה לדבר ההוא מעניני העולם ומביאו לשלימות הגמורה... זה נקרא מלאכת המשכן, שעושה משכן לבורא בכל העולם ומלואו בכל הל"ט מלאכות שהן חללי דעלמא כולו.

וכן בדיבור ומחשבה - כשמדבר דיבורים אפילו בדברים ארציים שהן הכרחים יהיה גם כן כך על דרך זה, שלא יהא שיחתו לצורך עצמו ולא יהיה בפירוד מהחיות העליון המשפיע לו החיות לדבר דיבורים. רק יכוין גם כן בבחינת "דע ה"ו [של שם הוי"ה] והבן...

וכל זה בשית יומין דחול, שאז הוא זמן בנין המשכן בל"ט מלאכות. אך בבוא השבת נאסרו הל"ט מלאכות שאז הוא זמן הקמת המשכן, כמו שנאמר "ויקם משה את המשכן" (שמות מ:יח) שהוא סוד הדעת מקים ומעלה את המשכן עם כל הבחינות הכלולים מא' ועד ת', שנבנה בששת ימי החול. ויש עלייה לכל הנבראים בקדושת שבת שמתפשט בכל העולמות ובכל הנבראים, ועל כן אין מלאכת המשכן דוחה שבת מפני שהעבודה היא במדריגה העליונה למעלה מן העולם...

מאור עינים ב'

(מפרשת כי תשא)

נודע האמור בזהר (ח"ב פח:): מהו שבת? שמא דקודשא בריך הוא, דאיהו שלים מכל סטרוי, וכיון שהוא שלם בכל מיני שלימות בודאי לא תחסר כל בה.

והנה העושה מלאכה הוא מפני שצריך לאותו דבר, וזולתה היה חסר ומשלים חסרונו על ידה. אמנם שבת דאיהו שלים מכל סטרוי ואינו חסר כלום אינה צריכה למלאכה להשלים איזה חסרון.

שבת

אור המאיר
(*מפרשת עקב*)

ככה השיבותי על מה שנשאלתי ממחותני החסיד הותיק הרב דקהלת קודש חמעלניק: מה שסדרו לנו בשמונה עשרה של שבת, "אלהינו ואלהי אבותינו... והנחילנו ה' אלהינו באהבה וברצון שבת קדשך," וככה אנחנו שואלים מלפניו יתברך בערבית ושחרית ומוסף ומנחה. ולכאורה תימה, הלא כבר פנה ועבר היום הקדוש, וביום הששי כבר קבלנו והוספנו מחול על הקודש, ואחר כך בקבלת שבת וקידוש היום, ואחר כך תפילת שחרית ומוסף וקידושא רבא, ומה לעשות עוד לאיש הישראלי שאנו שואלים אחר כל אלה "והנחילנו ה' אלהינו באהבה וברצון שבת קדשך," ומה שעשוי עשוי!

... [השיבותי] שיש הפרש גדול בין שבת שלנו שאנו מקיימים בעולם הזה, לשבת של הקדוש ברוך הוא, הגנוזה בבית גנזיו, אור הנעלם מעיני כל חי. ולזה אנו שואלים ומתפללים: עשינו מה שמוטל עלינו, עשה מה שמוטל עליך "והנחילנו ה' אלהינו שבת קדשך" דייקא, ליתן לנו לב טהור להשיג במושכלות במצות שבת שאתה מקיים בעצמך ובכבודך!

מאור עינים א'
(*מפרשת ויקהל*)

ענין מלאכת המשכן בל"ט מלאכות שהוא סוד העבודה השלימה לקיים "בכל דרכיך דעהו" (משלי ג:ו), לבנות כל הדברים שנפלו בשבירה בל"ט מלאכות שהוא בחינת משכן השוכן בתחתונים, ולהביאן לשרשן העליון,

הקדמה

קדושת לוי

(*חנוכה, קדושה שניה*)

... והנה כך הוא הסדר, שביום טוב מעצמו על ידי קדושת היום טוב נפתחו שערי האורות והחסדים למעלה, רק שכל אחד על ידי עשיותינו המצוות הנאמרים ביום טוב הוא ממשיך החסדים והאורות למטה, כגון בפסח נפתח שערי החסד, ובשבועות תפארת. ותליא בכוונתנו, אם מכוין הרבה בה וישמח במצוות הנאמרים ביום טוב זה מאד, הוא ממשיך שפע רב לכל העולמות ולכל ההיכלות ולכל הנשמות ולכל המלאכים...

והרי זה דומה למלך שפתח שערי אוצרות ביום אחד בשנה, ובאותו היום כל הרוצה ליקח מאוצרות המלך את שנפשו חפץ יקח. ואוי לכסיל אשר בזה היום ששערי אוצרות המלך נפתחים ולא פנה אליהם, רק ישן כל היום. לכן בשבת ויום טוב ראוי כל האדם רק לשמוח בעבודתו ולא בהבלי עולם, רק בעבודת ה׳ יתברך ב״ה ישמח כל היום.

ואפשר שהאורות נפתחין בשבת ויום טוב הוא על ידי נרות של שבת ויום טוב, כי הנר של שבת היא המצוה הראשונה בכניסת שבת קודם התפילה של ערבית, וקידוש אחרי כן. ועל ידי הנרות נפתחין האורות למעלה...

שבועות (ע' קמד-קמט)

ע' קמד **תורת המגיד** - דכולי עלמא בשבת ניתנה תורה (שבת פו:).

קמה **אור המאיר** - ויאמר ה' אל משה הנה אנכי בא אליך בעב הענן בעבור ישמע העם בדברי עמך... (שמות יט:ט); אנכי עומד בין ה' וביניכם... אנכי ה' אלהיך אשר הוצאתיך מארץ מצרים... (דברים ה:ה-ו).

קמז **קדושת לוי א'**

קמז **קדושת לוי ב'**

קמח **עבודת ישראל א'** - בחודש השלישי לצאת בני ישראל מארץ מצרים ביום הזה באו מדבר סיני (שמות יט:א).

קמט **עבודת ישראל ב'** - ויוצא משה את העם לקראת האלהים מן המחנה ויתיצבו בתחתית ההר... (שמות יט:יז).

תשעה באב (ע' קן-קנב)

קן **אור המאיר**

קנא **מאור עינים** - משחרב בית המקדש התקין רבי יוחנן בן זכאי שיהא לולב ניטל במדינה כל שבעה זכר למקדש (סוכה מא.); להגיד בבוקר חסדך ואמונתך בלילות (תהלים צב:ג).

קנב **עבודת ישראל** - בונה ירושלם ה'... (תהלים קמז:ב).

שבת זכור (ע' קלב-קלג)

ע' קלב **מעיין החכמה** - ויאמר ה' אל משה כתוב זאת זכרון בספר ושים באזני יהושע כי מחה אמחה את זכר עמלק מתחת השמים (שמות יז:יד).

קלג **תשואות חן** - זכור את אשר עשה לך עמלק בדרך בצאתכם ממצרים: אשר קרך בדרך... ואתה עיף ויגע ולא ירא אלהים... והיה בהניח ה'... תמחה את זכר עמלק מתחת השמים לא תשכח (דברים כה:יז-יט).

פורים (ע' קלד-קלז)

קלד **אור האמת** - איש יהודי היה בשושן הבירה... (אסתר ב:ה).

קלד **תפארת עוזיאל** - אסתר ירקרוקת היתה וחוט של חסד משוך עליה (מגילה יג.).

קלה **קדושת לוי א'**

קלו **קדושת לוי ב'**

פסח (ע' קלח-קמג)

קלח **דברת שלמה** - ... מועדי ה' אשר תקראו אותם... ששת ימים תעשה מלאכה וביום השביעי שבת שבתון... והניף את העומר לפני ה' לרצונכם ממחרת השבת יניפנו הכהן (ויקרא כג:א-ג,יא).

קלט **קדושת לוי** - חכם מה הוא אומר: מה העדות והחוקים והמשפטים אשר ציוה ה' אלהינו אתכם? (הגדה של פסח).

קמ **פרי חיים** - חכם מה הוא אומר... אף אתה אמור לו כהלכות הפסח: אין מפטירין אחר הפסח אפיקומן (הגדה של פסח).

קמא **תפארת עוזיאל** - מצה זו שאנו אוכלים... מרור זה... (הגדה של פסח).

קמב **מאור עינים** - בכל דור ודור חייב אדם לראות את עצמו כאילו הוא יצא ממצרים... שלא את אבותינו בלבד גאל הקדוש ברוך הוא, אלא אף אותנו גאל עמהם... (הגדה של פסח).

יום הכפורים (ע' קטו-קיט)

ע' קטו **מבשר צדק** - מי אל כמוך נושא עון ועובר על פשע לשארית נחלתו לא החזיק לעד אפו כי חפץ חסד הוא: ישוב ירחמנו יכבוש עונתינו ותשליך במצולות ים כל חטאותם (מיכה ז:יח-יט).

קטז **אורח לחיים** - אך בעשור לחודש השביעי הזה יום הכפורים הוא מקרא קודש יהיה לכם ועניתם את נפשותיכם... (ויקרא כג:כז).

קיז **דברת שלמה**

קיז **מאור עינים** - ... ועניתם את נפשותיכם בתשעה לחודש... (ויקרא כג:לב).

סוכות (ע' קכ-קכג)

קכ **אור האמת**

קכ **אור המאיר** - ולקחתם לכם ביום הראשון פרי עץ הדר כפת תמרים... (ויקרא כג:מ).

קכב **קדושת לוי** - ולקחתם לכם ביום הראשון פרי עץ הדר... (ויקרא כג:מ).

קכג **צמח ה' לצבי** - ולקחתם לכם ביום הראשון פרי עץ הדר... (ויקרא כג:מ).

שמיני עצרת ושמחת תורה (ע' קכד-קכה)

קכד **מאמרי אדמו"ר הזקן** - ביום השמיני עצרת תהיה לכם... (במדבר כט:לה).

קכד **מאור עינים**

חנוכה (ע' קכו-קלא)

קכו **מאור עינים א'** - תנו רבנן מאי חנוכה? דתנו רבנן בכ"ה בכסלו... כשנכנסו יוונים להיכל... (שבת כא:).

קכז **מאור עינים ב'**

קכז **קדושת לוי**

קכט **סידור הרב**

שבת (ע׳ ק-קו)

ע׳ ק **אור המאיר**

ק **מאור עינים א׳**

קא **מאור עינים ב׳**

קב **מאור עינים ג׳**

קג **מאור עינים ד׳**

קד **לקוטים יקרים**

קה **קדושת לוי** - ויאמר ה׳ אל משה לאמר: ואתה דבר אל בני ישראל לאמר אך את שבתותי תשמורו... (שמות לא:יא-יב).

קו **צמח ה׳ לצבי**

ראש חודש (ע׳ קז-קח)

קז **חיים וחסד** - ובראשי חדשיכם תקריבו עולה לה׳... (במדבר כח:יא).

קז **קדושת לוי א׳** - החדש הזה לכם ראש חדשים ראשון הוא לכם לחדשי השנה (שמות יב:ב).

קח **קדושת לוי ב׳** - ברכי נפשי את ה׳" (תהלים קד).

ראש השנה (ע׳ קט-קיד)

קט **אור האמת** - אל תבוא במשפט עמנו כי לא יצדק לפניך כל חי (סליחות לערב ראש השנה).

קט **שמועה טובה**

קי **אור המאיר**

קיא **קדושת לוי** - זמרו אלהים זמרו זמרו למלכנו זמרו (תהלים מז:ז).

קיא **אורח לחיים** - ואמרו לפני בראש השנה מלכיות זכרונות ושופרות. מלכיות כדי שתמליכוני עליכם, זכרונות כדי שיעלה זכרונכם לפני לטובה. ובמה? בשופר (ראש השנה טז.).

קיב **תורי זהב** - רבי ברכיה פתח: "תקעו בחודש שופר" (תהלים פא:ד)... בחודש הזה שפרו מעשיכם. אמר להן הקדוש ברוך הוא לישראל אם שפרתם מעשיכם הריני נעשה לכם כשופר הזה... (ויקרא רבה כט:ג).

קיג **מאור עינים** - מרחוק ה׳ נראה לי ואהבת עולם אהבתיך על כן משכתיך חסד (ירמיה לא:ב).

שבת
ומועדים

הגדול והנורא. וידוע משה זכה וזיכה הרבים, אז זכות הרבים תלויה בו. ולימד דעת כל ישראל, נמצא כל מה שאחד מישראל יעבוד הבורא ב"ה ויעשה איזה מצוה לשמו יחשבו כאילו הוא עובד ה'. [וזה **וימת שם משה עבד ה'**], שעדיין עובד לבורא ב"ה, והוא על ידי בני ישראל התלמידים שלו.

ישמח לב

ויקבור אותו בגיא בארץ מואב מול בית פעור ולא ידע איש את קבורתו עד היום הזה (דברים לד:ו).

שענין הקבורה הוא גניזת הדעת, שהיא בחינת משה שנגנז בתורה, כמו שאמרו (חגיגה יב:): [אור שברא הקדוש ברוך הוא ביום ראשון] - ראה שאין העולם כדאי, עמד וגנזו לעתיד לבוא. כי הדעת השלמה בכל השלימות אי אפשר עוד להשיג מהתורה כי אם לעתיד לבוא. על כן כתיב **ולא ידע איש את קבורתו**. פירוש, הדעת גנוזה **עד היום הזה**, כי אם כל אחד לפי טוב מדריגתו ובחינתו ותיקון מעשיו מתגלה לו מן הדעת ההיא הגנוזה בתורה כשיעור תיקון מעשיו ושפלותו, כי העיקר הוא השפלות לבוא לדעת הגנוזה על ידי זה. כי משה רבינו ע"ה זכה לדעת הגדולה לעצמו להמשיכו בתוך כל ישראל עבור השפלות והענוה, שהיה "עניו מכל האדם" (במדבר יב:ג). ולכך גם הדעת שנתגלתה לו היא יותר מכל האדם... עיקר הדעת הוא על ידי שנעשה לבבו בחינת שני לוחות, ימין ושמאל, משכן לבורא ב"ה, ועל ידי המשכת אלהותו יתברך בתוכו נמשך גם הדעת בתוך לבבו שהוא גם כן אלהותו יתברך, שהוא שמו הגדול ממש.

ונודע שאין הבורא ב"ה משכין שכינתו יתברך כי אם על נמוכי הרוח, כמו שכתוב "אשכון את דכא ושפל רוח" (ישעיה נז:טו). לכן כפי שיעור השפלות שבו כך הוא צמצום השראת אלהותו בתוכו, וכך היא אצלו התגלות הדעת שהיא אור הגנוז בתורה כפי שיעור שפלותו. לכן כתוב **ויקבור אותו בגיא**, בגיא דייקא שגנזו הקדוש ברוך הוא לדעת במי שיש בו שפלות...

תם ונשלם ספר דברים

- צ"ח -

תפארת עוזיאל ב'

שמעתי מפי מורי ורבי הגאון החסיד מורנו הרב דוב בער זצוק"ל נבג"ע על מאמר: **תורה צוה לנו משה, מורשה [קהילת יעקב]** (דברים לג:ד) - אל תקרי מורשה אלא מאורסה (פסחים מט:). לקרב הדבר אל הענין, כי מדרך העולם שאינו ראוי לאדם שאינו נכבד לחזוק בבת מלך ולרקד עמה במחול בבי הילולא כדרך העולם; כי אין מהראוי לו להתקרב אליה, מכל שכן לאחוז בה ולרקד עמה. מה שאין כן כשהבת מלך נכנסת לנשואין, אז מדרך העולם שהותר הקשר ורשאי אף הקל שבקלים לרקד עמה במחול.

כן הענין בנידון תורתנו הקדושה, היא בת מלך מלכי המלכים הקדוש ברוך הוא, ואם כן היה מן הראוי שלא להתקרב אליה כל מי שרוצה. אף על פי כן הותר לנו, שתורה נמשלה למים - מה מים הפקר, אף היא הפקר... כמאמרם ז"ל (במדבר רבה א:ז). והיא לנו דוגמת בת המלך ביום נשואין כשהיא מאורסה שהיא מופקרת לכל, כך היא לנו. וזה שרומז במתק לשונו "אל תקרי מורשה אלא מאורסה," רוצה לומר שהתורה היא לנו כמו ביום הנשואין שניתן רשות לכל לרקד עמה, כי ניתן גם כן לנו לכל לעסוק בתורה.

מבשר צדק

וימת שם משה עבד ה'... (דברים לד:ה).

כבר פרשתי לך המשנה "אם אין אני לי, מי לי" (מ' אבות א:יד), היינו דהנה "ימי שנותינו בהם שבעים שנה" (תהלים צ:י), ומה יוכל האדם בחומר שלו לעבוד הבורא ב"ה באלו המעט שנים ורעים. ולאחר המיתה כבר "לא המתים יהללו יה" (תהלים קטו:יז), ונעשה חפשי [מן התורה ומן המצוות] (שבת ל.).

אך כשאדם רוצה ללמד תורה לישראל ולהעמיד תלמידים, אז שפתותיו דובבות [בקבר] (יבמות צז.), וכל מה שהם יעשו אחר כך מצוות ה' לשמו של הצדיק יחשבו ונמצא עובד ה' אף אחר מיתתו.

וזה "אם אין אני לי" - כשאיני עושה ולומד רק לעצמי אלא שאני מלמד לתלמידים, אז "מי לי" - כל מי שיעשה יהיה לי אף אחר פטירתי. וכשאני לעצמי ואיני מקים תלמידים, אז "מה אני" ומה חיי נגד עבודת הבורא ב"ה

- צ"ז -

פרשת וזאת הברכה

תפארת עוזיאל א'

וזאת הברכה אשר ברך משה איש האלהים את בני ישראל לפני מותו (דברים לג:א).

במדרש רבה מקשה (דברים רבה יא:ד): אם איש, למה אלהים? ואם אלהים, למה איש? ועוד קשה דפתח **וזאת הברכה** ומסיים "ויאמר ה' מסיני בא" (דברים לג:ב), ומה ברכה היא זו?

ונראה לתרץ דידוע ד"זה" הוא לשון זכר ו"זאת" היא לשון נקבה. והנה ה' יתברך הוא נותן כל ההשפעות וכל החסדים כי מאתו הוא. והנה אף על פי כן רוצה ה' יתברך בתפילתנו ומקבל מאתנו הבקשות. ולפום ריהטא הוא תמוה האיך שמן הדכר יעשה נוקבא, כי הנותן ומשפיע לאחרים הוא נקרא דכר והמקבל הוא נקרא נוקבא כידוע.

וה' יתברך הוא הנותן הנקרא דכר, והאיך הוא נעשה נוקבא ומקבל מאתנו התפילות? ולזה כיוון דוד המלך ע"ה "מאת ה' היתה זאת, היא נפלאת בעינינו" (תהלים קיח:בג). רוצה לומר שמאת ה' היתה זאת - היא נוקבא - היא נפלאת בעינינו שהיכי תמצא מדכר נוקבא? אלא ש"אין חקר לתבונתו" (תהלים קמז:ה), שאף על פי שהוא במידת דכר, אף על פי כן בידו הכל ונקרא גם כן נוקבא.

וזהו **וזאת הברכה**, רוצה לומר שברך משה שיהיה הקדוש ברוך הוא נקרא גם כן במידת נוקבא, שיקבל תפילת הצדיקים. **אשר ברך משה איש האלהים**, רוצה לומר שמשה, איש, ברך שיהא אלהים נקרא במידת נוקבא...

"נעשה ונשמע" (שמות כד:ז) נעשו כתפוח שפריו קודם לעליו, ונדמה גם הקדוש ברוך הוא לתפוח.

מגיד דבריו ליעקב (ס' קכ)

כנשר יעיר קנו על גוזליו ירחף... (דברים לב:יא).

... כי בכל יש האלהות המחיה הכל, ועיקר החיות הוא מפני שיש לו התחברות עם תחילת המחשבה. ועיקר ההתחברות הוא מפני שהוא באפס בלתי החיות ואין בו אלא החיות. והחיות הוא אחד עם תחילת המחשבה, אחדות פשוטה. ואם האדם ירצה לעשות הכנה שישרה עליו אלהות, אזי עיקר הכל שיבין וישיג מאד שאין בו אלא האלהות המחיה אותו ובלתי זה הוא כאפס ממש, ואז יש הכנה שיוכל לשרות עליו.

והשריה היא **כנשר יעיר קנו... ירחף**, נוגע ואינו נוגע. דהיינו שההכרח בלתי שישיג האדם אז את זה, כי אם ישיג אזי יהיה בטל ממציאות ממש. ואם יש לאדם אפילו נידנוד קצת מגדלות קצת, שמחזיק את עצמו למאומה, אזי אין הוא קשור ומחובר עם האלהות, כיון שאינו באפס...

ליקוטי מהרי"ן

כנשר יעיר קנו על גוזליו ירחף... (דברים לב:יא).

הנה אדוני אבי מורנו הרב [לוי יצחק מברדיצ'ב] אמר: ...עיין רש"י, "אינו מכביד עצמו עליהם אלא מחופף, נוגע ואינו נוגע. כי האדם העובד ה' ח"ו שיאמר כי הוא מרוחק מן הקדוש ברוך הוא ותפילתו ועשיית מצוותיו ולימוד תורתו אינו מקובל לפני ה' - ח"ו וח"ו מלומר כן! כי ישראל עם קרובו [והוא] שומע תפילת עמו ישראל ברחמים.

וכן שיאמר האדם שהוא משיג גדולת הבורא ב"ה, זה גם כן חלילה לאדם לאמר כן, כנאמר "גדול ה' [ומהולל מאוד] ולגדולתו אין חקר" (תהלים קמה:ג). כי כל מה שהצדיק עובד ה' יתברך יותר במדריגה גדולה יותר ויותר, משיג יותר ויותר שאין מושג לו כלל...

דברת שלמה
(מפרשת חקת)

כי חלק ה׳ עמו... (דברים לב:ט).

כל עיקר בריאת עולמות ויחודי השמות הקדושים, וכן המדריגות העליונות הם נעשו הכל רק בשביל ישראל. כי בו יתברך לא שייך שום תמונת אות ואפילו קוצו של יוד, כמו שאיתא בזהר הקדוש (ח״א כא.), וכמו שאיתא בתיקונים: לית מחשבה תפיסא בך כלל (יז.). רק כל האותיות והשמות, ואפילו אותיות שם הוי״ה ב״ה, הם נעשו ונמשכו הכל בשביל ישראל. וזהו שנאמר **כי חלק ה׳**, רוצה לומר התחלקות לאותיות שם הוי״ה ב״ה היא בשביל ישראל **עמו**.

ובזה יתורץ קושית התוספות במסכת שבת (פח.) על מה שאמרו: מאי דכתיב ״כתפוח בעצי היער, כן [דודי בין הבנים]״ (שיר השירים ב:ג) - למה נמשלו כנסת ישראל לתפוח? [לומר לך מה תפוח זה פריו קודם לעליו, אף ישראל הקדימו נעשה לנשמע]. והקשו תוספות: הא קרא משתעי בהקדוש ברוך הוא, כמו שכתוב ״כן דודי״. ולפי דברינו על נכון, כי הקדוש ברוך הוא אין בו שום תמונה ואפילו קוצו של אות כנזכר לעיל, רק מתדמה כפי תפיסת ועשיות ישראל.

כמו שאיתא בתנא דבי אליהו (פ׳ יח): מאי [שפכי כמים לבך] נוכח פני ה׳ (איכה ב:יט)? מכאן כשאדם לומד ומתפלל הקדוש ברוך הוא לומד ומתפלל כנגדו. ובזה יובן מה שאמרו חז״ל: על הים נדמה להם כבחור בעל מלחמה, ובמתן תורה נדמה כזקן ששערותיו לבנים (פסיקתא רבתי פ׳ כא). כי על הים היה תיכף כשיצאו ממצרים ממ״ט שערי טומאה כעובר הנשמט ממעי אמו, וכשגדלו קצת ורצו לומר שירה ברוח הקודש כמו שאמרו באמת (שמות רבה כג:ב), והיו להם מלחמות עצומות עם היצר ותאוותיו ומחשבותיו הרעים, וכבשו ונצחו אותו, כן גם הקדוש ברוך הוא נדמה להם [כבחור בעל מלחמה].

אמנם במתן תורה כבר גדלו ועשו פרי, ובמ״ט ימי הספירה נתלבנו ונטהרו ונכנסו למ״ט שערי קדושה, וביום החמישים קבלו התורה, גם הקדוש ברוך הוא נדמה להם כזקן שנתלבנו שׂערותיו, שהוא לשון ״שׁער״, שהם חמישים שערי בינה וקדושה. כן גם כן על ידי שאמרו

ואם ח"ו האדם לומד שלא לשמה בלא לב, אמרו רז"ל על זה: לא זכה, נעשה לו סם המות (יומא עב:). כי התורה נמשלה למטר, ויש גשמי ברכה ויש גשמי קללה. כן על דרך זה כשלומד כראוי נעשה סם חיים ובהיפוך נעשה סם המות. וכתיב "חברים מקשיבים לקולך השמיעני" (שיר השירים ח:יג) שהמלאכים חושקים לשמוע ומתחברים למי שמדבר דברי תורה. והענין כי כיון שעל ידי התורה נבראו הכל וחיותם היא אותיות התורה שבזה נתהוו וביד ישראל נמסרו לגמור העשייה, נמצא כשאדם מדבר דברי תורה ומתדבק בו יתברך הוא גומר תיקונם ועשייתם כאילו בוראם הוא ומשפיע להם חיותם. לכן כל חשקם לשמוע קול העוסקים כי זה הוא בריאתם.

וזהו **האזינו השמים ואדברה**, רוצה לומר שתעשו ותעסקו בתורה בענין ראוי ונכון עד שתגרמו שיאזינו השמים, עולם השמים, והמלאכים כולם לקולך. ואמר איך יהיה זה? באופן ש**ואדברה**, רוצה לומר שידע האדם שדיבורו בתורה הוא עצמו דבר ה' הנשפע בו בעת אשר "בדבר ה' שמים נעשו" (תהלים לג:ו) וכל אשר בעולם והאדם בכלל כי הוא עיקר. נמצא דבריו הם דברי ה' ובזה [בורא] עולמות גם כן כאמור.

ותשמע הארץ אמרי פי, רוצה לומר כי אמרו רז"ל (לפי זבחים קטז.): בשעה שאמר הקדוש ברוך הוא "אנכי ה' אלהיך" (שמות כ:ב) היו שומעין מכל המקומות קול שואג "אנכי ה' אלהיך" אפילו אבן מקיר. ולא היה מקום פנוי שלא היה נשמע משם "אנכי". כי באמת דבר ה', אנכי ה', ממלא הכל, כי "מלא כל הארץ כבודו" (ישעיה ו:ג). והוא שוכן בכל דבר, נמצא לא היה מקום פנוי שלא יאמר "אנכי".

ויובן על דרך זה כשהאדם מקדש עצמו ומדבר בקדושת התורה כראוי, אז אפילו מן הארץ אשר נתקדש סביביו בהשפעת קדושה ישמע קול קדושת התורה, וכפי ערך גודל יכולתו לקדש המקום ישכון בו השכינה. וזהו **ותשמע הארץ** גם כן **אמרי פי**.

פרשת האזינו

מאור עינים

(לקוטים)

האזינו השמים ואדברה ותשמע הארץ אמרי פי (דברים לב:א).

... ידוע כי העולם הזה נברא בה', כדכתיב "בהבראם" (בראשית ב:ד), ודרשו רז"ל: בה' בראם (מנחות כט:), שהוא דיבורו כביכול בה' [חמש] מוצאות הפה, היא התורה שעל ידי התורה נברא הכל, כמאמר רז"ל בזהר אסתכל באורייתא וברא עלמא (ח"א ה.). והכל נברא בענין זה כל התורה כולה כמו שהיא מראש עד סוף בה [ברא] הקדוש ברוך הוא הכל דרך משל, כשדיבר הקדוש ברוך הוא אותיות התורה בה נברא כל עולם ועולם התלוי בבחינת האותיות ההם, ומסר לנו התורה שהיא בנין העולמות, כי כתיב "אשר ברא אלהים לעשות" (בראשית ב:ג), רוצה לומר שעדיין נשאר לעשות ולהגמר על ידי ישראל. וישראל כשעוסקים בתורה בדחילו ורחימו אזי מתקנים וגומרים העשייה של העולמות, כגוונא דאנא במילולא דילי עבדית שמיא וארעא, אף הכי אנת [זכאין אינון דמשתדלי באורייתא] [כמו שאני בדיבורי עשיתי שמים וארץ, אף אתה! אשרי העוסקים בתורה] (זהר ח"א ה.)

וצריך האדם להיות בבחינת ענוה בתכלית, כי כמו שהקדוש ברוך הוא הלביש מידת ענוה על ידי שנתצמצם והלביש עד ערך שיוכלו להשיגו ובזה נבנו העולמות, כן צריך האדם להיות בבחינת ענוה, ואז יקנה חכמה היא התורה ויוכל לברוא עולמות גם כן. ובתורה כלולות ל"ב [32] נתיבות חכמה חמישים שערי בינה, שהכל כלול בתורה. וכל אחד ואחד ידרוך בנתיב שרשו ובחינתו הראויה לו, וכל חד כפום מה דמשער בליביה בחינה הראויה לו משערי שיעור הבינה, ואיש לבב יקנה לב על ידי ל"ב נתיבות וילבב לבבו לאהבה ולדבקה בו בחכמת לב.

בשכינה ונכנס לחיי עולם, וזה נקרא חי] (זהר ח"א קלא:). וזהו שנאמר **וילך משה**, כאדם אשר הולך מחדר אל חדר דלא טעם טעם מיתה כלל.

עוד יש לפרש דאיתא בזהר הקדוש באדרא זוטא (ח"ג רפח.): פתח רבי שמעון ואמר, "אני לדודי ועלי תשוקתו" (שיר השירים ז:יא) - בכל יומא דאתקטרנא ביה בהאי עלמא בחד קטירא איתקטרנא ביה בקודשא בריך הוא, והשתא "ועלי תשוקתו" - עד כאן [בכל יום שהייתי קשור בעולם הזה עדיין הייתי קשור בהקדוש ברוך הוא בקשר אחד, ועכשיו "ועלי תשוקתו"]. וזהו שנאמר **וילך משה**, רוצה לומר שהלך עם כל חלקי נשמתו ואינו מקושר עוד בהאי עלמא כלום...

והנה נודע סגולת האהבה היא התקשרות גדולה בכל חיותו וכחותיו שיש לו בכל מקום, הן כל מה שעסק בתורה, הן כל מעשיו הטובים, והן כל ימיו שהוא חי וכל דיבוריו, הם כולם נתקשרים על ידי גודל אהבה זו בהבורא ב"ה... וזהו שנאמר **וידבר את** כל **הדברים האלה אל כל ישראל ויאמר אליהם**. ולכאורה הוא כפל לשון, ולפי דברינו על נכון, שכל הדברים שאמר היום היה בהם כלול כל הדיבורים שדיבר כל ימי חייו. וזהו שנאמר **בן מאה ועשרים שנה אנכי היום**, רוצה לומר שהיום נתאחדו כל המאה ועשרים שנה שהיה חי עד הנה.

- צ"א -

ממקום נפילתו לבא למדריגה גבוהה יותר מהקדום. והטעם לזה כי "יתרון האור מן החושך" (קהלת ב:יג), כי מן בחינת חשכות יבא ליתרון אור. כי בחינת העדר צריך להיות קודם להויה, כמו בבריאת העולם שהוצרך להיות מקודם תהו ובוהו, ובונה עולמות ומחריבן (בראשית רבה ג:ט), ואחר כך היתה הוית העולמות - וכמו כן בהאמור גם כן.

ונודע (ראש השנה כא:) כי מ"ט שערי בינה נמסרו למשה חוץ מאחד, שנאמר "ותחסרהו מעט מאלהים" (תהלים ח:ו). הכוונה שהשיג את מ"ט שערי בינה שאפשר לנבראים להשיג, ומשם ולמעלה אי אפשר לשום נברא להשיג מחמת ששער החמישים הוא עצם אלהותו של אין סוף ב"ה שאי אפשר בשום פנים להשיגו, אפילו מלאכי מעלה כמו שנאמר "איה מקום כבודו?" (קדושת מוסף של שבת).

ולפי זה השיג משה רבינו ע"ה כל מה שאפשר להשיג לנברא ולא הניח דבר מכל מה שאפשר להשיג, ובוודאי בשעת הליכתו כשהיה הולך ממדריגה למדריגה קודם שבא למדריגה זו שאין למעלה הימנה בוודאי היה מוכרח לצאת ממדריגתו הקדומה בבחינת נפילה כאמור, ואחר כך עלה יותר כאמור. וזהו שאמר קודם הסתלקותו מן העולם **לא אוכל עוד לצאת ולבוא** כי עד עכשיו הוצרכתי תמיד לצאת מדרגא הקודמת ולבא למדריגה יותר גבוהה עד שעליתי למדריגה הגבוהה שאני כהיום בה שאי אפשר לעלות ולהשיג לפנים ממנה, שהיא סתימא דכל סתימין כאמור, וזהו שנסתמו מעיינות החכמה - והבן.

דברת שלמה

וילך משה וידבר את הדברים האלה אל כל ישראל: ויאמר אליהם בן מאה ועשרים שנה אנכי היום לא אוכל עוד לצאת ולבוא... (דברים לא:א-ב).

תיבת **וילך** צריך להבין, כמו שדקדק בספר אור החיים. ונראה דאיתא בזהר הקדוש: משה לא אסתאב ולא מית אלא איתדבק בשכינה ועייל לחיי העולם, והא חי אקרי - עד כאן [משה לא נטמא ולא מת, אלא נדבק

פרשת וילך

קדושת לוי

וילך משה וידבר את הדברים האלה אל כל ישראל (דברים לא:א).

יבואר על פי מה שאמרו חז״ל פעמים ״היורד״ לפני התיבה (שבת כד:), ופעמים ״העובר״ לפני התיבה (ברכות לד.). כי הצדיק בשעה שמתפלל לפני ה׳ יתברך צריך לדבק עצמו בתיבות מהתפילה, והתיבות הקדושות הן הן המנהיגות אותו. ויש צדיקים גדולים אשר הם למעלה ממדריגה זו, אשר הם מנהיגים את התיבה. וזהו מדריגת משה שהוא בעלה דמטרוניתא, כנאמר בזהר הקדוש (ח״ג רעה:).

וזהו ״היורד לפני התיבה,״ שהתיבה מנהיגה אותו והוא למטה מן התיבה. ויש צדיק העובר לפני התיבה, שהוא מנהיג התיבה והוא למעלה מן התיבה, וזהו ״העובר לפני התיבה.״

וכאן שהיה סוף ימיו של משה, ונסתם ממנו מעיין החכמה כמבואר במדרש (סוטה יג:), והיה בבחינה הראשונה שהתיבה היתה מנהיגה אותו. וזה **וילך משה וידבר** - הלך אל הדיבור, שהתיבה היתה למעלה ממנו.

מאור עינים

... לא אוכל עוד לצאת ולבוא... (דברים לא:ב).

במסכת סוטה (יג:): **לא אוכל עוד לצאת ולבוא**, מלמד שנסתמו ממנו מעיינות החכמה. ולהבין מאי זה לשון לצאת ולבא, אם הוא על דברי תורה.

דנודע כי הצדיק שהולך ממדריגה למדריגה אינו יכול לבא למדריגה גבוהה מהראשונה כי אם שיפול תחילה ממדריגתו הקדומה **ולצאת** ממנה לגמרי. ואז אחר כך על ידי שיאחז צדיק דרכו בתוקף חוזק התקשרותו

מבשר צדק ב'

כי המצוה הזאת אשר אנכי מצוך היום לא נפלאת היא ממך ולא רחוקה היא (דברים ל:יא).

איתא בגמרא: [אמר ר' יהושע בן לוי, מאי דכתיב "אשר אנכי מצוך **היום** לעשותם" (דברים ז:יא)? היום לעשותם ולא למחר לעשותם, היום לעשותם] למחר לקבל שכרם (עירובין כב.). ואיתא תו בגמרא: חייב אדם לטעום תבשיל של שבת בערב שבת (שיבלי הלקט ס' פב, מחזור ויטרי בשם הירושלמי).

ונראה פירוש הגמרא דידוע דעולם הזה נקרא ערב שבת, שמכין ליום השבת. וצריך האדם בעת עשיית מצוות ה' לעשותם כל כך בבהירות ובזכות עד שישיג מתענוגי עולם הבא בזאת המצוה בעולם הזה. והוא רק טעימה בעלמא נגד התענוג העליון, כי הוא "עין לא ראתה אלהים זולתך" (ישעיה סד:ג). וזהו חייב אדם לטעום [תבשיל של שבת בערב שבת], והיינו על ידי גודל האהבה.

וזהו: גדול הנהנה מיגיע כפו [יותר מירא שמים] (ברכות ח.) גם כן כנזכר לעיל, שיקבל הנאה ותענוג ממצוותיו שעושה, והוא על ידי אהבה יותר מיראת שמים, שכשעובד ביראה אינו מקבל תענוג.

וזהו **כי המצוה הזאת אשר אנכי מצוך היום**, היינו אף שאני אומר לך **היום** דרשינן מיניה היום לעשותם ולמחר לקבל שכר. אבל **לא נפלאת היא ממך**, היינו שאינו מכוסה ממך השכר - אף שאתה בזה העולם בעת עשייתך המצוות גם כן תוכל להתענג בתענוג המצוה מעין עולם הבא וכנזכר לעיל.

ומפרש הפסוק **ולא רחוקה היא** ממך, שאין דבר רחוק להשיג תענוגי המצוות, כי בקל יכולין להשיג על ידי עשייתו בדחילו ורחימו ובהשתוקקות גדול, אז יהנה מיגיע כפו וכנזכר לעיל.

- פ"ח -

מבשר צדק א'

ושב ה' אלהיך את שבותך ורחמך ושב וקבצך מכל העמים אשר הפיצך ה' אלהיך שמה (דברים ל:ג).

הענין הוא דידוע מה שאנו תכופים בעול הגלות הוא מחמת הניצוצות הקדושים שנפלו, וצריכין אנחנו לבררן. וצריך האדם לראות לתקן זה, וכשיתקן במהרה בימינו אז יקבץ אותנו הקדוש ברוך הוא מבין העמים.

ולכן האדם העושה תשובה תהיה כוונתו ותשובתו רק למען הניצוצות הקדושים שנפלו על ידי עוונותינו. וכשנעלה אותן, אזי נהיה נגאלין. וזהו **ושב ה' אלהיך את שבותך**, היינו עם תשובתך, רוצה לומר שה' יתברך כביכול יהיה בשוב [ישוב] על ידי תשובתך, היינו הניצוצות הקדושים. ואז **ורחמך** שירחם עליך **ושב וקבצך מכל העמים**, כי אז תהיה הגאולה. ומפרש הפסוק **אשר הפיצך**, מה שהבורא ב"ה הפיץ אותך בין העמים הוא מחמת **ה' אלהיך שמה**, רוצה לומר הניצוצות הקדושים נפלו שמה. ואם תעלה אותן בתשובתך, אזי תיכף תהיה הגאולה, ובא לציון גואל במהרה בימינו - אמן, סלה.

מאמרי אדמו"ר הזקן

אם יהיה נדחך בקצה השמים משם יקבצך ה' אלהיך ומשם יקחך (דברים ל:ד).

ולכאורה איך שייך לשון יחיד על כנסת ישראל? דמה שנאמר "ואהבת [את ה' אלהיך]" (דברים ו:ה) שייך על כל אחד ואחד מישראל, אבל **משם יקבצך** האיך שייך לשון "קיבוץ" לאדם אחד?

הענין שהאדם מפוזר ומפורד, שכל אדם אינו בשלימותו לפי ערך שכלו מידותיו. כי יש אדם שחסרה לו מידה אחת, ובמידה הזאת אם היתה לו היה שלם בכולו, ואם חסר הרי חסר לו אבר אחד כידוע. ויש שחסרונו ימצא באדם אחר, ועם אותו האדם נעשה שלם. ויש שהאדם הזה הוא רחוק מאוד ממנו, והוא לא יכול היות שלם בלתו. וזהו **אם יהיה נדחך** בלשון יחיד **משם יקבצך** ויהיה אחד. וזהו ענין הגלות...

- פ"ז -

שהוא לשון "אצלו" שהאדם עומד אצלו יתברך ממש, כביכול. וזה בתפילת שמונה עשרה שהאדם עומד אז בעולם האצילות ואין שום מסך וחלל מפסיק בין האדם לקונו. רק האור אין סוף מקיף את האדם מכל צדדיו ולפני ה' ישפוך שיחו...

על כן כשאנו באים למדריגת העמידה כנזכר לעיל הוא יתברך מתיצב כביכול לפנינו. ורוצה לומר, כמו שאנו עומדים לפניו ומדבקים את מחשבותינו אל נקודה האמצעית שהוא אלהותו יתברך שהוא שורש לכל, והנקודה הפנימיות המחיה את כל, כך הקדוש ברוך הוא מצמצם עצמו ועומד על נקודת עושי רצונו שהיא נקודת מחשבתו שבשבילם ברא העולמות כולם. והם עיקר המחשבה והם יסוד לכל העולמות ובעבורם נברא הכל.

ומזה תבין מה שאמר הכתוב "הנני עומד שם," רוצה לומר כמו שאתה עומד במחשבתך דבוק אצלי ממש, כן אני עומד על הצור, רוצה לומר הציור של עושי רצונו שהוא המחשבה להטיב להם אשר בשבילם נבראו כל החסדים והשפעות טובות. וזה שנאמר "והכית בצור," רוצה לומר שתכה בזה הצור ותעורר מחשבה עליונה ודביקות אלהים בכנסת ישראל, ומכונה בשם צור, אז ויצאו מים; משם ממשיך כל השפעות וחסדים לכנסת ישראל והבן.

ובזה יתפרש הכתוב **אתם נצבים היום כולכם לפני ה' אלהיכם**, שמשה רבינו ע"ה הסתכל בישראל וראה שהם בבחינת נצבים עומדים ואמר: אל תתמה מה שאתם נצבים היום, הוא מחמת שאתם במדריגה גדולה לפני ה' אלהיכם שאתם קשורים בדביקות עליונה פנים בפנים עם ה' אלהיכם ואין שום מסך ומבדיל ביניכם, ואתם קרובים אל מלך מלכי המלכים, ושם לא יצטייר כלל הליכה, כי אם עמידה.

- פ"ו -

פרשת נצבים

שמן הטוב

(על פי קדושת לוי פ' בשלח)

אתם נצבים היום כולכם לפני ה' אלהיכם (דברים כט:ט).

"הנני עומד לפניך שם על הצור בחורב והכית בצור ויצאו ממנו מים ושתה העם" (שמות יז:ו). הקושיא מפורסמת, דאיך שייך אצלו יתברך דעומד שם?! הא מלא כל הארץ כבודו, ולית אתר פנוי מניה, ואיך יתכן לומר שעומד שם על הצור, דמשמע דלא היה עומד רק במקום הזה חלילה.

אך דשורש הדבר הוא כך: דידוע דברי חז"ל (ברכות ו:) דאין עמידה אלא תפילה, שנאמר "ויעמוד פנחס ויפלל" (תהלים קו:ל). ולכאורה אינו מובן, דכי לא מצינו שום עמידה באדם זולת זה אלא תפילה דווקא? ובוודאי כוונו לאיזה דבר שכל ולא כפי פשטות הענין. אבל באמת בוודאי חז"ל לא דיברו מאנשים פחותי ערך, רק מאנשים השלמים ביראת ה' ובתורתו, ובאלו אמרו חז"ל דלא שייך אצלם עמידה כי אם תפילה. דהם הולכים כל ימיהם בשכלם ומחשבתם ממדריגה למדריגה ומעולם לעולם עליון. כי כשאדם רוצה לקבל את הבורא ב"ה, ולבוא לעבודת האמת ולהיות דבוק אצלו יתברך, צריך האדם לחפש יומם ולילה על ידי תורה ומצוות ועל ידי צרופי שמות אותיות ותיבות הקדושות, ועל ידי המלאכים הקדושים שבכל עולם ועולם ובכל מדה הקדושה, ואי אפשר להיות כלול במעמד אחד. ולזה הצדיקים נקראו מהלכים ולא יצויר כלל עמידה זולת בתפילה, דהיא הדביקות וחיבור אל הבורא יתברך.

עד שאדם מגיע לתפילת העמידה, הוא הולך דרך השתלשלות העולמות, על ידי שירות ותשבחות שאומר מפסוקי דזמרה, אז בכל פעם משיג אדם שכל יותר דרך המידות הקדושות שעדיין לא הגיע לדבר אל המלך בעצמו ולהיות דבוק אצלו ממש בלי הפסק ומסך וחלל, אפילו של קדושה עליונה, זולת אורו של האין סוף הפשוט לבד, ולכך נקרא עולם "אצילות"

- פ"ה -

מעוררים תחילה עם דיבורים שלנו. וזהו ״ישקני מנשיקות פיהו״ - הוא מנשק אותי מנשיקות פי. תחילה הם נשיקות פי, ואחר כך הוא ישקני. ונמצא אנו גורמים לפה של מעלה לדבר ואחר כך באים הדיבורים שלנו. וזהו פירוש הפסוק **את ה׳ האמרת היום**, מלשון אמירה ממש, ואחר כך **האמירך** כנזכר לעיל.

- פ"ד -

קדושת לוי

... בדרך אחד יצאו אליך ובשבעה דרכים ינוסו לפניך (דברים כח:ז).

הכלל כי ישראל עם קדוש, יש להם יראת ה' ואהבה לה' והתפארות הבורא ב"ה. וכן יש להם כל שבע המידות להבורא ב"ה, בכדי ליתן שפע טוב לישראל שיש להם כל המידות להבורא ב"ה.

וכמו כן לעומת זה יש יראה חיצונית, וכן אהבה ושאר המידות. והחילוק הוא בקדושה יכול להיות כל המידות ביחד באחדות הפשוטה, ורחמנא לשזבן בחיצונים אינו יכול להיות להם כל שבע המידות ביחד, כיון שיש לו יראה אינו יכול להיות אהבה עמו, וכן שאר המידות. אבל בקדושה יכול לעבוד עם כל המידות ביחד באחדות פשוטה.

וזהו הרמז **בדרך אחד יצאו אליך**, כי החיצונים אין להם אלא מידה אחת, או אהבה או יראה או שאר מידה אחת משבע מידות, אבל אינם יכולים להיות כל השבע מידות ביחד.

אבל אתה שאתה הוא בקדושה, ואתה יכול לעבוד בקדושה את הבורא ב"ה בכל שבע המידות ביחד. וזהו הרמז **בדרך [אחד]**, שהאויב אינו יכול לבוא עליך רק במידה אחת, אבל אתה יש לך כל שבע המידות. לכך ינוסו לפניך, וזהו **ובשבעה דרכים ינוסו לפניך**.

שארית ישראל

את ה' האמרת היום להיות לך לאלהים... וה' האמירך היום להיות לו לעם סגולה (דברים כו:יז-יח).

והענין הוא דכתיב "ישקני מנשיקות פיהו" (שיר השירים א:ב), והיה ראוי לכתוב פיו - מהו פיהו?

רק כי אנו כביכול עושין דיבור למעלה, שה' יתברך ב"ה מדבר בשמנו. וכביכול אנו גורמים אל פה של מעלה לדבר, ואחר כך באה התעוררות לפה של מטה לדבר דיבורים. ונמצא כל השפעות באות עלינו מחמת שאנו

- פ"ג -

פרשת כי תבוא

תפארת עוזיאל

ארור האיש אשר לא יקים את דברי התורה הזאת... (דברים כז:כו).

מאמרם ז"ל (על פי סנהדרין קיא.): שאפיקורסים אומרים לנו ארורים אתם מאלהיכם, וכי אפשר לשום אדם לקיים את כל התורה כולה? אבל נראה שהבל יפצה פיהם, כי ידוע מאמר רבי יוחנן: "ופערה פיה לבלי חוק" (ישעיה ה:יד) למי שלא קיים אפילו חוק, אבל מי שמקיים אפילו חוק אחד הוא בכלל ברוך. וזה טעם נראה כי כל מצוה כלולה מתרי"ג מצוות. נמצא בעשיית מצוה אחת מקיים כל התרי"ג. אלא לפי זה קשה עליו יתברך שאמר "והיה אם לא תשמע בקול ה' אלהיך לשמור לעשות את כל מצוותיו וחוקותיו... ובאו עליך כל הקללות האלה..." (דברים כח:טו). הלא כל אדם עושה מצוה אחת על כל פנים ומקיים כל התורה כולה, ולמה באה התוכחה?

אך ראיתי במפרשים בשם הרמב"ם שדווקא כשאדם עושה מצוה בשמחה נכללות כל התרי"ג במצוה אחת, מה שאין כן כשעושה בלי שמחה. והטעם נראה כי תפילה בלא כוונה כגוף בלא נשמה, כי אותיות התורה ותפילה ומעשה המצוה הוא הגוף, והנשמה היא הכוונה ומחשבה ושמחה בעשיית רצון קונו. ובמעשה הגשמיות באמת חלוקה כל מצוה בפני עצמה - תפילין הוא מעור, וציצית הוא מצמר וכדומה, אין ענין זה לזה. אבל מחשבת ושמחת המצוה הכל אחד כי נקשר מאחדות הבורא יתברך ונכלל כל התרי"ג.

וזה שמסיים שם "תחת אשר לא עבדת את ה' אלהיך בשמחה" (דברים כח:מז), פירוש מחמת שלא עשית בשמחה ולא נכלל כל התרי"ג במצוה אחת נמצא שלא עשית כל התורה, ובעבור זה באה התוכחה...

- פ"ב -

כנזכר לעיל. ואז **וכבא השמש**, רוצה לומר כשתבא לו הבהירות והתלהבות **יבא אל תוך המחנה**, פירוש אז יבא אל פנימיות המחנה הם הסודות העליונים, וקל להבין.

- פ"א -

נועם אלימלך

כי יהיה בך איש אשר לא יהיה טהור מקרה לילה ויצא אל מחוץ למחנה לא יבא אל תוך המחנה: והיה לפנות ערב ירחץ במים וכבא השמש יבא אל תוך המחנה (דברים כג:יא-יב).

על דרך הרמז שהתורה הקדושה מרמזת על איש צדיק ההולך בדרכי ה' יתברך, אבל עדיין אינו טהור בכל מחשבותיו. וזהו **כי יהיה... מקרה לילה**, שאירע לו מקרה של שפלות וחטאים חלילה הנקראים לילה. דהיינו שאין גופו טהור לגמרי שיהיה נשמר מטומאת קרי ח"ו, ועיניו מלהסתכל הסתכלות לא טובות ומלראות ברע, ואזניו משמוע ופיו מלדבר דבר שאינו צורך גבוה לעבודתו ויראתו יתברך שמו.

ויצא אל מחוץ למחנה, פירוש הכתוב משיאו עצה מאחר שיצא חוץ למחנה קדושים, צריך לתקן עצמו במדריגות תחתונות, שלא יאחוז בדרכי הצדיקים הקדושים האמיתים העוסקים בסודות עליונים ביראתם ובאהבתם שלימה בלי שום סיג ונדנוד חטא והרהור עון כלל. ולא כן הוא, שמחשבתו פגומה ואינה צלולה בקדושה ואבריו אינם מתוקנים, ואיך יכנוס בהיכלא דמלכא לחפש ולפשפש באוצרות המלך, הם סודות התורה הקדושים העליונים? ואדרבה ח"ו קנאים פוגעים בו, הם הקליפות החיצונים ומתאחזים בו להחטיאו ולהכשילו יותר חלילה.

ולכן צריך לתקן את נפשו ואבריו באיזה ענינים שהם מחוץ למחנה הקדושה העליונה, דהיינו שיסגף עצמו באיזה סיגוף ויתחרט וישוב ויזהר וישמר עצמו מהדברים המביאים אותו לידי חטאים הנזכרים לעיל. ויראה להתאמץ ולהתחזק להצליל את מחשבותיו ולדקדק במעשיו ולהסתכל בהם, אם הם עשויים באמת בלב שלם בלי שום תערובות חמץ וסיג ופסולת, ושיהיו מעשיו בדרך אמת בלי שום ערבוב טוב ורע, ולדבק עצמו בתורה הקדושה ולעסוק בה בטהרה ולטבול עצמו בעת שצריך טבילה. ואז יתלהב לבו בקרבו לדבקות והתלהבות בהירות קדושה עליונה.

וזהו כוונת הפסוק **והיה לפנות ערב**, רוצה לומר כאשר יפנה את תערובות הרע שיהיו בו כנזכר לעיל **ורחץ במים**, רמז להתורה הקדושה הנקראת מים, וגם מים כפשוטו שיעסוק בתורה בטהרה בטובלו במים

יד:ט). ואם כן אתה יכול לעשות אותנו בריה חדשה וליתן לנו לב טהור כנזכר לעיל...

והנה מה שהקדוש ברוך הוא צוה אותנו **לא תקח האם על הבנים** הוא אינו מצד הרחמנות שלו, שאם היה מצד הרחמנות לא היה צריך לצוות אותנו, והיה בעצמו יכול להציל את האם, כי באמת הרבה ריוח והצלה לפניו. רק היתה כוונתו בכדי שנעורר מידת הרחמנות במה שאנו מרחמין על קן ציפור כנזכר לעיל. ואם כן זה פירוש הפייט "מחשבותיך לרחמנו מפעלותיך לרוממנו," פירוש אתה צוית כדי שנעורר הרחמנות ותרחם עלינו.

אור תורה

כי תבנה בית חדש ועשית מעקה לגגך ולא תשים דמים בביתך כי יפול הנופל ממנו (דברים כב:ח).

פירוש אדם האומר פירוש חדש על איזה ענין בתורה. **ועשית מעקה לגגך**, רוצה לומר דאילו לפי הפשט, היה צריך לכתוב ועשית מעקה לגגו, והוה קאי על הבית אשר בנה. ולפי פירוש הנזכר אתי שפיר. וכך פירושו: **ועשית מעקה**, רצה לומר מחיצה, **לגגך**, רצה לומר לגדלות שלך, שלא תהיה לך פניה בזה, שלא יגבה לבך בזה שאמרת תורה חדשה שלא שמעה אוזן מעולם - כי לא לך הגדלות, כי הכל מאתו יתברך.

כי יפול הנופל ממנו, ראוי הוא ליפול, כי ידעת שהשבירה כבר היתה בשביל גדלות, שכל אחד אמר "אנא אמלוך", ודי למבין.

וכן כשמתגאה על המקבל נקרא תועבה, כמו שאמרו רז״ל (מכילתא יתרו פ׳ ט). וכתוב בהדיא ״תועבת ה׳ כל גבה לב״ (משלי טז:ה), ועל כן אמר הכתוב **כי תועבת ה׳ אלהיך כל עושה אלה.**

קדושת לוי

(מפרשת בלק)

כי יקרא קן צפור לפניך בדרך בכל עץ או על הארץ אפרוחים או ביצים והאם רובצת על האפרוחים או על הביצים לא תקח האם על הבנים: שלח תשלח את האם ואת הבנים תקח לך למען ייטב לך והארכת ימים (דברים כב:ו-ז).

...איתא בגמרא: האומר ״עד קן צפור יגיעו רחמיך״... משתקין אותו (ברכות לג:), מפני שמשוה מידותיו של הקדוש ברוך הוא רחמים, והן גזירת מלך על עבדיו. והקשו התוספות, לפי זה מפני מה יסד הפייט כן, דכתיב ״צדקו אותו ואת בנו בל תשחטו (ויקרא כב:כח), מחשבותיך לרחמנו, מפעלותיך לרוממנו״ (שחרית של פסח יום ב׳).

ונראה דאמרו חכמים: כל המרחם על הבריות, מרחמין עליו מן השמים (שבת קנא:). ושורש הדבר הוא דאיתא בזהר הקדוש: באיתערותא דלתתא איתער עובדא דלעילא (ח״א עז:), נמצא כאשר האדם מרחם עצמו על הבריות הוא מעורר מידת הרחמנות, ומרחמין עליו גם כן.

וידוע הוא ד״חסדי ה׳ כי לא [תמנו כי לא] כלו [רחמיו]״ (איכה ג:כב), והקדוש ברוך הוא תמיד משפיע עלינו חסדים ורחמים וטובות. ומה שאנו חסרים לפעמים מטובות ח״ו, המניעה הוא מאיתנו שאין אנו ראוים לקבל הטובות. אבל הקדוש ברוך הוא ברוב רחמיו וחסדיו יכול להפוך את לבנו וליתן לנו לב טהור וחזק ואמיץ לעבדו באמת, ונהיה אנו ראוין לקבל הטובות.

ועל זה אנו מתפללין (תהלים מ:יב): ״אתה ה׳ לא תכלא רחמיך ממנו,״ פירוש שלא תהיה המניעה ממנו, כי ״חסדך ואמתך תמיד יצרוני,״ שהקדוש ברוך הוא יוצר את האדם בכל עת ורגע, כפי מאמר הגמרא: ״כל הנשמה תהלל יה״ (תהלים קנ:ו) - על כל נשימה ונשימה (בראשית רבה

- ע״ח -

לעיל, כי בוודאי האדם יקבל על עצמו יסורים רגע קטן כדי שיגיע לרחמים גדולים כנזכר לעיל.

ואף בעבודת ה' לא יתכן שיעבוד בדרך שאם הוא פועל בעבודתו שמונע ונפטר ממידה רעה אז טוב לו, ובהיפוכו צר לו מאד. כי נראה שאז הוא איש בפני עצמו ואינו הוי"ה אלהיך שיהיה כולא חד, אבל צריך שיהיה הוי"ה אלהיך ויהיה בעיניו כלא חשיב. ואז **ושבית שביו**, מה שהיה המלך אסור ברהטים, וזהו **שביו** שלו כו', ודי למבין.

אורח לחיים

לא יהיה כלי גבר על אשה ולא ילבש גבר שמלת אשה כי תועבת ה' אלהיך כל עושה אלה (דברים כב:ה).

ונראה דהנה ידוע דכל מה שהאדם משפיע לחבירו הוא מקבל ממנו יותר, כמאמרם ז"ל: יותר ממה שבעל הבית עושה עם העני, העני עושה עם בעל הבית (ויקרא רבה לד:י), וכן בתורה אמרו: הרבה תורה למדתי מרבותי... ומתלמידי יותר מכולם (תענית ז.). ואם כן צריך המשפיע לראות שלא להתגאות במחשבתו על המקבל ממנו, לומר בלבו שהוא המשפיע וחבירו צריך לו ומקבל ממנו, כיון שהוא מקבל יותר מחבירו המקבל ממנו.

וכלי גבר נקרא כלים של המשפיע. וזהו **לא יהיה כלי גבר**, הכלי של השכל המשפיע, לא יהיה במחשבתו במעלה על איש המקבל ממנו, שהוא בחינת אשה. אלא יחשוב בשעת השפעה לחבירו, הן בשכל והן בממון, שהוא מקבל יותר ממנו.

ולא ילבש גבר שמלת אשה, נראה דבא להזהיר שבשעת עבודה בלימוד או בעשית המצוה, שלא יהיה מחשבתו להנאת עצמו. כי כשהוא מכווין להנאת עצמו בעשית המצוה, נמצא שהוא מלובש בשכלו כדי לקבל מהמצוה הזאת, והוא בחינת אשה. וזהו **לא ילבש גבר שמלת אשה**, רק יכווין לעשות נחת רוח ליוצרו. ונמצא הוא בחינת משפיע, שמשפיע תענוג גדול למעלה, על דרך "תנו עוז לאלהים" (תהלים סח:לה). אבל אם מכוון להנאת עצמו נמצא עובד את עצמו, וזהו עבודה זרה ח"ו.

פרשת כי תצא

מאמרי אדמו״ר הזקן

כי תצא למלחמה על אויביך ונתנו ה׳ אלהיך בידך ושבית שביו (דברים כא:י).

דהנה מחשבות האדם בדברים זרים נקראות ״מלך אסור ברהטים״ (שיר השירים ז:ו) ברהיטי מוחין שהוא אסור בהם (תיקוני זוהר ת׳ ו כא:). כי יש דברים שאינו יכול לסובלם, ובעל כורחו אסור בהם. והעושה תשובה דהיינו תשוב ה׳, וכיצד יעשה תשובה לתקן זה?

הנהֿ כתיב ״ברגע קטן עזבתיך וברחמים גדולים אקבצך״ (ישעיה נד:ז). ותמוה שגודל אריכת הגלות י״ז מאות שנה קוראו רגע קטן!

והענין ידוע שה׳ יתברך עושה בראשית, ופירוש עושה תמיד בכל רגע יש מאין, ותתר״ף [1080] רגעים בשעה היינו תתר״ף נשימות שבאדם, שהלב בכל רגע מתחדש חיות בתוכו, כמו שנאמר ״והחיות רצוא ושוב״ (יחזקאל א:יד). ולמעלה ממנו יש יום שהשעה מקבלת חיות ממנו, כי היום מתחלק לי״ב שעות והוא מקבל חיות משבת, ששת ימי המעשה מקבלין משבת תתאה, ותתאה מעילאה עד שבת העליונה ששם הכל רגע קטן. וזהו ״עולת שבת בשבתו חודש בחדשו״ (במדבר כח:י,יד), שהשבת עולה לשבתו הגבוה ממנה, וכן החודש כנזכר לעיל.

וזהו ״מלכותך מלכות כל עולמים וממשלתך [בכל דור ודור]״ (תהלים קמה:יג), שלמעלה הוא מלכות ומשתלשל למטה עד שנקרא ״מלכות כל עולמים,״ וכן ״בכל דור ודור.״ הוא דכתיב ״אלף שנים כיום אתמול״ (תהלים צ:ד) הוא רק למטה אבל למעלה הוא רק רגע קטן.

וזהו ״ברגע קטן עזבתיך״ והוא ״ברחמים גדולים אקבצך,״ שאביא אותך לבחינת רחמים גדולים - המתקת הדינים. וכאשר יתבונן האדם שכל העולם הוא רגע קטן יסבול רגע קטן כדי שיגיע לרחמים גדולים כנזכר

וכדומה מצרכי ישראל המרובים, המבלים רוב שנותם רק בעבור האוכל והכסות, ועיקר עבודתם שנבראו בשבילה נשכח מלוח לבם.

מול זה בא הרמז בתורה **והיה** יגיד שמחה, **כקרבכם אל המלחמה**, וכתיב בה' הידיעה, היינו המלחמה הידועה, מלחמתה של תורה ותפילה, שמחה ודאי לפניו יתברך, בקרבם בני ישראל ללחום נגד צר הצורר, הוא היצר הרע. וישימו לב להכין את עצמם בכל מיני קרבא, לירות חצים חזקים, ומבטיחו הכתוב "חציך שנונים עמים תחתיך יפלו" (תהלים מה:ו)... לומר תשים אל לבך וידוע תדע שמחשבות זרות הבאות בתוך התפילה, ושאר מונעים עבדות בוראך, המה אויבי המלך מלכו של עולם... כשנפטר מספר תורה ויצא לפעלו, שם עיקר השמירה מאויב הצופה להחטיאו, ולחטוף אותיות בקליפות, והם כלי המלחמה שלא יהיה לו במה ללחום מלחמתה של תורה ותפילה.

אמנם מי הוא המלומד מלחמה להורות דרכי העבודה, אומר הכתוב **ונגש הכהן**, הוא העובד, כי על הכהנים להורות, ועליו מוטל **לדבר אל העם... ואמר אליהם שמע ישראל אתם קרבים היום למלחמה**, ופירש רש"י: אפילו אין בהן זכות אלא קריאת שמע בלבד, כדאי אתם שיושיע אתכם. ומובן על פי הדברים הנאמרים שרומז למלחמתה של תורה ותפילה, ועיקר התפילה מדאורייתא הוא הקריאת שמע, ושם עיקר היחוד כנזכר בכוונות. ולכן צריך למסור את עצמו עם כל נפשו ומאודו להיות בתכלית הזכות לפנות מחשבות מעולם הזה, וינענע ראשו לשית סטרין...

ולזה העמיק רש"י אפילו אין זְכות - לשון זַכות ובהירות - אלא קריאת שמע, ששם עיקר הכוונה ומסירת הנפש, כדאי אתם שיושיע אתכם.

- ע"ה -

הגוף, אז תהיה **עם ה' אלהיך**, כלומר שה' יתברך הוא השורה בתוך העולם הטבעי בלי פירוד, ומלא כל העולם ומנהיג כרצונו. כך אתה תהיה תמים, ושתנהיג הנשמה את הגוף מן העולם הטבעי, ואז תהיה דבוק עם ה' אלהיך.

אור המאיר

והיה כקרבכם אל המלחמה ונגש הכהן ודבר אל העם: ואמר אליהם שמע ישראל אתם קרבים היום למלחמה על אויביכם אל ירך לבבכם אל תיראו ואל תחפזו ואל תערצו מפניהם (דברים כ:ב-ג).

יש להבין מה לשון "והיה" שיגיד שמחה (בראשית רבה מב:ג), ובכאן שמחה מה זו עושה כיון שמקרבים את עצמם למלחמה? ודרך הארץ כשהולכים למלחמה, אפילו מלומדי מלחמה ייראו לנפשם אם יהיו מהמנצחים או מהמנוצחים... כל זה צריך ביאור.

והנראה שכאן הרמז בעניני התורה ותפילה, שהם עיקר מלחמתו של אדם כל ימי חיים חיותו. "ואשרי הגבר מלא את אשפתו מהם" (תהלים קכז:ה), לזרוק חצים לגבי סמא"ל, ולהיות חצים שנונים בידו, דהיינו להוציא אותיות מלאים מאהבה ויראה בהתעוררות גדולה, אזי יהיה לבו בטוח שיהיה מהמנצחים ולא מהמנוצחים.

כאשר עינינו רואות רובן דעלמא בגשתם אל עבודה שבלב זו תפילה, "אין אומר ואין דברים בלי נשמע קולם" (תהלים יט:ד). רק ינוע כעצי היער, ובאמת אנשים אלו המלחמה כבדה בידם, ומורך בלבבם מפני האויב. והצר השוכן בקרבם, הוא היצר הרע, הלוקח מאתם כלי המלחמה, הם האותיות, ועושה צרופים בקליפות, ומבלבל מחשבתם לשוט בהבלי עולם. וממילא אין חצים לירות במו אופל, לנצח ולהרחיק הצפוני מלבו, ונעשה מנוצח מלפניו. וכאשר בא לתורה ולתפילה כן הולך ומאומה אין בידו.

והכל בעבור שאין איש שם על הלב עיקר בואו בעולם הזה ומה מעשהו. ומצד הסברא בוודאי לא בא רק לפרנס את עצמו ולפרנס אשתו ובניו,

וזהו "תורת ה' תמימה משיבת נפש" (תהלים יט:ח), כשלומד בענין זה שמבואר אל שלימות היראה שהיא תמימה, משיבת נפש. אין בה שבירה, אז משיבת נפש - הוא משיב נפשו שהוא במדריגה התחתונה בבחינת נפש, שהוא משוקע במדריגה פחותה ומשיב על ידי הבאת השראת היראה עליו משיבת נפשה גם כן.

וזהו **תמים תהיה [עם ה' אלהיך]**, כשתהיה במדריגת שלימות היראה שהיא **תמים, תהיה עם ה' אלקיך**. ולכך הוא ת' רבתי, כי יש אתוון רברבין ואתוון זעירין, הזעירין הם שהזערו ונתצמצמו על ידי צמצומים רבים, והרברבין שלא הוצרכו לצמצם כנזכר לעיל. וכשבא אל היראה התמימה בא אל אתוון רברבין שלא היו בצמצום, ויובן.

אורח לחיים

תמים תהיה עם ה' אלהיך (דברים יח:יג).

דהנה ה' יתברך ברא אדם מן העליון ומן התחתונים, נשמה מעליונים וגוף מתחתונים. ואמרו רז"ל: הני חמשי [אלה החמשה] "ברכי נפשי" כנגד מי אמרן דוד? לא אמרן אלא כנגד הקדוש ברוך הוא וכנגד הנשמה - מה הקדוש ברוך הוא מלא כל העולם, אף הנשמה מלאה את כל הגוף וכו'. יבא מי שיש בו חמשה דברים הללו וישבח למי שיש בו חמשה דברים הללו (ברכות י.).

וכתבתי פירוש "ה' הוא האלהים" (מלכים א יח:לט) דהנה הטבע בגימטריא אלהים, וה' יתברך הוא מנהיג את העולם הגשמי הטבעי, שמתנהג על פי הטבע כרצונו וחפצו, "כי מלא כל הארץ כבודו" (ישעיה ו:ג), וכמו שאמרו הקדוש ברוך הוא מלא כל העולם. וזהו "ה' הוא האלהים," הוא השוכן בתוך הטבע ומנהיגה כרצונו, ואין הטבע נפרד ממנו, אלא הוא יתברך השוכן בתוך העולם הטבעי ומנהיגו כרצונו.

וכך צריך האדם לדמות ליוצרו, שיהיו הנשמה והגוף אחדות גמורה בלי פירוד, ותהא הנשמה מנהיגה הגוף, אבל לא כחמר גמל, שתהא הנשמה מושכת לכאן והגוף לצד אחר. וזהו **תמים תהיה עם ה' אלהיך**, כלומר אם תהיה בעצמך תמים, הנשמה והגוף ביחד בלי פירוד, והנשמה תוליך

ולכן המלאכים שמשיגין יותר גדולתו יתברך, נתן להם הקדוש ברוך הוא יראה ופחד גדול, עד שנהר דינור יוצא מזיעתן מפחד ה' ומהדר גאונו, כדי שלא יבואו לביטול ממציאותן... וידוע דהמלאכים נקראין אחים לישראל... וגם נקראים "עומדים" (זכריה ג:ז), כי אינם הולכין ממדריגה למדריגה...

וזהו **וכי יבא הלוי**, היינו מי שדבוק בהבורא ב"ה נקרא לוי, מלשון "הפעם ילוה אישי [אלי]" (בראשית כט:לד), דהוא דביקות והתחברות. **מאחד שעריך**... היינו מעולם הזה... **ובא בכל אוות נפשו**, היינו באהבה והתלהבות גדולה לבד **אל המקום אשר יבחר ה'**, אל עבודות הבורא ב"ה. וקאמר הפסוק **ושרת בשם ה' אלהיו**, היינו שיראה לשרת עבודתו בשם הוי"ה דהוא אהבה, אלהיו הוא יראה, בשניהם כאחד. **ככל אחיו הלוים העומדים לפני ה'**, היינו המלאכים שנקראין אחיו ועומדים כנזכר לעיל שעובדין ביראה הגדולה שברא להם הקדוש ברוך הוא כדי שלא יתבטלו, גם הוא יעשה כן, כי גם האדם יוכל לבא באהבה לביטול ממציאות.

תורת המגיד

(*מפרשת בא, מכתב יד של ר' שמעלקי*)

תמים תהיה עם ה' אלהיך (דברים יח:יג).

והנה הלומד תורה שבעל פה צריך לדעת שכל התורה והדיבורים נלקחו מדיבור הראשון, שהוא "בדבר ה' שמים נעשו" (תהלים לג:ו). ונמצא השורש הוא הפה העליון דיבור הראשון והכל מקבלים ממנו מדיבור זה, והדיבור הראשון שהוא מדריגת בעל שממנו מקבלים כולם. וזהו תורה שבעל פה - שהפה העליון הוא הבעל.

ונמצא כשלומד ומדבר צריך שיבוא למדריגת דיבור ראשון, והוא היחוד שמייחד הכל אל הבעל שהוא הפה דיבור הראשון. כי אז שורה עליו יראה השלימה, כי התורה מחכמה נפקת, וכתיב "ראשית חכמה יראת ה'" (תהלים קיא:י)... ושרשא דכל עלמין שהוא דיבור הראשון.

- ע"ב -

פרשת שופטים

מבשר צדק

וכי יבא הלוי מאחד שעריך מכל ישראל אשר הוא גר שם ובא בכל אוות נפשו אל המקום אשר יבחר ה': ושרת בשם ה' אלהיו ככל אחיו הלוים העומדים שם לפני ה' (דברים יח:ו-ז).

על פי מה שכתבתי לעיל לפרש המשנה אבות: הוי מתפלל בשלומה של מלכות, [שאלמלא מוראה איש את רעהו חיים בלעו] (מ' אבות ג:ב). והוא דהנה בעבדות הבורא ב"ה יש בחינת יראה ובחינת אהבה, ואיתא בזהר: מלתא דלא מתאמרי בתרין גדפין דאיהו דחילו ורחימו לא פרחת לעילא [דבר שאינו נאמר בשני כנפיים, שהם יראה ואהבה, אינו פורח למעלה] (תיקוני זהר ת' י כה:). ולכאורה אינו מובן, הלא יותר טוב לעבוד [רק] באהבה ובהתלהבות. אך דהאמת היא דבאהבה יכולין לבא לידי ביטול ממציאות, ותהיה חיותו נבלעת בשורש. לכן צריכין ליראה שתכבה להאהבה.

וזהו "החיות רצוא ושוב" (יחזקאל א:יד), היינו חיות האדם הוא על ידי רצוא ושוב, והוא שוב ביראה, כי בלא זה היתה חיותו נבלעת בדביקות בשורש. וזהו שפרשתי "ואהבת את ה' אלהיך" (דברים ו:ה), היינו שבגודל האהבה שתהיה לך, חזק עצמך ביראה, דהוא "אלהיך".

וידוע דמלכות היא כלולה מיראה ואהבה. וזהו "הוי מתפלל בשלומה של מלכות," בשלימות של מידת המלכות, דהיא כלולה [מ]אהבה ויראה. "שאלמלא מוראה," דבלא היראה, "איש את רעהו," היינו האדם בדביקותו אל הקדוש ברוך הוא, והוא נקרא "רעך ורע אביך" (משלי כז:י). "חיים בלעו," היתה חיותו נבלעת בשורש, ולכן יתפלל במידת יראה גם כן. והנה כל מי שמבחין יותר גדולת הבורא ב"ה צריך לחיזוק יותר ביראה שלא יתבטל ממציאות.

- ע"א -

זורעים, מונע אותו מליתן צדקה בשביל זה שיכין לעצמו שיהיה לו מה יאכל בשנה השביעית כי חייו קודמים.

אבל אם יהיה לו לב טוב להאמין בו יתברך בוודאי ישפיע לו שפע מן השמים כאומרו "וכי תאמרו מה נאכל בשנה השביעית הן לא נזרע [ולא נאסף את תבואתנו]. וצויתי את ברכתי [לכם בשנה הששית ועשת את התבואה לשלש השנים]" (ויקרא כה:כ-כא).

והתורה נקראת דבר, כמו "דבר צוה לאלף דור" (דברי הימים טז:טו). וזהו **כי יהיה דבר**, כלומר שיהיו לך דברי תורה שפטור אתה מליתן צדקה, כי חייך קודמין, **עם לבבך בליעל**, כלומר מחמת שבלבבך בליעל. אתה שומע לטענת היצר המראה לך דברי תורה שפטור אתה מליתן.

אבל אם היה לך לב טוב היית מאמין בו יתברך כנזכר לעיל, רק מחמת שבלבבך בליעל חפץ אתה בדברי תורה אלו ותאמר **קרבה שנת השמיטה** ואינן זורעין **ורעה עיניך באחיך האביון**, לאמר "חייך קודמין"...

- ע -

"ועצר את השמים ולא יהיה מטר" (דברים יא:יז). פותח ידו המטר יורד, שנאמר "יפתח ה' לך את אוצרו [הטוב את השמים]" (דברים כח:יב), וכן הוא אומר "פותח את ידך ומשביע [לכל חי רצון]."

והנפקא מינה בדבר שאצל בשר ודם שהשפעתו אינה דבוקה במקורה, והוא רק כמו ספוג שנספגו לתוכו מים, ושוב נעקרו המים ממקורם. והספוג הוא המחזירם כל זמן שידו פתוחה, ואינם יוצאים ממנה כי אם על ידי עצירה. אבל במידת הקדוש ברוך הוא שהשפעתו דבוקה במקורה, ולכן נקרא "פלג אלהים" שהיא דבוקה באלהים. כל זמן שידו פתוחה יוצאת לעולם מן מקורה, שהמקור ההוא הוא אין סוף, והספוג הפעל שלה הפכיות. כשרוצה להחזיר ההשפעה למקורה שלא תרד, אזי הוא עוצרה וסופגה בספוג. ולמדנו ה' יתברך דרכיו ליתן צדקה בפתיחת המקור, שלא כמידת בשר ודם, ודבק במידותיו יתברך.

וזהו **פתוח** הוא מקור בלשון המדקדקים, וכן "נתון תתן" פרוש כן (דברים טו:י). **תפתח את ידך**, ותהיה משפיע בפתיחת היד ולא בקפיצת היד. ורוצה לומר שתהיה פותח בצדקה זו שאתה נותן את מקור ההשפעה המשפעת "לכל חי רצון"...

אורח לחיים ב'

השמר לך פן יהיה דבר עם לבבך בליעל לאמר קרבה שנת השבע שנת השמיטה ורעה עינך באחיך האביון ולא תתן לו וקרא עליך אל ה' והיה בך חטא: נתון תתן לו ולא ירע לבבך בתתך לו כי בגלל הדבר הזה יברכך ה' אלהיך בכל מעשך ובכל משלח ידך (דברים טו:ט-י).

ולכאורה הוה ליה למימר "פן יהיה בלבבך בליעל לאמר קרבה וכו'"? ומאי **דבר עם** - והוא מיותר.

ונראה דהנה היצר הרע כשבא לאדם ורוצה להעבירו מן הדרך ולמנוע מליתן צדקה לאדם הולך בדרך הישר ומראה לו דברים מן התורה שלא יתן, כגון "חייך קודמין" (בבא מציעא סב.). ובפרט בעת השמיטה שאין

ולכך בכל דבר, אף שהוא בסוף המדריגה שהוא רחוק מאור שפעת אורו אין סוף ב"ה, צריך לקרב את עצמו עם אותו סוף המדריגה שהוא בחינת ת', אל הא', שהוא אלופו של עולם, ולהגביה הדבר ולהעלותו מתתא לעילא אל שורש הכל בחינת האלף... וכמו שנאמר "ובחרת בחיים," שיבחר החיות והטוב שבדבר ההוא שהוא צמצום אלהותו, ולא שימשך אחר הרע שבהדבר. כנודע שמחטא אדם הראשון נעשה התערבות טוב ורע, שבכל הדברים שהוא רואה בעיניו יוכל לראות הטוב או הרע שיש שם. והאדם גם כן הוא מעורב מטוב ורע כנודע שהוא בחינת היצר טוב ויצר הרע שבאדם. והרע שבו נמשך אחר הרע שבהדבר, והטוב נמשך אחר הטוב שבהדבר שרואה אותו מדברי עולם הזה...

וזהו **ראה אנכי נותן לפניכם**, בכל מה שאתה רואה בדברים שבעולם תדע ששם **אנכי נותן לפניכם ברכה וקללה**, שהוא בחינת טוב ורע המעורב בכל הדברים כנזכר לעיל. **את הברכה**, פירוש על ידי בחינת את שהוא יחוד א' עם בחינת ת' שהוא סוף המדריגה כאמור לעיל. על ידי שרואה הטוב שבכל דבר ומקרבו לאלופו של עולם הברכה באה על ידי זה...

ועל כן גבי קללה לא נאמר תיבת **את**, כי כל עיקר ביאת הקללה הוא על ידי שאין שם יחוד "את" שהוא יחוד ת', שהוא סוף המדריגה, אל הא'...

צמח ה' לצבי ב'

כי יהיה בך אביון מאחד אחיך באחד שעריך בארצך אשר ה' אלהיך נותן לך לא תאמץ את לבבך ולא תקפוץ את ידך מאחיך האביון: כי פתוח תפתח את ידך לו... (דברים טו:ז-ח).

על דרך המדרש וזה הלשון (שמות רבה כה:ג): "פותח את ידך [ומשביע לכל חי רצון]" (תהלים קמה:טז). בא וראה שלא כמידת הקדוש ברוך הוא מידת בשר ודם: בשר ודם - כל זמן שהספוג בידו, פותח ידו אין טיפה יורדת, קפץ ידו הוא מוריד מים. אבל הקדוש ברוך הוא אינו כן - הספוג בידו שנאמר "פלג אלהים מלא מים" (תהלים סה:י), אם עצר אין המים יורדים, שנאמר "הן יעצור במים ויבשו" (איוב יב:טו). וכן הוא אומר

החסדים והתענוגים ויש בהן ברכה וקללה ביחד. **את הברכה** שיש בהן **אשר תשמעו אל מצוות ה' אלהיכם.**

ולשון **תשמעו** מלשון "וישמע שאול את העם" (שמואל א טו:ד), כלומר שתקבץ הדברים, הן עשיות המצוות הן תענוגי רשות הגשמיים שיהיו הכל **אל מצוות ה' אלהיכם**, שתהיה כוונתכם בעשיותם לעבודת ה' יתברך ויהיה הכל מצוות ה' אלהיכם. והקללה שיש בהם **אם לא תשמעו אל מצוות ה' אלהיכם**, שלא תהיה כוונתכם בעשית דברים הגשמיים שיהיו מצוות ה' אלהיכם. וסוף תהיה **וסרתם מן הדרך [אשר אנכי מצוה אתכם היום]** - תעבור ח"ו גם כן עבירות.

ואמר **נותן לפניכם**, כלומר הבחירה בידכם לבחור בטוב ובתמים.

מאור עינים

ראה אנכי נותן לפניכם היום ברכה וקללה: את הברכה אשר תשמעו אל מצוות ה' אלהיכם אשר אנכי מצוה אתכם היום: והקללה אם לא תשמעו אל מצוות ה' אלהיכם וסרתם מן הדרך אשר אנכי מצוה אתכם היום ללכת אחרי אלהים אחרים אשר לא ידעתם (דברים יא:כו-כח).

להבין הענין, מהו לשון **ראה** שמראה באצבע כאלו הדבר מוכן לפני עין הרואה? ועוד להבין שאצל הברכה אמר לשון "את" כמו שכתוב **את הברכה אשר** וכו' ואצל הקללה לא נאמר תיבת "את".

ונקדים פסוק הכתוב בפרשת נצבים "ראה נתתי לפניך היום את החיים ואת הטוב ואת המות ואת הרע," ואחר זה נאמר שם "ובחרת בחיים" (דברים ל:טו,יט). כי נודע שבריאת כל העולמות ומלואן היתה בתורה, שהן האותיות שמא' ועד ת', שהבורא ב"ה צמצם את עצמו בהאותיות. ותחילת צמצומו ואצילותו היא באות א', ואחר זה צמצם את עצמו כביכול והאציל אור שפעת קדושתו מאות אל אות עד ת', שהוא סוף המדריגה כנודע שהוא מקום הבחירה, כמו שאמרו: ת' תחיה ת' תמות (שבת נה.).

אורח לחיים א'

ראה אנכי נותן לפניכם היום ברכה וקללה: את הברכה אשר תשמעו אל מצוות ה' אלהיכם אשר אנכי מצוה אתכם היום: והקללה אם לא תשמעו אל מצוות ה' אלהיכם וסרתם מן הדרך אשר אנכי מצוה אתכם היום ללכת אחרי אלהים אחרים אשר לא ידעתם (דברים יא:כו-כח).

להבין מלת היום הוא מיותר, וגם שכלל ברכה וקללה ביחד, ושם אמר "נתתי לפניך היום את החיים ואת הטוב ואת המות ואת הרע ובחרת בחיים" (דברים ל:טו)...

ונראה דכתוב בשולחן ערוך (אורח חיים ס' רלא) וזה הלשון: "בכל דרכיך דעהו" (משלי ג:ו), אמרו חכמים כל מעשיך יהיו לשם שמים (מ' אבות ב:טו), שאפילו דברים של רשות כגון האכילה והשתיה וההליכה והשינה והקימה והתשמיש וכל צרכי גופך יהיו כולם לעבודת בוראך...

וכלל הדברים כי כל עבודת ה' יתברך ב"ה אחר כוונת הלב הן הן הדברים, ורחמנא לבא בעי (רש"י על סנהדרין קו:). ואפילו אם עושה המצוה ואינו מכוין לעבודת הבורא יתברך נקרא פושע, כמו שאמרו רז"ל (נזיר כג.): שנים שצלו את פסחיהם אחד אכלו לשום מצוה ואחד לשום אכילה גסה - על זה נאמר "צדיקים ילכו בם ופושעים יכשלו בם" (הושע יד:י).

וזאת הבחירה אשר ניתנה לאדם לנטות ימין או שמאל. ואם מכוין בכל מעשיו לשם שמים, עובד את בוראו תמיד ועושה מצוות תמיד, ואם ח"ו להיפך הוא להיפך. ובבחינת הדעת שבאדם יבחין איזה דרך יבחר ולהבדיל בין טוב לרע, כמו שאמרו רז"ל: אם אין דעה, הבדלה מניין (ירושלמי ברכות ה:ב)? ונמצא בכל דברים, בעשיית מצוות ובכל האהבות היינו התענוגים, יש בהן שני דרכים: היינו ברכה וקללה. אם יכוין בהם לעבודת בוראו הוא ממשיך ברכה, ואם ח"ו להיפך הוא להיפך. וכל החסדים והתענוגים מכונים בשם יום, כמו שנאמר "יומם יצוה ה' חסדו" (תהלים מב:ט), ומשה רבינו ע"ה היה בחינת הדעת של כללות ישראל. וזה שנאמר **ראה אנכי**, בחינת הדעת הוא **נותן לפניכם היום**, הן

פרשת ראה

צמח ה' לצבי א'

(מפרשת כי תבוא)

ראה אנכי נותן לפניכם היום... את הברכה אשר תשמעו אל מצוות ה' אלהיכם אשר אנכי מצוה אתכם היום (דברים יא:כו-כז).

על דרך הזהר (ח"א יב.-יב:): "וידעת היום והשבות אל לבבך כי ה' הוא האלהים" (דברים ד:לט) - למינדע דאינון חד, שמא דאלהים ושמא דהוי"ה - דאינון חד ולית בהו פרודא [לדעת ששם אלהים ושם הוי"ה הם אחד - הם אחד ואין בהם פירוד]. "וידעת" זאת מן היום, דאיהו לילה ויום, "ערב ובוקר יום אחד" (בראשית א:ה). וזהו שנאמר "וידעת היום," מן יומא אתה ידעת, "אל לבבך," דאיהו יצר טוב ויצר הרע ואינון אקרו לב, ואינון שתי לבבות ואינון חד.

וזהו שנאמר **ראה אנכי נותן לפניכם היום**, שהוא יום ולילה, ימינא ושמאלא, מן זה נמשכו ברכה וקללה. **את הברכה אשר תשמעו אל מצוות ה' אלהיכם** (דברים יא:כז), רוצה לומר תשמעו לשון "השמע לי" (יומא לה:) - לייחד - שתהיו מיין דכורין ומיין נוקבין "אל מצוות ה' אלהיכם," לייחד קודשא בריך הוא ושכינתיה. **אשר אנכי מצוה אתכם היום**, רוצה לומר בכח הייחוד שאנכי מצווה ומייחד לכם היום ימינא ושמאלא...

אור תורה

... לאהבה את ה' אלהיכם ללכת בכל דרכיו ולדבקה בו (דברים יא:כב).

ואמרו רבותינו ז"ל: וכי אפשר לדבק עצמו בהקדוש ברוך הוא? והלא "אש אוכלה הוא" (דברים ד:כד)! אלא הדבק במידותיו - מה הוא רחום, אף אתה רחום (שבת קלג:).

פירוש כי לעבוד את ה' בהתלהבות, וזהו דביקות גמורה בו יתברך, זה אי אפשר להיות תמיד, רק מטי ולא מטי [נוגע ואינו נוגע] כדרך אש. כי כמו אש שאם מנפחין אותה תחילה היא נכבית, ואחר כך גדלה המדורה, והאש גופה יורדת מעלה ומטה ומתנענעה. כן ההתלהבות היא מטי ולא מטי, כי תענוג תמידי אינו תענוג.

וזהו שמקשה בגמרא והלא "אש אוכלה הוא." רוצה לומר ההתלהבות נמנעת ממך, וזהו במטי ולא מטי. וכי אפשר לדבק בו יתברך? ותירץ הדבק במידותיו, פירוש בלבושיו - באותיותיו. רוצה לומר כי זה אפשר תמיד להיות במחשבתו לחשוב באותיות התורה, והתורה לבושו יתברך. ואפילו כשמדבר עם בני אדם לא יחשוב רק באותיות הדברים ההם, והם גם כן מכ"ב אותיות התורה.

מה הוא רחום, פירוש כי רחום אותיות "חומר," רוצה לומר כי להקדוש ברוך הוא אי אפשר לרחם על חומר עכור, והיאך יכול להיות במחשבה הדקה מן הדקה חומר עב עכור? רק אם יצמצם את עצמו יתברך להיות במחשבתו חומר, אז מרחם עליו. ומהיכן בא הצמצום הלז? זה בא אם אדם הוא רחום, אז הוא פועל שהקדוש ברוך הוא מלביש עצמו בלבושים ומצמצם את עצמו כביכול, וגם כן מרחם עלינו. וזהו מה הוא רחום [אף אתה רחום], וזה הוא מביא רחמנות.

נועם אלימלך

ועתה ישראל מה ה' אלהיך שואל מעמך כי אם ליראה את ה' אלהיך ללכת בכל דרכיו ולאהבה אותו ולעבד את ה' אלהיך בכל לבבך ובכל נפשך: לשמור את מצוות ה' ואת חוקתיו אשר אנכי מצוך היום לטוב לך (דברים י:יב-יג).

הדקדוק מפורש, מה המקרא חסר עוד מלפרשו שחושב ומונה כל העובדות הללו יראה ואהבה וללכת בכל דרכיו? ומה יש עוד לעשות, שאמר הכתוב **שואל מעמך כי אם** כו'? ונראה לפרש, דהנה הבורא ב"ה לא ברא את עולמו רק להטיב לברואים. אך שצריך לזה כלי נכון ומוכשר שיוכל לקבל ההטבה.

והנה המשל: מי שרוצה לשלוח לחבירו יין או דבש ואין לו כלי נאה ויפה, שואל מחבירו זה שיש לו כלי נאה של כסף וממלא אותה יין או דבש ושולח לזה שהכלי שלו. והנמשל מובן, שהאדם הוא הכלי לקבל. וזה הוא הכשרו ותיקונו של הכלי, דהיינו האדם, שיהיה מוכשר לקבל הטובות והשפעות הבורא ב"ה, הוא היראה ואהבה וקיום מצוות ה' וחוקותיו וכל דרכיו. ואז הוא כלי נאה ויפה ושואל ה' יתברך הכלי הזה וממלא אותו כל טוב.

וזה **מה ה' אלהיך שואל מעמך**, רוצה לומר אימתי ה' יתברך שואל מה שיש עמך, דהיינו הכלי שלך, כדי למלא אותו משפעת טובו וברכותיו? **כי אם ליראה** כו', רוצה לומר זה בלתי אפשרי, כי אם שתעבוד אותו בכל העובדות המנויים והמפורשים בפסוק, ואז תהיה כלי יפה ונאה ומוכשר לקבל וישאל ממך הכלי שלך, דהיינו את עצמך. **לטוב לך** כדי שייטיב לך ועל ידך יבואו טובות והשפעות לכל ישראל, וקל להבין.

- ס"ג -

הנמשל, כשישראל ראוין לקבל השפעתו יתברך ושואבים ממנו יתברך השפעתם, מזה מתברך שמו יתברך, על דרך שכתוב "ושאבתם מים בששון ממעיני הישועה" (ישעיה יב:ג). רוצה לומר שצריך [המעיין, היינו הקדוש ברוך הוא] לתשועה, והתשועה הוא ממה ששואבים ממנו. נמצא האכילה והשביעה הוא גם כן מצוה מעשית. וזו **ואכלת ושבעת**, רוצה לומר מצוה מעשית, **וברכת**, מצוה שבדיבור.

אור האמת

... מה ה' אלהיך שואל מעמך כי אם ליראה את ה' אלהיך... (דברים י:יב).

על דרך משל, כל זמן שהאב הולך עם בנו ביחד, אין הבן עושה מעשה נערות מיראת האב. אבל פעם אחת היה האב מתרחק ממנו, אז היה התינוק מתדבק עם שאר קטנים והיה משחק עמהם, עד אשר הוזק באבן נגף. ובתחילה לא היה לו מכאוב כי אם מעט, וכאשר בא אביו וראה נתחלחל מאוד, כי הבין בדעתו כי אם יתרבה השחפת יהיה יותר מכאוב ויתקלקל ח"ו שאר הגוף. אז לקח אותו אביו בחזקה והוציא ממנו הקוץ.

נמצא לפי דעת התינוק הוא אכזריות גדולה אצלו, כי היה לו עינוי גדול בהוצאת הקוץ יותר מהעינוי כשהוא בתוך הגוף, והאמת שהוא רפואה גדולה אצלו. וכשאביו רוצה להוכיח אותו, אומר לו "'שמע בני מוסר אביך' (משלי א:ח), ואל תתחזק במעשי נערות ואם לאו אייסר אותך כמו שיסרתי אותך בהוצאת הקוץ."

נמצא יראת התינוק אינו דומה ליראת האב, כי האב ירא מההיזק. לכך מפחיד אותו בעינוי גדולה לפי דעתו, דהיינו הוצאת הקוץ. אבל התינוק אינו ירא מההיזק אלא מהרפואה, דהיינו הוצאת הקוץ. ואם היה התינוק מבין, היה גם כן ירא כמו שהאב ירא.

וזו **מה ה' שואל מעמך כי אם ליראה את ה' אלהיך**, ואת הוא כמו עם. רוצה לומר שתאחז בזאת היראה מה שאביך בשמים ירא, דהיינו ההיזק מעבירה, וזו "ויהי מורא שמים עליך" (מ' אבות א:ג)...

פרשת עקב

צמח ה' לצבי א'

... כי לא על הלחם לבדו יחיה האדם כי על כל מוצא פי ה' יחיה האדם (דברים ח:ג).

פירוש על דרך משל, עבד שהמלך נותן לו ממאכלו ממה שהמלך עצמו סועד, ולוקח מפיו ממש ונותן להעבד, אזי אותו העבד שמח ומתענג יותר בזה מה שזכה שהמלך נותן לו בכבודו ובעצמו ממאכלו מפיו, יותר מן הנאת המאכל עצמו, אף שהוא מעדן גדול. ובזה יש לו חיות יותר ממה שהוא מקבל חיות מן המאכל עצמו. וזהו שנאמר **כי לא על הלחם... כי על כל מוצא פי ה'**, שהלחם הוא מוצא פי ה' כידוע.

ועל דרך זה יתפרש הפסוק: "כי ה' יתן חכמה מפיו" (משלי ב:ו), "כי החכמה תחיה" (קהלת ז:יב), נמצא החיות של האדם מפיו יתברך. וזו מזונא דאורייתא כנזכר בזהר (ח"ב סב.). ועל דרך דאיתא במסכת נדה (ע:): "כי ה' יתן חכמה מפיו" - תני ר' חייא, משל למלך בשר ודם שעשה סעודה לעבדיו ומשגר לאוהביו ממה שלפניו - עד כאן לשונם.

ועל דרך זו נקרא לחם הפנים, רוצה לומר שמשפיע מאור פני מלך חיים. ועל דרך "פה אל פה אדבר בו" (במדבר יב:ח), ועל דרך "פנים בפנים דבר ה' אל כל קהלכם" (דברים ה:ד), וגם נקרא "לחם מן השמים" כידוע (שמות טז:ד).

צמח ה' לצבי ב'

ואכלת ושבעת וברכת את ה' אלהיך... (דברים ח:י).

פירוש על דרך משל: המעיין הנובע כששואבים ממנו תמיד, אזי מתגבר ונובע תמיד ומתברך. על דרך שאמרו רז"ל: נהרא מכיפיה מתברך (נדרים מ.), וכשאין שואבים ממנו אזי חוזר המקור לאחוריו.

מאור עינים ב׳

ואהבת את ה׳ אלהיך בכל לבבך ובכל נפשך ובכל מאדך (דברים ו:ה).

ודרשו רז״ל: בשני יצריך - ביצר הטוב, וביצר הרע (ברכות נד.). ולהבין איך אפשר לאהוב לאהוב ה׳ יתברך ביצר הרע. אבל הענין הוא שה׳ יתברך צוה לאהוב אותו יתברך, ואיך אפשר לאהוב דבר שלא נודע מהותו? לכן יעצה לנו התורה ביצר הרע והוא שה׳ יתברך ברא בעולם משל שממנו נוכל להבין הנמשל, דהיינו כל התענוגים שבעולם כמו אכילה ושתיה ומשגל, שיבין מפני מה אני אוהב אותו דבר. הלא הוא רק אהבה נפולה מעולם האהבה, כנזכר אצלנו כמה פעמים. ועל אחת כמה וכמה שיש לי לאהוב הבורא ב״ה שהוא מקור כל התענוגים.

וזהו שאמר דוד המלך ע״ה "ואהי להם למשל" (תהלים סט:יב), רוצה לומר שהם סוברים שאני אוחז במשל לבדו, ואין אני לוקח הנמשל. אבל באמת אינו כך! אך יש יצר הרע שמסמא עיניו בל יראה ליקח הנמשל, רק לאחוז במשל לבדו. העצה לזה הוא עסק התורה כמאמר רז״ל: אם פגע בך מנוול זה, משכהו לבית המדרש (קדושין ל:). ולהבין למה קורא כאן בשם מנוול דוקא. הענין הוא כי כל התענוגים הם תענוגים שבורים ואינם שלימים שהם רק לפי שעה ואחר כך בטל, נמצא הוא שבור ואינו שלם וסופם הוא דבר מאוס, כמו אכילה נעשה אחר כך דבר מאוס, וכן שאר כל התאוות. וזהו אם פגע בך מנוול זה שמסיתך לדברים המאוסים, משכהו לבית המדרש. כי התורה היא תבלין ליצר הרע, כמאמר "בראתי יצר הרע בראתי תורה תבלין" (שם).

וזהו נקרא תשובה מאהבה, שמשיב עצמו מהתאוות עצמם לאהוב ה׳ יתברך. וזדונות נעשים לו כזכיות (יומא פו:), שמכל עבירה נעשית מצות אהבה, שלוקח מהם הנמשל לאהוב ה׳ יתברך, ולכן נקרא התורה תבלין. כמו תבלין שממתקים אותו התבשיל עצמו, כך על ידי התורה מהזדונות עצמן נעשים זכיות, והבן.

- ס -

נקראים כן. והנה שכל האנושי מחייב שיותר יכול האדם להתקרב ולבקש בקשתו משרי מעלה שהם קרובים במעלה אלינו יותר מה' שהוא גבוה מאוד, כמו שנאמר "כי גבוה מעל גבוה שומר" (קהלת ה:ז). וזה היה הטעות של דור הפלגה.

אבל האמת אינו כן, כי ה' הוא ממלא כל עלמין וסובב [כל עלמין], ואיהו בתוך כל עלמין. ואם כן הוא יתברך קרוב אלינו יותר מהשרים שהם רק במקום אחד ותו לא. וזה שנאמר **כי מי גוי גדול אשר לו אלהים קרובים**, פירוש שרי מעלה שקרובים לתחתונים. **כה' אלהינו** שהוא גבוה מאוד מהתחתונים ואף על פי כן הוא קרוב אלינו יותר.

מאור עינים א'

(*מפרשת יתרו*)

...וההר בוער באש עד לב השמים... (דברים ד:יא).

הנה ענין השני לוחות שהוריד משה היה שהוריד לישראל לב, שיהיה להם לב לאביהם שבשמים, שלב נקרא לוח, כמו שנאמר "כתבם על לוח לבך" (משלי ג:ג). ואמרו רז"ל (זהר ח"ב קז:): שני חללים יש בלב - של ימין משכן יצר טוב, ושל שמאל משכן ליצר הרע ,והן הן השני לוחות.

וזהו **וההר בוער באש**, כי "הלא כה דברי כאש" (ירמיה כג:כט), שהשיגו ישראל האור והפנימיות של התורה **עד לב השמים**, עד שהיה להם לב לאביהם שבשמים. כי ה' יתברך נקרא שמים כמו שנאמר "ואתה תשמע השמים" (מלכים א ח:לד).

והנה אחר שעשו את העגל ניטל מהם הלב, ואז התחילה הנהגה על ידי תשובה שצריכה לב נשבר, כמאמר "לב נשבר ונדכה [אלהים לא תבזה]" (תהלים נא:יט). כי אם היה להם לב נלבב לה' יתברך לא היו חוטאים, ולא היו צריכים לתשובה ולשבור הלב. וזהו בי"ז בתמוז, דהיינו ביום שירד מן ההר כשעשו את העגל, נשתברו הלוחות - דהיינו שהוצרכה לתשובה שצריכה לב נשבר כנזכר לעיל.

פרשת ואתחנן

קדושת לוי

ראה למדתי אתכם חוקים ומשפטים כאשר צוני ה' אלהי לעשות כן בקרב הארץ אשר אתם באים שמה לרשתה (דברים ד:ה).

יבואר על פי מה שבארנו "ויעשו בני ישראל כאשר צוה ה' את משה" (שמות יב:כח). הכלל, ה' יתברך אמר למשה המצוות לומר לישראל, ובאמת אינו דומה שומע מפי הרב [לשומע מפי התלמיד] (כתובות קיא.). ולא קבלו באותו שכל הגדול שאמר ה' למשה. רק כאשר עשו מצוות ה' אז מחמת עשיות המצוות השיגו זה השכל... וזהו "ויעשו בני ישראל כאשר צוה ה' את משה," באותו השכל אשר צוה ה' את משה...

משה אמר להם באותו שכל שקיבל המצוה ההיא מפי ה'. וזהו שאמר **ראה למדתי אתכם חוקים ומשפטים כאשר צוני ה' אלהי**, כלומר בזה השכל אני אומר לך המצוה ההיא. ושמא תאמר מחמת שעשה משה המצוות לכך השיג, וזהו שאמר **לעשות כן בקרב הארץ**. משה לא בא לארץ ולא עשה המצוות, בוודאי הוא שהשיג מעצמו השכל איך שאמר לו ה' המצוות בלא שום עשיות אותן המצוות.

תורת המגיד

(*מכתב יד מרבי חיים חייקא מאמדור*)

כי מי גוי גדול אשר לו אלהים קרובים אליו כה' אלהינו בכל קראנו אליו (דברים ד:ז).

... הנה יש לדקדק שינוי לשון בפסוק, שמתחילה אמר **אשר לו אלהים קרובים אליו**, ואחר כך הזכיר שם המיוחד **כה' אלהינו**. אך הענין הוא כי אלהים הוא שם משותף, דאפילו דיין נקרא אלהים, וכן כל שרי מעלה

- נ"ח -

מבשר צדק

אוכל תשברו מאתם בכסף ואכלתם... (דברים ב:ו).

שמעתי בשם הרב המגיד איש אלהים מורנו דוב בער זלה"ה על פסוק זה, על דרך דאיתא בשולחן ערוך (אורח חיים ס׳ תקעא, מגן אברהם): כשאדם רואה שתאוותו מתגברת עליו באכילתו, אזי יפסיק מלאכול ומשבר התאוה, עד כאן לשונו. וזהו **אוכל תשברו מאתם בכסף**, כסף הוא לשון "חמדה," על דרך "נכסוף נכספתי" (לפי בראשית לא:ל) והיינו כשאוכל בחמדה **תשברו**, היינו על דרך הנזכר בשולחן ערוך שיפסיק מלאכול וישבר התאוה - עד כאן דבריו הקדושים.

ולי נראה לפרש בדרך זה, דהנה ידוע ד"אוכל" בגימטריא שני שמות - "אל" הוי"ה [57]. וכשהאדם בעת אכילתו שׂם אל לבו איך שאוכל מאכל אשר שריא ביה קדושה גדולה כל כך שאוכל גימטריא שני שמות הקדושים. ונמצא האוכל בעצמו משבר לו תאוותו וחמדתו, ואוכל ביראה ובושה גדולה ובקדושה גדולה, וכוונתו להעלות הניצוצות הקדושות ששריא במאכל.

וזהו בחינת הקרבת קרבן כנודע, וזאת מצוה לאכול כמו שמצוה עליו ללמוד, כיון שגם זה נקרא אצלו עבודת הבורא ב"ה. ונמצא כשאדם זוכר גודל קדושת האוכל ממילא נפסק מאתו החמדה, ואז הוא בחינת מקריב קרבנות ומצוה לו לאכול.

וזהו **אוכל תשברו מאתם בכסף**, היינו כשהאוכל בעצמו משבר לו את תאוותו... ואז **ואכלתם**, היינו שמצוה עליכם לאכול. וזהו **ואכלתם** דייקא, כי הוא כמקריב קרבנות באכילתו כנזכר לעיל, ומעלה ניצוצות הקדושה ששריא ביה.

תורי זהב

רב לכם סוב את ההר הזה פנו לכם צפונה (דברים ב:ג).

נראה לי בדרך רמז דנודע דלצדיקים היצר הרע נדמה להר (סוכה נב.). ושמעתי אומרים בשם החסיד המובהק המופלא מורנו הרב רבי נחמן קאסיוור "קדשי קדשים שחיטתן בצפון" (מ' זבחים ה:א), דיצר הרע מסית לאדם לעבירות חמורות. וכשהאדם צדיק וכובש אותו כמה וכמה פעמים, אז מתחיל להסיתו למצוות שהן באמת עבירות גדולות, כגון שמצוה למוסרו לעכו"ם או לביישו והדומה לו. או שמטיל בו פניה דקה שאי אפשר להרגיש בה עד שיחקור אחריה בחקירות גדולות, ואז ירגישה. ועל זה צריך הצדיק שלא להעלים השגחה זו ממנו אף רגע אחד, כמאמר החסיד: אתה ישן והוא ער לך; אתה מתעלם והוא משגיח עלך להטרידך פתאום משני עולמות (חובות הלבבות שער יחוד המעשה פ' ה).

וזה אמר "קדשי קדשים" שהם הצדיקים גדולים "שחיטתן" של היצר הרע השוחטן "בצפון", היינו בדברים הצפונים כנזכר לעיל, שיודע שלא יציית אותו בעבירה נגלית. מה שאין כן "קדשים קלים," שהם המוני עם שהם קלי הדעת, "שחיטתן בכל מקום" (מ' זבחים ה:ז), בכל עבירה הנגלית גם כן יכול לשוחטן. עד כאן שמעתי, ודברי פי חכם חן.

ובזה אפשר לפרש **רב לכם סוב את ההר**, שאתם לוחמים תמיד ומרחיקים את עצמיכם ומסבבים אותו, על דרך [שאומרים לנזיר] "סחור סחור לכרמא לא תקרב" (נזיר נח:), מעבירות גדולות שהוא הר. **פנו לכם צפונה** להשגיח על דברים צפונים, על עבירות ופניות שהם דקים וצפונים, רוצה לומר שאין משגיחים רק לסבב ולהרחיק מעבירות גדולות... שתגיע עת שתעבדו לה' יתברך באמת ותמים שלא ימצא בכם גם הצפונים.

נועם אלימלך

ותקרבון אלי כולכם ותאמרו נשלחה אנשים לפנינו ויחפרו לנו את הארץ... ואומר אליכם לא תערצון ולא תיראון מהם: ה' אלהיכם ההולך לפניכם הוא ילחם לכם ככל אשר עשה אתכם במצרים לעיניכם... ובדבר הזה אינכם מאמינים בה' אלהיכם: ההולך לפניכם בדרך לתור לכם מקום לחנתכם (דברים א:כב,כט-ל,לב-ג).

נראה לבאר הטעם שילוח מרגלים, ובפרט על אשר הוטב בעיני משה אדון הנביאים. לפי שכוונתו היתה לטובה - לפי שהיו צריכין לפנות להם הדרך לפניהם ולבער הקליפות אשר היו בארץ כנען, למען היות להם בנקל להלחם באויביהם ולהרוג אותם. כי יחשבו לפגרים מתים באין כח וחיות עוד להם מהקליפות.

ולזה רצו לבחור להם המובחר והחשוב שבהם, כולם אנשים צדיקים שיהיה להם כח לבער הקליפות מגודל קדושתם. ולזה שלחו איש אחד מכל שבט, המעולה שבהם. ובאותה השעה כשרים היו, כפירוש רש"י ז"ל. אבל אחר כך כשקלקלו הוכיחם משה רבינו ע"ה באמור להם באמת כוונתכם היתה לטוב, אבל היה לכם להאמין בה' אלהיכם אשר עשה לכם הניסים הנפלאות הנוראים האלה "במדבר הגדול והנורא" אשר היה מקום "נחש [שרף ועקרב]" (דברים ח:טו), הם הקליפות, והוא הלך לפניכם ובער אותם, כן יעשה בוודאי לכל הממלכות אשר תעברו שם לילך לפניכם. ו"**לתור לכם** מנוחה" (במדבר י:לג, דברים א:לג) כדי שיהא קל לכם להנקם מאויביכם ולשרש אחריהם לבלתי השאיר להם כל חי.

וזהו שאמר **ותקרבון אלי [כולכם ותאמרו] נשלחה אנשים לפנינו**, הוא הפירוש כנזכר לעיל שיהא להם לעזר לפנות להם הדרך מכל מכשול, כיון שכל הקליפות חונים שם עדיין. **ואומר אליכם לא תערצון [ולא תיראון]... ובדבר הזה אינכם מאמינים בה' אלהיכם ההולך לפניכם לתור לכם** מנוחה, ומוטב היה לכם להאמין בו יתברך, כי הוא יפנה הדרך לפניכם והוא ינחיל לכם את הארץ, וקל להבין.

- נ"ה -

של התורה ובין לומדיה. כי על כן נקרא מ"ט פנים טמא ומ"ט פנים טהור, כי על ידי הבאורים ההם מתגלין פני התורה שהיו מכוסין במכסה הקליפות המבדיל, כן ראה הבורא ב"ה בחכמתו הבלתי מושגת שלא היה אפשר לסלקן ולהכריתן כי אם על ידי נסיעת ישראל דרך אותם המדבריות דווקא באותו הזמן שהיתה תחילת התגלות התורה...

גם היום הוא כן ענין הקושיות הוא על ידי שהקליפות מכסות בזה המקום ונעשה אצלו קושיא, ואחר שמביא את עצמו למידת בינה ומתחיל לצער עצמו על זה, ורואה להבין בבינה, על ידי זה מסלק ומכרית הקליפות ההן ונתגלה אליו האמת, שבאמת המכסה ההוא הוא דינים שלו שגורם להיות מכסה ומבדיל בינו ובין האמת. וכשבא להתבונן ואוחז את עצמו במידת בינה, על ידי זה מביא את הדינים האלו וממתיקן בשרשן כנודע...

ואחר שהן הכריתו וסלקו הקליפה הכללית צריך כל אחד מלומדי התורה לסלק הדינים הבאים מצידו שלא יבדילו בינו ובין הפנים של התורה וכנזכר לעיל.

ונודע שארץ מואב הוא חנייה אחרונה אחר כל נסיעתן בהמדבריות, וכמבואר בכתוב "ויחנו בערבות מואב מעבר לירדן" (במדבר כב:א), שהוא אצל גבול ארץ ישראל...

כי עד עכשיו לא היתה התגלות התורה כי אם למשה לבדו מחמת גודל מעלתו, וכהיום יכלו להשיג גם כן כל ישראל כי כעת כבר נבדל המסך המבדיל כאמור...

- נ"ד -

פרשת דברים

מאור עינים

בעבר הירדן בארץ מואב הואיל משה באר את התורה הזאת לאמר (דברים א:ה).

איתא במדרש (רבינו בחיי על התורה): התורה נדרשת במ"ט פנים טהור ובמ"ט פנים טמא, וזהו מואב בגמטריא מ"ט הוא, והיינו דכתיב "אם תבקשנה ככסף וכ**מט**מונים [תחפשנה]" (משלי ב:ד).

ולהבין מה שייכות ארץ מואב למ"ט [49] פנים שהתורה נדרשת בהן להכניסן בגמטריא של תיבת מואב. לבאר זה הוא על פי מה שנודע ענין שלא ניתנה התורה לישראל כי אם אחר שבעה שבועות ואחר הליכתן דרך ים סוף ודרך כמה מסעות במדבר, כמו שמפורש בכתוב כמה מסעות שנסעו ישראל קודם בואם להר סיני. כל זה היה כדי להכרית הקליפות והחיצוניות שהיו מסך מבדיל על התורה שבכתב שהיו ישראל משוקעים בטומאות וקליפות כנודע, ועל ידי נסיעתן באותן המדבריות שקודם בואם להר סיני ועל ידי ראיית הנסים והנפלאות בקריעת ים סוף ושאר נסים שראו שם ונתקע אמונתו יתברך בלבן, היתה יכולת בידם על ידי נסיעתן במדבריות ההם, שהוא מקום חרוב מקום דירת הקליפות היה כח בידם להכריתן ולסלקן בכדי שלא יעכבו להיות מסך מבדיל בין התורה שבכתב ובין ישראל.

והנה התורה ניתנה למשה בסיני בכללותיה ובפרטותיה שבכתב ושבעל פה, אפילו מה שתלמיד ותיק עתיד לחדש (ויקרא רבה כב:א). אך עדיין לא היתה התגלות התורה שבעל פה, שהיא ביאור התורה שבכתב, לכל ישראל ולהיות אפשר לבאר להם מצפוניה וביאורה כי אם אחר שיסולק מסך התכסות הקליפות שמכסה על התורה שבעל פה...

ישראל לא היה באפשרי להן לבאר ולגלות התורה כי אם אחר נסיעתן באותן המדבריות מקום הקליפות, ועל ידי נסיעתן ועבודתן לה' יתברך באלה המסעות הכריתו אותן הקליפות והמכסים שמפסיקים בין הפנים

(ע' צב-צה) האזינו

ע' צב **מאור עינים** - האזינו השמים ואדברה ותשמע הארץ אמרי פי (דברים לב:א).

צד **דברת שלמה** - כי חלק ה' עמו... (דברים לב:ט).

צה **מגיד דבריו ליעקב** - כנשר יעיר קנו על גוזליו ירחף... (דברים לב:יא).

צה **ליקוטי מהרי"ן** - כנשר יעיר קנו על גוזליו ירחף... (דברים לב:יא).

(ע' צו-צח) וזאת הברכה

צו **תפארת עוזיאל א'** - וזאת הברכה אשר ברך משה איש האלהים את בני ישראל לפני מותו (דברים לג:א).

צז **תפארת עוזיאל ב'**

צז **מבשר צדק** - וימת שם משה עבד ה'... (דברים לד:ה).

צח **ישמח לב** - ויקבור אותו בגיא בארץ מואב מול בית פעור ולא ידע איש את קבורתו עד היום הזה (דברים לד:ו).

ע' עה **קדושת לוי** - כי יקרא קן צפור לפניך בדרך בכל עץ או על הארץ אפרוחים או ביצים... שלח תשלח את האם ואת הבנים תקח לך למען ייטב לך והארכת ימים (דברים כב:ו-ז).

עט **אור תורה** - כי תבנה בית חדש ועשית מעקה לגגך ולא תשים דמים בביתך כי יפול הנופל ממנו (דברים כב:ח).

פ **נועם אלימלך** - כי יהיה בך איש אשר לא יהיה טהור מקרה לילה ויצא אל מחוץ למחנה לא יבא אל תוך המחנה: והיה לפנות ערב ירחץ במים וכבא השמש יבא אל תוך המחנה (דברים כג:יא-יב).

כי תבוא (ע' פב-פד)

פב **תפארת עוזיאל** - ארור האיש אשר לא יקים את דברי התורה הזאת... (דברים כז:כו).

פג **קדושת לוי** - ... בדרך אחד יצאו אליך ובשבעה דרכים ינוסו לפניך (דברים כח:ז).

פג **שארית ישראל** - את ה' האמרת היום להיות לך לאלהים... וה' האמירך היום להיות לו לעם סגולה (דברים כו:יז-יח).

נצבים (ע' פה-פח)

פה **שמן הטוב** - אתם נצבים היום כולכם לפני ה' אלהיכם (דברים כט:ט).

פז **מבשר צדק א'** - ושב ה' אלהיך את שבותך ורחמך ושב וקבצך מכל העמים אשר הפיצך ה' אלהיך שמה (דברים ל:ג).

פז **מאמרי אדמו"ר הזקן** - אם יהיה נדחך בקצה השמים משם יקבצך ה' אלהיך ומשם יקחך (דברים ל:ד).

פח **מבשר צדק ב'** - כי המצוה הזאת אשר אנכי מצוך היום לא נפלאת היא ממך ולא רחוקה היא (דברים ל:יא).

וילך (ע' פט-צא)

פט **קדושת לוי** - וילך משה וידבר את הדברים האלה אל כל ישראל (דברים לא:א).

פט **מאור עינים** - ... לא אוכל עוד לצאת ולבוא... (דברים לא:ב).

צ **דברת שלמה** - וילך משה וידבר את הדברים האלה אל כל ישראל: ויאמר אליהם בן מאה ועשרים שנה אנכי היום לא אוכל עוד לצאת ולבוא... (דברים לא:א-ב).

ראה (ע' סה-ע)

ע' סה **צמח ה' לצבי א'** - ראה אנכי נותן לפניכם היום... את הברכה אשר תשמעו אל מצוות ה' אלהיכם אשר אנכי מצוה אתכם היום (דברים יא:כו-כז).

סו **אורח לחיים א'** - ראה אנכי נותן לפניכם היום ברכה וקללה: את הברכה אשר תשמעו אל מצוות ה' אלהיכם... והקללה אם לא תשמעו... וסרתם מן הדרך... (דברים יא:כו-כח).

סז **מאור עינים** - ראה אנכי נותן לפניכם היום ברכה וקללה: את הברכה אשר תשמעו אל מצוות ה' אלהיכם... והקללה אם לא תשמעו... וסרתם מן הדרך... (דברים יא:כו-כח).

סח **צמח ה' לצבי ב'** - כי יהיה בך אביון מאחד אחיך באחד שעריך בארצך אשר ה' אלהיך נותן לך לא תאמץ את לבבך ולא תקפוץ את ידך מאחיך האביון: כי פתוח תפתח את ידך לו... (דברים טו:ז-ח).

סט **אורח לחיים ב'** - השמר לך פן יהיה דבר עם לבבך בליעל לאמר קרבה שנת השבע שנת השמיטה ורעה עינך באחיך האביון... נתון תתן לו ולא ירע לבבך בתתך לו... (דברים טו:ט-י).

שופטים (ע' עא-עה)

עא **מבשר צדק** - וכי יבא הלוי מאחד שעריך מכל ישראל אשר הוא גר שם ובא בכל אות נפשו אל המקום אשר יבחר ה': ושרת בשם ה' אלהיו ככל אחיו הלוים העומדים שם לפני ה' (דברים יח:ו-ז).

עב **תורת המגיד** - תמים תהיה עם ה' אלהיך (דברים יח:יג).

עג **אורח לחיים** - תמים תהיה עם ה' אלהיך (דברים יח:יג).

עד **אור המאיר** - והיה כקרבכם אל המלחמה ונגש הכהן ודבר אל העם: ואמר אליהם שמע ישראל אתם קרבים היום למלחמה על אויביכם אל ירך לבבכם אל תיראו ואל תחפזו ואל תערצו מפניהם (דברים כ:ב-ג).

כי תצא (ע' עו-פא)

עו **מאמרי אדמו"ר הזקן** - כי תצא למלחמה על אויביך ונתנו ה' אלהיך בידך ושבית שביו (דברים כא:י).

עז **אורח לחיים** - לא יהיה כלי גבר על אשה ולא ילבש גבר שמלת אשה כי תועבת ה' אלהיך כל עושה אלה (דברים כב:ה).

דברים (ע' נג-נז)

ע' נג **מאור עינים** - בעבר הירדן בארץ מואב הואיל משה באר את התורה הזאת לאמר (דברים א:ה).

נה **נועם אלימלך** - ותקרבון אלי כולכם ותאמרו נשלחה אנשים לפנינו ויחפרו לנו את הארץ... ובדבר הזה אינכם מאמינים בה' אלהיכם: ההולך לפניכם בדרך... (דברים א:כב,כט-ל,לב-ג).

נו **תורי זהב** - רב לכם סוב את ההר הזה פנו לכם צפונה (דברים ב:ג).

נז **מבשר צדק** - אוכל תשברו מאתם בכסף ואכלתם... (דברים ב:ו).

ואתחנן (ע' נח-ס)

נח **קדושת לוי** - ראה למדתי אתכם חוקים ומשפטים כאשר צוני ה' אלהי לעשות כן בקרב הארץ אשר אתם באים שמה לרשתה (דברים ד:ה).

נח **תורת המגיד** - כי מי גוי גדול אשר לו אלהים קרובים אליו כה' אלהינו בכל קראנו אליו (דברים ד:ז).

נט **מאור עינים א'** - ...וההר בוער באש עד לב השמים... (דברים ד:יא).

ס **מאור עינים ב'** - ואהבת את ה' אלהיך בכל לבבך ובכל נפשך ובכל מאדך (דברים ו:ה).

עקב (ע' סא-סד)

סא **צמח ה' לצבי א'** - ... כי לא על הלחם לבדו יחיה האדם כי על כל מוצא פי ה' יחיה האדם (דברים ח:ג).

סא **צמח ה' לצבי ב'** - ואכלת ושבעת וברכת את ה' אלהיך... (דברים ח:י).

סב **אור האמת** - ... מה ה' אלהיך שואל מעמך כי אם ליראה את ה' אלהיך... (דברים י:יב).

סג **נועם אלימלך** - ועתה ישראל מה ה' אלהיך שואל מעמך כי אם ליראה את ה' אלהיך ללכת בכל דרכיו... לשמור את מצוות ה' ואת חוקתיו אשר אנכי מצוך היום לטוב לך (דברים י:יב-יג).

סד **אור תורה** - ... לאהבה את ה' אלהיכם ללכת בכל דרכיו ולדבקה בו (דברים יא:כב).

ספר
דברים

אחרונה של הוי"ה, ולחברה במוצאה ליה"ו שבשם כידוע. וזה **מסעיהם למוצאיהם**, וכן כל ההעלאות אכילה ושתיה וכיוצא, כולם נקראו **מסעיהם למוצאיהם**.

אור תורה

ויסעו ממרה ויבואו אלימה... (במדבר לג:ט).

..."[ויבואו מרתה] ולא יכלו לשתות מים ממרה כי מרים הם" (שמות טו:כג). מים המרים נקרא השכל שבמדריגות התחתונות. מים התחתונים בוכים "אנא בעי למיהוי קדם מלכא" [אני רוצה להיות לפני המלך] (תקוני זהר ת' ה יט:). וזהו כמו במי סוטה שנלקח מקרקע המשכן שנתמשכן בשבירה (תנחומא פקודי ב), ואם [האדם] לא טמא הוא, נהפכה המחשבה זרה אצלו לזרע, שמכחה נתחזק לעבודתו יתברך, כידוע שבכל דברים רעים יש דבר טוב. אבל אם הוא טמא ח"ו אזי רע לו.

וזהו "ויבואו מרתה," שנפלו לדבר רע, "ולא יכלו לשתות," שהאהבה שבגבורה לא נתגלה להם. "כי מרים הם," פירוש העם לא היו טובים. שאם היו טובים, היה אדרבא משם בא להם טובה יתירה, שבכל דין יש בתוכו חסד, ואם היו שוברין הדין היו באים להטוב.

וזהו **ויסעו ממרה ויבואו אלימה**, כי אלימה הוא אותיות אלהים, רק הצירוף הוא כך אלי מה, נקרא דבר שאינו מושג, והחסד שבדין אינו מושג...

תם ונשלם ספר במדבר

המסעות שנסעו בני ישראל במדבר הגדול והנורא, מאת ה׳ היתה זאת לברר נצוצות הקדושים שנפלו שם בקליפות, ולהוציא בלעו מפיו [של הסטרא אחרא]. והוא הטעם שהיו ישראל חונים במקום אחד זמן רב ובמקום אחר זמן מועט, שהוא כפי מה שהיה צריך לברר הנצוצות שבמקום ההוא.

והנה במ״ב מסעות שנסעו בני ישראל כתיב ״ויחנו בחרדה״ (במדבר לג:כד), ״ויחנו במתקה״ (במדבר לג:כח), ״ויחנו בהר שפר״ (במדבר לג:כג), כלומר כשהיו ישראל חונים באיזה מקום שהיו שם יראות רעות רחמנא ליצלן, אזי היו עובדים לה׳ יתברך ביראת הרוממות, לירא מפני פחדו והדר גאונו. וזו ״ויחנו בחרדה,״ מידת היראה, שהיו צריכין לעבוד הבורא במקום ההוא במידת היראה. וכשהיו חונים באיזה מקום שהיו שם אהבות רעות שנפלו שם מהשבירה כידוע, היו צריכין לעבוד ה׳ יתברך במידת האהבה אמיתית. וזו ״ויחנו במתקה״ מידת אהבה. וכן ״ויחנו בהר שפר״ הוא מידת התפארות. ובזה היו מעלים כל הניצוצות שנפלו שם והעלו אותם לשרשן למקום הקדושה, וזו היתה עיקר נסיעתם במדבר.

צמח ה׳ לצבי

ויכתב משה את מוצאיהם למסעיהם על פי ה׳ ואלה מסעיהם למוצאיהם (במדבר לג:ב).

מה שהקשו על לשון ההיפוך בפסוק זה, אמרתי על דרך שכתבתי בדרוש לפסח ענין יציאת מצרים עליונה, כי בה היו כל ההפכים מעורבים אלו באלו, ומשם יצאו ונקבעו כל אחד ואחד במקומו.

וזהו **ויכתב משה את מוצאיהם**, רוצה לומר יציאת הנשמות ממצרים העליונה. **למסעיהם**, כלומר לפי השתלשלותם מעולם לעולם, ונקבעו כל אחד ואחד במקומו כנ״ל. ובענין זה צריך האדם להעלות את נשמתו למקום שחוצבה משם באור חוזר. וזהו שנאמר **ואלה מסעיהם**, רוצה לומר ליסע למעלה, **למוצאיהם**, למקום המוצא שיצאה הנשמה משם.

וכידוע שהדיבור מתפשט בכל ענייני עולם הזה, וצריך האדם להעלות הדיבורים בכ״ב אתוון, וכ״ב אתוון לה׳ [חמש] מוצאות הפה, שהיא ה׳

- נ״א -

ואלה מסעיהם למוצאיהם, פירוש מסעות של האבות הם סימן לבנים. **ואלה מסעיהם** של כל אדם אפילו בדורות האחרונים הוא **למוצאיהם**, על ידי מוצאות והרפתקאות ויסורין, ולפום צערא אגרא (מ' אבות ה:כב). ולפי היסורין שמקבל אדם על עצמו בשביל לבוא לעבודת ה' יתברך בשלימות כך הוא נוסע לדביקות למנוחה מתמדת.

דברי אמת

ויכתב משה את מוצאיהם למסעיהם על פי ה' ואלה מסעיהם למוצאיהם (במדבר לג:ב).

איתא בחובות הלבבות שיש שתי מדריגות טובות: מי שעל ידי התורה משיג הדביקות הגדולה בו יתברך, כמו הנביאים, והדביקות נקראת חובת הלבבות. ויש מדריגה יותר גבוהה מזה שעיקר שלו הוא דביקות בו יתברך על ידי זה משיג התורה כמו אברהם אבינו ע"ה, שהשיג כל התורה עד שלא ניתנה, כי אם בגלות מצרים נתגשמו אבותינו הוצרכנו לקבל אל [את] התורה להשיג הדביקות בו יתברך.

זה **ויכתב משה את מוצאיהם למסעיהם**, פירוש הכתיבות התורה [תורה שבכתב] הוא מוצא לדביקות להיות הולכים ונוסעים מחיל לחיל כנ"ל. **ועל פי ה'**, פירוש על ידי התורה שבעל פה, שהיא ביאור התורה שבכתב, וכמו שפירשו רז"ל "על פי הדברים האלה כרתי אתך ברית" (שמות לד:כז) קאי על תורה שבעל פה (גיטין ס:). **ואלה** מוסיף על ענין ראשון **מסעיהם למוצאיהם**, שיש להם דביקות עצמם שעל ידי הדביקות משיגים התורה.

קדושת לוי

ויכתב משה את מוצאיהם למסעיהם על פי ה' ואלה מסעיהם למוצאיהם (במדבר לג:ב).

צריך לדקדק שינוי הלשון מתחילה כתיב **מוצאיהם** ואחר כך **למסעיהם**, ואחר כך הקדים **מסעיהם למוצאיהם**. ונראה כי מודעת זאת שכל

פרשת מסעי

אור הגנוז לצדיקים

אלה מסעי בני ישראל אשר יצאו מארץ מצרים לצבאותם ביד משה ואהרן: ויכתב משה את מוצאיהם למסעיהם על פי ה' ואלה מסעיהם למוצאיהם (במדבר לג:א-ב).

... מאי נפקא מינה בסיפורים אלו בתורה להיות צריך לדורות עולם להיות מורה דרך לעבודת ה' בשמה תורה? דמאי דהוה הוה.

בשם הבעש"ט ז"ל: כשאדם הולך בדרך ואינו יכול להתפלל וללמוד כדרכו וצריך לעבדו יתברך באופנים אחרים, אל יצער עצמו בזה. כי ה' יתברך צריך שיעבדוהו בכל האופנים, פעמים באופן זה [ופעמים באופן אחר]. לכן הזדמן לפניו לילך בדרך, בכדי לעבוד אותו יתברך באופן זה.

וזהו שנאמר **אלה מסעי בני ישראל**, פירוש גם המסעות של ישראל היו לעבודת ה' יתברך - על כן נכתבו בתורה. **אשר יצאו מארץ מצרים**, ששם לא היו נגד ארץ ישראל עליונה ששם שרשי הנשמות שנקרא **צבאותם**, על כן **יצאו לצבאותם. ביד משה ואהרן**, שהיו כלולים מכל הנשמות של ישראל.

וכל המסעות היו הדרגות ובחינות עליונות כדי לזכות לבוא לארץ ישראל. אלמלא לא חטאו בעגל ובמרגלים לא היו צריכין כל כך מסעות והדרגות, אלא בהדרגות מועטות היו זוכין לבוא לארץ ישראל. אבל מפני החטא הוצרכו לכל כך מסעות שהם מדריגה אחר מדריגה לבוא לארץ ישראל.

וכן בכל אדם על ידי שכל מסעותיו הם לשם שמים, או לפי מעשיו הטובים יש לך אדם שזוכה על ידי מסעות מועטות שהם לשם שמים זוכה לבוא למנוחה מתמדת בין [ב]עולם הזה בין [ל]עולם הבא, "ומעבירין ממנו עול מלכות ועול דרך ארץ" (מ' אבות ג:ה) ובא למנוחה מתמדת.

- מ"ט -

הטוב, ולהרגיל בנו במעשים טובים ולשמור את פיו מדברים רעים, ומכל שכן שלא ירגילו אותו בידים בדברים רעים...

וביותר להזהיר אותו על השתיקה מלשון הרע ורכילות ומניבול פה. וזה שכתוב **ושמע אביה**, הוא אביו של הילד, היינו שמיעה בלב, שיחשוב אביו וישים על לבו את נדרה ואסרה של הנשמה שכבר נשבעה על נפשה בהיותה נפש בלא גוף בגן עדן. **והחריש לה אביה**, היינו שירגיל אותו בשתיקה שהוא סייג לחכמה, וממילא יהיה **וקמו כל נדריה** וכ׳ **על נפשה יקום**, יהיה קיום לנשמה במידות טובות.

שעובד ה' בכח ההוא כאמור ומדבר דיבורים... יש עלייה להאותיות הנפולין שהן ניצוצות הקדושים...

וזהו **איש כי ידור נדר לה'**... **לאסור איסר על נפשו**, שאוסר על ידי זה על נפשו לבלי קרבה אל הקדושה כנ"ל, דהיינו הנפש המלובשת בדבר ההוא ששייך לחלק נפשו שהיה יכול לקשרו ולקרבו למעלה, ועתה אסרו מבלי שיקורב. לכך אמרה תורה **לא יחל דברו**, שהוא מוצא פי ה' הניצוץ המלובש שם לא ישאירנו חולין. אך **ככל היוצא מפיו** של הבורא יתברך, שהוא דבר גבוה וככל כוונת הבורא ב"ה מהניצוץ הזה שהלבישו שם במאכל ובמשקה ההיא - יעשה ויתקן!

גנזי יוסף

ואשה כי תדור נדר לה' ואסרה איסר בבית אביה בנעוריה: ושמע אביה... והחריש לה אביה וקמו כל נדריה וכל איסר אשר אסרה על נפשה יקום (במדבר ל:ד-ה).

הוא רמז על הנשמה, שהיא נקראת בתו של אברהם אבינו ע"ה, שקודם צאתה לאויר העולם מלמדין אותה כל התורה כולה, ואינה יוצאת משם עד שמשביעין אותה. מהו השבועה? תהי צדיק ואל תהי רשע, ואפילו כל העולם אומרים שהוא צדיק תהיה בעיניך כרשע (נדרים ל:).

וזהו **ואשה כי תדור נדר [לה'] ואסרה איסר בבית אביה**, שהנשמה קודם ביאתה לעולם מראין לה בגן עדן שורות צדיקים וכבודם ומקבלת עליה מידות טובות של הצדיקים. זהו **ואסרה איסר בבית אביה**, שעדיין היא בגן עדן שהוא בית אביה, שהקדוש ברוך הוא בא בכל לילה בחצות ומשתעשע שם עם הצדיקים. וזהו **בנעוריה**, שהוא ימי נעורים של הנשמה שאז שרויה בטובה יותר מכל ימיה.

ושמע אביה. הענין הכתוב בזהר, ורזא דמלה אוליפנא דמשמע דאב ואם אית לנשמתא כמה דאית אב ואם לגופא [וסוד הענין למדנו פירושו שיש אב ואם לנשמה כמו שיש לגוף] (זהר ח"ב יב.). והעיקר שיצר הרע "לפתח חטאת רובץ" (בראשית ד:ז) שבא מיד כשנולד, ויצר טוב בא בשנת י"ג. אם כן, עד י"ג שנים על האב מוטל החיוב להיות במקום יצר

- מ"ז -

שהן מדברים שנפלו בשבירה בזה העולם השפל כנודע מחטא אדם הראשון, וגם בדורות שאחריו שכמה וכמה ניצוצי נשמות הנפולין מלובשין בדברים מזה העולם במיני מאכל ומשתה וכיוצא בהן ממיני העולם, שאין לך דבר מזה העולם שאין בו ניצוץ הקדוש שנאצל מדיבורו של הקדוש ברוך הוא המחיה אותו הדבר, והוא הטעם שבדבר ההוא המתוק לחיך, כמו שנאמר "טעמו וראו כי טוב ה'" (תהלים לד:ט) רוצה לומר מה שאתם טועמין ורואין כי טוב הוא ה', שהוא ניצוץ הקדוש שבדבר ההוא המלובש בו כמו שנראה לעין.

כי לאחר שאכל האדם המאכל ונשאר החיות בקרבו שהפסולת נדחה לחוץ מבלי חיות, והוא דבר נפסד וגרוע כי עיקר המזון שהאדם ניזון ממנו ומוסיף לו כח הוא הניצוץ הקדוש שבמאכל ההוא, שהוא הטעם הטוב שהאדם טועם במאכל ובמשקה ההוא. ולכן בשעה שאוכל האדם המאכל נתייחד הניצוץ ההוא אל חיותו של האדם ההוא האוכלו וניתוסף בו כח.

וכשמאמין אמונה שלימה וגמורה שזהו מזון רוחני שהוא אלהותו יתברך המלובש שם, ונותן דעתו ולבו על הפנימיות ומדבק את עצמו עם כל חיותו ומוחו ועם זה הכח והחיות שניתוסף בו על ידי הניצוץ הקדוש שבא בקרבו לשורש הכל שממנו נאצלה כל החיות, אזי מביא גם כן הניצוץ הקדוש שהיה עד עכשיו בשבירה ובגלות אליו יתברך, שהוא מתענג מאוד מזה כנודע. כי זה כל עיקר עבודתנו לקרב כל הניצוצות הקדושים מן קליפות שהן בשבירה אל מקום הקדושה, שיהא עליית הקדושה מן השבירה.

ובפרט שכל עבודתו ותורתו שמדבר דיבורים, מחמת זה הכח והחיות שקיבל מטעם המאכל שהוא הניצוץ הקדוש כאמור. וכשמייחד דיבורו אל דיבור הקדוש יש עלייה גם לאותו הניצוץ שהוא גם כן דבר ה' כאמור לעיל, שהן הכל אותיות נפולין כנודע.

על כן צריך כל עובד ה' לראות על פנימיות הדבר האמור, שיהיו כל מעשיו לשם שמים באכילה ושתיה גם כן להעלות ניצוצי הקדושה מן השבירה שהוא בחינת שביה וגלות אל הקדושה העליונה, על ידי הברכות שמברך וממליך את הבורא יתברך שמו על הדבר ההוא. וגם אחר זה

פרשת מטות

נועם אלימלך

וידבר משה אל ראשי המטות לבני ישראל לאמר זה הדבר אשר צוה ה' (במדבר ל:ב).

דהנה הצדיק הרוצה להמשיך השפעות על ישראל צריך לחבר עמו שאר צדיקים, שעל ידי הדיבור המדבר עמהם הוא משפיע לכל ישראל. והם המסייעים אותו אל הטוב ההוא להסתים פי המקטרג מעליו בזכות הרבים. מה שאין כן כשהוא לבדו, צריך כח גדול ויד חזקה להשקיט המקטרג לבל ישלוט בו.

וזהו שאמר משה רבינו ע"ה "איכה אשא לבדי [טרחכם ומשאכם וריבכם]" (דברים א:יב), פירוש כשאני לבדי בלא התחברות שאר צדיקים הוא למשא עלי להמשיך לכם צורכיכם. וזהו **וידבר משה אל ראשי המטות**, פירוש שחיבר עצמו עם הצדיקים. **לבני ישראל**, כמו בשביל ישראל להמשיך להם שפע, וקל להבין.

מאור עינים

איש כי ידור נדר לה'... לאסור איסר על נפשו לא יחל דברו ככל היוצא מפיו יעשה (במדבר ל:ב-ג).

ונקדים מה שאמרו רז"ל על מה שנאמר גבי נזיר "וכיפר עליו הכהן מאשר חטא על הנפש" (במדבר ו:יא), וכי באיזה נפש חטא? אלא זה שציער עצמו מן היין (תענית יא.).

להבין הענין דנודע כי כל העולם ומלואו "בדבר ה' שמים נעשו וברוח פיו כל צבאם" (תהלים לג:ו), כי על ידי הדיבור נתהוו כל המציאות, דבר קטן וגדול. והוא המקיימם ומחיה אותם, כמו שנאמר "ואתה מחיה את כולם" (נחמיה ט:ו), ולולא החיות שבתוך הדבר היה נעדר מן המציאות. אלא

אם חטא אדם כנגדו בלילה צריך למחול קודם אור השמש כנודע מזהר (ח"א רא:), ולא לכבוש כעסו על חבירו שנה תמימה.

וזהו שנאמר **ואמרת להם זה האשה אשר תקריבו לה'**, שתעשו לו נחת רוח מזה. **כבשים בני שנה**, רוצה לומר זה הדבר אשר כבוש בלבכם שנה תמימה עד ערב יום הכפורים - לא תעשו כן! אלא **שנים ליום**, שתי פעמים ליום, **את הכבש אחד תעשה בבוקר** מה שכבוש בלבכם. **תעשו** לשון תיקון, כמו "ובן הבקר אשר עשה" (בראשית יח:ח). **ואת הכבש השני תעשה** - תתקן - **בין הערבים**, קודם השינה. עד כאן שמעתי, ודברי פי חכם חן.

ואני פרשתי על ענין זה באופן אחר: דרוב המוני עם אינם משגיחים על תפילתם שתהיה בכוונה כל השנה, רק בימים נוראים מחזקים את עצמם בכל כחם להתפלל כראוי בכוונה שלימה. ושמעתי מפי קדוש איש אלקי מורנו הרב דובער ממזריטש זצללה"ה על הא דאיתא: ישראל מפרנסים לאביהם שבשמים (זהר ח"ג ז:), דמי שהוא בחינת ישראל שהוא צדיק שעובד לה' יתברך ביראה ואהבה ובוער בו אש ההתלהבות בעבודתו לה' יתברך, זהו כביכול פרנסה של ה' יתברך. כי השעשועין ותענוג שמקבל ה' יתברך מעבודתו זה נקרא פרנסה אצלו יתברך, כמו "ויחזו את האלהים ויאכלו וישתו" (שמות כד:יא), ומתרגם "וחדו בנפשיהן כאילו אכלו ושתו." וזהו שנאמר "כי ה' אלהיך אש אוכלה הוא" (דברים ד:כד), רוצה לומר האש של התלהבות שאדם מתלהב בעבודתו לה' יתברך חשוב אצלו יתברך לאכילה. עד כאן שמעתי מפה קדוש בעצמו.

וזהו שנאמר **ואמרת אליהם את קרבני** ההתקרבות שלכם שהוא **לחמי לאשי**, שהוא פרנסה שלי לאש ההתלהבות שלכם אלי. **תשמרו להקריב לי במועדו... זה האשה**, זה האש והתלהבות בדביקות **אשר תקריבו לה'**. זה שהוא **כבשים בני שנה**, שכבוש אצליכם שנה תמימה על ימים נוראים - לא תעשו כן, אלא **שנים ליום עולם תמיד**. **את הכבש אחד תעשה בבוקר**, בתפילת שחרית, **ואת הכבש השני תעשה בין הערבים**, שהוא מנחה וערבית.

שאתה אלהי הרוחות לכל בשר ואתה מלמד זכות עליהם, כן פקוד **איש על העדה**, שמנהיג לישראל יהיה גם כן מלמד זכות על ישראל.

קדושת לוי ב׳

...אל אלהי הרוחות לכל בשר... (במדבר טז:כב).

הכלל: נפש אדם עיקר התאוה שלו לעבודת ה׳, רק הגוף הוא שיש לו תאוות הגשמיות, ובאמת הגוף והנשמה שניהם מעשה ה׳, וכאשר יש כח בנשמה מן ה׳ על עבודתו יתברך, כן היכולת ביד ה׳ שיהיה הגוף גם כן עיקר תאותו לעבודת ה׳.

ונמצא יש לנו טענה אל הקדוש ברוך הוא לסלוח לנו עוונותינו, כיון שהכח ביד הקדוש ברוך הוא שיתן הכח בהגוף לשעבד אותו לעבודתו יתברך. והנה הנפש המתאוה לעבודת ה׳ נקרא רוח כנאמר, ״רוח ה׳ דיבר בי״ (שמואל ב כג:ב), והגוף נקרא בשר. וזהו **אל אלהי הרוחות** אתה המתאוים לעבודתך, כן תהיה **לכל בשר**, זהו הגוף כנ״ל.

תורי זהב

צו את בני ישראל ואמרת אליהם את קרבני לחמי לאשי ריח ניחוחי תשמרו להקריב לי במועדו: ואמרת להם זה האשה אשר תקריבו לה׳ כבשים בני שנה תמימים שנים ליום עולה תמיד: את הכבש אחד תעשה בבקר ואת הכבש השני תעשה בין הערבים (במדבר כח:ב-ד).

שמעתי אומרים בדרך מוסר בשם הוותיק וחסיד ומופלא איש אלקי מורנו הרב יצחק הנקרא ר׳ איצק דראביטשיר זצללה״ה, דעולם נוהג שמעכבים כעסם על חבריהם עד יום ערב יום הכפורים, ואז מפייסים זה את זה. ואין זה הדרך יחלק אור, כי צריך האדם למחול לחבירו קודם השינה על כל שעשה לו חבירו דבר שאינו הגון באותו יום, ולומר ״שארי ליה מארי לכל מאן דמצער לי״ [יסלח האדון לכל מי שמצער אותי; מגילה כח.]. וכן

האיש, אם כן מה לך ליתן התורה בארץ? 'תנה הודך על השמים'" (תהלים ח:ב) דייקא, רוצה לומר שהתורה תהא נתונה בשמים, ומי מבני אדם אשר יחפוץ לקיים התורה יעלה למעלה ויעסוק בתורה וירד וילמוד לחבירו וחבירו לחבירו....

אמר הקדוש ברוך הוא למשה, "החזר להם תשובה!" [ואמר משה], "למצרים ירדתם? יצר הרע יש ביניכם?" ואם כן אין התורה שייכת לעליונים כלל, רק תחתונים...

ואפשר זה רימז הכתוב "והאיש משה עניו מאוד," ומפרש הלא הביא ראיה למלאכים "מכל אדם אשר פני האדמה" (במדבר יב:ג). רוצה לומר שאין דומים מלאכי השרת לבני אדם. ולמה לא השיב תשובה אחרת, היינו שאי אפשר לאדם אחר זולתו לעלות למעלה ולירד וממילא היה נסתר טענות המלאכים כנ"ל. אלא שלא רצה לישא על שפתיו תשובה זו כי הוא זה יורה מעלתו הגדולה על כל בני אדם, ומזה מוכח ש"האיש משה עניו מאוד."

קדושת לוי א'

יפקוד ה' אלהי הרוחות לכל בשר איש על העדה (במדבר כז:טז).

הכלל: יש ללמוד זכות על ישראל מה שאינם עושין רצון הבורא בתמידות כמלאכים, מחמת שהם טרודים בפרנסתם. וזהו שאברהם אבינו היה איש חסד והיה מלמד זכות, ולכך נתן להם להמלאכים לאכול (בראשית יח:ה-ח), להראות להם הצטרכות בשר ודם כדי שלא ילמדו חובה על ישראל.

וזה שאמר משה **אל אלהי הרוחות לכל בשר** (במדבר טז:כב), שהאדם מחמת שהוא בשר ודם הצטרכות של אדם בפרנסתו, ומחמת זה הוא לפעמים אינו עובד ה' בתמידות.

וזהו שאמר **יפקוד ה' אלהי הרוחות לכל בשר**, כלומר שופט ומנהיג שילמד תמיד זכות על ישראל, כמו שאתה לומד זכות על האדם שאינו עובד אותך בתמידות. כן ביקש משה שיעמוד מנהיג לישראל שילמד תמיד זכות על ישראל. וזהו **יפקוד ה' אלהי הרוחות לכל בשר**, כמו

- מ"ב -

דביקותו בבורא עולם יתברך שמו, כי כשהקדוש ברוך הוא רוצה שיפעול צדיק, נותן לו חשק ורצון גדול כמו שכתוב "רצון יראיו יעשה..." כדי "ואת שועתם ישמע [ויושיעם]" (תהלים קמה:יט), וכמו שאמרו חז"ל על פסוק (ברכות לא.; ויקרא רבה טז:ט): "תכין לבם תקשיב אזנך" (תהלים י:יז). מה שאין כן בנות צלפחד, שהיו להם חשק ורצון גדול לפי ערכן על ידי תביעות ירושה ודבקו את עצמן לאותיות הירושה שלהם. זה שאיתא: [יפה תבעו בנות צלפחד] שכך כתובה [פרשה לפני במרום] (ספרי פ' קלד), וזה שפירש רש"י ז"ל: ראתה עינם מה שלא ראה עינו של משה...

אור פני משה

יפקוד ה' אלהי הרוחות לכל בשר איש על העדה: אשר יצא לפניהם ואשר יבא לפניהם ואשר יוציאם ואשר יביאם ולא תהיה עדת ה' כצאן אשר אין להם רועה (במדבר כז:טז-יז).

יאמר כרבי משה אלשיך זלה"ה על מאמר חז"ל (ילקוט משלי): "מי עלה שמים וירד" (משלי ל:ד) זה משה ז"ל. אף שגם חנוך ואליהו עלו שמים, מכל מקום לא ירדו פה מטה כאשר עלו, רק נעשו הגופים לפידות (תורת משה שמות ט). ואפשר זה שנאמר **יפקוד... איש על העדה** שיהא במדריגה זו **אשר יצא לפניהם** בגוף ויעלה לרקיע, ובמדריגה זו **ואשר יבא** מן הרקיע **לפניהם**, וידע בנפשו שזה אי אפשר לשום ילוד אשה להיות במדריגה זו רק הוא לבדו. וחשב שיחזיר ה' יתברך את עטרה ליושנה ויבטל הגזירה... **ואשר יוציאם**, רוצה לומר מי אשר הוציאם ממצרים, היינו משה הוא **ואשר יביאם** [אל ארץ ישראל]...

והשתא אתי שפיר בלשון זה על חנוך לא הקשו מלאכי השרת, כי הוא נעשה גופו לפידים ולא ירד מן השמים. אמנם משה רבינו ע"ה ראו אותו עומד בשמים ממעל וגופו לא נשתנה ומוכן לירד, וזה שאלו (שבת פח:-פט.), "מה לילוד אשה" דייקא, להיות במראה ילוד אשה בגוף ולעמוד "בינינו" דייקא, ולמה לא נתהפך גופו ללפידים כמו חנוך? והשיב ה' יתברך, "לקבל את התורה הוא בא," וצריך להוריד עוז מבטחה לישראל, וצריך להיות בהתחברות הגוף. ושאלו המלאכים, "אם כן איפה אחר שגזרת שהתחתונים יעלו למעלה ויוכלו לירד כמו שאנו רואין במשה זה

- מ"א -

אליהו אל אלו הנשמות, ולכך תמיד הוא היחוד והתשוקה שעל ידו יהיה היחוד השלם...

כללו של דבר: כל מקום שיש יחוד נקרא שלום על שם שלימות, ולכך תורה ותפילה הם שלום. וסיום התפילה הוא בשלום מאחר שנעשה יחוד הדיבור והמחשבה...

וזהו "הנה אנכי שולח לכם" - תמיד בהווה - "את אליהו"...

דברת שלמה

ויאמר ה׳ אל משה לאמר: כן בנות צלפחד דוברות נתון תתן להם אחוזת נחלה בתוך אחי אביהם והעברת את נחלת אביהן להן (במדבר כז:ו-ז).

... דהנה כתוב למעלה "ויקרב משה את משפטן לפני ה׳" (במדבר כז:ה), וצריך להבין דהוה ליה למימר "עמדו ואשמעה [מה יצוה ה׳ לכם]" (במדבר ט:ח) כמו בפרשת בהעלותך.

אך הענין הוא דבנות צלפחד חבבו ארץ ישראל מאוד, כמו שאמרו חז"ל (רש"י על במדבר כו:סד; תנחומא ז), ועל ידי חיבה זו נתעורר גם בכל ישראל חיבה גדולה אל ארץ ישראל. וזהו שנאמר "ויקרב משה [את משפטן], רוצה לומר שהקריב משפטן, רוצה לומר גודל החיבה שלהן ועל ידן אצל כל ישראל,"לפני ה׳", כדי שעל ידי גודל התשוקה והחיבה ההיא ימהר ה׳ לתת להם ארץ ישראל. כנודע שעיקר הכל הוא החשק והרצון לדבר ה׳, והוא העושה פעולה בבחינת מיין נוקבין. וזה שנאמר **נתון תתן להם**, רוצה לומר שכבר פתחו מקור הנתינה של ארץ ישראל לישראל, כי תיבת נתון הוא מקור, ולכן **תתן להם**.

ואפשר לומר שחשוקת משה רבינו ע"ה אל ארץ ישראל, לפי ערך גודל צדקתו, לא היתה כל כך בשלימות. כי אילו היה בשלימות, בוודאי "לא יגרע מצדיק עיניו" (איוב לו:ז) והיה הקדוש ברוך הוא מביאו לשם. אף על פי שנגזר עליו, כמו שכתוב "ותגזר אומר [ויקם לך]" (איוב כב:כח) - צדיק גוזר [מלמטה והקדוש ברוך הוא מקיים מאמרו מלמעלה] (תענית כג.). רק מה׳ היתה זאת, שלא היה לו כל כך חשק לפי ערכו וגודל

ידי בחינת אליהו, שהוא המבשר לכל דבר שהוא שלימות, כגון תורה ותפילה שהוא יחוד שלם כנודע במחשבה ודיבור, שהוא יחוד גמור. ומקודם זה צריך תשוקה גדולה וחשק גדול, וזה הוא על ידי בחינת אליהו המעורר התשוקה מקודם ואחר כך הוא בחינת משיח.

כי בודאי בכל תפילה ההגונה שהיא ביחוד מחשבה ודיבור נעשה תיקון בחינת משיח, כמו שבביאת משיח צדקינו במהרה בימינו יהיה יחוד ושלימות גמורה בתמידות, כי אז תהיה עליית כל המחשבות והאותיות שהוא הדיבור. כך הוא בכל אדם בשעת התפילה ותורה בחינת משיח. היחוד הזה שהוא סוד בנין קומת משיח, כמאמר הבעל שם טוב נבג"מ שצריך כל אחד מישראל לתקן ולהכין חלק קומת משיח השייך לנשמתו, כנודע ש"אדם" הוא ראשי תיבות **א**דם **ד**וד **מ**שיח, שקומתו של אדם הראשון מסוף העולם ועד סופו היה, שהיו כלולין בקומת אדם הראשון כל הנשמות של ישראל, ואחר כך על ידי החטא נתמעטה קומתו. וכמו כן יהיה משיח קומה שלימה מכל נשמות ישראל כלולה מששים ריבוא, כמו שהיה קודם החטא של אדם הראשון.

על כן צריך כל אחד מישראל להכין חלק בחינת משיח השייך לחלק נשמתו... וזה אי אפשר אם לא על ידי התשוקה שמקודם שהוא בחינת המבשר בחינת אליהו, ולכך נקרא משיח, כי משיח [= מֵשִׂיחַ] הוא לשון דיבור... ולכך בכל עת שהוא יחוד המחשבה עם הדיבור הוא תיקון בחינת משיח, רק שהוא אינו בתמידות כמו שיהיה בתיקון ביאת המשיח במהרה בימינו. ולכך קודם השלימות הגמורה תהיה בשורת אליהו ז"ל לעורר תשוקת ישראל קודם ביאת משיח.

והסיבה לזה שאליהו הוא המעורר התשוקה הוא כי נודע כי פנחס שהוא אליהו זכה לנשמות של נדב ואביהוא בני אהרן. ונודע שסיבת מיתתן היה על ידי השתוקקות רבה בהתלהבות גדולה בעבודתן להבורא ב"ה, עד שמחמת דביקתן באור בהיר וזך ותשוקה חזקה נפרדו נשמותיהן מגופן. וזהו שנאמר "ותצא אש מלפני ה' ותאכל אותם וימותו לפני ה'" (ויקרא י:יב) - לפני ה' דייקא, שנתקרבו מאוד בהתלהבות גדולה המכונה לאש "מלפני ה'." ואומר בקרבתם לפני ה' "וימותו" מחמת גודל הקירוב באש ההתלהבות והתשוקה נדבקה נשמתן באור הזך. ואחר כך זכה פנחס שהוא

ובכאן שכבר הפעיל האף פעולתו כולו וגם החימה התחילה ונפלו כ״ד אלף, נתרשלו ידיו ובכו, כמו שכתוב ״והמה בוכים״ (במדבר כה:ו). וחידש פנחס סברא זו, שראה שאי אפשר לבטל קנאת ה׳ יתברך שכבר התחילה לעשות פעולתה, ואפילו אם היה גם הוא מקנא קנאת ה׳ צבאות לבד לא היה עושה כלום, כי זה לא ניחי קמיה דקודשא בריך הוא, כנ״ל. על כן התחיל לקנא קנאת ה׳ והרג את זמרי וחבטן בקרקע ואמר, על אלו יפלו כ״ד אלף מישראל? הרי שקנא גם כן קנאת ישראל שלא יפלו על ידי החוטאים הללו, ובזה חבר קנאת ה׳ צבאות וקנאת ישראל בחבור אחד.

וזהו ״ויעמוד פנחס ויפלל.״ וזהו חבור, כמו שכתב רש״י על ״נפתולי אלהים נפתלתי עם אחותי״ (בראשית ל:ח) - נתחברתי. ולא כתיב ויתפלל כי זה פירושו תפילה לה׳ לבד, רק ויפלל וכמו שאמרו רז״ל עשה פלילות עם קונו (סנהדרין מד.), רוצה לומר שחבר קנאת ישראל לקנאת ה׳ צבאות, והשווה אצלו אהבתם לאהבתו יתברך. וזה שכתבו בספרי היראים, כשמקיים ״ואהבת לרעך כמוך״ (ויקרא יט:יח), מקיים ״ואהבת את ה׳״ (דברים ו:ה). וזהו פלילות עם קונו, על דרך: חברותא [כלפי שמיא] נמי איכא (ברכות לד., אבל במקור כתוב ״מי איכא״).

וזהו **בקנאו קנאתי בתוכם**, רוצה לומר שקנאתי בתוך קנאתם. וזהו **השיב את חמתי מעל בני ישראל... לכן אמור [הנני נותן לו את בריתי שלום]**, רוצה לומר שעל ידי שחבר ותווך שלום בין שתי קנאות הנ״ל, ועשה שלום בין ישראל לאביהם שבשמים, **הנני נותן לו את בריתי שלום**...

מאור עינים

לכן אמור הנני נותן לו את בריתי שלום (במדבר כה:יא-יב).

במדרש תנחומא (פנחס ס׳ א): גדול השלום שסיום התפילה הוא בשלום, והתורה נקראת שלום, שנאמר ״וכל נתיבותיה שלום״ (משלי ג:יז). והבא בדרך נותנין לו שלום. להבין הענין נקדים הפסוק ״הנה אנכי שולח לכם את אליהו הנביא לפני בא [יום ה׳ הגדול והנורא]״ (מלאכי ג:כג), דלשון שולח הוא לשון הווה, דמשמע אף עכשיו מדלא כתיב אשלח לכם וכו׳. דהאמת הוא שכל השתוקקות ישראל עובדי ה׳ לאביהם שבשמים הוא על

פרשת פנחס

צמח ה' לצבי

פינחס בן אלעזר בן אהרן הכהן השיב את חמתי מעל בני ישראל בקנאו את קנאתי בתוכם ולא כליתי את בני ישראל בקנאתי: לכן אמור הנני נותן לו את בריתי שלום (במדבר כה:יא-יב).

על דרך שאמרו רז"ל (סנהדרין מד.): בא וחבטן בקרקע, ואמר "רבונו של עולם! על אלו יפלו כ"ד אלף מישראל? וזה "ויעמוד פנחס ויפלל" (תהלים קו:ל), עד כאן לשונם. ולהבין ענין תפילה זו.

דאיתא (תנא דבי אליהו זוטא פ' ח): כשאמר אליהו "קנא קנאתי וכו'" (מלכים א יט:י), סלקו הקדוש ברוך הוא לרקיע, אמר אין אתה והם יכולים להיות בעולם אחד, שאתה מלמד קטגוריא על בני. וכן בהושע, ובישעיה (פסחים פז:). כי ה' יתברך רוצה באהבת בניו, על דרך שכתוב "ותפילת ישרים רצונו" (משלי טו:ח), שזהו רצונו יתברך לבקש בעד ישראל. ולכן משה רבינו ע"ה מסר נפשו עליהם, כי זהו רצון ה' יתברך כנ"ל, ואמר "למה ה' יחרה אפך [בעמך]" (שמות לב:יא), וכמו שכתוב במדרש (שמות רבה מג:ו):

[בשעה שעשו ישראל אותו מעשה [חטא העגל], עמד לו משה מפייס את האלהים. אמר, "רבון העולם! עשו לך סיוע ואתה כועס עליהם. העגל הזה שעשו יהיה מסייעך. אתה מזריח את החמה והוא הלבנה, אתה הכוכבים והוא המזלות, אתה מוריד את הטל והוא משיב רוחות, אתה מוריד גשמים והוא מגדל צמחים." אמר הקדוש ברוך הוא, "משה! אף אתה טועה כמותם? והלא אין בו ממש." אמר לו, "אם כן, למה אתה כועס על בניך," הוי "למה ה' יחרה אפך בעמך."]

נמצא עשה משה את קנאת ה' יתברך ללא כלום בשביל אהבת ישראל...

- ל"ז -

ועוד כי על ידי יראת הבורא ב"ה ממילא באים לידי אהבה ודביקות הבורא ב"ה, כמו ששמעתי ממורי זללה"ה (על קדושין ב:): כי דרכו של איש, שהוא אהבה בחינת דכר, לחזור אחר אשה, שהיא יראה, כמו שכתוב "אשה יראת [ה' היא תתהלל] (משלי לא:ל), ועל ידי אהבה ודביקות הבורא ב"ה זו, נמשך חסדים ורחמים גדולים בכל העולמות ממקור החסדים, שהוא אין סוף ב"ה, ולכן נמתקין הדינים.

וזהו **כי מראש צורים אראנו**, כי צור הוא לשון חוזק וצמצום, **וראש צורים** הוא צמצום הראשון כנ"ל. וכן הוא **מגבעות**, שהן האמהות (במדבר רבה ט:יג) גם כן מסטרא דיראה הקדושה בחינת נוקבא, רוצה לומר שהם דבוקים בשורש הצמצום הראשון שהיא היראה הגדולה, ועל ידי זה הם דבוקים באחדות הבורא ב"ה ואינם מעלמא דפרודא, שהם בחינת מספר וחשבון. וזה שנאמר **הן עם לבדד ישכון**, שהוא בחינת אחדות. **ובגוים לא יתחשב**, שהם בחינת חשבון.

אור תורה

וישא בלעם את עיניו וירא את ישראל שוכן לשבטיו (במדבר כד:ב).

ודרשו רז"ל: ראה פתחיהן שאינם מכוונים זה כנגד זה, אמר ראוים אלו שתשרה עליהם שכינה (בבא בתרא ס.). הוא רמז לכמה תלמידי חכמים שיושבים במסיבה אחת, וכל אחד אומר דרוש על איזה פסוק או על איזה מימרא דהש"ס. זה אומר כך פירושו, וזה אומר כך פירושו. ואם ח"ו מתכוונים לקנטר, לאמר פירוש שלי יותר טוב מפירושי האחרים, בוודאי אוי להם ולנפשם, מוטב שתהפוך שלייתם על פניהם. אבל אם כל אחד מתכוון רק להגדיל תורה ולהאדירה, אז אשרי להם ולנשמתם.

וזהו ראה שאין פתחיהן, רוצה לומר פיהם, כי הפה נקרא פתח כמו "שמור פתחי פיך" (מיכה ז:ה). וראה שאין פתחיהן של כל אחד ואחד מכוונין זה כנגד זה, רוצה לומר שאין כוונתם להיות מתנגדים זה לזה, רק כל אחד אומר דרוש ופירוש שלו לשם שמים, אמר ראוים אלו שתשרה עליהם שכינה.

דברת שלמה

מה אקוב לא קבה אל ומה אזעם לא זעם ה׳: כי מראש צורים אראנו ומגבעות אשורנו הן עם לבדד ישכון ובגוים לא יתחשב (במדבר כג:ח-ט).

פירוש כי קבה הוא לשון קללה, מפני שהוא לשון צימצום לשון ״קב,״ והוא כלי קטן מצומצם מאוד. וכן לשון זעם הוא גם כן לשון קללה וצימצום מאוד, ולכן אמרו חז״ל: כמה זעמו? רגע (ברכות ז.), רוצה לומר מצומצם מאוד. וההיפך לזה שהוא הביטול המבטל אותו כשדבקים במקור החסדים והרחמים שהוא בחינת התפשטות גדול עד אין סוף, וזה שנאמר **מה אקוב לא קבה אל**, ששם זה הוא שורש החסדים, כמו שכתוב ״חסד אל כל היום״ (תהלים נב:ג), כמו שנאמר בספר לקוטי אמרים [מאת הרב המגיד] על פסוק ״אל מוציאם ממצרים״ (במדבר כג:כב).

ומה אזעם לא זעם ה׳, רוצה לומר כשמדבקים בו יתברך אז כל הדינים בטלים, והגם שיש דינים וצמצומים והכל הוא מאתו יתברך, אמנם מהיכן באו הדינים? מן מה שצמצם הבורא ב״ה כביכול גודל בהירותו האין סוף וברא על ידי כ״ב אותיות התורה בגין דישתמודעין ליה, כמו שאיתא בתיקוני זוהר: ובהון אתכסיאת מבני נשא [ובהן אתה מתכסה מבני אדם (הקדמה אחרת יז.).

וכמו ששמעתי ממורי [ר׳ דוב בער] זללה״ה על מאמר חז״ל (בראשית רבה ג:ד): מהיכן נברא האור? נתעטף הקדוש ברוך הוא באור וברא אור, שנאמר ״עוטה אור כשלמה״ (תהלים קד:ב), וצמצום הזה נמשך ממדריגה למדריגה עד למטה מטה, ונעשה בחינת גיהנם ודינים קשים, רחמנא לצלן, ועלמא דפירודא, אשר ממנה נמשכים בחינת הסטרא אחרא והרשעים ההולכים אחר תאות לבם שבעולם הזה. ומה שאין כן ישראל הקדושים שקבלו התורה הקדושה ומצוותיו, ועל ידי זה הם דבקים בבורא עולם ויראים ממנו מאוד. נמצא הם דבקים בשורש הצמצום הראשון, שנדבק בו יתברך שממנו נמשכים כל הצמצומים והדינים כנ״ל, ועל ידי היראה הגדולה יראת הרוממות של הבורא ב״ה בטלים כל הדינים והצמצומים הנמשכים ממנה, ונקרא סוספיתא דדהבא, שהם סיגים של זהב, כמו שכתב האריז״ל שהמתקת הדינים בשרשם.

- ל״ה -

תשואות חן

(*מפרשת בלק/מסעי*)

ויען בלעם ויאמר אל עבדי בלק אם יתן לי בלק מלוא ביתו כסף וזהב לא אוכל לעבור את פי ה׳ אלוהי... (במדבר כב:יח).

מי מנה עפר יעקב ומספר את רובע ישראל... (במדבר כג:י).

הנה יש באדם ארבע יסודות: אש, רוח, מים, עפר. ודוגמת ארבע יסודות אלו יש ארבעה חלוקי בני אדם בישראל, והם חסידים, צדיקים, בינונים, רשעים...

והבין שהקדוש ברוך הוא מריח אפילו ריח בוגדיו (בראשית כז:כז, סנהדרין לז.), שאפילו מן העבירות של ישראל יוצא דבר גדול מאוד, כמבואר במדרש שמן מכירת יוסף יצא להחיות עם רב, ומחטא העגל שקלי המשכן, וכדוגמתן (ר׳ בראשית נ:כ , תנחומא ישן ס׳ ח ,תנחומא כי תשא ס׳ י). ולזה אנו מתפללין "מלפניך משפטינו יצא," כי הקדוש ברוך הוא מסתכל בהיוצא מן העבירה...

והנה עיקר בחינת האדם הוא לחבר עולם תחתון לעליון, ולעשות מן החובות זכויות ומגשמיות רוחניות, ובחינה זאת נקראת חיבור הוי"ה ואדנ"י. וזה פירוש הפסוק **לא אוכל לעבר את פי**, הוא בחינת המלכות, בחינה התחתונה של שבעה ימי הבנין והוא אדנ"י. על דרך אמרם ז"ל: לא כשאני נקרא אני נכתב, נכתב בהוי"ה ונקרא בפה באדני (פסחים נ.).

והיה בלעם רוצה לקלל את ישראל מצד מדריגה הרביעית המכונים בשם עפר, ולא היה יכול כי הקדוש ברוך הוא מריח ריח בוגדים היוצא מעבירות שלהם, כנזכר. וזהו **לא אוכל לעבר את פי ה׳**, שאיני יכול לפרוד הוי"ה מאדנ"י [= מלכות, פה], כי הם מעלים אפילו מדריגות התחתונות שלהם.

- ל"ד -

קדושת לוי

ויגר מואב מפני העם מאוד כי רב הוא ויקץ מואב מפני בני ישראל (במדבר כב:ג).

נראה במאי דדייק הכתוב מקודם **העם** ואחר כך **בני ישראל**, דידוע במדרש (שמות רבה מב:ו) ובזהר הקדוש (ח"ב מה:) ד"עם" הוא ערב רב. וזהו **ויגר מואב מפני העם מאד**, מחמת העם ערב רב פחד, שראה שכל מקום שישראל שוכנים מתגיירים להם גרים, כמו ערב רב שנתגיירו לישראל, גלל כן פחד שיבואו בני ישראל לגבולו, אולי יתגיירו מאומתו גם כן להם.

ושלא תאמר מאי אכפת להו, לזה אמר הכתוב **ויקץ מואב מפני בני ישראל**, שהיה שונא מאד לישראל...

והנה נפש הבעל תשובה, דהיינו הגרים, להם יותר בנקל להעלות הניצוץ ממי שהוא צדיק מנעוריו. והנה זה הרשע בלק היה לו פחד מישראל, מחמת שישראל בהליכתם העלו נצוצות, וזה הרשע היה שונא מאוד להקדושה.

וזהו הרמז **ויקוצו [ויקץ מואב] מפני בני ישראל**, שזה קץ בעיני אותו הרשע להיות ישראל. וזהו הרמז **ויגר מואב מפני העם מאד**, כי כל מקום שכתוב העם הוא הרמז על הערב רב, הגרים שהיו בישראל. וזהו **כי רב הוא**, היינו הגרים, שלא יעלו אותם כנ"ל, כי הם מסוגלים יותר להעלות הניצוץ...

- ל"ג -

~ פרשת בלק ~

גנזי יוסף

וירא בלק בן ציפור את כל אשר עשה ישראל לאמורי (במדבר כב:ב).

הנה איתא בזהר: בלק הוא "בא לק," שבא לקותא [קללה], ובזה היה בלק רוצה לנצח את ישראל. ובלעם הוא "בל עם," להעביר עם ישראל [מן העולם] (זהר ח"ג קצט:).

הנה בלק הרמז ליצר הרע שהוא אורב לאדם ופורש פח לרגליו, כמו שנאמר "וכצפרים האחוזות בפח כהם יוקשים בני האדם" (קהלת ט:יב). וראשית מלחמת יצר הרע נכנס במחשבה של אדם, שזה הוא קל ליצר הרע להביא את האדם לידי הרהור, כמו שאמרו חז"ל שאין אדם ניצול מזה בכל יום (בבא בתרא קסד:). ומהרהור הולך לדיבורים, כמו שאמרו חז"ל אבק לשון הרע אין אדם ניצול בכל יום. ומדיבור הולך ח"ו לידי מעשה, כמו שכתוב "אל תתן את פיך לחטיא את בשרך" (קהלת ה:ה).

וירא בלק, הוא היצר הרע שהוא רואה להכשיל את האדם. **בן צפור**, כמו שנאמר "וכצפרים האחוזות בפח"...

ואחר שמוציא מחשבתו הרעה לדיבור ממילא בא לידי מעשה. וזהו **את כל אשר עשה ישראל לאמורי**, הם באים באמירות הדברים שהם בלבו של אדם, כמו שנאמר "ויאמר בלבו" (בראשית כז:מא). וכך כתיב "תנה בני לבך לי" (משלי כג:כו), כי הכל תלוי בלב.

- ל"ב -

לטובות ישראל, עושהו ויקבל עליו אף להיות בגיהנם עבורם, כי כל תשוקתו להטיבם.

ובאמת הצדיק יכול להמשיך השפע על ידי דיבורו הקדוש בלי שום פעולה גשמיות כלל, רק שלפעמים צריך הצדיק דווקא לעשות פעולה גשמית, כי בדיבור אינו יכול לפעול כי אם לבני אדם המאמינים בזה שהצדיק יכול לפעול בדיבור, אבל אותם שאין מאמינים בזה צריך הצדיק להמשיך לו בדרך הטבע, ולזה צריך לפעולה גשמית. בדרך משל אל החולה שאינו יכול לקבל הרפואות הטובים לו מחמת שהם חריפים ביותר וצריך לבקש לו רפואה קלה לפי טבעו שיהיה יכול לסבול, אף אם היה לוקח הרפואה החריפה היה יותר בריא מה לעשות לו כיון שאינו יכול לסבול, והנמשל מובן.

וכוונת משה רבינו ע"ה גם כן שסבר אמת אם אדבר אל הסלע יהיה כרצון הבורא ב"ה, אבל לא אהיה יכול לפעול כי אם לאנשים הצדיקים, כאשר בארנו. לכך מוטב אעשה פעולה גשמית ויהיה טוב לכולם והכל שוין בטובה. ולזה הסכים הקדוש ברוך הוא על ידו בראותו כוונתו הטובה מאוד, ולזה כתיב **ויצאו מים רבים**, פירוש רבים שהיו בשביל רבים די לכולם כנ"ל.

- ל"א -

בדברים קשים אינו בבחינה הזאת. והנה זה שמוכיח את ישראל בטוב ומספר תמיד בגדולת ישראל וצדקתם, אז כל הדברים הנבראים בעולם צריכין לעשות מעצמם הרצון של ישראל לדבר שנבראו, דהיינו בשביל ישראל, אבל אם אינו מספר ומעלה צדקת ישראל, אז צריך להכריח כל הנברא בהכרח גדול לעשות מה שנברא, דהיינו לעשות רצון ישראל.

והנה משה אמר בכאן "שמעו נא המורים," הוכיח את ישראל בדברים קשים, ולכך הוצרך להכות את הסלע לעשות מה שנברא, כי אילו היה מעלה את ישראל כנ"ל, וכמו שהיה כוונת הקדוש ברוך הוא **ודברתם אל הסלע**, כי אז היה מדבר אל הסלע: אתה שנבראת בשביל ישראל והם במעלה גדולה, צריך אתה לעשות מה שנבראת, דהיינו להוציא מים לישראל. אבל עתה שהוכיח את ישראל בדברים קשים "שמעו נא," הוצרך להכות את הסלע לעשות רצון ישראל...

וזהו הרמז **יען לא האמנתם בי להקדישני לעיני בני ישראל**, כי זה שמוכיח את ישראל בטוב יכול גם הוא להשיג את העם זה השכל. וזה הרמז **להקדישני לעיני בני ישראל**, כמאמר חז"ל (שיר השירים רבה א:טו) "עיני עדה" - חכמי עדה, שגם הם ישיגו זה השכל.

נועם אלימלך
(*מפרשת בלק*)

וירם משה את ידו ויך את הסלע במטהו פעמיים ויצאו מים רבים ותשת העדה ובעירם (במדבר כ:יא).

...יש להקשות למה נענש משה רבינו ע"ה במי מריבה בהכותו הסלע? הלא הסכים הקדוש ברוך הוא על ידו, דכתיב **ויצאו מים רבים**, וכיון שעשה שלא כהוגן לא היה להסלע להוציא מים, וכי עביד רחמנא ניסא לשקרי (ברכות נח.)?

אלא נראה בוודאי חלילה לו ל"איש האלהים" (דברים לג:א) שלא לעשות רצון הבורא ב"ה, אלא שדרך הצדיק תמיד לחזור אחר טובות ישראל, ואף שנראה לו איזה דבר קצת עבירה בעשותו הדבר ההוא, אך שיהיה

(לפי בראשית מח:ו), דהיינו בדיבור לבד היה יוצא מים כמו דור המדבר, ובזה היו גם הם מבחינת דור דעה כנ"ל. ומזה שהכה הסלע גרם שכחה, דהיינו נפילה מן הדיבור אל העובדא, וזה פירוש הזהר הנ"ל - עד כאן לשון העתקות.

נמצא אם היו כל ישראל רואים את הדיבור כנ"ל, לא היתה נפילה, כי כך הסדר שנמשך מן הדעת אל הדיבור. אך על ידי שלא ראו הדיבור רק ההכאה, נפלו מן הדעת אל העובדא...

נמצא כל הכוונה היתה כדי להמשיך אור מדעת עליון לנוה אפריון, שהיא השכינה שהיא עולם הדיבור. אך שעל ידי שכעס משה... שאמרו רז"ל: כל הכועס שכינה מסתלקת ממנו (נדרים כב:).

קדושת לוי

... ודברתם אל הסלע לעיניהם... יען לא האמנתם בי להקדישני לעיני בני ישראל (במדבר כ:ח,יב).

הנה רש"י והרמב"ן חולקים בחטא של משה. אחד [רמב"ן] מפרש על שאמר לישראל "שמעו נא [המורים]" (במדבר כ:י), ואחד [רש"י] מפרש על שהכה את הסלע. והנראה שטעם אחד הוא, כי זה גרם זה.

והנה יש שתי בחינות במוכיח שמוכיח את ישראל שיעשו רצון הבורא ב"ה, אחד שמוכיח בדברים טובים, דהיינו שאומר לכל איש ישראל גודל מעלתו ומקום מקור מחצב נשמתו, אשר באמת נשמת ישראל חצובה למעלה מכסא הכבוד, וגודל הנחת רוח אשר להבורא יתברך כביכול ממצוות כל איש ישראל, וגודל השמחה אשר בכל העולמות בעשות איש ישראל מצוות הבורא ב"ה. ובזה התוכחה מטה את לב בני ישראל לעשות רצון הבורא ב"ה, לקבל כל איש מישראל עול מלכות שמים עליו. ויש שמוכיח את ישראל בדברים קשים ובדברי ביושים, עד שהם מוכרחים לעשות רצון הבורא.

והחילוק שביניהם, זה שמוכיח את ישראל בטוב מעלה את נשמת ישראל למעלה למעלה, ומספר תמיד בצדקת ובגדולת ישראל כמה גדול כוחם למעלה, וראוי הוא להיות מנהיג על ישראל, וזה שמוכיח את ישראל

לשרשו לא יוציא מים. ולכן **ויך את הסלע** דהוא מדריגה קטנה, ואז **ותשת העדה**, אף המון עם.

יען לא [האמנתם בי] להקדישני לעיני בני ישראל, היינו עיני העדה דהוא הצדיק, ואף שלהמון עם לא הייתם פועלים, אף על פי כן היה לכם **להקדישני** בפני עיני העדה הכשרים. לכן, **לא תביאו**... ובאמת כוונת משה רבינו ע"ה היה רק למען טובת ישראל המון העם וכנ"ל.

צמח ה' לצבי

...ודברתם אל הסלע לעיניהם... (במדבר כ:ח).

פירוש על דרך שכתוב "וראו כל בשר יחדיו כי פי ה' דבר" (ישעיה מ:ה), רוצה לומר על דרך "וכל העם רואים את הקולות" (שמות כ:טו), שהיו מרגישים הקול בחוש הראות מגודל קדושתם. וכן על דרך זה "ויברך דוד [את ה'] לעיני כל הקהל" (דברי הימים א כט:י). וזהו שנאמר בכאן **לעיניהם**, שיראו כל ישראל את הדיבור ההוא. ולכן היה הצווי למשה ולאהרן ששניהם ידברו, כמו שכתוב **ודברתם אל הסלע**, על דרך שאמרו רז"ל: שנים שעוסקים בתורה שכינה שרויה ביניהם (מ' אבות ג:ב), וכל הכוונה היתה שתהיה שם השראת השכינה.

ועל דרך זה מה שכתוב בזהר: אם היה משה מדבר אל הסלע, לא היתה שכחה (תיקוני זהר ת' כא מד.), שהשכחה היא הנפילה מן הדעת, וכמו שכתוב בהעתקות [כתבי יד של דרשות המגיד]... וטעם לזה, שמשה רבינו ע"ה כל נסים שנעשו על ידו לא היה רק על ידי הדיבור, ולא היה שייך לעובדא כידוע. על דרך "הרם את מטך" (שמות יד:טז), ובדיבור לבד נכנע הים, לאפוקי יהושע כנודע. כי משה היה מבחינת דעת ונמשך אל הדיבור, וגם דורו היו דור דעה, ועל זה נקראו דור המדבר (סנהדרין קח.) לשון דיבור הנמשך מן הדעת, וקבלו התורה בדיבור...

והנה כאשר תמו דור הראשון דור המדבר דור דעה ובא דור אחר, סבר משה רבינו ע"ה שבחינתם הם עובדות דווקא, שהם באים לרשת הארץ, ועל כן הכה את הסלע. ובאמת אמר לו הקדוש ברוך הוא כי אדרבה צריך הוא להקים את הדור השני ולהרימם, "על שם אביהם יקראו בנחלתם"

מבשר צדק

וידבר ה' אל משה לאמר: קח את המטה והקהל את העדה אתה ואהרן אחיך ודברתם אל הסלע לעיניהם ונתן מימיו... ויקהילו משה ואהרן את הקהל אל פני הסלע ויאמר להם שמעו נא המורים המן הסלע הזה נוציא לכם מים: וירם משה את ידו ויך את הסלע במטהו פעמיים ויצאו מים רבים ותשת העדה ובעירם: ויאמר ה' אל משה ואל אהרן יען לא האמנתם בי להקדישני לעיני בני ישראל לכן לא תביאו את הקהל הזה אל הארץ אשר נתתי להם (במדבר כ:ז-יב).

דהנה כשהאדם הצדיק רוצה לפעול איזה השתנות מסדר הבריאה, צריך לילך לשורש של הדבר שרצה לשנותו. על דרך משל, כשהיוצר עושה איזה כלי על ידי חומר, ואדם רוצה לשנות זה הכלי על איזה כלי אחר, צריך לילך להיוצר ולבקש מאתו שישנה זה הכלי ויעשה כרצונו.

ולכן כשרצה משה רבינו ע"ה לפעול הנס שהסלע יוציא מים להעם, אז הוצרך להעלות העם לשורש של הסלע, ואז יכולין לפעול שאף הסלע יוציא מים, כי בשורש של כל דבר יכולין להשתנות. וכך היתה כוונת הקדוש ברוך הוא אל משה שיעלה הבני ישראל, ואז בדיבורא בעלמא סגי - וכן עשה משה רבינו ע"ה. אך שאף המון עם היו צריכין למים, ולא היה ביכלתו להעלות אף המון עם למדריגה עליונה לשורש העליון, ולכן לא עלתה בידו, והוכרח להכות הסלע. והיא מדריגה קטנה, כדאיתא בליקוטי תורה מהאריז"ל.

ועונש הצדיק היה אף שלא היה באפשרי להעלות המון עם, הוי לו להעלות את הצדיקים הנקראים עיני העדה (שיר השירים רבה א:טו), כדי שיקודש ה' יתברך בפניהם. וזהו פירוש הפסוק **ויקהילו משה ואהרן את הקהל**, אף המון עם, **אל פני הסלע**, רוצה לומר לפנימיות מהסלע דהיא השורש שלו, ולא עלתה בידו, כי להמון עם אינו ביכלתו להעלות. וכיון שראה משה איך המון עם אין כוונתן אל השרש רק על סלע זה דלמטה, **ויאמר להם שמעו נא המורים המן הסלע הזה נוציא [לכם מים]**, היינו מסלע שאתם רואין זהו אי אפשר. וכיון שאינכם ראוים למדריגת העלאה

לעומת זה עשה אלהים, וכמו שיש שבע ספירות שהם שבעה ימים דקדושה, כן יש שבע ספירות שהם שבעת ימי הטומאה בקליפה. וידוע דקליפה סובבת לפרי... וצריך האדם לעבור דרך כל הקליפות ולשברם עד שיבא אל האהל הפנימי שהוא מלכות דקדושה - תורה שבעל פה, מידת היראה. ומשם לתפארת, תורה שבכתב, מידת האהבה.

ולזה צריך מסירות נפש שימית את עצמו, דהיינו כל חלקי הרע והקליפות שבעצמו ובגופו, כמו שמשבר את התאוות ופניות ושאר שטותים של קליפות של עצמו, עד שיבא לחיות הפנימית של הנשמה, חלק [אלוה] ממעל. כן משבר כל הקליפות למעלה עד שיבא אל האהל פנימי ליראה ואהבה באמת בלי פניה רק לשמו יתברך.

ומקודם שישבר כל מעבר הקליפות אינו לומד ועובד לשמו יתברך כי הוא עדיין בתוך הקליפות של עצמו... מה שאין כן אם יש לו מסירות נפש על כל עובדא... ואז בא על ה"*לִשמה*." ואם כן השכל נותן שלא יאמר אדם שכעת אני בחומריות ועביות ואי אפשר לי לשבר את עצמי שאבוא אל ה"*לִשמה*," ואם כן מה לי ללמוד בחנם כשאני יודע בעצמי שאי אפשר לי ללמוד לשמה? רק דזה אינו שאי אפשר לי לבא מתחילת הלימוד ל"*לִשמה*," הואיל שהוא צריך לעבור דרך קליפות, שהוא שלא לשמה. ולאחר זמן, כשיחזק את עצמו לשבר כל הקליפות, יעשה לו דרך ומעבר שלא יבלבלו אותו, אז ילמוד לשמה, וכשלא יתחיל כלל ללמוד הואיל שהוא אינו יכול לבא ל"*לִשמה*," אם כן לעולם לא ילמוד לשמה כי סוף סוף צריך לעבור דרך שם ולעשות לו דרך כבושה, וצריך על כן שיהיה תחילה שלא לשמה.

ובזה פרשתי "...ודברת בם בשבתך בביתך [ובלכתך בדרך] ובשכבך ובקומך" (דברים ו:ז), רוצה לומר הן בזמן שכיבה והוא כשאדם בקטנות המוחין לעבדו ביראה ואהבה ובשמחה, הן "ובקומך" והוא בזמן שיש לך קימה שתוכל ללמוד לשמו יתברך בדחילא ורחימא ובשמחה גדולה, ואין לך רשות לומר הואיל שאתה בזמן שכיבה לא תלמוד, אלא למוד, ומהשכיבה יבא לקימה...

והתורה נקראת על שם משה כמו שכתוב "זכרו תורת משה עבדי" (מלאכי ג:כב), וצריך ליקח בעת עסקו בתורה גם בחינת אין האמור להדביקו לבחינת תורה דאתגליא שנקרא תורת משה, בכדי שתהא שלימות התורה כפי כוונת הבורא יתברך, ויאיר ויופיע אור הזך ומצוחצח בהאותיות שנקרא תורת משה.

וזהו **דבר אל בני ישראל ויקחו אליך**, פירוש אל בחינת התורה שנקראת על שמך תורה דאתגליא תורת משה יקחו **פרה אדומה**, הבחינה שנקראת בשם פרה שהוא מקור השופע ומאיר בהתורה, **ואדומה** על שם זהרורית הגדולה ואור הזך שאי אפשר להשיגו. ואז **תמימה** תהיה שלימות גמורה ככוונת הבורא יתברך. וגם אפשר שנקראת בחינה זו על שם שעדיין היא תמימה, כמאמר הבעל שם טוב כי אור הגנוז עדיין הוא תמים שלא הגיע לו שום אדם כי אם מעט מזעיר, כמו שנאמר "תורת ה' תמימה" (תהלים יט:ח) - "תורת ה'" פירוש בחינת התורה שנקראת על שם ה' ולא על שם משה, תמימה שלא דרכו בה רבים ולא באו לזו המדריגה.

אך בדורות הללו צריך כל אדם השלם להתאמץ ולהגיע לזה כאמור. וזהו **אשר אין בה מום** הוא לשון חסרון, פירוש בחינת אין הוא חסר בה בבחינת תורת משה כל זמן שלא יתעורר האדם השלם לדבק את עצמו לבחינת אין הנ"ל. ומפני מה? מפני אשר **לא עלה עליה עול**, שלא קיבל עליו עול מלכות שמים כראוי ולא הגיע לשלימות, אך בודאי שאי אפשר לבא לידי שלימות הגמורה כי אם בענין זה. וזהו שתרגם אונקלוס "דא גזירת אורייתא די פקיד ה'," שצריך לבא לבחינה שהתורה נגזרה ונחקקה משם ואז נקרא עובד ה' הגמור.

תורי זהב

זאת התורה אדם כי ימות באהל כל הבא אל האהל וכל אשר באהל יטמא שבעת ימים (במדבר יט:יד).

ודרשינן בגמרא: אין התורה מתקיימת אלא במי שממית עצמו עליה (ברכות סג.). ולפי דרשה זו צריך להבין לפרש סוף הפסוק, מאי **כל הבא אל האהל... שבעת ימים**. ונראה לי על פי שפרשתי: לעולם ילמוד אדם תורה אפילו שלא לשמה, שמתוך שלא לשמה בא לשמה (סוטה כב:), דזה

פרשת חקת

מאור עינים

וידבר ה' אל משה ואל אהרן לאמר: זאת חקת התורה אשר צוה ה' לאמר דבר אל בני ישראל ויקחו אליך פרה אדומה תמימה אשר אין בה מום אשר לא עלה עליה עול (במדבר יט:א-ב).

דנודע שהתורה היא אותיות ונקודות וטעמים ותגין. אך זה הוא בחינת התורה דאתגליא, כי כל זה אפשר לשכל אנושי להשיג כל אחד לפי מדריגתו. אך המאור שבה שעליו אמרו חז"ל: המאור שבה מחזירן למוטב (איכה רבה פתיחתא ב) הוא בחינת אין, שאין לו תפיסה מפני שהוא למעלה מן הטעם. והוא המקור שממנו נביעת התורה שהוא הבורא ב"ה שעל ידי זה הוא והתורה אחד.

וצריך כל אחד העוסק בתורה לדבק את חיותו בהמאור שבה דייקא, הנקרא אין, שהוא למעלה מן הטעם. כי לכך נקראו הטעמים של הנגינות טעמים, מפני שהן עדיין בבחינה שאפשר להשיג ולתת טעם אף שהם דבר גבוה. אבל הפנימיות נקרא אין שאין לו טעם ותפיסה. וצריך הלומד לדבק באור הנשפע מבחינת אין ואז בוודאי מחזירו למוטב, מאחר שנדבק פנימיותיו באור פנימיות התורה נעשה כסא להשראתו יתברך השורה בתורה ושופע בתוכה. ואף שצריך בעת לימודה להבין מה שלומד ולהטעים בכדי שיבין הטעם, מכל מקום צריך גם כן להאמור בכדי שיהא שלימות הגמורה כי זה הוא "אור הגנוז לצדיקים" (חגיגה יב.)...

על כן צריך כל אחד שרוצה שתפעול בו התורה להחזירו למוטב לחפש האור השופע שהתורה נגזרה ממנו, וזה נקרא בחינת פרה, על דרך שאמרו רז"ל: יותר ממה שהעגל רוצה לינק פרה רוצה להניק (פסחים קיב.), שהמשפיע מכונה בשם פרה, ואף זה האור הגנוז השופע בהתורה יכונה בשם פרה.

- כ"ד -

צמח ה' לצבי

... עבודת מתנה אתן את כהונתכם והזר הקרב יומת (במדבר יח:ז).

פירוש על דרך משל, מלך נותן לשריו במתנה עיירות וכפרים, והנאהב אצלו ביותר אינו נותן לו כלום מזה, ואומר לו שיקרב אצלו ושישמשו וישרתו ויערוך שולחן לפני המלך ויאיר נר לפניו וכל מה שצריך למלך עצמו. לימים אמר עבד זה למלך, "למה לכל שרים אתה נותן מתנות ואחוזות ולי אין אתה נותן?" והשיב, הם משמשים ועובדים את בחינת מלכות שלי במסים וארנונות, אבל אתה משמש הגוף שלי. וכי יש שכר גדול מזה, שזכית לדבק למלך גופא? ואינך צריך לשום שכר. וכל השרים הרואים את כבודך ישתחוו לך ויתנו לך מה שתרצה, ועבודתך שאתה עובד הוא השכר.

וזהו שנאמר "בארצם לא תנחל וחלק לא יהיה לך [בתוכם] אני חלקך [ונחלתך בתוך בני ישראל]" (במדבר יח:כ). **עבודת מתנה אתן את כהונתכם**, רוצה לומר המתנה היא העבודה. למה? לפי שהיא כהונתכם, רוצה לומר שכירתכם. כי **הזר הקרב יומת**, ואתה מקורב, ואין לך כבוד גדול מזה.

מאמרי אדמו"ר הזקן

ועבד הלוי הוא... (במדבר יח:כג).

עבודת הלויים היתה בשיר לעורר המידות, כי בשיר כלולות כל המידות, כגון אהבה ויראה ושמחה וכו'. ובאתערותא דלתתא תהיה אתערותא דלעילא. וזהו בחינת בינה - התבוננות, שהמידות באות מהתבוננות. אבל בחינת כהן הוא בחינת חכמה למעלה מן המידות, שהמידות אינן ממדריגת "אין עוד," אבל כשרואה "אין עוד מלבדו" (דברים ד:לה) והכל בטל במציאות באמת ואין מי לאהוב או ליראה או שארי מידות. זהו כהנא ברעותא דלבא [כהן עובד בתשוקת הלב] (זהר ח"ג לט.), שלמעלה מן המידות. וזהו "סייג לחכמה שתיקה" (מ' אבות ג:יג), שהוא למעלה מבחינת קול, שהוא השיר עבודת הלויים, שאינו יכול להרים קולו מפני שהוא בטל במציאות.

- כ"ג -

לעשות על ידי אחר, ולא יחשוב שהוא ראוי לזה יותר מחבירו, כי זה גבהות...

וצריך האדם ללמוד מזה ולא להתקוטט עבור מצוה שיש בה צד שררה ח"ו, ולברוח ממנה. ואם יהיה ראוי לה ה' יתברך יכריח כל העולם להזמין לידו הנהגה זו וכדומה. וצריך לשקול דבר זה תמיד בשכל עמוק וצדק וזך ולשאול מה' יתברך על זה עזר שיעזרנו שלא יסיתנו היצר הרע בזה לצד ההיפוך ח"ו, רק ידריכנו ה' יתברך בדרך האמת והטוב.

חסד לאברהם המלאך

ויחר למשה מאוד ויאמר אל ה' אל תפן אל מנחתם לא חמור אחד מהם נשאתי ולא הרעותי את אחד מהם (במדבר טז:טו).

ואמרינן בגמרא: לא חמד (מגילה ט:). והיה אפשר לומר על דרך שאמרה השונמית "כי באת אלי להזכיר את עווני" (מלכים א יז:יח). פירוש שאדם צדיק מעורר תמיד צד הטוב שלו, וכשאין מתעורר אזי ח"ו מתעורר צד הרע שלו. וכשאדם שהוא במדריגה התחתונה הוא ביחד עם איש צדיק שהוא במדריגה עליונה, אזי אין איש הקטן יכול לעורר צד הטוב שלו, מדריגה התחתונה, מפני גדולתו של הצדיק, ואז ח"ו מתעורר צד הרע שלו. וזהו "באת אלי להזכיר את עווני."

אך כשהצדיק הוא במדריגת ענווה, אזי אין מזיק לאדם כלל. ומשה היה עניו מכל האדם, וזהו פירוש **לא חמור אחד מהם נשאתי**, פירוש לא גרמתי לשום אדם להנשא חומר שלו. ואמרינן בגמרא לא חמד, פירוש התאוות של האדם לא נשאתי. **ולא הרעותי את אחד [מהם]**, פירוש החיות שלכם שהוא אחדות שלכם.

פרשת קרח

יושר דברי אמת (ס' ל)

... ומדוע תתנשאו על קהל ה' (במדבר טז:ג).

ועניין זה קרה לקרח עם משה כי באמת משה רבינו ע"ה היתה לו תכלית השפלות, כמו שהעידה התורה (במדבר יב:ג), ואף על פי כן היתה לו גבהות בכמה דברים שעשה, שהיה מלך על ישראל והנהיג כמלך על עמו. רק באמת היה זה לעבודת הבורא להדריך העם לעבודת ה' יתברך, כי לא היה אפשר בלתי זה שיהיה איש אשר יצא לפניהם. ואף על פי כן לא רצה בתחילה זה כנודע שסרב, ואמר "שלח נא ביד תשלח" (שמות ד:יג) עד שהכריחו ה' יתברך לזה שתהיה לו שררה זו.

וקרח אף על פי שפקח היה והיה לו רוח הקודש, עם כל זה ניצוץ קנאה נשארה בו ולא נטהר לבו ממנה בכל מכל כל. וקנאה היא מצד גבהות, ואמונה לא היתה לו שיעשה משה הכל מפי ה' יתברך ויהיה באמת מצדו בתכלית השפלות והענוה. רק שחשב שמשה השתמש בגבהות להיפך ולנגד האמת שחשב שמשה נטה מן האמת וטעה בגבהות שעל ידי הגבהות שיש בלבו התנשא על קהל ה' יתברך כמו שנאמר **ומדוע תתנשאו על קהל ה'**.

ועל עצמו לא דימה שתהיה לו גבהות, רק חשב שמה שלבו נוטה לזה להיות נשיא הכל הוא מצד האמת, כמו שנאמר לעיל בפסוק "ויגבה לבו בדרכי ה'" [דברי הימים ב יז:ו], כי זו הגאוה הותרה. ולא רצה לתלות הפחיתות בו בגבהותו, והאמת הישרה של הגבהות שמותר הוא במשה, רק חשב להיפוך מפני הקנאה של הרע, שהפך לבו לאמור על הרע טוב ועל טוב רע...

ולזה נחלקו כי זה דבר עמוק, וצריך לזה האמונה לתלות החסרון תמיד בו [בעצמו] ולחפוץ תמיד בכניעות ושפלות, אפילו לדבר מצוה. פן ואולי הוא מצד הגבהות של הקליפה לעשות מצוה שאינה מוטלת עליו ושיוכל

דאמר למדני כל התורה כשאני עומד על רגל אחת, אמר לו [הלל] "ואהבת לרעך כמוך," דסני לך לחברך לא תעביד (שבת לא.)...

וזהו שאמר כאן **וזכרתם את כל מצוות ה'**, שהוא "ואהבת לרעך" כנ"ל, **ולא תתורו [אחרי עיניכם] אשר אתם זונים אחריהם**, **זונים** דייקא שהוא הפך "ואהבת." ועל ידי זה תזכו למדריגה היותר גדולה שהוא "בכל דרכיך דעהו," שהוא כולל כל התורה...

ובאמת "בכל דרכיך דעהו" מרומז ונכלל בפסוק "ואהבת לרעך כמוך," וכמו שפירש רש"י - "רעך," זה הקדוש ברוך הוא (שבת לא.)...

וזהו שנאמר "כי עין בעין יראו בשוב ה' ציון" (ישעיה נב:ח), ורוצה לומר אף שעיני ה' משוטטים וממלאים כל הארץ, ומונחה על עין האדם ממש, אף על פי כן "יראו" מפני שיהיה להם אור בעצמות העין...

וזו בתחילה ביראה לחוד. **ועשו להם ציצית**, רוצה לומר שימשיכו אור שיסתכלו על ידו על ה' יתברך, וזה לא יכול להיות רק מרחוק, על דרך שכתוב "מרחוק ה' נראה לי" (ירמיה לא:ב), כי בקרוב לא יוכלו לראות מפני שאין להם אור בעצמותם. ואחר כן כשיבא למדריגת רקיע [ראיה] שהיא מאהבה, אמר **והיה לכם לציצית**, רוצה לומר שתעשו את עצמכם להסתכלות, דהיינו שיהיה אור בעצמותיכם כנ"ל, ועל ידי זה **וראתים אותו** מקרוב.

צמח ה' לצבי ג'

והיה לכם לציצית וראיתם אותו וזכרתם את כל מצוות ה' ועשיתם אותם ולא תתורו אחרי לבבכם ואחרי עיניכם אשר אתם זונים אחריהם (במדבר טו:לט).

רוצה לומר שיהיו בהם מידות הענוה ושפלות זה לפני זה. וזהו **להם ציצית**, רוצה לומר שיעשו את עצמם לציצית, שיהיו נגררים זה אחר זה על כנפי בגדיהם... ועל ידי מידת הענוה תקיים בוודאי מצות "ואהבת לרעך כמוך" (ויקרא יט:יח), שהוא כולל כל התורה (שבת לא.). וזהו **וזכרתם את כל מצוות ה'**, דהיינו מצות ואהבת לרעך, והוא דרך כלל.

וכשאדם מקיים "ואהבת לרעך כמוך," פירוש שתאהב לרעך כאילו הוא אתה, נמצא כשנותן צדקה לחבירו הדומה לו כאילו נותן לעצמו, ואינו רוצה בביושו של חבירו כמו בבושתו. על ידי זה זוכה ורואה פני השכינה ולא בהית לאיסתכולי באפיה [לא מתבייש להסתכל בפניה]. וזו ציצית, לשון "מציץ מן החרכים" (שיר השירים ב:ט) לשון הסתכלות...

וראיתם אותו וזכרתם את כל מצוות ה'. וידוע מה שאמרו רז"ל: איזה פרשה קטנה שכל גופי התורה תלוין בה? "בכל דרכיך דעהו" (משלי ג:ו), הרי שכל התורה תלויה בזה (ברכות סג.). גם אמרו רז"ל בהאי גיורא

היתה רוח אחרת, היינו אף שדיבר עמהם אף על פי כן לא נפל ממדריגתו, ואדרבה **וימלא אחרי** לגמרי, וקל להבין.

צמח ה' לצבי ב'

דבר אל בני ישראל ואמרת אליהם ועשו להם ציצית על כנפי בגדיהם לדורותם... והיה לכם לציצית וראיתם אותו... (במדבר טו:לח-ט).

קשה, היה לו לומר "ועשו ציצית על כנפי [בגדיהם]," ולמה לי **להם**? אך רומז על הכוונה שיעשו לעצמם הסתכלות על ה' יתברך, כמו שפירש רש"י כמו "[הנה זה עומד אחר כתלנו משגיח מן החלנות] מציץ [מן החרכים]" (שיר השירים ב:ט). כדי ליראה את ה' יתברך, כי יראה אותיות ראיה, ולזה אם [טלית] מונחה בקופסא פטורה מן ציצית (מנחות מא.), כי עיקר המצוה הוא **להם** דייקא...

כי מתחילה ביראה לבד אמר **ועשו להם**, לשון נסתר, כי דרך הירא להסתיר עצמו מן המלך. וכשאוהב, מחבר את עצמו למלך. וזהו **וראיתם אותו**, מוסב על ה' יתברך...

ועל שבתחילה אמר **ועשו להם ציצית**, פירושו שיעשו לעצמם הסתכלות, ואחר זה אמר **והיה לכם לציצית**, משמע שיעשו את עצמם להסתכלות.

יבואר על פי מה שכתוב במדרש שמואל [פירוש ר' שמאול אוזידה לפרקי אבות]: "עין רואה" (מ' אבות ב:א), שבאדם הגשמי אין עין רואה, רק שהאור מבהיק על עינו ועל ידי האור הוא רואה. ונראה הנפקותא בזה, על דרך שאמרו הפילוסופים טעם שאין אדם רואה את האוויר, מפני שהאוויר מלא כל המקומות והוא מונח על העין... [וגם] שהשכינה "מלא כל הארץ כבודו" (ישעיה ו:ג), לכן אי אפשר לראותה. ולזה הנפקותא הנ"ל הוא כך, שאדם הגשמי אין לו אור בעצמות העין רק שרואה מן האור הנעלם, ולזה אם מונח על העין ממש אינו רואה מפני שמבדיל בינו לבין האור, אכן אם היה לו אור בעצמות העין היה רואה גם את האוויר...

צמח ה' לצבי א'

ואולם חי אני וימלא כבוד ה' את כל הארץ (במדבר יד:כא).

אמרו רז"ל (חולין פט.): מה יעשה אדם ויחיה? יעשה עצמו כאלם. יכול אפילו לדברי תורה כן? תלמוד לומר "צדק תדברון" (תהלים נח:ב)....

שחיות האלם הוא על ידי דברי תורה, שהוא ו' מן השם - אילנא דחיין. ועל דרך שכתוב בזהר (ח"ג ב.): "ונתתם לי אות אמת והחייתם" (יהושע ב:יב-יג), דא ו' דמתמן חיין תלויין. וזה שנאמר **ואולם**, אותיות אלם ו', שעל ידי ו' נמשך לה חיין.

וימלא כבוד ה' את כל הארץ. על דרך שאמרו רז"ל: "מי כמוכה באלים" (שמות טו:יא) - באלמים (גיטין נו:), שהוא שומע גידופו ושותק. ובזה מתמלא כבוד ה' את הארץ, אפילו במקום חירופים וגידופים, שכבוד ה' שם ששומע ושותק. וזה שורש אלם ששותק ואינו מרגיש לחרופים, והשתוות אצלו לשבח ולגנות, וזה מן המעלות הרמות והמשבוחות.

וזה שנאמר "הרחב פיך ואמלאהו" (תהלים פא:יא), שנעשה מן אותיות אלם - "'מלא' ברכת ה'" (דברים לג:כג). וזהו שנאמר **וימלא כבוד ה' [את כל הארץ]**.

נועם אלימלך

ועבדי כלב עקב היתה רוח אחרת עמו וימלא אחרי... (במדבר יד:כד).

דהנה יש שני גווני צדיקים, דהיינו יש צדיקים שמוכרחים להיות פרושים ומובדלים מבני אדם, כי כאשר יהיו בין העולם יוכל להיות שיפלו ממדריגתם הנכונה להם. ויש צדיקים שמעורבים בין העולם ומדברים עמהם, ואף על פי כן אינו נופל ממדריגתו, ואדרבה הוא מחזירם למוטב.

על דרך ששמעתי הפירוש מרבי ומורי הרב הגאון הקדוש המנוח מורנו דוב בער דק"ק ראווני נב"ע "ולא הסריח בשר קודש מעולם" (מ' אבות ה:ה), ופירש מי שהוא בשר קודש שהוא צדיק גמור אינו מסריח מ"עולם," אף כשהוא מעורב עמהם ומדבר עמם. וזהו **ועבדי כלב עקב**

כאשר יוכל שאת לערך הכרתו ותבונתו, כמו כן מכביד עליו העבודה, החזק הוא הרפה. ובלבד שיכוין את לבו לשמים, גורם גם כן בחינת עליה ומעלה גם כן איברי השכינה למקומה הרמתה. וזהו שרומז הכתוב **ויאמר עלה נעלה**, לא כמו שאמרתם **אפס כי עז העם היושב עליה**, ומי שאין הכרתו חזקה הרי הוא כעץ יבש, ותועלתו מעט להעלות מדריגות התחתונים. כי אם **עלה נעלה** והכליל עצמו עמהם, אשר כולנו יתכן לנו על כל אחד ואחד לערכו, כמו כן מעלה את השכינה. וזהו **עלה נעלה וירשנו אותה**, כלומר כולנו איש אחד נחנו לירש אות "ה" אחרונה.

כי אין לך אחד מישראל שלא יהיה לו אחיזה בקומת השכינה, ולערך אחיזתו כמו כן יכול לתקן במקום עליון. ונקל לו המעשה אשר יעשה, כי לא נברא בעולם יותר על כחו ממה שנברא בעולם לתקן... ולזה השתיק את כולם, ואמר **כי יכול נוכל לה**, ואין הקדוש ברוך הוא מכביד העבודה על בני אדם.

אור תורה

(*מפרשת מסעי*)

...ארץ אוכלת יושביה היא... (במדבר יג:לב).

שבכל דבר יש עשר המידות. וזהו פירוש כל התורה שעשוע של הקדוש ברוך הוא, אפילו המעשיות המדברים מאיזה מידה, מאהבה או מיראה, וזהו התלבשות הקדוש ברוך הוא. רק האדם צריך ליזהר בכל מחשבה ומחשבה שיעלה אותה, הן למידת אהבה אם הוא דבר של אהבה, או למידת יראה. אבל לא **ישב** בתוכה בקביעות, כי זהו שטות גדול.

כמשל אדם שנוסע לעיר לסחורה, וישב שם ועזב את בני ביתו, וכי יש שטות גדול מזה? כך הקדוש ברוך הוא שלח לאדם המחשבה שיעלה אותה, ואם **ישב** בה ולא ישיב אותה להקדוש ברוך הוא, היש שטות גדול מזה?

וזהו **ארץ**, ארציות, **אוכלת**, מכלה את **היושב** בה בקביעות.

- ט"ז -

פרשת שלח לך

אור המאיר

ויספרו לו ויאמרו באנו אל הארץ אשר שלחתנו וגם זבת חלב ודבש היא וזה פריה: אפס כי עז העם היושב בארץ... ויהס כלב את העם אל משה ויאמר עלה נעלה וירשנו אותה כי יכול נוכל לה (במדבר יג:כז-ח,ל).

הכוונה כלפי דברינו אשר כוונת משה לתור את ארץ כנען ללמד את ישראל איך שיתורו כללות האותיות המלובשים בארציות כמדובר. לזה השיבו ויאמרו **באנו אל הארץ אשר שלחתנו**, בוודאי רצוננו לראות את מלכנו, ולהשיג אלהותו יתברך אפילו מבחינת ארציות ותענוגות בני אדם, לבלתי עשות מלאכתנו מלאכת ה' ברמיה, לעשות מעשינו זר ונכריה עבודתנו. אמנם קשה עלינו המעשה אשר יעשון, כי לאו כל מוחא סביל דא, לעשות בתחתון ולרמוז בעליון, וקרוב הדבר שיפול הנופל ונשאר שקוע שם עם ראשו ורובו. ולא די שאינו מעלה משם כלום, כי אם אדרבה הגבוה השפיל, מוריד לשם ח"ו אותיות התורה ועושה צרופים בקליפות, כי "בני עליה מועטים" (סוכה מה:) אשר כח בהם להעלות אותיות מארציות.

וזהו "ויוציאו דיבת הארץ אשר תרו אותה אל בני ישראל לאמר, הארץ אשר עברנו בה לתור אותה, ארץ אוכלת יושביה" (במדבר יג:לב). ושמעתי מהמגיד זללה"ה שביאר סגולת הארציות שמכלה אותם היושבין ושוהין שם, להתענג את נפשם בתענוגי הארציות. כי מלת "יושביה" משמעו לשון עכבה... ומכלה את האדם מ[עולם ה]זה ומ[עולם ה]בא, בהיותו מעכב את עצמו לשהות בבחינת ארציות...

ויהס כלב את העם אל משה, ויאמר עלה נעלה וירשנו אותה, כי יכול נוכל לה. ופירש רש"י: השתיק את כולם, להיות ש"כלב רוח אחרת היתה בו" (במדבר יד:כד). ולבו תמים באמת את האלהים, נפשו יודעת מאד שאין הקדוש ברוך הוא בא בטרוניא עם בני אדם, כי אם לכל אחד ואחד

- ט"ו -

כלל שום תאוה מתאוות העולם הזה, ומכיר ויודע שהם כולם בהירות הבורא ב"ה, ואב אחד לכולנו.

וזה שנאמר "ותשב בפתח עינים" (בראשית לח:יד), ואמרו חז"ל שכל עינים צופות אליו יתברך (בראשית רבה פה:ז), ולכן כתוב "הנה עין ה' אל יראיו" (תהלים לג:יח), שנכללין כולם באחדותו יתברך.

- י"ד -

שיש בגופניות שלכם, וללחום מלחמת יצר הרע **הצורר אתכם**. וזה שנאמר **על הצר הצורר אתכם**, שהוא היצר הרע הבא לאבד לאדם משני עולמות, הוא הצר הביתי הפנימי בתוך האדם.

והרעותם בחצוצרות, על פי ששמעתי בשם הוותיק והחסיד המפורסם מורנו הרב דוב בער זללה"ה מ"מ דק"ק מזריטש שתיבת חצוצרות נוטריקון חצי צורות - עד כאן שמעתי. ונראה לי לפרש דבריו על דרך "כי יד על כס יה [מלחמה לה' בעמלק מדור דור]" (שמות יז:טז) - שאין השם והכסא שלם (רש"י), והם חצי צורות. וזה שנאמר **והרעותם** היינו שתשברו עצמכם, לא בשביל שלא יבא עליכם ח"ו איזה צרה, אלא למען שמו הגדול שיתמלא ויהיה שמו וכסאו שלם. וזה שנאמר **והרעותם** בחצי צורות, רוצה לומר בשביל חצי צורות שיתמלאו ויהיו שלמים...

דברת שלמה

(*מפרשת כי תבוא*)

והמן... ועינו כעין הבדלח (במדבר יא:ז).

דהנה העולמות נבראו באותיות ודיבורים, כמו שנאמר "בדבר ה' [שמים נעשו]" (תהלים לג:ו). והוא החיות של כל דבר המחיה אותו. והבהירות הזאת היא נקראת עין של כל דבר, כי עין הוא לשון "בהירות," כמו שנאמר **ועינו כעין הבדולח** (במדבר יא:ז). וזה הוא מתנוצץ בהירות וחיות הבורא ב"ה, כמו שמתנוצץ החיות של המוח של האדם דרך עין. וזה שנאמר בכל הנבראים "וירא אלהים כי טוב"...

ואחר עינים אלו יכול אדם להתפתות בתאוות עולם, וזה שנאמר "ותשא אשת אדוניו את עיניה אל יוסף" (בראשית לט:ז). וזה שאמרו חז"ל: אפילו הוא מלא עינים כמלאך המות (עבודה זרה כ.-כ:), רוצה לומר שמפריד כל תאוה בפני עצמה כאלו הוא מלא עינים, וזהו נקרא מ"ה [מלאך המות].

וזה שאיתא בגמרא: ואי הוינא נסבנא בר תריסר, הוה אמינא "גירא בעינא דשטנא" [אם הייתי מתחתן בגיל שתים-עשרה, הייתי אומר "חץ בעין השטן"] (קדושין כט:-ל.). [עינא] דייקא, רוצה לומר שלא הייתי מחשב

וזהו "על דמות הכסא," שהוא יתברך מכוסה שם, על דרך "וענן ואש מתלקחת." וענן, פירוש מקודם חשכות שורה באדם שאינו יכול להתפלל בהתלהבות. ואחר כך "ואש מתלקחת," שבא להתלהבות. וזהו "דמות הכסא," שהוא יתברך מכוסה. כמו "מראה אדם" - כמו שנתעורר בו כך נתעורר אצלו יתברך. אם נתעורר בצדיק אהבה נתעורר למעלה אהבה, וכן כל המידות. וזהו כשמביא את עצמו בהזדככות גדולה למעלה מכל העולמות ויהיה אחדות עמו יתברך...

וזהו **שתי חצוצרות כסף**. שהאדם הוא חצי צורה שהוא רק "דם." ו"א" לבד כביכול גם כן אינו צורה שלימה. אמנם כשיתדבקו יחד נעשה צורה שלימה. **כסף** לשון תאוה, שתהא אתה מתאוה לקדוש ברוך הוא, והקדוש ברוך הוא יאהב אותך...

תורי זהב

וכי תבאו מלחמה בארצכם על הצר הצורר אתכם והרעותם בחצוצרות ונזכרתם לפני ה' אלהיכם ונושעתם מאויביכם (במדבר י:ט).

"קרבה אל נפשי גאלה למען אויבי פדני" (תהלים סט:יט). דנודע שהגלות היא באדם עצמו, במידות ותאוות רעות. וכשאדם מבקש על הגאולה כללית צריך להיות בעצמו גאולה פרטית מכל מידות ותאוות רעות. וממילא סרו מנו כל המקטרגים וכל השונאים נהפכו לאוהבים, "וברצות ה' דרכי איש גם אויביו ישלים אותו" (משלי טז:ז). וממילא נפדה מכל צרות כי כל הדינים נמתקים מעליו, ואז יש לו לבקש על הגאולה כללית של כל ישראל. מה שאין כן כשהוא בעצמו בגלות ובקליפות של מידות ותאוות רעות, איך יבקש על הגאולה כללית? וזה שנאמר "קרבה אל נפשי גאלה," שתסייע לי שאהיה אוכל לשבר הקליפות שלי של תאוות ומידות רעות. ואז ממילא "למען אויבי פדני," שיהיה לי פדיון מכל האויבים.

וזה שנאמר **וכי תבאו**, רוצה לומר כשתרצו לבא אצלי, אזי תראו תחילה **מלחמה בארצכם**, היינו שתעשו מלחמה בארציות, בתאוות רעות ומגונות

כו׳, ובדבר משה לבני ישראל לא נאמר רק **וידבר משה** כו׳ **לעשות הפסח**, ואחר כך בעשייה נאמרו גם כן כל הסימנים כמו בצוו[י] ה׳ יתברך. ממה נפשך אם אין מן הצורך לפרש בצוואת משה לבני ישראל כל העיתים, כי בוודאי ציוה אותם כאשר ציוה ה׳ אותו, אם כן גם בעשיה אין צורך לפרש, כי עשו בוודאי כאשר נצטוו! וגם כן **עשו** הוא מיותר שכבר התחיל הכתוב **ויעשו בני ישראל**.

אך הענין הוא דכל מצוות זמניות כגון פסח סוכה שופר ולולב צריך האדם לעשות המצוה הזאת בבחינה גדולה בשמחה ובדביקות העליון, כדי שעל ידי זה יתקשר בקדושה בלי שום הפסק לכל זמן. ולזה רמז מלת **במועדו** ולא אמר בזמנו לרמז להנ״ל גם כן שיעשה המצוה בשמחה ודביקות כנ״ל. **ומועדו** סובל שני פרושים: לשון זמן, ויום טוב - דהיינו שמחה ודביקות. ונמצא עשיית המצוה זמנית היא בפועל בזמן ההוא ובכח לאחר זמן, דהיינו הארת קדושה שתשאר בו.

ולזה כיון משה רבינו ע״ה שאמר סתם ל**בני ישראל לעשות הפסח**, לרמז הנזכר לעיל שיעשו תמיד הפסח, דהיינו בזמנו בפועל ולאחר זמן בכח קדושה שנתקשר בה ומעוררן תמיד לעבודתו יתברך. ולכן בעשייה נאמר **ויעשו** כו׳ **במועדו [לא נאמר בפסוקנו]**, דהיינו שעשו באופן הנזכר לעיל בשמחה ובדביקות העליון.

ולזה כפל [**ויעשו**] **כן עשו** להורות שהיתה עשייה כפולה בפועל בזמנו ובכח לעתיד לאחר זמן והבן.

אור תורה ב׳

עשה לך שתי חצוצרות כסף... (במדבר י:ב).

פירוש שתי חצי צורות, על דרך ״על דמות הכסא דמות כמראה אדם עליו מלמעלה״ (יחזקאל א:כו). כי האדם הוא רק ד׳ מ׳, דיבור מלכות שורה בו. וכשמתדבק בקדוש ברוך הוא, שהוא אלופו של עולם, נעשה אדם.

והקדוש ברוך הוא עשה כמה צמצומים דרך כמה עולמות כדי שיהיה אחדות עם האדם, שלא יכול לסבול את בהירותו. והאדם צריך לפרוש את עצמו מכל הגשמיות עד שיעלה דרך כל העולמות ויהיה אחדות עם הקדוש ברוך הוא עד שיבוטל ממציאות, ואז יקרא אדם.

- י״א -

פרשת בהעלותך

אור תורה א'

דבר אל אהרן ואמרת אליו בהעלותך את הנרות אל מול פני המנורה יאירו שבעת הנרות (במדבר ח:ב).

על דרך "כי נר מצוה [ותורה אור]" (משלי ו:כג), המצוה היא כנר שבו שורה אור, כך הפנימיות היא אהבה ויראה.

וזהו **בהעלותך** את עצמך, **את הנרות**, פירוש עם המצוות, **אל מול פני המנורה יאירו שבעת הנרות**. על דרך "וידבר אלהים את כל הדברים האלה לאמר: אנכי [ה' אלהיך אשר הוצאתיך מארץ מצרים]" (שמות כ:א-ב). פירוש על ידי כל המצוות תחשוב "אנכי" ו"לא יהיה לך," פירוש אהבה ויראה של אנכי [שאנכי] הוא אהבה "אשר הוצאתיך מארץ מצרים" מכל צרות. ו"לא יהיה לך אלהים אחרים," פירוש שלא תלך אחר תאוות, שהוא אל אחר. "על פני," פירוש על פנימיות, שהפנימיות היא הקדוש ברוך הוא וראוי [ליראה לפניו]. וזהו **אל מול פני המנורה** - הפנימיות, **יאירו שבעת הנרות**, שבעת ימי הבנין [שבע המידות], אהבה ויראה ותפארת וכו'.

נועם אלימלך

וידבר ה' אל משה... ויעשו בני ישראל את הפסח במועדו: בארבעה עשר יום בחודש הזה בין הערבים... וידבר משה אל בני ישראל לעשות הפסח: ויעשו את הפסח בראשון... בין הערבים... ככל אשר צוה ה' את משה כן עשו בני ישראל (במדבר ט:א-ה).

ולכאורה יש לדקדק מה טעם בציוו[י] ה' יתברך נאמרו כל הסימנים הללו באיזה זמן יעשו הפסח **בחודש הראשון, בארבעה עשר בין הערבים**

וזהו **ולבני קהת לא נתן... בכתף ישאו**, כי על בני קהת שהיו צדיקים היה עבודת הקודש חל עליהם, ומה היה עבודת הקודש? בכתף ישאו, שהיו צריכין להוריד השפע הנקרא כתף כנ"ל, ודוק היטב ותהיה מתוק לחיך.

- ט -

לשמה [ממצוה שלא לשמה] (נזיר כג:). וקשה, מה זה שייכות אצל עבירה לשמה, וכי מי צוה לעשות עבירה שיהא שייך אצלה "לשמה"?

אבל נראה דהאמת הוא כך, דהנה כל מה שברא הקדוש ברוך הוא בעולמו לא בראו כי אם להטיב לברואיו על ידי השפעות השפע מעילא לתתא, אלא שלזה צריך התערותא דלתתא על ידי מיין נוקבין...

השפע אינו [נמשך] כי אם על ידי הצדיק המשפיע. והצדיק אשר הוא רוצה להשפיע לבני אדם צריך הוא לדבק עצמו עמהם כדי להשפיע כל דבר הצורך לטובתם, כי מי שרוצה לעשות איזה טובה לחבירו אינו יכול לעשות לו הטובה בשלימות כי אם על ידי שידבק עמו באחדות גמורה. ואם כן הצדיק צריך לדבק עצמו בכל ישראל כדי להטיב להם, ואיך הוא עושה עם הבעל עבירה חלילה? הלא אף שהוא בעל עבירה אף על פי כן צריך להשפעה ולחיות, ואיך יתקשר הצדיק עמו? לזה אמרה הגמרא גדולה עבירה לשמה, שהצדיק עושה גם כן איזה עבירה אלא שהיא לשמה, ועל ידי זה יכול להתקשר עם הבעל עבירה גם כן ויטיב לו גם כן.

וענין עבירה לשמה הוא כך כמו אצל שאול... היה נראה לו זה שיהרוג הבהמות של עמלק עבירה גדולה, אבל אם היה יכול לעשות עבירה לשמה היה עושה והורג את הבהמות גם כן, כיון שצוה המקום ב"ה מה לך שנראה לך עבירה יהיה עבירה לשמה. אלא שמרוב צדקותיו שלא היה בו שום דופי לא היה יכול לעשות אפילו עבירה לשמה, וממילא כיון שלא היה יכול לעשות עבירה לשמה, לא היה יכול להתחבר עם הבעל עבירה להמשיך עליהם השפעה, כי במה היה דבוק עמהם?

והמלך צריך להטיב לכל ישראל לכולם שוין, אפילו לבעלי עבירה חס וחלילה. וזהו שאמרו מפני מה לא נמשכה [מלכות שאול]? מפני שלא היה בו שום דופי, ולא היה בידו להטיב לכולם וכנ"ל. ולזה נאמר אצל שאול שהיה "משכמו ומעלה גבוה מכל העם," פירוש כי השכם הם הכתפיים ונרמזים אל החסדים המגולים... ושאול עם החסדים שלו שהיה צריך להשפיע גבוה מכל העם, כי לא היה בו שום דופי. נמצא שלא יכול להאחד עמהם כלל, כי היה למעלה מהם ולא היה יכול להשפיע אליהם כי אם שהם יתאחדו עמו, פירוש שיהיו צדיקים ויתאחדו עמו במדריגתו, אבל הוא לא היה יכול להוריד עצמו אליהם...

הבורא ב"ה אוהב את בניו ורוצה לעשות שלום ואהבה בין אדם לחבירו, זה הכל של שורש אהבה.

ומזה בא לברך את ישראל, מפני אהבה. וזה **אל אהרן ואל בניו לאמר**, פירוש ראוין לאמר לשון כה כי אהרן ובניו הם תלמידיו של אהרן הנקראים בנים, טבע שלהם לברך - ראוי לאמר **כה תברכו**...

חיים וחסד

ישא ה' פניו אליך וישם לך שלום (במדבר ו:כו).

וקשה, וכי ח"ו יש דמיון או פנים להקדוש ברוך הוא? אלא הפירוש להיפך, כי **הפנים** בא מצד המקבלים, לפי זיכוך שלהם כך הם מציירין האור של ה' יתברך. וזהו **ישא ה' פניו אליך**, פירוש בחינת שלך.

וזה שנאמר שעל הים נדמה להם כבחור ובמעמד סיני כזקן מלא רחמים בליבון שערות (פסיקתא רבתי כא). פירוש כי בשעת יציאת מצרים היו ישראל בקטנות, כבחינת בחור שהוא בקטנות, ובזה הפנים היתה השגתן באור ה' יתברך. אבל בשעת מעמד הר סיני היו בגדלות והיו משיגין לבנות האור ובהירתו, והיו באותה העת בבחינת פנים של זקן בליבון שערות. על כן אמר שבאותם פנים נדמה להם הקדוש ברוך הוא כזקן מלא רחמים.

נועם אלימלך

ולבני קהת לא נתן כי עבודת הקודש עליהם בכתף ישאו (במדבר ז:ט).

נראה לפרש כי נאמר אצל שאול "משכמו ומעלה גבוה מכל העם" (שמואל א ט:ב)... ובגמרא: מפני מה לא נמשכה מלכות שאול? מפני שלא נמצא בו שום דופי (יומא כב:). ותמוה, אדרבה בשביל שלא היה בו שום דופי היה טוב שימשך עדי עד! ונראה כי בגמרא איתא גדולה עבירה

מפני שהכהנים הם מידת חסד ואהבה, וכאשר מעוררין עצמן באהבה לברך את ישראל, אז מעוררין גם כן אהבה לעילא לעילא במקור עליון להשפיע כל טוב וכל הברכות על ישראל. ועל כן תקנו בברכה "וצונו לברך את עמו ישראל באהבה," כי על ידי שמעוררים מידתם אהבה להשפיע ולברך את ישראל, מעוררים אהבה והשפעה ממקור עליון עד מידת מלכות הנקראת כנסת ישראל, ומקבלין כללות ישראל וכל העולמות והברואים אשר נכללין במידת מלכות השפעה ממקור עליון...

והיאך היו יכולין לבוא למדריגת אהבה גמורה? על כרחך היו צריכין לשוב בתשובה שלימה ולראות בשפלותן, כמו בסיני שהיו ישראל במדריגת אהבה ואחדות על ידי התשובה.

וזהו **דבר אל אהרן ואל בניו לאמר**, ואמירה הוא בלב, כמו "כי תאמר בלבבך" (דברים ז:יז), ובינה לִבָּא והוא עולם התשובה, כלומר שיעשו תשובה ואז יכולין לבא אל מידת אהבה אל ישראל.

אמור להם, אמור לשון מחשבה והניקוד של אָמור קמץ חולם, ניקוד של מקור. וזהו **אמור להם**, להמשיך שפע **אל ישראל** ומידת מלכות ממקור העליון, ויברכו כל העולמות וכל הברואים אשר נכללין במידת מלכות ממקור עליון.

דברי אמת

דבר אל אהרן ואל בניו לאמר כה תברכו את בני ישראל אמור להם (במדבר ו:כג).

קשה לשון "כה", הלא בפרשת בהעלותך כתיב "קח את הלויים [מתוך בני ישראל] וטהרת אתם, וכה תעשה להם לטהרם..." (במדבר ח:ו-ז), זה ניחא שקודם אמר "וטהרת אותם" אחר כך "כה תעשה לטהרם." מה שאין כן כאן, האיך שייך לשון **כה תברכו** כיון שלא כתיב קודם צווי.

אך הנה ידוע שאיתא שאהרן מעשיו הביאו אותו למדריגתו, שהיה תמיד אוהב שלום ועשה שלום בין אדם לחבירו. על כן זכה לעשות שלום בין ישראל לאביהם שבשמים, כדאיתא בזהר (ח"ג פח.). וזה בא מאהבת

בעת גשתו אל עבודה זו תפילה, כחו יפה בפיו לענות אמן כראוי. ואפשר לרמוז בדבריהם שהעמיקו בלשונם, העונה אמן יהא שמיה רבה בכל כחו, לרמוז את האמור בכל בחינות כ"ח העתים הנראים הפכיים גם משם עונה אמן לחבר דין ברחמים - הוי"ה ואדנ"י. ולזה עיקר שאלתנו ובקשתנו, "מרן די בשמיא יהא בסעדהון," ועיקר הסעד ונאמר אמן, שיתן לנו לב לדעת איך לומר אמן בכל בחינת הכ"ח...

סוף דבר הכל נשמע מדברינו הנ"ל, אשר כללות מעשה אדם ומעלליו אינו שלם עם בוראו כי אם בהשתדלו בעבודתו באימוץ רב כל כך עד שגורם שאפילו מלאך רע עונה אמן. ומעתה תחזה איך שהעמיקו בדבריהם, ואמרה האשה **אמן אמן**, הוא קבלת שבועה היינו קבלת עול מלכות שלימה לגרום יחוד בשלימות שני שמות הוי"ה ואדנ"י, בלתי אפשרי להיות כי אם בהתאמצו והשתדלו בעבודה כל כך עד שאפילו מלאך רע עונה אמן. וזהו **אמן** אם מאיש, זה כינוי לשם הוי"ה ב"ה הנקרא איש, **אמן** אם מאיש אחר, מוסב לסטרא אחרא הנקרא אחר, גם הוא עונה אמן בעל כרחו כנזכר, והבן הדברים.

אורח לחיים

וידבר ה' אל משה לאמר: דבר אל אהרן ואל בניו לאמר כה תברכו את בני ישראל אמור להם (במדבר ו:כב-ג).

להבין מלת **לאמר**, וגם כיון דאמר **תברכו** לשון רבים, הוה ליה למימר אמרו להם - מה לשון **אמור**? ורש"י ז"ל כתוב אָמוֹר כמו זָכוֹר ושָׁמוֹר, שהוא בדקדוק לשון מקור פקוד בניקוד קמץ חולם.

ונראה דידוע בספרים שה' יתברך ברא כל העולמות כדי שתתגלה מלכותו על ישראל. ובשבילם נבראו כל העולמות בהשתלשלות עד העולם הזה ועל ידם תתגלה מלכותו. ומידת מלכות היא מידה האחרונה מעילא לתתא, וכל האורות והעולמות העליונים בה מתחזיין והיא דמיון ומראה דכולא, כמו שנאמר בתיקונים (ת' יח לא:).

והנה הברכות מסר הקדוש ברוך הוא לאברהם אבינו, והוא מסר ליצחק, ויצחק מסר ליעקב, ויעקב לבניו, והקדוש ברוך הוא מסר הברכה לכהנים

~ פרשת נשא ~

אור המאיר

ובאו המים המאררים האלה במעיך לצבות בטן ולנפל ירך ואמרה האשה אמן אמן (במדבר ה:כה).

ופירש רש"י קבלת שבועה, אמן אם מאיש זה, אמן אם מאיש אחר. יש לרמוז על דרך מאמרם ז"ל: תניא רבי יוסי ברבי יהודה אומר, שני מלאכי השרת מלוין לו לאדם בערב שבת מבית הכנסת לביתו, אחד טוב ואחד רע. וכשבא לביתו ומצא נר דלוק ושולחן ערוך ומטתו מוצעת מלאך טוב אומר "יהי רצון שתהא לשבת אחרת כך," ומלאך רע עונה אמן בעל כרחו. ואם לאו מלאך רע אומר "יהי רצון וכו'," ומלאך טוב עונה אמן בעל כרחו (שבת קיט:). וידוע כי יש לכל מצוות שבתורה מלאכים ממונים עליהן, האחד מסטרא דימינא ואחד מסטרא דשמאלא. ובעשות האדם מצוותיו בדחילו ורחימו אזי נכלל שמאל בימין...

וכבר נודע: תיבת אמן מורה יחוד שני שמות הוי"ה אדנ"י, דין ורחמים כנודע למבינים (תיקוני זהר ת' י כה:)... הגם שחכמים הגידו: העונה "אמן יהא שמיה רבה..." בכל כוחו [קורעין לו גזר דינו] (שבת קיט:), כבר נודע ומפורסם שלא באמירה והרמת קול לבד תולה, כי אם הפה הולך אחר פנימיות מחשבתו. כאשר עם לבבו לדעת ולהכיר אחדותו ויחודו יתברך, אפילו בעוסקו בצרכי ההכרחים שבלתי אפשרי זולתם, גם שם עיקר מגמתו לדרוש יחודו יתברך ואחדותו, ואינו נפרד עם מחשבתו מרוממותו יתברך אפילו כמעט רגע. כי אם בכל מקום בואו רואה ומשיג משם התלבשות אלהות הן המה איברי השכינה, הכינוי בשם אדנ"י, להעלות משם הוי"ה ברוך הוא. ונמצא איש משכיל כזה עונה אמן, פירוש גורם יחוד שני שמות הנ"ל.

אפילו בעוסקו בבחינת הכ"ח [28] עתים הידועים (על פי קהלת ג), י"ד [14] עתים לטובה וי"ד [14] עתים לרעה, בכל הכ"ח עתים עובד עמהם את הבורא ב"ה ומעלה משם איברי השכינה. ואיש אשר אלה לו בוודאי

דבזה שהיה מונה משה את ישראל היה מעורר הארת שורש ישראל למעלה והשרה עליהם אור גדול. והגביה והגדיל אותם עד רום מעלה ביראה ואהבה, שיכוונו לבם למקום. לכך כתיב **שאו** לשון "וישאו ישראל את עיניהם" (שמות יד:י).

וזה **שאו את ראש**, דהיינו שהגביה את ישראל לראש שורש שלהם. **לבית אבותם**, מקור נשמותיהם. ואמר הכתוב **במספר שמות**, מספר הוא [לשון] ספירות וזהירות. **שמות** שהשם של אדם הוא חיות שלו, ובזה המספר מאירים בשרשם העליון והשמות [ובשמות] שהוא חיות שלהם.

קדושת לוי

כאשר צוה ה' את משה ויפקדם במדבר סיני (במדבר א:יט).

ויש לדקדק, הוי ליה למימר "ויפקדם במדבר סיני כאשר צוה ה' את משה." ונראה דהנה ה' יתברך נתן התורה לישראל, ונשמת ישראל הם גוף התורה כי ישראל הם ששים רבוא אותיות לתורה. נמצא ישראל הם התורה, כי כל אחד מישראל הוא אות מהתורה.

נמצא מה שפקד משה את ישראל למד את התורה. וזהו הרמז **כאשר צוה ה' את משה**, הרמז שציווי התורה אשר צוה ה' את משה הוא בעצמו מה שספר את ישראל. ומזה הטעם נראה הא דכתיב: "אך את מטה לוי לא תפקוד ולא תשא בתוך בני ישראל" (במדבר א:מט), כי ישראל הם נגד התורה שבכתב, ומטה לוי הם נגד התורה שבעל פה. וזהו בלוים "על פי ה' פקד אותם" (במדבר ד:מט).

רב ייבי

וידבר ה׳ אל משה במדבר סיני באהל מועד באחד לחודש השני בשנה השנית לצאתם מארץ מצרים לאמר (במדבר א:א).

נראה לפרש בעזרת ה׳ יתברך דהנה לא מצינו בתורה שנקרא מדבר סיני, רק הר סיני. אלא הפירוש כמו שנאמר בזהר ובתיקונים סיני בגימטריא סלם שהוא ק״ל [130], כן סיני הוא ק״ל (זהר ח״א קמט.), לכך כשירד ה׳ על הר סיני ליתן תורה לישראל נקרא הר סיני. היינו מה שהוא גבוה מאד מאד, ה׳ יתברך גבוה על גבוה, התפשט לארץ, כמשל לשבר האוזן כמו בר נש שיורד מן השמים לארץ יורד ב״סולם מוצב ארצה וראשו מגיע השמימה״ (בראשית כח:יב), כן נקרא הר סיני שהוא הר סלם מוצב ארצה וראשו מגיע השמימה, כמו שנאמר ״וירד ה׳ על הר סיני״ (שמות יט:יא).

ולפעמים נקרא **מדבר סיני**, שהאדם זוכה להידבק בהקדוש ברוך הוא וזוכה לרוח הקודש על ידי דיבורו. כי כל אות מאלף בית וכל כ״ב אותיות דבוקים למעלה בה׳ יתברך, וכשאדם מדבר למטה דיבורו על ידי כ״ב אתוון [אותיות] מגיע שורשן של כ״ב אתוון למעלה ונעשה דיבורו כמו ״סולם מוצב ארצה וראשו מגיע השמימה.״ ועולה דיבורו למעלה לפני ה׳ יתברך, זהו נקרא **מדבר סיני**.

גנזי יוסף

וידבר ה׳ אל משה במדבר סיני... לאמר: שאו את ראש כל עדת בני ישראל למשפחותם לבית אבותם במספר שמות כל זכר לגולגלתם (במדבר א:א-ב).

פירש רש״י, מתוך חיבתן לפניו מונה אותן בכל שעה. הענין עיקר מנין של ישראל הוא רומז למעלה בשרשם העליון בשש קצוות [שש ספירות מחסד עד יסוד], שהם עולים לששים רבוא ומשם מקור נשמת ישראל. ולכך כתיב **שאו את ראש בני ישראל** ולא כתיב ספור או מנה, משום

פרשת במדבר

נועם אלימלך

וידבר ה' אל משה במדבר סיני באהל מועד באחד לחודש השני בשנה השנית לצאתם מארץ מצרים לאמר (במדבר א:א).

נראה דהתורה מלמדת לאדם [איך] שיתנהג עצמו, כי להיות שהתורה ניתנה **בסיני** למען ילמד אדם להיות תמיד מוכנע גדול ונבזה בעיניו, כדרך שעשה ה' יתברך ב"ה שמאס בהרים הגבוהים ובחר בהר סיני הנמוך מכולם. וזהו **במדבר סיני**.

רק לזה צריך האדם שלא יתעצב [כי] מחמת גודל הכנעה יפול בעצבות, וזאת היא מניעה גדולה מעבודת הבורא יתברך. לכן הזהירה תורה עליו שיראה להיות תמיד בשמחה, כי אין השכינה שורה מתוך עצבות. וזהו **באהל מועד**, פירוש שיכניס עצמו לאהלו של מועד הוא לשון שמחה, כי מועד הוא לשון יום טוב.

באחד לחדש השני, פירוש ואם יאמר האדם "ואיך אוכל לשמוח כיון שהרביתי לפשוע," ולזה אמרה תורה אף על פי כן יראה לעשות תשובה בשמחה ויתחזק עצמו לאמר "הרי אני כאילו נולדתי היום הזה ולא אשוב עוד לכסלה." וזה נקרא חידוש שנתחדש כבריה חדשה. וזהו **באחד לחדש השני** כי האדם הזה הוא נתחדש שתי פעמים - האחד ביום שנולד, והשני ביום שעושה התשובה ונתכפר לו.

בשנה השנית לצאתם מארץ מצרים, גם כן על הדרך זה, כי ה' יתברך ב"ה הוציאנו ממצרים, הם הקליפות גדולות מ"ט שערי טומאה, ותמיד כשאדם עושה תשובה על חטאיו הוא יוצא מהקליפה אל הקדושה ונקרא גם כן יציאת מצרים. וזה נקרא **בשנה השנית**, כי העולם נקרא שנה כנזכר בספר יצירה (פ' ו:א), לומר שגם **בשנה השנית** פירוש בעולם עכשיו גם כן יש יציאת מצרים שנית, והיינו בשעה שעושה אדם תשובה כנ"ל והבן.

- א -

ע' מג **קדושת לוי ב'** - ...אל אלהי הרוחות לכל בשר... (במדבר טז:כב).

מג **תורי זהב** - צו את בני ישראל ואמרת אליהם את קרבני לחמי לאשי... את הכבש אחד תעשה בבקר ואת הכבש השני תעשה בין הערבים (במדבר כח:ב-ד).

מטות (ע' מה-מח)

מה **נועם אלימלך** - וידבר משה אל ראשי המטות לבני ישראל לאמר זה הדבר אשר צוה ה' (במדבר ל:ב).

מה **מאור עינים** - איש כי ידור נדר לה'... לאסור איסר על נפשו לא יחל דברו ככל היוצא מפיו יעשה (במדבר ל:ב-ג).

מז **גנזי יוסף** - ואשה כי תדור נדר לה' ואסרה איסר בבית אביה בנעוריה: ושמע אביה... והחריש לה אביה וקמו כל נדריה וכל איסר אשר אסרה על נפשה יקום (במדבר ל:ד-ה).

מסעי (ע' מט-נב)

מט **אור הגנוז לצדיקים** - אלה מסעי בני ישראל אשר יצאו מארץ מצרים לצבאותם ביד משה ואהרן: ויכתב משה את מוצאיהם למסעיהם על פי ה' ואלה מסעיהם למוצאיהם (במדבר לג:א-ב).

נ **דברי אמת** - ויכתב משה את מוצאיהם למסעיהם על פי ה' ואלה מסעיהם למוצאיהם (במדבר לג:ב).

נ **קדושת לוי** - ויכתב משה את מוצאיהם למסעיהם על פי ה' ואלה מסעיהם למוצאיהם (במדבר לג:ב).

נא **צמח ה' לצבי** - ויכתב משה את מוצאיהם למסעיהם על פי ה' ואלה מסעיהם למוצאיהם (במדבר לג:ב).

נב **אור תורה** - ויסעו ממרה ויבואו אלימה... (במדבר לג:ט).

ע׳ כח **צמח ה׳ לצבי** - ...ודברתם אל הסלע לעיניהם... (במדבר כ:ח).

כט **קדושת לוי** - ... ודברתם אל הסלע לעיניהם... יען לא האמנתם בי להקדישני לעיני בני ישראל (במדבר כ:ח,יב).

ל **נועם אלימלך** - וירם משה את ידו ויך את הסלע במטהו פעמיים ויצאו מים רבים ותשת העדה ובעירם (במדבר כ:יא).

בלק (ע׳ לב-לו)

לב **גנזי יוסף** - וירא בלק בן ציפור את כל אשר עשה ישראל לאמורי (במדבר כב:ב).

לג **קדושת לוי** - ויגר מואב מפני העם מאוד כי רב הוא ויקץ מואב מפני בני ישראל (במדבר כב:ג).

לד **תשואות חן** - ויען בלעם ויאמר אל עבדי בלק אם יתן לי בלק מלוא ביתו כסף וזהב לא אוכל לעבור את פי ה׳ אלוהי... (במדבר כב:יח). מי מנה עפר יעקב ומספר את רובע ישראל... (במדבר כג:י).

לה **דברת שלמה** - מה אקוב לא קבה אל ומה אזעם לא זעם ה׳: כי מראש צורים אראנו ומגבעות אשורנו הן עם לבדד ישכון ובגוים לא יתחשב (במדבר כג:ח-ט).

לו **אור תורה** - וישא בלעם את עיניו וירא את ישראל שוכן לשבטיו (במדבר כד:ב).

פנחס (ע׳ לז-מד)

לז **צמח ה׳ לצבי** - פינחס בן אלעזר בן אהרן הכהן השיב את חמתי מעל בני ישראל בקנאו את קנאתי בתוכם... לכן אמור הנני נותן לו את בריתי שלום (במדבר כה:יא-יב).

לח **מאור עינים** - לכן אמור הנני נותן לו את בריתי שלום (במדבר כה:יא-יב).

מ **דברת שלמה** - ויאמר ה׳ אל משה לאמר: כן בנות צלפחד דוברות נתון תתן להם אחוזת נחלה בתוך אחי אביהם והעברת את נחלת אביהן להן (במדבר כז:ו-ז).

מא **אור פני משה** - יפקוד ה׳ אלהי הרוחות לכל בשר איש על העדה: אשר יצא לפניהם ואשר יבא לפניהם ואשר יוציאם ואשר יביאם ולא תהיה עדת ה׳ כצאן אשר אין להם רועה (במדבר כז:טז-יז).

מב **קדושת לוי א׳** - יפקוד ה׳ אלהי הרוחות לכל בשר איש על העדה (במדבר כז:טז).

שלח לך (ע' טו-כ)

ע' טו **אור המאיר** - ויספרו לו ויאמרו באנו אל הארץ אשר שלחתנו וגם זבת חלב ודבש היא וזה פריה: ...ויהס כלב את העם אל משה ויאמר עלה נעלה וירשנו אותה כי יכול נוכל לה (במדבר יג:כז-ח,ל).

טז **אור תורה** - ...ארץ אוכלת יושביה היא... (במדבר יג:לב).

יז **צמח ה' לצבי א'** - ואולם חי אני וימלא כבוד ה' את כל הארץ (במדבר יד:כא).

יז **נועם אלימלך** - ועבדי כלב עקב היתה רוח אחרת עמו וימלא אחרי... (במדבר יד:כד).

יח **צמח ה' לצבי ב'** - דבר אל בני ישראל ואמרת אליהם ועשו להם ציצית על כנפי בגדיהם לדורותם... והיה לכם לציצית וראיתם אותו... (במדבר טו:לח-ט).

יט **צמח ה' לצבי ג'** - והיה לכם לציצית וראיתם אותו וזכרתם את כל מצוות ה' ועשיתם אותם ולא תתורו אחרי לבבכם ואחרי עיניכם אשר אתם זונים אחריהם (במדבר טו:לט).

קרח (ע' כא-כג)

כא **יושר דברי אמת** - ... ומדוע תתנשאו על קהל ה' (במדבר טז:ג).

כב **חסד לאברהם המלאך** - ויחר למשה מאוד ויאמר אל ה' אל תפן אל מנחתם לא חמור אחד מהם נשאתי ולא הרעותי את אחד מהם (במדבר טז:טו).

כג **צמח ה' לצבי** - ... עבודת מתנה אתן את כהונתכם והזר הקרב יומת (במדבר יח:ז).

כג **מאמרי אדמו"ר הזקן** - ועבד הלוי הוא... (במדבר יח:כג).

חקת (ע' כד-לא)

כד **מאור עינים** - וידבר... זאת חקת התורה אשר צוה ה' לאמר דבר אל בני ישראל ויקחו אליך פרה אדומה תמימה אשר אין בה מום אשר לא עלה עליה עול (במדבר יט:א-ב).

כה **תורי זהב** - זאת התורה אדם כי ימות באהל כל הבא אל האהל וכל אשר באהל יטמא שבעת ימים (במדבר יט:יד).

כז **מבשר צדק** - וידבר... קח את המטה והקהל את העדה אתה ואהרן אחיך ודברתם אל הסלע לעיניהם ונתן מימיו... ויאמר ה' אל משה ואל אהרן יען לא האמנתם בי... (במדבר כ:ז-יב).

במדבר (ע׳ א-ג)

ע׳ א **נועם אלימלך** - וידבר ה׳ אל משה במדבר סיני באהל מועד באחד לחודש השני בשנה השנית לצאתם מארץ מצרים לאמר (במדבר א:א).

ב **רב ייבי** - וידבר ה׳ אל משה במדבר סיני באהל מועד באחד לחודש השני בשנה השנית לצאתם מארץ מצרים לאמר (במדבר א:א).

ב **גנזי יוסף** - וידבר ה׳ אל משה במדבר סיני... לאמר: שאו את ראש כל עדת בני ישראל למשפחותם לבית אבותם במספר שמות כל זכר לגולגלתם (במדבר א:א-ב).

ג **קדושת לוי** - כאשר צוה ה׳ את משה ויפקדם במדבר סיני (במדבר א:יט).

נשא (ע׳ ד-ט)

ד **אור המאיר** - ובאו המים המאררים האלה במעיך לצבות בטן ולנפל ירך ואמרה האשה אמן אמן (במדבר ה:כב).

ה **אורח לחיים** - וידבר ה׳ אל משה לאמר: דבר אל אהרן ואל בניו לאמר כה תברכו את בני ישראל אמור להם (במדבר ו:כב-ג).

ו **דברי אמת** - דבר אל אהרן ואל בניו לאמר כה תברכו את בני ישראל אמור להם (במדבר ו:כג).

ז **חיים וחסד** - ישא ה׳ פניו אליך וישם לך שלום (במדבר ו:כו).

ז **נועם אלימלך** - ולבני קהת לא נתן כי עבודת הקודש עליהם בכתף ישאו (במדבר ז:ט).

בהעלותך (ע׳ י-יד)

י **אור תורה א׳** - דבר אל אהרן ואמרת אליו בהעלותך את הנרות אל מול פני המנורה יאירו שבעת הנרות (במדבר ח:ב).

י **נועם אלימלך** - ... ויעשו בני ישראל את הפסח במועדו: ... ככל אשר צוה ה׳ את משה כן עשו בני ישראל (במדבר ט:א-ה).

יא **אור תורה ב׳** - עשה לך שתי חצוצרות כסף... (במדבר י:ב).

יב **תורי זהב** - וכי תבאו מלחמה בארצכם על הצר הצורר אתכם והרעותם בחצוצרות ונזכרתם לפני ה׳ אלהיכם ונושעתם מאויביכם (במדבר י:ט).

יג **דברת שלמה** - והמן... ועינו כעין הבדלח (במדבר יא:ז).

ספר

במדבר

אומרים תורה:
סביב שלחנו של המגיד

לקוטי תורות מפי מרן ר׳ דב בער ממזריטש ותלמידיו

לקט תרגם ופירש אברהם יצחק גרין

בהשתתפות:

אריאל אבן-מעשה　　אבן דוד לידר　　אור נסתר רוז

כרך ב: במדבר　דברים　שבת ומועדים

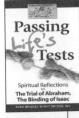

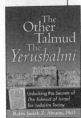

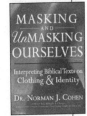

Congregation Resources

Jewish Megatrends: Charting the Course of the American Jewish Future
By Rabbi Sidney Schwarz; Foreword by Ambassador Stuart E. Eizenstat
Visionary solutions for a community ripe for transformational change—from fourteen leading innovators of Jewish life.
6 x 9, 288 pp, HC, 978-1-58023-667-6 **$24.99**

Relational Judaism: Using the Power of Relationships to Transform the Jewish Community *By Dr. Ron Wolfson*
How to transform the model of twentieth-century Jewish institutions into twenty-first-century relational communities offering meaning and purpose, belonging and blessing.
6 x 9, 288 pp, HC, 978-1-58023-666-9 **$24.99**

Revolution of Jewish Spirit: How to Revive *Ruakh* in Your Spiritual Life, Transform Your Synagogue & Inspire Your Jewish Community
By Rabbi Baruch HaLevi, DMin, and Ellen Frankel, LCSW; Foreword by Dr. Ron Wolfson
A practical and engaging guide to reinvigorating Jewish life. Offers strategies for sustaining and expanding transformation, impassioned leadership, inspired programming and inviting sacred spaces.
6 x 9, 224 pp, Quality PB Original, 978-1-58023-625-6 **$19.99**

Building a Successful Volunteer Culture: Finding Meaning in Service in the Jewish Community *By Rabbi Charles Simon; Foreword by Shelley Lindauer; Preface by Dr. Ron Wolfson*
6 x 9, 192 pp, Quality PB, 978-1-58023-408-5 **$16.99**

The Case for Jewish Peoplehood: Can We Be One?
By Dr. Erica Brown and Dr. Misha Galperin; Foreword by Rabbi Joseph Telushkin
6 x 9, 224 pp, HC, 978-1-58023-401-6 **$21.99**

Empowered Judaism: What Independent Minyanim Can Teach Us about Building Vibrant Jewish Communities *By Rabbi Elie Kaunfer; Foreword by Prof. Jonathan D. Sarna*
6 x 9, 224 pp, Quality PB, 978-1-58023-412-2 **$18.99**

Finding a Spiritual Home: How a New Generation of Jews Can Transform the American Synagogue *By Rabbi Sidney Schwarz*
6 x 9, 352 pp, Quality PB, 978-1-58023-185-5 **$19.95**

Inspired Jewish Leadership: Practical Approaches to Building Strong Communities
By Dr. Erica Brown 6 x 9, 256 pp, HC, 978-1-58023-361-3 **$27.99**

Jewish Pastoral Care, 2nd Edition: A Practical Handbook from Traditional & Contemporary Sources *Edited by Rabbi Dayle A. Friedman, MSW, MAJCS, BCC*
6 x 9, 528 pp, Quality PB, 978-1-58023-427-6 **$35.00**

Jewish Spiritual Direction: An Innovative Guide from Traditional and Contemporary Sources
Edited by Rabbi Howard A. Addison, PhD, and Barbara Eve Breitman, MSW
6 x 9, 368 pp, HC, 978-1-58023-230-2 **$30.00**

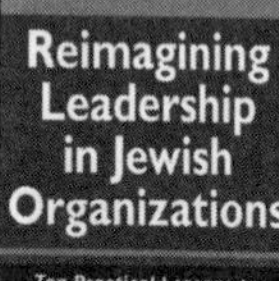

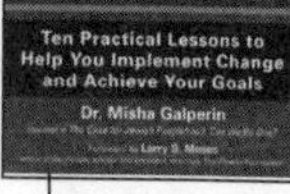

A Practical Guide to Rabbinic Counseling
Edited by Rabbi Yisrael N. Levitz, PhD, and Rabbi Abraham J. Twerski, MD
6 x 9, 432 pp, HC, 978-1-58023-562-4 **$40.00**

Professional Spiritual & Pastoral Care: A Practical Clergy and Chaplain's Handbook
Edited by Rabbi Stephen B. Roberts, MBA, MHL, BCJC
6 x 9, 480 pp, HC, 978-1-59473-312-3 **$50.00**

Reimagining Leadership in Jewish Organizations: Ten Practical Lessons to Help You Implement Change and Achieve Your Goals *By Dr. Misha Galperin*
6 x 9, 192 pp, Quality PB, 978-1-58023-492-4 **$16.99**

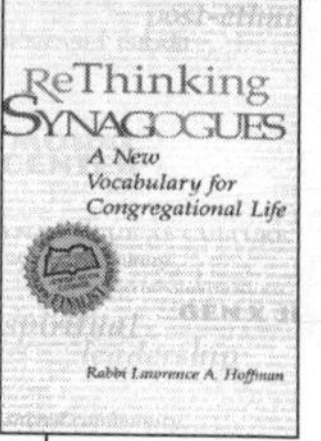

Rethinking Synagogues: A New Vocabulary for Congregational Life
By Rabbi Lawrence A. Hoffman, PhD 6 x 9, 240 pp, Quality PB, 978-1-58023-248-7 **$19.99**

Spiritual Community: The Power to Restore Hope, Commitment and Joy
By Rabbi David A. Teutsch, PhD
5½ x 8½, 144 pp, HC, 978-1-58023-270-8 **$19.99**

Spiritual Boredom: Rediscovering the Wonder of Judaism *By Dr. Erica Brown*
6 x 9, 208 pp, HC, 978-1-58023-405-4 **$21.99**

The Spirituality of Welcoming: How to Transform Your Congregation into a Sacred Community *By Dr. Ron Wolfson* 6 x 9, 224 pp, Quality PB, 978-1-58023-244-9 **$19.99**

Bar / Bat Mitzvah

The Mitzvah Project Book
Making Mitzvah Part of Your Bar/Bat Mitzvah ... and Your Life
By Liz Suneby and Diane Heiman; Foreword by Rabbi Jeffrey K. Salkin; Preface by Rabbi Sharon Brous
The go-to source for Jewish young adults and their families looking to make the world a better place through good deeds—big or small.
6 x 9, 224 pp, Quality PB Original, 978-1-58023-458-0 **$16.99** *For ages 11–13*

The Bar/Bat Mitzvah Memory Book, 2nd Edition: An Album for Treasuring the Spiritual Celebration
By Rabbi Jeffrey K. Salkin and Nina Salkin
8 x 10, 48 pp, 2-color text, Deluxe HC, ribbon marker, 978-1-58023-263-0 **$19.99**

For Kids—Putting God on Your Guest List, 2nd Edition: How to Claim the Spiritual Meaning of Your Bar or Bat Mitzvah *By Rabbi Jeffrey K. Salkin*
6 x 9, 144 pp, Quality PB, 978-1-58023-308-8 **$15.99** *For ages 11–13*

The Jewish Prophet: Visionary Words from Moses and Miriam to Henrietta Szold and A. J. Heschel *By Rabbi Dr. Michael J. Shire*
6½ x 8½, 128 pp, 123 full-color illus., HC, 978-1-58023-168-8 **$14.95**

Putting God on the Guest List, 3rd Edition: How to Reclaim the Spiritual Meaning of Your Child's Bar or Bat Mitzvah *By Rabbi Jeffrey K. Salkin*
6 x 9, 224 pp, Quality PB, 978-1-58023-222-7 **$16.99**

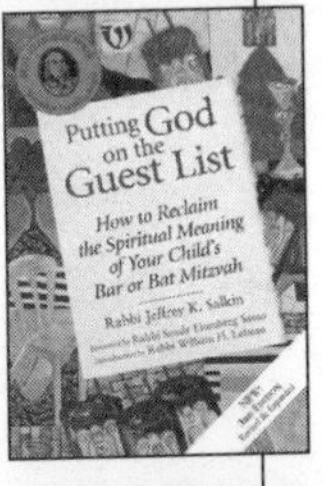

Putting God on the Guest List Teacher's Guide
8½ x 11, 48 pp, PB, 978-1-58023-226-5 **$8.99**

Teens / Young Adults

Text Messages: A Torah Commentary for Teens
Edited by Rabbi Jeffrey K. Salkin
Shows today's teens how each Torah portion contains worlds of meaning for them, for what they are going through in their lives, and how they can shape their Jewish identity as they enter adulthood.
6 x 9, 304 pp (est), HC, 978-1-58023-507-5 **$24.99**

Hannah Senesh: Her Life and Diary, the First Complete Edition
By Hannah Senesh; Foreword by Marge Piercy; Preface by Eitan Senesh; Afterword by Roberta Grossman
6 x 9, 368 pp, b/w photos, Quality PB, 978-1-58023-342-2 **$19.99**

I Am Jewish: Personal Reflections Inspired by the Last Words of Daniel Pearl
Edited by Judea and Ruth Pearl 6 x 9, 304 pp, Deluxe PB w/ flaps, 978-1-58023-259-3 **$19.99**
Download a free copy of the ***I Am Jewish Teacher's Guide*** at www.jewishlights.com.

The JGirl's Guide: The Young Jewish Woman's Handbook for Coming of Age
By Penina Adelman, Ali Feldman and Shulamit Reinharz
6 x 9, 240 pp, Quality PB, 978-1-58023-215-9 **$14.99** *For ages 11 & up*

The JGirl's Teacher's and Parent's Guide
8½ x 11, 56 pp, PB, 978-1-58023-225-8 **$8.99**

Tough Questions Jews Ask, 2nd Edition: A Young Adult's Guide to Building a Jewish Life *By Rabbi Edward Feinstein*
6 x 9, 160 pp, Quality PB, 978-1-58023-454-2 **$16.99** *For ages 11 & up*

Tough Questions Jews Ask Teacher's Guide
8½ x 11, 72 pp, PB, 978-1-58023-187-9 **$8.95**

Pre-Teens

Be Like God: God's To-Do List for Kids
By Dr. Ron Wolfson
Encourages kids ages eight through twelve to use their God-given superpowers to find the many ways they can make a difference in the lives of others and find meaning and purpose for their own.
7 x 9, 144 pp, Quality PB, 978-1-58023-510-5 **$15.99** *For ages 8–12*

The Book of Miracles: A Young Person's Guide to Jewish Spiritual Awareness
By Lawrence Kushner, with all-new illustrations by the author.
6 x 9, 96 pp, 2-color illus., HC, 978-1-879045-78-1 **$16.95** *For ages 9–13*

Children's Books

Around the World in One Shabbat

Jewish People Celebrate the Sabbath Together

By Durga Yael Bernhard

Takes your child on a colorful adventure to share the many ways Jewish people celebrate Shabbat around the world.

11 x 8½, 32 pp, Full-color illus., HC, 978-1-58023-433-7 **$18.99** *For ages 3–6*

It's a … It's a … It's a Mitzvah

By Liz Suneby and Diane Heiman; Full-color Illus. by Laurel Molk

Join Mitzvah Meerkat and friends as they introduce children to the everyday kindnesses that mark the beginning of a Jewish journey and a lifetime commitment to *tikkun olam* (repairing the world). 9 x 12, 32 pp, Full-color illus., HC, 978-1-58023-509-9 **$18.99** *For ages 3–6*

What You Will See Inside a Synagogue

By Rabbi Lawrence A. Hoffman, PhD, and Dr. Ron Wolfson; Full-color photos by Bill Aron

A colorful, fun-to-read introduction that explains the ways and whys of Jewish worship and religious life. 8½ x 10½, 32 pp, Full-color photos, Quality PB, 978-1-59473-256-0 **$8.99** *For ages 6 & up*

(A book from SkyLight Paths, Jewish Lights' sister imprint)

Because Nothing Looks Like God

By Lawrence Kushner and Karen Kushner

Real-life examples of happiness and sadness—from goodnight stories, to the hope and fear felt the first time at bat, to the closing moments of someone's life—invite parents and children to explore, together, the questions we all have about God, no matter what our age. 11 x 8½, 32 pp, Full-color illus., HC, 978-1-58023-092-6 **$18.99** *For ages 4 & up*

The Book of Miracles: A Young Person's Guide to Jewish Spiritual Awareness

Written and illus. by Lawrence Kushner

Easy-to-read, imaginatively illustrated book encourages kids' awareness of their own spirituality. Revealing the essence of Judaism in a language they can understand and enjoy. 6 x 9, 96 pp, 2-color illus., HC, 978-1-879045-78-1 **$16.95** *For ages 9–13*

In God's Hands *By Lawrence Kushner and Gary Schmidt*

Brings new life to a traditional Jewish folktale, reminding parents and kids of all faiths and all backgrounds that each of us has the power to make the world a better place—working ordinary miracles with our everyday deeds.

9 x 12, 32 pp, Full-color illus., HC, 978-1-58023-224-1 **$16.99** *For ages 5 & up*

In Our Image: God's First Creatures

By Nancy Sohn Swartz

A playful new twist to the Genesis story, God asks all of nature to offer gifts to humankind—with a promise that the humans would care for creation in return. 9 x 12, 32 pp, Full-color illus., HC, 978-1-879045-99-6 **$16.95** *For ages 4 & up*

The Jewish Family Fun Book, 2nd Ed.

Holiday Projects, Everyday Activities, and Travel Ideas with Jewish Themes

By Danielle Dardashti and Roni Sarig

The complete sourcebook for families wanting to put a new spin on activities for Jewish holidays, holy days and the everyday. It offers dozens of easy-to-do activities that bring Jewish tradition to life for kids of all ages.

6 x 9, 304 pp, w/ 70+ b/w illus., Quality PB, 978-1-58023-333-0 **$18.99**

The Kids' Fun Book of Jewish Time *By Emily Sper*

A unique way to introduce children to the Jewish calendar—night and day, the seven-day week, Shabbat, the Hebrew months, seasons and dates.

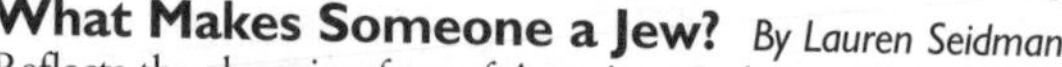

9 x 7½, 24 pp, Full-color illus., HC, 978-1-58023-311-8 **$16.99** *For ages 3–6*

What Makes Someone a Jew? *By Lauren Seidman*

Reflects the changing face of American Judaism. Helps preschoolers and young readers (ages 3–6) understand that you don't have to look a certain way to be Jewish. 10 x 8½, 32 pp, Full-color photos, Quality PB, 978-1-58023-321-7 **$8.99** *For ages 3–6*

When a Grandparent Dies: A Kid's Own Remembering Workbook for Dealing with Shiva and the Year Beyond *By Nechama Liss-Levinson*

8 x 10, 48 pp, 2-color text, HC, 978-1-879045-44-6 **$15.95** *For ages 7–13*

Children's Books by Sandy Eisenberg Sasso

The *Shema* in the Mezuzah: Listening to Each Other
Introduces children ages 3 to 6 to the words of the *Shema* and the custom of putting up the mezuzah. Winner, National Jewish Book Award
9 x 12, 32 pp, Full-color illus., HC, 978-1-58023-506-8 **$18.99**

Adam & Eve's First Sunset: God's New Day
Explores fear and hope, faith and gratitude in ways that will delight kids and adults—inspiring us to bless each of God's days and nights.
9 x 12, 32 pp, Full-color illus., HC, 978-1-58023-177-0 **$17.95** *For ages 4 & up*

Also Available as a Board Book: **Adam and Eve's New Day**
5 x 5, 24 pp, Full-color illus., Board Book, 978-1-59473-205-8 **$7.99** *For ages 0–4*
(A book from SkyLight Paths, Jewish Lights' sister imprint)

But God Remembered: Stories of Women from Creation to the Promised Land Four different stories of women—Lilith, Serach, Bityah and the Daughters of Z—teach us important values through their faith and actions.
9 x 12, 32 pp, Full-color illus., Quality PB, 978-1-58023-372-9 **$8.99** *For ages 8 & up*

For Heaven's Sake
Heaven is often found where you least expect it.
9 x 12, 32 pp, Full-color illus., HC, 978-1-58023-054-4 **$16.95** *For ages 4 & up*

God in Between
If you wanted to find God, where would you look? This magical, mythical tale teaches that God can be found where we are: within all of us and the relationships between us. 9 x 12, 32 pp, Full-color illus., HC, 978-1-879045-86-6 **$16.95** *For ages 4 & up*

God Said Amen
An inspiring story about hearing the answers to our prayers.
9 x 12, 32 pp, Full-color illus., HC, 978-1-58023-080-3 **$16.95** *For ages 4 & up*

God's Paintbrush: Special 10th Anniversary Edition
Wonderfully interactive, invites children of all faiths and backgrounds to encounter God through moments in their own lives. Provides questions adult and child can explore together. 11 x 8½, 32 pp, Full-color illus., HC, 978-1-58023-195-4 **$17.95** *For ages 4 & up*

Also Available as a Board Book: **I Am God's Paintbrush**
5 x 5, 24 pp, Full-color illus., Board Book, 978-1-59473-265-2 **$7.99** *For ages 0–4*
(A book from SkyLight Paths, Jewish Lights' sister imprint)

Also Available: **God's Paintbrush Teacher's Guide**
8½ x 11, 32 pp, PB, 978-1-879045-57-6 **$8.95**

God's Paintbrush Celebration Kit
A Spiritual Activity Kit for Teachers and Students of All Faiths, All Backgrounds
9½ x 12, 40 Full-color Activity Sheets & Teacher Folder w/ complete instructions
HC, 978-1-58023-050-6 **$21.95**
8-Student Activity Sheet Pack (40 sheets/5 sessions), 978-1-58023-058-2 **$19.95**

In God's Name
Like an ancient myth in its poetic text and vibrant illustrations, this award-winning modern fable about the search for God's name celebrates the diversity and, at the same time, the unity of all people.
9 x 12, 32 pp, Full-color illus., HC, 978-1-879045-26-2 **$16.99** *For ages 4 & up*

Also Available as a Board Book: **What Is God's Name?**
5 x 5, 24 pp, Full-color illus., Board Book, 978-1-893361-10-2 **$7.99** *For ages 0–4*
(A book from SkyLight Paths, Jewish Lights' sister imprint)

Also Available in Spanish: **El nombre de Dios**
9 x 12, 32 pp, Full-color illus., HC, 978-1-893361-63-8 **$16.95** *For ages 4 & up*

Noah's Wife: The Story of Naamah
9 x 12, 32 pp, Full-color illus., HC, 978-1-58023-134-3 **$16.95** *For ages 4 & up*

Also Available as a Board Book: **Naamah, Noah's Wife**
5 x 5, 24 pp, Full-color illus., Board Book, 978-1-893361-56-0 **$7.95** *For ages 0–4*
(A book from SkyLight Paths, Jewish Lights' sister imprint)

Judaism / Christianity / Interfaith

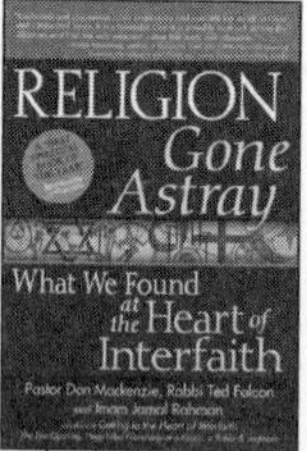

Christians & Jews—Faith to Faith: Tragic History, Promising Present, Fragile Future *By Rabbi James Rudin*
A probing examination of Christian-Jewish relations that looks at the major issues facing both faith communities.
6 x 9, 288 pp, Quality PB, 978-1-58023-717-8 **$18.99** HC, 978-1-58023-432-0 **$24.99**

Religion Gone Astray: What We Found at the Heart of Interfaith
By Pastor Don Mackenzie, Rabbi Ted Falcon and Imam Jamal Rahman
Probes more deeply into the problem aspects of our religious institutions—specifically exclusivity, violence, inequality of men and women, and homophobia—to provide a profound understanding of the nature of what divides us.
6 x 9, 192 pp, Quality PB, 978-1-59473-317-8 **$16.99***

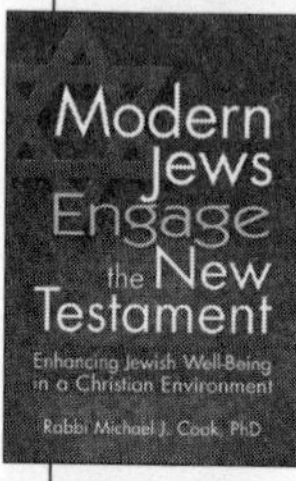

Getting to the Heart of Interfaith: The Eye-Opening, Hope-Filled Friendship of a Pastor, a Rabbi and an Imam
By Rabbi Ted Falcon, Pastor Don Mackenzie and Imam Jamal Rahman
Presents ways we can work together to transcend the differences that have divided us historically. 6 x 9, 192 pp, Quality PB, 978-1-59473-263-8 **$16.99***

How to Do Good & Avoid Evil: A Global Ethic from the Sources of Judaism
By Hans Küng and Rabbi Walter Homolka 6 x 9, 224 pp, HC, 978-1-59473-255-3 **$19.99***

Claiming Earth as Common Ground: The Ecological Crisis through the Lens of Faith *By Rabbi Andrea Cohen-Kiener* 6 x 9, 192 pp, Quality PB, 978-1-59473-261-4 **$16.99***

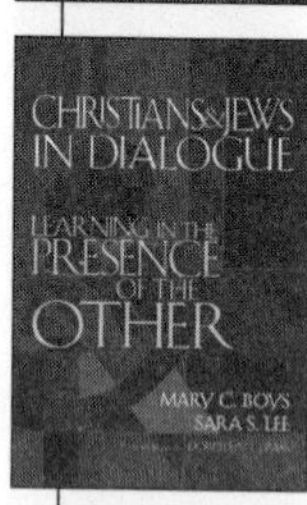

Modern Jews Engage the New Testament: Enhancing Jewish Well-Being in a Christian Environment *By Rabbi Michael J. Cook, PhD* 6 x 9, 416 pp, HC, 978-1-58023-313-2 **$29.99**

The Changing Christian World: A Brief Introduction for Jews
By Rabbi Leonard A. Schoolman 5½ x 8½, 176 pp, Quality PB, 978-1-58023-344-6 **$16.99**

Christians & Jews in Dialogue: Learning in the Presence of the Other
By Mary C. Boys and Sara S. Lee 6 x 9, 240 pp, Quality PB, 978-1-59473-254-6 **$18.99***

Disaster Spiritual Care: Practical Clergy Responses to Community, Regional and National Tragedy *Edited by Rabbi Stephen B. Roberts, BCJC, and Rev. Willard W. C. Ashley Sr., DMin, DH*
6 x 9, 384 pp, HC, 978-1-59473-240-9 **$40.00***

How to Be a Perfect Stranger, 5th Edition: The Essential Religious Etiquette Handbook *Edited by Stuart M. Matlins and Arthur J. Magida*
6 x 9, 432 pp, Quality PB, 978-1-59473-294-2 **$19.99***

InterActive Faith: The Essential Interreligious Community-Building Handbook
Edited by Rev. Bud Heckman with Rori Picker Neiss
6 x 9, 304 pp, Quality PB, 978-1-59473-273-7 **$16.99**; HC, 978-1-59473-237-9 **$29.99***

Introducing My Faith and My Community
The Jewish Outreach Institute Guide for the Christian in a Jewish Interfaith Relationship
By Rabbi Kerry M. Olitzky 6 x 9, 176 pp, Quality PB, 978-1-58023-192-3 **$16.99**

The Jewish Approach to Repairing the World (*Tikkun Olam*)
A Brief Introduction for Christians *By Rabbi Elliot N. Dorff, PhD, with Rev. Cory Willson*
5½ x 8½, 256 pp, Quality PB, 978-1-58023-349-1 **$16.99**

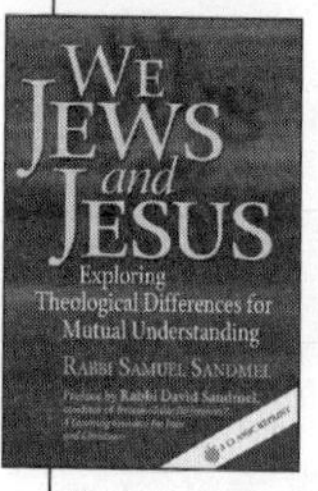

The Jewish Connection to Israel, the Promised Land: A Brief Introduction for Christians *By Rabbi Eugene Korn, PhD* 5½ x 8½, 192 pp, Quality PB, 978-1-58023-318-7 **$14.99**

Jewish Holidays: A Brief Introduction for Christians *By Rabbi Kerry M. Olitzky and Rabbi Daniel Judson* 5½ x 8½, 176 pp, Quality PB, 978-1-58023-302-6 **$16.99**

Jewish Ritual: A Brief Introduction for Christians *By Rabbi Kerry M. Olitzky and Rabbi Daniel Judson* 5½ x 8½, 144 pp, Quality PB, 978-1-58023-210-4 **$14.99**

A Jewish Understanding of the New Testament *By Rabbi Samuel Sandmel; Preface by Rabbi David Sandmel* 5½ x 8½, 368 pp, Quality PB, 978-1-59473-048-1 **$19.99***

Righteous Gentiles in the Hebrew Bible: Ancient Role Models for Sacred Relationships *By Rabbi Jeffrey K. Salkin; Foreword by Rabbi Harold M. Schulweis; Preface by Phyllis Tickle*
6 x 9, 192 pp, Quality PB, 978-1-58023-364-4 **$18.99**

We Jews and Jesus: Exploring Theological Differences for Mutual Understanding
By Rabbi Samuel Sandmel; Preface by Rabbi David Sandmel
6 x 9, 192 pp, Quality PB, 978-1-59473-208-9 **$16.99**

**A book from SkyLight Paths, Jewish Lights' sister imprint*

Spirituality / Crafts

Jewish Threads: A Hands-On Guide to Stitching Spiritual Intention into Jewish Fabric Crafts *By Diana Drew with Robert Grayson*
Learn how to make your own Jewish fabric crafts with spiritual intention—a journey of creativity, imagination and inspiration. Thirty projects.
7 x 9, 288 pp, 8-page color insert, b/w illus., Quality PB Original, 978-1-58023-442-9 **$19.99**

Beading—The Creative Spirit: Finding Your Sacred Center through the Art of Beadwork *By Wendy Ellsworth*
Invites you on a spiritual pilgrimage into the kaleidoscope world of glass and color.
7 x 9, 240 pp, 8-page full-color insert, b/w photos and diagrams, Quality PB, 978-1-59473-267-6 **$18.99***

Contemplative Crochet: A Hands-On Guide for Interlocking Faith and Craft *By Cindy Crandall-Frazier; Foreword by Linda Skolnik*
Will take you on a path deeper into your crocheting and your spiritual awareness.
7 x 9, 208 pp, b/w photos, Quality PB, 978-1-59473-238-6 **$16.99***

The Knitting Way: A Guide to Spiritual Self-Discovery
By Linda Skolnik and Janice MacDaniels
Shows how to use knitting to strengthen your spiritual self.
7 x 9, 240 pp, b/w photos, Quality PB, 978-1-59473-079-5 **$16.99***

The Painting Path: Embodying Spiritual Discovery through Yoga, Brush and Color *By Linda Novick; Foreword by Richard Segalman*
Explores the divine connection you can experience through art.
7 x 9, 208 pp, 8-page full-color insert, b/w photos, Quality PB, 978-1-59473-226-3 **$18.99***

The Quilting Path: A Guide to Spiritual Self-Discovery through Fabric, Thread and Kabbalah *By Louise Silk* Explores how to cultivate personal growth through quilt making. 7 x 9, 192 pp, b/w photos, Quality PB, 978-1-59473-206-5 **$16.99***

Travel / History

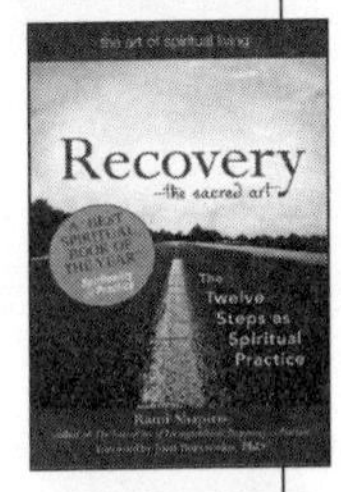

Israel—A Spiritual Travel Guide, 2nd Edition: A Companion for the Modern Jewish Pilgrim *By Rabbi Lawrence A. Hoffman, PhD*
Helps today's pilgrim tap into the deep spiritual meaning of the ancient—and modern—sites of the Holy Land.
4¾ x 10, 256 pp, Illus., Quality PB, 978-1-58023-261-6 **$18.99**
Also Available: **The Israel Mission Leader's Guide** 5½ x 8½, 16 pp, PB, 978-1-58023-085-8 **$4.95**

On the Chocolate Trail: A Delicious Adventure Connecting Jews, Religions, History, Travel, Rituals and Recipes to the Magic of Cacao
By Rabbi Deborah R. Prinz
Take a delectable journey through the religious history of chocolate—a real treat!
6 x 9, 272 pp w/ 20+ b/w photographs, Quality PB, 978-1-58023-487-0 **$18.99**

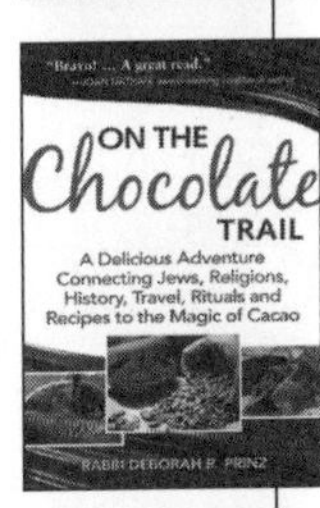

Twelve Steps

Recovery—The Sacred Art: The Twelve Steps as Spiritual Practice
By Rami Shapiro; Foreword by Joan Borysenko, PhD
Draws on insights and practices of different religious traditions to help you move more deeply into the universal spirituality of the Twelve Step system.
5½ x 8½, 240 pp, Quality PB Original, 978-1-59473-259-1 **$16.99***

100 Blessings Every Day: Daily Twelve Step Recovery Affirmations, Exercises for Personal Growth & Renewal Reflecting Seasons of the Jewish Year *By Rabbi Kerry M. Olitzky; Foreword by Rabbi Neil Gillman, PhD* 4½ x 6½, 432 pp, Quality PB, 978-1-879045-30-9 **$16.99**

Recovery from Codependence: A Jewish Twelve Steps Guide to Healing Your Soul *By Rabbi Kerry M. Olitzky* 6 x 9, 160 pp, Quality PB, 978-1-879045-32-3 **$13.95**

Twelve Jewish Steps to Recovery, 2nd Edition: A Personal Guide to Turning from Alcoholism & Other Addictions—Drugs, Food, Gambling, Sex...
By Rabbi Kerry M. Olitzky and Stuart A. Copans, MD; Preface by Abraham J. Twerski, MD
6 x 9, 160 pp, Quality PB, 978-1-58023-409-2 **$16.99**

**A book from SkyLight Paths, Jewish Lights' sister imprint*

Life Cycle

Marriage / Parenting / Family / Aging

The New Jewish Baby Album: Creating and Celebrating the Beginning of a Spiritual Life—A Jewish Lights Companion
By the Editors at Jewish Lights; Foreword by Anita Diamant; Preface by Rabbi Sandy Eisenberg Sasso
A spiritual keepsake that will be treasured for generations. More than just a memory book, *shows you how—and why it's important*—to create a Jewish home and a Jewish life. 8 x 10, 64 pp, Deluxe Padded HC, Full-color illus., 978-1-58023-138-1 **$19.95**

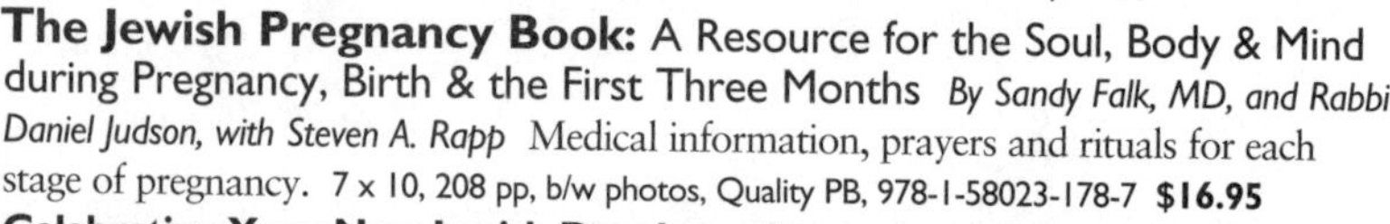

The Jewish Pregnancy Book: A Resource for the Soul, Body & Mind during Pregnancy, Birth & the First Three Months *By Sandy Falk, MD, and Rabbi Daniel Judson, with Steven A. Rapp* Medical information, prayers and rituals for each stage of pregnancy. 7 x 10, 208 pp, b/w photos, Quality PB, 978-1-58023-178-7 **$16.95**

Celebrating Your New Jewish Daughter: Creating Jewish Ways to Welcome Baby Girls into the Covenant—New and Traditional Ceremonies *By Debra Nussbaum Cohen; Foreword by Rabbi Sandy Eisenberg Sasso* 6 x 9, 272 pp, Quality PB, 978-1-58023-090-2 **$18.95**

The New Jewish Baby Book, 2nd Edition: Names, Ceremonies & Customs—A Guide for Today's Families *By Anita Diamant* 6 x 9, 320 pp, Quality PB, 978-1-58023-251-7 **$19.99**

Parenting as a Spiritual Journey: Deepening Ordinary and Extraordinary Events into Sacred Occasions *By Rabbi Nancy Fuchs-Kreimer, PhD*
6 x 9, 224 pp, Quality PB, 978-1-58023-016-2 **$17.99**

Parenting Jewish Teens: A Guide for the Perplexed
By Joanne Doades Explores the questions and issues that shape the world in which today's Jewish teenagers live and offers constructive advice to parents.
6 x 9, 176 pp, Quality PB, 978-1-58023-305-7 **$16.99**

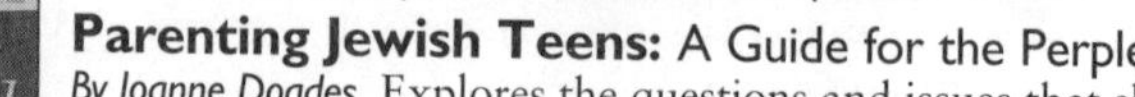

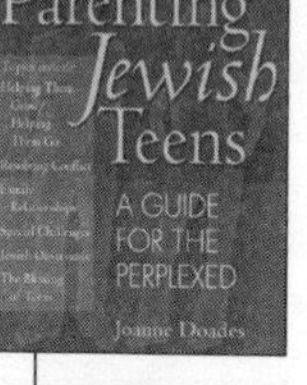

Judaism for Two: A Spiritual Guide for Strengthening and Celebrating Your Loving Relationship *By Rabbi Nancy Fuchs-Kreimer, PhD, and Rabbi Nancy H. Wiener, DMin; Foreword by Rabbi Elliot N. Dorff, PhD*
Addresses the ways Jewish teachings can enhance and strengthen committed relationships. 6 x 9, 224 pp, Quality PB, 978-1-58023-254-8 **$16.99**

The Creative Jewish Wedding Book, 2nd Edition: A Hands-On Guide to New & Old Traditions, Ceremonies & Celebrations *By Gabrielle Kaplan-Mayer*
9 x 9, 288 pp, b/w photos, Quality PB, 978-1-58023-398-9 **$19.99**

Divorce Is a Mitzvah: A Practical Guide to Finding Wholeness and Holiness When Your Marriage Dies *By Rabbi Perry Netter; Afterword by Rabbi Laura Geller*
6 x 9, 224 pp, Quality PB, 978-1-58023-172-5 **$16.95**

Embracing the Covenant: Converts to Judaism Talk About Why & How
By Rabbi Allan Berkowitz and Patti Moskovitz 6 x 9, 192 pp, Quality PB, 978-1-879045-50-7 **$16.95**

The Guide to Jewish Interfaith Family Life: An InterfaithFamily.com Handbook
Edited by Ronnie Friedland and Edmund Case
6 x 9, 384 pp, Quality PB, 978-1-58023-153-4 **$18.95**

A Heart of Wisdom: Making the Jewish Journey from Midlife through the Elder Years
Edited by Susan Berrin; Foreword by Rabbi Harold Kushner
6 x 9, 384 pp, Quality PB, 978-1-58023-051-3 **$18.95**

Introducing My Faith and My Community: The Jewish Outreach Institute Guide for the Christian in a Jewish Interfaith Relationship
By Rabbi Kerry M. Olitzky 6 x 9, 176 pp, Quality PB, 978-1-58023-192-3 **$16.99**

Making a Successful Jewish Interfaith Marriage: The Jewish Outreach Institute Guide to Opportunities, Challenges and Resources *By Rabbi Kerry M. Olitzky with Joan Peterson Littman*
6 x 9, 176 pp, Quality PB, 978-1-58023-170-1 **$16.95**

A Man's Responsibility: A Jewish Guide to Being a Son, a Partner in Marriage, a Father and a Community Leader *By Rabbi Joseph B. Meszler*
6 x 9, 192 pp, Quality PB, 978-1-58023-435-1 **$16.99**

So That Your Values Live On: Ethical Wills and How to Prepare Them
Edited by Rabbi Jack Riemer and Rabbi Nathaniel Stampfer
6 x 9, 272 pp, Quality PB, 978-1-879045-34-7 **$18.99**

Holidays / Holy Days

Prayers of Awe Series

An exciting new series that examines the High Holy Day liturgy to enrich the praying experience of everyone—whether experienced worshipers or guests who encounter Jewish prayer for the very first time.

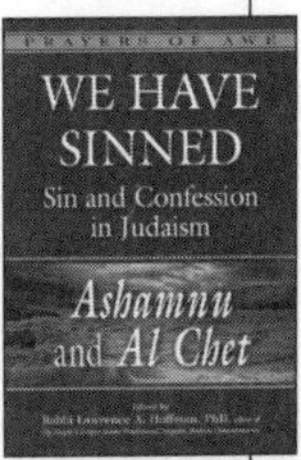

We Have Sinned—Sin and Confession in Judaism: *Ashamnu* and *Al Chet*
Edited by Rabbi Lawrence A. Hoffman, PhD
A varied and fascinating look at sin, confession and pardon in Judaism, as suggested by the centrality of *Ashamnu* and *Al Chet*, two prayers that people know so well, though understand so little. 6 x 9, 304 pp, HC, 978-1-58023-612-6 **$24.99**

Who by Fire, Who by Water—*Un'taneh Tokef*
Edited by Rabbi Lawrence A. Hoffman, PhD 6 x 9, 272 pp, HC, 978-1-58023-424-5 **$24.99**

All These Vows—*Kol Nidre*
Edited by Rabbi Lawrence A. Hoffman, PhD 6 x 9, 288 pp, HC, 978-1-58023-430-6 **$24.99**

Rosh Hashanah Readings: Inspiration, Information and Contemplation
Yom Kippur Readings: Inspiration, Information and Contemplation
Edited by Rabbi Dov Peretz Elkins; Section Introductions from Arthur Green's These Are the Words
Rosh Hashanah: 6 x 9, 400 pp, Quality PB, 978-1-58023-437-5 **$19.99**
Yom Kippur: 6 x 9, 368 pp, Quality PB, 978-1-58023-438-2 **$19.99**; HC, 978-1-58023-271-5 **$24.99**

Reclaiming Judaism as a Spiritual Practice: Holy Days and Shabbat
By Rabbi Goldie Milgram 7 x 9, 272 pp, Quality PB, 978-1-58023-205-0 **$19.99**

The Sabbath Soul: Mystical Reflections on the Transformative Power of Holy Time
Selection, Translation and Commentary by Eitan Fishbane, PhD
6 x 9, 208 pp, Quality PB, 978-1-58023-459-7 **$18.99**

Shabbat, 2nd Edition: The Family Guide to Preparing for and Celebrating the Sabbath
By Dr. Ron Wolfson 7 x 9, 320 pp, Illus., Quality PB, 978-1-58023-164-0 **$19.99**

Hanukkah, 2nd Edition: The Family Guide to Spiritual Celebration
By Dr. Ron Wolfson 7 x 9, 240 pp, Illus., Quality PB, 978-1-58023-122-0 **$18.95**

Passover

My People's Passover Haggadah
Traditional Texts, Modern Commentaries
Edited by Rabbi Lawrence A. Hoffman, PhD, and David Arnow, PhD
A diverse and exciting collection of commentaries on the traditional Passover Haggadah—in two volumes!
Vol. 1: 7 x 10, 304 pp, HC, 978-1-58023-354-5 **$24.99**
Vol. 2: 7 x 10, 320 pp, HC, 978-1-58023-346-0 **$24.99**

Freedom Journeys: The Tale of Exodus and Wilderness across Millennia
By Rabbi Arthur O. Waskow and Rabbi Phyllis O. Berman
Explores how the story of Exodus echoes in our own time, calling us to relearn and rethink the Passover story through social-justice, ecological, feminist and interfaith perspectives. 6 x 9, 288 pp, HC, 978-1-58023-445-0 **$24.99**

Leading the Passover Journey: The Seder's Meaning Revealed, the Haggadah's Story Retold *By Rabbi Nathan Laufer*
Uncovers the hidden meaning of the Seder's rituals and customs.
6 x 9, 224 pp, Quality PB, 978-1-58023-399-6 **$18.99**

Creating Lively Passover Seders, 2nd Edition: A Sourcebook of Engaging Tales, Texts & Activities *By David Arnow, PhD* 7 x 9, 464 pp, Quality PB, 978-1-58023-444-3 **$24.99**

Passover, 2nd Edition: The Family Guide to Spiritual Celebration
By Dr. Ron Wolfson with Joel Lurie Grishaver 7 x 9, 416 pp, Quality PB, 978-1-58023-174-9 **$19.95**

The Women's Passover Companion: Women's Reflections on the Festival of Freedom
Edited by Rabbi Sharon Cohen Anisfeld, Tara Mohr and Catherine Spector; Foreword by Paula E. Hyman
6 x 9, 352 pp, Quality PB, 978-1-58023-231-9 **$19.99**; HC, 978-1-58023-128-2 **$24.95**

The Women's Seder Sourcebook: Rituals & Readings for Use at the Passover Seder
Edited by Rabbi Sharon Cohen Anisfeld, Tara Mohr and Catherine Spector
6 x 9, 384 pp, Quality PB, 978-1-58023-232-6 **$19.99**

Social Justice

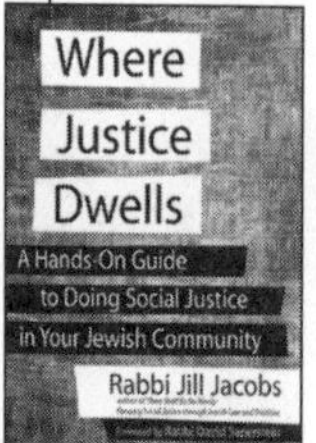

Where Justice Dwells
A Hands-On Guide to Doing Social Justice in Your Jewish Community
By Rabbi Jill Jacobs; Foreword by Rabbi David Saperstein
Provides ways to envision and act on your own ideals of social justice.
7 x 9, 288 pp, Quality PB Original, 978-1-58023-453-5 **$24.99**

There Shall Be No Needy
Pursuing Social Justice through Jewish Law and Tradition
By Rabbi Jill Jacobs; Foreword by Rabbi Elliot N. Dorff, PhD; Preface by Simon Greer
Confronts the most pressing issues of twenty-first-century America from a deeply Jewish perspective. 6 x 9, 288 pp, Quality PB, 978-1-58023-425-2 **$16.99**

There Shall Be No Needy Teacher's Guide 8½ x 11, 56 pp, PB, 978-1-58023-429-0 **$8.99**

Conscience
The Duty to Obey and the Duty to Disobey
By Rabbi Harold M. Schulweis
Examines the idea of conscience and the role conscience plays in our relationships to government, law, ethics, religion, human nature, God—and to each other.
6 x 9, 160 pp, Quality PB, 978-1-58023-419-1 **$16.99**; HC, 978-1-58023-375-0 **$19.99**

Judaism and Justice
The Jewish Passion to Repair the World
By Rabbi Sidney Schwarz; Foreword by Ruth Messinger
Explores the relationship between Judaism, social justice and the Jewish identity of American Jews. 6 x 9, 352 pp, Quality PB, 978-1-58023-353-8 **$19.99**

Spirituality / Women's Interest

New Jewish Feminism
Probing the Past, Forging the Future
Edited by Rabbi Elyse Goldstein; Foreword by Anita Diamant
Looks at the growth and accomplishments of Jewish feminism and what they mean for Jewish women today and tomorrow.
6 x 9, 480 pp, HC, 978-1-58023-359-0 **$24.99**

The Divine Feminine in Biblical Wisdom Literature
Selections Annotated & Explained
Translation & Annotation by Rabbi Rami Shapiro
5½ x 8½, 240 pp, Quality PB, 978-1-59473-109-9 **$16.99**
(A book from SkyLight Paths, Jewish Lights' sister imprint)

The Quotable Jewish Woman
Wisdom, Inspiration & Humor from the Mind & Heart
Edited by Elaine Bernstein Partnow
6 x 9, 496 pp, Quality PB, 978-1-58023-236-4 **$19.99**

The Women's Haftarah Commentary
New Insights from Women Rabbis on the 54 Weekly Haftarah Portions, the 5 Megillot & Special Shabbatot
Edited by Rabbi Elyse Goldstein
Illuminates the historical significance of female portrayals in the Haftarah and the Five Megillot. 6 x 9, 560 pp, Quality PB, 978-1-58023-371-2 **$19.99**

The Women's Torah Commentary
New Insights from Women Rabbis on the 54 Weekly Torah Portions
Edited by Rabbi Elyse Goldstein
Over fifty women rabbis offer inspiring insights on the Torah, in a week-by-week format.
6 x 9, 496 pp, Quality PB, 978-1-58023-370-5 **$19.99**; HC, 978-1-58023-076-6 **$34.95**

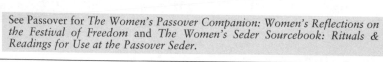

See Passover for *The Women's Passover Companion: Women's Reflections on the Festival of Freedom* and *The Women's Seder Sourcebook: Rituals & Readings for Use at the Passover Seder.*

Ecology / Environment

A Wild Faith: Jewish Ways into Wilderness, Wilderness Ways into Judaism
By Rabbi Mike Comins; Foreword by Nigel Savage 6 x 9, 240 pp, Quality PB, 978-1-58023-316-3 **$16.99**

Ecology & the Jewish Spirit: Where Nature & the Sacred Meet
Edited by Ellen Bernstein 6 x 9, 288 pp, Quality PB, 978-1-58023-082-7 **$18.99**

Torah of the Earth: Exploring 4,000 Years of Ecology in Jewish Thought
Vol. 1: Biblical Israel & Rabbinic Judaism; Vol. 2: Zionism & Eco-Judaism
Edited by Rabbi Arthur Waskow Vol. 1: 6 x 9, 272 pp, Quality PB, 978-1-58023-086-5 **$19.95**
Vol. 2: 6 x 9, 336 pp, Quality PB, 978-1-58023-087-2 **$19.95**

The Way Into Judaism and the Environment *By Jeremy Benstein, PhD*
6 x 9, 288 pp, Quality PB, 978-1-58023-368-2 **$18.99**; HC, 978-1-58023-268-5 **$24.99**

Graphic Novels / Graphic History

The Adventures of Rabbi Harvey: A Graphic Novel of Jewish Wisdom and Wit in the Wild West *By Steve Sheinkin* 6 x 9, 144 pp, Full-color illus., Quality PB, 978-1-58023-310-1 **$16.99**

Rabbi Harvey Rides Again: A Graphic Novel of Jewish Folktales Let Loose in the Wild West *By Steve Sheinkin* 6 x 9, 144 pp, Full-color illus., Quality PB, 978-1-58023-347-7 **$16.99**

Rabbi Harvey vs. the Wisdom Kid: A Graphic Novel of Dueling Jewish Folktales in the Wild West *By Steve Sheinkin*
Rabbi Harvey's first book-length adventure—and toughest challenge.
6 x 9, 144 pp, Full-color illus., Quality PB, 978-1-58023-422-1 **$16.99**

The Story of the Jews: A 4,000-Year Adventure—A Graphic History Book
By Stan Mack 6 x 9, 288 pp, Illus., Quality PB, 978-1-58023-155-8 **$16.99**

Grief / Healing

Facing Illness, Finding God: How Judaism Can Help You and Caregivers Cope When Body or Spirit Fails *By Rabbi Joseph B. Meszler*
Will help you find spiritual strength for healing amid the fear, pain and chaos of illness. 6 x 9, 208 pp, Quality PB, 978-1-58023-423-8 **$16.99**

Midrash & Medicine: Healing Body and Soul in the Jewish Interpretive Tradition *Edited by Rabbi William Cutter, PhD; Foreword by Michele F. Prince, LCSW, MAJCS*
Explores how midrash can help you see beyond the physical aspects of healing to tune in to your spiritual source.
6 x 9, 352 pp, Quality PB, 978-1-58023-484-9 **$21.99**

Healing from Despair: Choosing Wholeness in a Broken World
By Rabbi Elie Kaplan Spitz with Erica Shapiro Taylor; Foreword by Abraham J. Twerski, MD
5½ x 8½, 208 pp, Quality PB, 978-1-58023-436-8 **$16.99**

Healing and the Jewish Imagination: Spiritual and Practical Perspectives on Judaism and Health *Edited by Rabbi William Cutter, PhD*
6 x 9, 240 pp, Quality PB, 978-1-58023-373-6 **$19.99**

Grief in Our Seasons: A Mourner's Kaddish Companion *By Rabbi Kerry M. Olitzky*
4½ x 6½, 448 pp, Quality PB, 978-1-879045-55-2 **$15.95**

Healing of Soul, Healing of Body: Spiritual Leaders Unfold the Strength & Solace in Psalms *Edited by Rabbi Simkha Y. Weintraub, LCSW*
6 x 9, 128 pp, 2-color illus. text, Quality PB, 978-1-879045-31-6 **$16.99**

Mourning & Mitzvah, 2nd Edition: A Guided Journal for Walking the Mourner's Path through Grief to Healing *By Rabbi Anne Brener, LCSW*
7½ x 9, 304 pp, Quality PB, 978-1-58023-113-8 **$19.99**

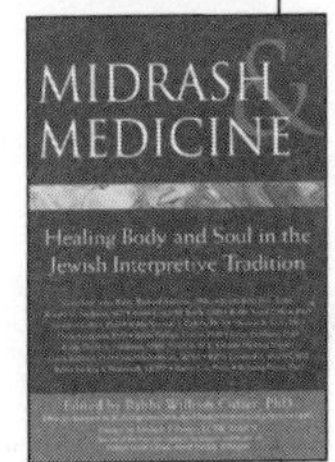

Tears of Sorrow, Seeds of Hope, 2nd Edition: A Jewish Spiritual Companion for Infertility and Pregnancy Loss *By Rabbi Nina Beth Cardin*
6 x 9, 208 pp, Quality PB, 978-1-58023-233-3 **$18.99**

A Time to Mourn, a Time to Comfort, 2nd Edition: A Guide to Jewish Bereavement *By Dr. Ron Wolfson; Foreword by Rabbi David J. Wolpe*
7 x 9, 384 pp, Quality PB, 978-1-58023-253-1 **$21.99**

When a Grandparent Dies: A Kid's Own Remembering Workbook for Dealing with Shiva and the Year Beyond *By Nechama Liss-Levinson, PhD*
8 x 10, 48 pp, 2-color text, HC, 978-1-879045-44-6 **$15.95** *For ages 7–13*

Theology / Philosophy

From Defender to Critic: The Search for a New Jewish Self
By Dr. David Hartman
A daring self-examination of Hartman's goals, which were not to strip halakha of its authority but to create a space for questioning and critique that allows for the traditionally religious Jew to act out a moral life in tune with modern experience.
6 x 9, 336 pp, HC, 978-1-58023-515-0 **$35.00**

The God Who Hates Lies: Confronting & Rethinking Jewish Tradition
A deeply personal look at the struggle between commitment to Jewish religious tradition and personal morality.
By Dr. David Hartman with Charlie Buckholtz 6 x 9, 208 pp, HC, 978-1-58023-455-9 **$24.99**

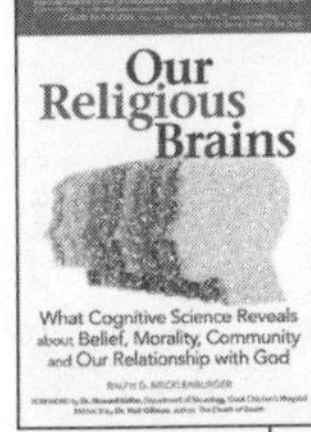

Our Religious Brains: What Cognitive Science Reveals about Belief, Morality, Community and Our Relationship with God
By Rabbi Ralph D. Mecklenburger; Foreword by Dr. Howard Kelfer; Preface by Dr. Neil Gillman
This is a groundbreaking, accessible look at the implications of cognitive science for religion and theology, intended for laypeople. 6 x 9, 224 pp, HC, 978-1-58023-508-2 **$24.99**

The Other Talmud—*The Yerushalmi*: Unlocking the Secrets of The Talmud of Israel for Judaism Today *By Rabbi Judith Z. Abrams, PhD*
A fascinating—and stimulating—look at "the other Talmud" and the possibilities for Jewish life reflected there. 6 x 9, 256 pp, HC, 978-1-58023-463-4 **$24.99**

The Way of Man: According to Hasidic Teaching
By Martin Buber; New Translation and Introduction by Rabbi Bernard H. Mehlman and Dr. Gabriel E. Padawer; Foreword by Paul Mendes-Flohr
An accessible and engaging new translation of Buber's classic work—*available as an e-book only.* E-book, 978-1-58023-601-0 Digital List Price **$14.99**

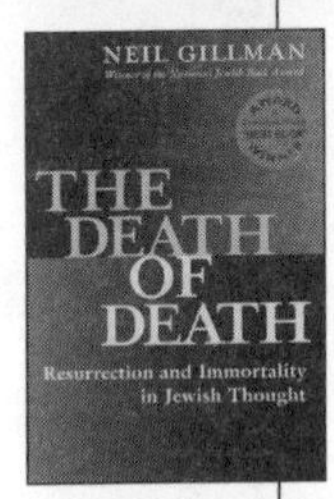

The Death of Death: Resurrection and Immortality in Jewish Thought
By Rabbi Neil Gillman, PhD 6 x 9, 336 pp, Quality PB, 978-1-58023-081-0 **$18.95**

Doing Jewish Theology: God, Torah & Israel in Modern Judaism *By Rabbi Neil Gillman, PhD*
6 x 9, 304 pp, Quality PB, 978-1-58023-439-9 **$18.99**; HC, 978-1-58023-322-4 **$24.99**

A Heart of Many Rooms: Celebrating the Many Voices within Judaism
By Dr. David Hartman 6 x 9, 352 pp, Quality PB, 978-1-58023-156-5 **$19.95**

Jewish Theology in Our Time: A New Generation Explores the Foundations and Future of Jewish Belief *Edited by Rabbi Elliot J. Cosgrove, PhD; Foreword by Rabbi David J. Wolpe; Preface by Rabbi Carole B. Balin, PhD* 6 x 9, 240 pp, Quality PB, 978-1-58023-630-1, **$19.99**; HC, 978-1-58023-413-9 **$24.99**

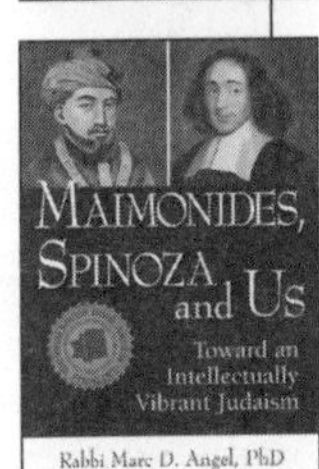

Maimonides—Essential Teachings on Jewish Faith & Ethics: The Book of Knowledge & the Thirteen Principles of Faith—Annotated & Explained
Translation and Annotation by Rabbi Marc D. Angel, PhD
5½ x 8½, 224 pp, Quality PB Original, 978-1-59473-311-6 **$18.99***

Maimonides, Spinoza and Us: Toward an Intellectually Vibrant Judaism
By Rabbi Marc D. Angel, PhD 6 x 9, 224 pp, HC, 978-1-58023-411-5 **$24.99**

Your Word Is Fire: The Hasidic Masters on Contemplative Prayer
Edited and translated by Rabbi Arthur Green, PhD, and Barry W. Holtz
6 x 9, 160 pp, Quality PB, 978-1-879045-25-5 **$16.99**

I Am Jewish

Personal Reflections Inspired by the Last Words of Daniel Pearl

Almost 150 Jews—both famous and not—from all walks of life, from all around the world, write about many aspects of their Judaism.
Edited by Judea and Ruth Pearl 6 x 9, 304 pp, Deluxe PB w/ flaps, 978-1-58023-259-3 **$19.99**
Download a free copy of the *I Am Jewish Teacher's Guide* at www.jewishlights.com.

Hannah Senesh: Her Life and Diary, The First Complete Edition
By Hannah Senesh; Foreword by Marge Piercy; Preface by Eitan Senesh; Afterword by Roberta Grossman
6 x 9, 368 pp, b/w photos, Quality PB, 978-1-58023-342-2 **$19.99**

**A book from SkyLight Paths, Jewish Lights' sister imprint*

Meditation

The Magic of Hebrew Chant: Healing the Spirit, Transforming the Mind, Deepening Love
By Rabbi Shefa Gold; Foreword by Sylvia Boorstein
Introduces this transformative spiritual practice as a way to unlock the power of sacred texts and make prayer and meditation the delight of your life. Includes musical notations. 6 x 9, 352 pp, Quality PB, 978-1-58023-671-3 **$24.99**

The Magic of Hebrew Chant Companion—The Big Book of Musical Notations and Incantations
8½ x 11, 154 pp, PB, 978-1-58023-722-2 **$19.99**

Jewish Meditation Practices for Everyday Life
Awakening Your Heart, Connecting with God
By Rabbi Jeff Roth
Offers a fresh take on meditation that draws on life experience and living life with greater clarity as opposed to the traditional method of rigorous study.
6 x 9, 224 pp, Quality PB, 978-1-58023-397-2 **$18.99**

Discovering Jewish Meditation, 2nd Edition
Instruction & Guidance for Learning an Ancient Spiritual Practice
By Nan Fink Gefen, PhD 6 x 9, 208 pp, Quality PB, 978-1-58023-462-7 **$16.99**

The Handbook of Jewish Meditation Practices
A Guide for Enriching the Sabbath and Other Days of Your Life
By Rabbi David A. Cooper 6 x 9, 208 pp, Quality PB, 978-1-58023-102-2 **$16.95**

Meditation from the Heart of Judaism
Today's Teachers Share Their Practices, Techniques, and Faith
Edited by Avram Davis 6 x 9, 256 pp, Quality PB, 978-1-58023-049-0 **$16.95**

Ritual / Sacred Practices

God in Your Body: Kabbalah, Mindfulness and Embodied Spiritual Practice
By Jay Michaelson
The first comprehensive treatment of the body in Jewish spiritual practice and an essential guide to the sacred. 6 x 9, 272 pp, Quality PB, 978-1-58023-304-0 **$18.99**

The Book of Jewish Sacred Practices: CLAL's Guide to Everyday & Holiday Rituals & Blessings *Edited by Rabbi Irwin Kula and Vanessa L. Ochs, PhD*
6 x 9, 368 pp, Quality PB, 978-1-58023-152-7 **$18.95**

The Jewish Dream Book: The Key to Opening the Inner Meaning of Your Dreams
By Vanessa L. Ochs, PhD, with Elizabeth Ochs; Illus. by Kristina Swarner
8 x 8, 128 pp, Full-color illus., Deluxe PB w/ flaps, 978-1-58023-132-9 $16.95

Jewish Ritual: A Brief Introduction for Christians
By Rabbi Kerry M. Olitzky and Rabbi Daniel Judson
5½ x 8½, 144 pp, Quality PB, 978-1-58023-210-4 **$14.99**

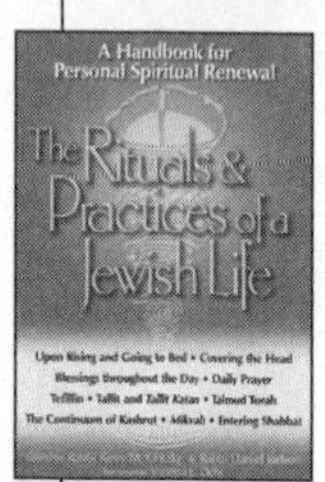

The Rituals & Practices of a Jewish Life: A Handbook for Personal Spiritual Renewal *Edited by Rabbi Kerry M. Olitzky and Rabbi Daniel Judson*
6 x 9, 272 pp, Illus., Quality PB, 978-1-58023-169-5 **$18.95**

The Sacred Art of Lovingkindness: Preparing to Practice
By Rabbi Rami Shapiro 5½ x 8½, 176 pp, Quality PB, 978-1-59473-151-8 **$16.99**
(A book from SkyLight Paths, Jewish Lights' sister imprint)

Mystery & Detective Fiction

Criminal Kabbalah: An Intriguing Anthology of Jewish Mystery & Detective Fiction *Edited by Lawrence W. Raphael; Foreword by Laurie R. King*
All-new stories from twelve of today's masters of mystery and detective fiction—sure to delight mystery buffs of all faith traditions.
6 x 9, 256 pp, Quality PB, 978-1-58023-109-1 **$16.95**

Mystery Midrash: An Anthology of Jewish Mystery & Detective Fiction
Edited by Lawrence W. Raphael; Preface by Joel Siegel
6 x 9, 304 pp, Quality PB, 978-1-58023-055-1 **$16.95**

Inspiration

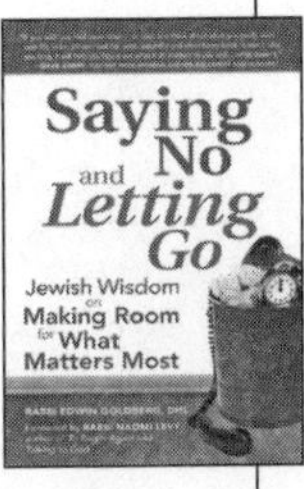

Saying No and Letting Go: Jewish Wisdom on Making Room for What Matters Most
By Rabbi Edwin Goldberg, DHL; Foreword by Rabbi Naomi Levy
Taps into timeless Jewish wisdom that teaches how to "hold on tightly" to the things that matter most while learning to "let go lightly" of the demands and worries that do not ultimately matter. 6 x 9, 192 pp, Quality PB, 978-1-58023-670-6 **$16.99**

The Magic of Hebrew Chant: Healing the Spirit, Transforming the Mind, Deepening Love *By Rabbi Shefa Gold; Foreword by Sylvia Boorstein*
Introduces this transformative spiritual practice as a way to unlock the power of sacred texts and make prayer and meditation the delight of your life. Includes musical notations. 6 x 9, 352 pp, Quality PB, 978-1-58023-671-3 **$24.99**

The Bridge to Forgiveness: Stories and Prayers for Finding God and Restoring Wholeness *By Rabbi Karyn D. Kedar* 6 x 9, 176 pp, Quality PB, 978-1-58023-451-1 **$16.99**

The Empty Chair: Finding Hope and Joy—Timeless Wisdom from a Hasidic Master, Rebbe Nachman of Breslov *Adapted by Moshe Mykoff and the Breslov Research Institute*
4 x 6, 128 pp, Deluxe PB w/ flaps, 978-1-879045-67-5 **$9.99**

A Formula for Proper Living: Practical Lessons from Life and Torah
By Rabbi Abraham J. Twerski, MD 6 x 9, 144 pp, HC, 978-1-58023-402-3 **$19.99**

The Gentle Weapon: Prayers for Everyday and Not-So-Everyday Moments—Timeless Wisdom from the Teachings of the Hasidic Master, Rebbe Nachman of Breslov
Adapted by Moshe Mykoff and S. C. Mizrahi, together with the Breslov Research Institute
4 x 6, 144 pp, Deluxe PB w/ flaps, 978-1-58023-022-3 **$9.99**

The God Upgrade: Finding Your 21st-Century Spirituality in Judaism's 5,000-Year-Old Tradition *By Rabbi Jamie Korngold; Foreword by Rabbi Harold M. Schulweis*
6 x 9, 176 pp, Quality PB, 978-1-58023-443-6 $15.99

God Whispers: Stories of the Soul, Lessons of the Heart *By Rabbi Karyn D. Kedar*
6 x 9, 176 pp, Quality PB, 978-1-58023-088-9 **$15.95**

God's To-Do List: 103 Ways to Be an Angel and Do God's Work on Earth
By Dr. Ron Wolfson 6 x 9, 144 pp, Quality PB, 978-1-58023-301-9 **$16.99**

Happiness and the Human Spirit: The Spirituality of Becoming the Best You Can Be
By Rabbi Abraham J. Twerski, MD
6 x 9, 176 pp, Quality PB, 978-1-58023-404-7 **$16.99**; HC, 978-1-58023-343-9 **$19.99**

Life's Daily Blessings: Inspiring Reflections on Gratitude and Joy for Every Day, Based on Jewish Wisdom *By Rabbi Kerry M. Olitzky* 4½ x 6½, 368 pp, Quality PB, 978-1-58023-396-5 **$16.99**

Restful Reflections: Nighttime Inspiration to Calm the Soul, Based on Jewish Wisdom
By Rabbi Kerry M. Olitzky and Rabbi Lori Forman-Jacobi 5 x 8, 352 pp, Quality PB, 978-1-58023-091-9 **$16.99**

Sacred Intentions: Morning Inspiration to Strengthen the Spirit, Based on Jewish Wisdom
By Rabbi Kerry M. Olitzky and Rabbi Lori Forman-Jacobi 4½ x 6½, 448 pp, Quality PB, 978-1-58023-061-2 **$16.99**

The Seven Questions You're Asked in Heaven: Reviewing and Renewing Your Life on Earth *By Dr. Ron Wolfson* 6 x 9, 176 pp, Quality PB, 978-1-58023-407-8 **$16.99**

Kabbalah / Mysticism

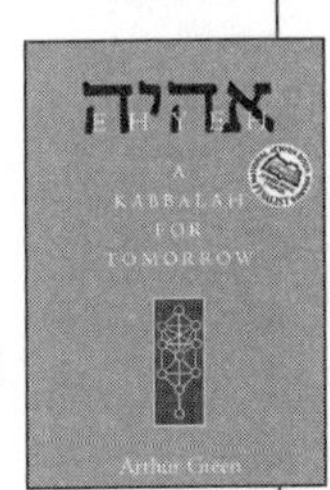

Jewish Mysticism and the Spiritual Life: Classical Texts, Contemporary Reflections *Edited by Dr. Lawrence Fine, Dr. Eitan Fishbane and Rabbi Or N. Rose*
Inspirational and thought-provoking materials for contemplation, discussion and action. 6 x 9, 256 pp, HC, 978-1-58023-434-4 **$24.99** Quality PB, 978-1-58023-719-2 **$18.99**

Ehyeh: A Kabbalah for Tomorrow
By Rabbi Arthur Green, PhD 6 x 9, 224 pp, Quality PB, 978-1-58023-213-5 **$18.99**

The Gift of Kabbalah: Discovering the Secrets of Heaven, Renewing Your Life on Earth
By Tamar Frankiel, PhD 6 x 9, 256 pp, Quality PB, 978-1-58023-141-1 **$16.95**

Seek My Face: A Jewish Mystical Theology *By Rabbi Arthur Green, PhD*
6 x 9, 304 pp, Quality PB, 978-1-58023-130-5 **$19.95**

Zohar: Annotated & Explained *Translation & Annotation by Dr. Daniel C. Matt; Foreword by Andrew Harvey* 5½ x 8½, 176 pp, Quality PB, 978-1-893361-51-5 **$16.99**
(A book from SkyLight Paths, Jewish Lights' sister imprint)

See also *The Way Into Jewish Mystical Tradition* in The Way Into... Series.

Spirituality / Prayer

Davening: A Guide to Meaningful Jewish Prayer
By Rabbi Zalman Schachter-Shalomi with Joel Segel; Foreword by Rabbi Lawrence Kushner
A fresh approach to prayer for all who wish to appreciate the power of prayer's poetry, song and ritual, and to join the age-old conversation that Jews have had with God. 6 x 9, 240 pp, Quality PB, 978-1-58023-627-0 **$18.99**

Jewish Men Pray: Words of Yearning, Praise, Petition, Gratitude and Wonder from Traditional and Contemporary Sources
Edited by Rabbi Kerry M. Olitzky and Stuart M. Matlins; Foreword by Rabbi Bradley Shavit Artson, DHL
A celebration of Jewish men's voices in prayer—to strengthen, heal, comfort, and inspire—from the ancient world up to our own day.
5 x 7¼, 400 pp, HC, 978-1-58023-628-7 **$19.99**

Making Prayer Real: Leading Jewish Spiritual Voices on Why Prayer Is Difficult and What to Do about It *By Rabbi Mike Comins* 6 x 9, 320 pp, Quality PB, 978-1-58023-417-7 **$18.99**

Witnesses to the One: The Spiritual History of the *Sh'ma*
By Rabbi Joseph B. Meszler; Foreword by Rabbi Elyse Goldstein
6 x 9, 176 pp, Quality PB, 978-1-58023-400-9 **$16.99**; HC, 978-1-58023-309-5 **$19.99**

My People's Prayer Book Series: Traditional Prayers, Modern Commentaries *Edited by Rabbi Lawrence A. Hoffman, PhD*
Provides diverse and exciting commentary to the traditional liturgy. Will help you find new wisdom in Jewish prayer, and bring liturgy into your life. Each book includes Hebrew text, modern translations and commentaries from all perspectives of the Jewish world.

Vol. 1—The *Sh'ma* and Its Blessings
7 x 10, 168 pp, HC, 978-1-879045-79-8 **$29.99**
Vol. 2—The *Amidah* 7 x 10, 240 pp, HC, 978-1-879045-80-4 **$24.95**
Vol. 3—*P'sukei D'zimrah* (Morning Psalms)
7 x 10, 240 pp, HC, 978-1-879045-81-1 **$29.99**
Vol. 4—*Seder K'riat Hatorah* (The Torah Service)
7 x 10, 264 pp, HC, 978-1-879045-82-8 **$29.99**
Vol. 5—*Birkhot Hashachar* (Morning Blessings)
7 x 10, 240 pp, HC, 978-1-879045-83-5 **$24.95**
Vol. 6—*Tachanun* and Concluding Prayers
7 x 10, 240 pp, HC, 978-1-879045-84-2 **$24.95**
Vol. 7—Shabbat at Home 7 x 10, 240 pp, HC, 978-1-879045-85-9 **$24.95**
Vol. 8—*Kabbalat Shabbat* (Welcoming Shabbat in the Synagogue)
7 x 10, 240 pp, HC, 978-1-58023-121-3 **$24.99**
Vol. 9—Welcoming the Night: *Minchah* and *Ma'ariv* (Afternoon and Evening Prayer) 7 x 10, 272 pp, HC, 978-1-58023-262-3 **$24.99**
Vol. 10—Shabbat Morning: *Shacharit* and *Musaf* (Morning and Additional Services) 7 x 10, 240 pp, HC, 978-1-58023-240-1 **$29.99**

Spirituality / Lawrence Kushner

I'm God; You're Not: Observations on Organized Religion & Other Disguises of the Ego
6 x 9, 256 pp, Quality PB, 978-1-58023-513-6 **$18.99**; HC, 978-1-58023-441-2 **$21.99**

The Book of Letters: A Mystical Hebrew Alphabet
Popular HC Edition, 6 x 9, 80 pp, 2-color text, 978-1-879045-00-2 **$24.95**
Collector's Limited Edition, 9 x 12, 80 pp, gold-foil-embossed pages, w/ limited-edition silkscreened print, 978-1-879045-04-0 **$349.00**

The Book of Miracles: A Young Person's Guide to Jewish Spiritual Awareness
6 x 9, 96 pp, 2-color illus., HC, 978-1-879045-78-1 **$16.95** *For ages 9–13*

God Was in This Place & I, i Did Not Know: Finding Self, Spirituality and Ultimate Meaning 6 x 9, 192 pp, Quality PB, 978-1-879045-33-0 **$16.95**

Honey from the Rock: An Introduction to Jewish Mysticism
6 x 9, 176 pp, Quality PB, 978-1-58023-073-5 **$16.95**

Invisible Lines of Connection: Sacred Stories of the Ordinary
5½ x 8½, 160 pp, Quality PB, 978-1-879045-98-9 **$16.99**

The Way Into Jewish Mystical Tradition
6 x 9, 224 pp, Quality PB, 978-1-58023-200-5 **$18.99**; HC, 978-1-58023-029-2 **$21.95**

Spirituality

Amazing Chesed: Living a Grace-Filled Judaism
By Rabbi Rami Shapiro
Drawing from ancient and contemporary, traditional and non-traditional Jewish wisdom, reclaims the idea of grace in Judaism.
6 x 9, 176 pp, Quality PB, 978-1-58023-624-9 **$16.99**

Jewish with Feeling: A Guide to Meaningful Jewish Practice
By Rabbi Zalman Schachter-Shalomi with Joel Segel
Takes off from basic questions like "Why be Jewish?" and whether the word God still speaks to us today and lays out a vision for a whole-person Judaism.
5½ x 8½, 288 pp, Quality PB, 978-1-58023-691-1 **$19.99**

The Jewish Lights Spirituality Handbook: A Guide to Understanding, Exploring & Living a Spiritual Life *Edited by Stuart M. Matlins*
What exactly is "Jewish" about spirituality? How do I make it a part of my life? Fifty of today's foremost spiritual leaders share their ideas and experience with us.
6 x 9, 456 pp, Quality PB, 978-1-58023-093-3 **$19.99**

Aleph-Bet Yoga: Embodying the Hebrew Letters for Physical and Spiritual Well-Being
By Steven A. Rapp; Foreword by Tamar Frankiel, PhD, and Judy Greenfeld; Preface by Hart Lazer
7 x 10, 128 pp, b/w photos, Quality PB, Lay-flat binding, 978-1-58023-162-6 **$16.95**

A Book of Life: Embracing Judaism as a Spiritual Practice
By Rabbi Michael Strassfeld 6 x 9, 544 pp, Quality PB, 978-1-58023-247-0 **$19.99**

Bringing the Psalms to Life: How to Understand and Use the Book of Psalms
By Rabbi Daniel F. Polish, PhD 6 x 9, 208 pp, Quality PB, 978-1-58023-157-2 **$16.95**

Does the Soul Survive? A Jewish Journey to Belief in Afterlife, Past Lives & Living with Purpose *By Rabbi Elie Kaplan Spitz; Foreword by Brian L. Weiss, MD*
6 x 9, 288 pp, Quality PB, 978-1-58023-165-7 **$18.99**

Entering the Temple of Dreams: Jewish Prayers, Movements and Meditations for the End of the Day *By Tamar Frankiel, PhD, and Judy Greenfeld*
7 x 10, 192 pp, illus., Quality PB, 978-1-58023-079-7 **$16.95**

First Steps to a New Jewish Spirit: Reb Zalman's Guide to Recapturing the Intimacy & Ecstasy in Your Relationship with God *By Rabbi Zalman M. Schachter-Shalomi with Donald Gropman* 6 x 9, 144 pp, Quality PB, 978-1-58023-182-4 **$16.95**

Foundations of Sephardic Spirituality: The Inner Life of Jews of the Ottoman Empire
By Rabbi Marc D. Angel, PhD 6 x 9, 224 pp, Quality PB, 978-1-58023-341-5 **$18.99**

God & the Big Bang: Discovering Harmony between Science & Spirituality
By Dr. Daniel C. Matt 6 x 9, 216 pp, Quality PB, 978-1-879045-89-7 **$18.99**

God in Our Relationships: Spirituality between People from the Teachings of Martin Buber *By Rabbi Dennis S. Ross* 5½ x 8½, 160 pp, Quality PB, 978-1-58023-147-3 **$16.95**

Judaism, Physics and God: Searching for Sacred Metaphors in a Post-Einstein World
By Rabbi David W. Nelson 6 x 9, 352 pp, Quality PB, inc. reader's discussion guide, 978-1-58023-306-4 **$18.99**; HC, 352 pp, 978-1-58023-252-4 **$24.99**

Meaning & Mitzvah: Daily Practices for Reclaiming Judaism through Prayer, God, Torah, Hebrew, Mitzvot and Peoplehood *By Rabbi Goldie Milgram*
7 x 9, 336 pp, Quality PB, 978-1-58023-256-2 **$19.99**

Repentance: The Meaning and Practice of Teshuvah
By Dr. Louis E. Newman; Foreword by Rabbi Harold M. Schulweis; Preface by Rabbi Karyn D. Kedar
6 x 9, 256 pp, HC, 978-1-58023-426-9 **$24.99** Quality PB, 978-1-58023-718-5 **$18.99**

The Sabbath Soul: Mystical Reflections on the Transformative Power of Holy Time
Selection, Translation and Commentary by Eitan Fishbane, PhD
6 x 9, 208 pp, Quality PB, 978-1-58023-459-7 **$18.99**

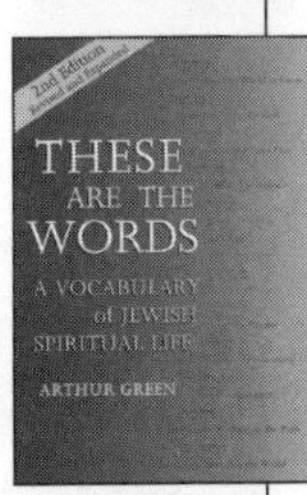

***Tanya*, the Masterpiece of Hasidic Wisdom:** Selections Annotated & Explained
Translation & Annotation by Rabbi Rami Shapiro; Foreword by Rabbi Zalman M. Schachter-Shalomi
5½ x 8½, 240 pp, Quality PB, 978-1-59473-275-1 **$16.99**

These Are the Words, 2nd Edition: A Vocabulary of Jewish Spiritual Life
By Rabbi Arthur Green, PhD 6 x 9, 320 pp, Quality PB, 978-1-58023-494-8 **$19.99**

JEWISH LIGHTS BOOKS ARE AVAILABLE FROM BETTER BOOKSTORES. TRY YOUR BOOKSTORE FIRST.

About Jewish Lights

People of all faiths and backgrounds yearn for books that attract, engage, educate, and spiritually inspire.

Our principal goal is to stimulate thought and help all people learn about who the Jewish People are, where they come from, and what the future can be made to hold. While people of our diverse Jewish heritage are the primary audience, our books speak to people in the Christian world as well and will broaden their understanding of Judaism and the roots of their own faith.

We bring to you authors who are at the forefront of spiritual thought and experience. While each has something different to say, they all say it in a voice that you can hear.

Our books are designed to welcome you and then to engage, stimulate, and inspire. We judge our success not only by whether or not our books are beautiful and commercially successful, but by whether or not they make a difference in your life.

For your information and convenience, at the back of this book we have provided a list of other Jewish Lights books you might find interesting and useful. They cover all the categories of your life:

Bar/Bat Mitzvah
Bible Study / Midrash
Children's Books
Congregation Resources
Current Events / History
Ecology / Environment
Fiction: Mystery, Science Fiction
Grief / Healing
Holidays / Holy Days
Inspiration
Kabbalah / Mysticism / Enneagram
Life Cycle
Meditation
Men's Interest
Parenting
Prayer / Ritual / Sacred Practice
Social Justice
Spirituality
Theology / Philosophy
Travel
Twelve Steps
Women's Interest

Stuart M. Matlins, Publisher

Or phone, fax, mail or e-mail to: **JEWISH LIGHTS Publishing**
Sunset Farm Offices, Route 4 • P.O. Box 237 • Woodstock, Vermont 05091
Tel: (802) 457-4000 • Fax: (802) 457-4004 • www.jewishlights.com
Credit card orders: **(800) 962-4544** (8:30AM–5:30PM EST Monday–Friday)
Generous discounts on quantity orders. SATISFACTION GUARANTEED. Prices subject to change.

For more information about each book, visit our website at www.jewishlights.com